Grand Theater Urbanism

Charlie Qiuli Xue

Editor

Grand Theater Urbanism

Chinese Cities in the 21st century

 Springer

Editor
Charlie Qiuli Xue
City University of Hong Kong
Kowloon, Hong Kong

ISBN 978-981-13-7867-6   ISBN 978-981-13-7868-3   (eBook)
https://doi.org/10.1007/978-981-13-7868-3

This Springer imprint is published by the registered company Springer Nature Singapore Pte Ltd.
The registered company address is: 152 Beach Road, #21-01/04 Gateway East, Singapore 189721, Singapore

Preface

A construction boom has swept through China since the 1980s, and landmark buildings are constantly emerging and frequently achieving new records. After the Shanghai Grand Theater was completed in 1998 and construction of the National Performing Art Center ("The Duck Egg") in Beijing began in 1999, cultural mega-structures sprang up like mushrooms throughout China. This phenomenon was described in my earlier book, *Building a Revolution: Chinese Architecture since 1980* (HKU Press, 2006). Motivated by curiosity, I started to record the grand theaters built in China in the twenty-first century. The number had reached 150 by early 2010.

For most Chinese people emerging from the darkness of the "cultural revolution" at the end of the 1970s, seeing a film or performance was a luxurious experience that required leisure time, money, the right mood, and a sufficient number of films and performances. In Mao's era, few theaters existed in towns and cities, and performances were infrequent, monotonous, and dull. Most people did not have the money, the leisure time, or the inclination to attend the theater. In the years of the open-door policy, many grandiose theaters were planned and built in a very short time and were filled with various colorful performances. This phenomenon illustrates the leaps forward in Chinese people's living standards, freedoms, civic life, and cultural production.

Fabulous cultural facilities and mega-structures are now part of the new town centers in many cities. The municipal government uses cultural buildings to boost the economy, people's confidence, and branding in fierce competition between cities. The precursor to this book, *Chinese Urbanism in the 21st Century* (edited by Li and Xue 2017), revealed various emerging trends in Chinese cities, including shopping malls, university cities, artists' loft spaces, and villages in cities. These are all new typologies for China in the new millennium. Although I myself was a member of the design team for theaters in Shanghai in the 1980s, I view the rise in grand theater construction as part of the urbanism movement in China. These facilities sometimes lead to the development of new towns and become sources of pride and symbols of progress and modernization. Based on this understanding, I tentatively term this trend "Grand Theater Urbanism."

The study of Grand Theater Urbanism has been echoed by colleagues, friends, and students. Thanks to the support of the Research Grant Council, Hong Kong Government (Project No., CityU 11658816), and particularly the kindness of five anonymous reviewers, we have traveled to and investigated grand theaters in more than ten Chinese cities of the first, second, and third tiers. In my travels to overseas cities, my study targets included theaters and opera houses. There is much pleasure to be had in wandering in the external and internal environments of these artistic palaces, enjoying performances at home and abroad, and accumulating an understanding of various cities, city centers, and cultural buildings.

Professor Lu Xiangdong, an authority in theater study, kindly contributed the chapter on Beijing. His seminal book on Chinese theaters was an inspiring resource for my initial research. Professor Chu Dongzhu gave advice on the development of Chongqing and provided an overview of the mountainous city. Li Lin, Xiao Jing, and Ding Guanghui were my partners in conceiving Chinese urbanism. I have greatly benefited from working closely with them. My students Sun Cong, Zhang Lujia, and Xiao Yingbo have carried on the study of grand theaters from different angles and with various examples, and our continuous discussions push forward the study of theaters and relevant architectural topics. Chang Wei and Wan Yan assisted in preparing materials and drawings. My colleagues Carmen Tsui, Lu Yi, Gianni Talamini, and Louie Sieh are panel members for doctoral students who are taking grand theaters and design institutions as their thesis topics. Their timely guidance and discussions have shaped students' theses and the direction of this theater study.

I am indebted to my mentors Profs. Dai Fudong, Sivaguru Ganesan, Stephen Lau, and Chris Abel, who introduced me to the field of architecture and urban design many years ago. I have learned a great deal from my discussions with friends and colleagues Profs. Gu Daqing, Pu Miao, Jia Beisi, Jianfei Zhu, Paul Sanders, Leigh Shutter, Zhonghua Gou, Stan Fung, Per-Johan Dahl, Longgen Chen, Tao Zhu, Zhu Jingxiang, Weijin Wang, Shiqiao Li, Tan Zheng, Zou Han, Yin Ziyuan, Liu Xin, Zang Peng, Wang Yijia, Wang Zhendong, Li Yingchun, and Wang Zhigang.

I am grateful to the theater designers and managers in Shanghai, Beijing, Shenzhen, and Zhengzhou. Their names are acknowledged in relevant chapters. Professors Matthew Carmona and David Grahame Shane took time out of their extremely busy schedules to read the manuscript and endorsed the book enthusiastically. Their many books and articles are valuable texts on urban design, to which I frequently refer and from which I draw inspiration. Thank you so much to the editorial team at Springer, Lydia Wang, Fiona Wu, and the two anonymous reviewers who gave kind encouragement and constructive suggestions.

On a personal note, I would like to dedicate this book to the memory of my father, who meant to treat his two sons to an Albanian film, one of the few entertainments during the stifled time of "Cultural Revolution," however, his wallet was stolen on the trolley bus in that hapless Sunday afternoon; and to my mother, who lavished her sons and family with expensive admission tickets and gave me the opportunity to see the Russian ballet *Swan Lake* at Shanghai Grand Theater in 2002.

Hong Kong   Charlie Qiuli Xue
Summer 2019

Introduction: Grand Theaters and City Branding—Boosting Chinese Cities

With the opening ceremony held on August 27, 1998, Shanghai Grand Theater marked the beginning of a unique movement of theater construction in China. Until 2015, the total number of new theaters including new additions is 364, in which 200 theaters are new constructions with an auditorium of 1200 seats or more (see Appendix A).

The name "grand theater" first appeared at a cultural center in 1989 in Shenzhen, a special economic zone bordering Hong Kong. In 1994, an international design competition of "grand theater" was held in Shanghai. Four years later, a French designed theater clad with crystal clear glass and flying roof monumentally stood at the People's Square—the heart of Shanghai. The design of Shanghai "grand theater" was selected through international architecture competition—its quality and image were well worth and admired as "grand" by people of Shanghai and China. Since then, grand theaters were planned and built in various Chinese cities, from coastal metropolis to provincial city, from prefecture city to rural town center. "Grand theater" in this context is not only an auditorium. It usually contains an opera house, a concert hall and a multi-functional theater. Most of these grand theaters have a gross floor area between 10,000 and 50,000 m^2, and the total construction cost is about RMB 100 billion yuan (around USD 16 billion).[1]

Half of these prominent landmark buildings in China were designed through competition and by overseas firms. As Shanghai Grand Theater is the first theater designed by a foreign architect since 1949, Fuzhou Strait Culture and Art Center, which was opened in October 2018, certainly is not the last one. The newly built grand theaters in China may outnumber the sum of similar buildings constructed in Western Hemisphere since World War II. No other country has constructed so many grand theaters and cultural buildings in such a short period, which raises a number of issues of general concern. Parallel with the heat of grand theater, China donated around 15 national theaters in Asia, Africa, and the Oceania in the

---

[1] The data is collected and calculated by the authors' team.

twenty-first century. These fabulous state gifts in overseas were designed and constructed by Chinese professionals.[2]

Performing art is part of entertainment activities of the human being. From ancient Greek to Shakespeare's era, dramas were played at amphitheaters which were semi-open environment. When Garnier's opera house was built in Paris in 1861, it was a high-class venue of performance and social life. Its Baroque image was part of the Parisians' pride. In the first half of the twentieth century, American and European cities had accumulated wealth from industrialization and built opera house and "movie theaters" in Art Deco style, to accommodate the burgeoning film industry and amazed audiences. Decorated with neon lighting, theaters are designed like palaces for showing off and enticing lust (Blundell-Jones 2016).

After Sydney Opera House erected in Bennelong Point of Sydney Harbor in 1973, municipal leaders and people began to learn how a cultural landmark had helped promoting the image of a city significantly (Murray 2004). In Europe, there is a trend to merge the competing interests of bourgeoisie and the working class after World War II. Cultural halls were extensively built as a "result of the transformation of public welfare from a collection of class-based civil-society initiatives to a bureaucratic state-led regime of mass provision" (Cupers 2015). In France, President de Gaulle believed that bringing high culture to the masses would contribute to creating a more educated and productive society (Grenfell 2004). In the 1980s, Mitterrand's state projects in Paris revitalized this economic and cultural capital of Europe. The old facilities were rebuilt, like the Louvre; and new facilities were constructed, like opera house in Bastille and the national library. The historical city emitted a refreshed and vital glow with these flagship projects. In 1997, the Guggenheim Museum in Bilbao, Spain, greatly revitalized the originally derelict industrial town, population around 250,000, and attracted more than one million tourists annually, creating the so-called Guggenheim effect. Cultural buildings and theaters have always been strongly tied with progression of urbanism and city status (Kong et al. 2015).

All those foreign landmarks, events, and city spectacles have been inspiring China when the country got away from political turmoil and returned to normal life in the 1980s. The movement of constructing grand theater in China is accompanied and fueled by constant economic growth, rapid urbanization, new town construction, and old town renewal. In 2017, China's gross domestic product (GDP) was recorded over RMB 80 trillion (US$13 trillion), second only to the USA. In the same year, GDPs of all four tier-1 cities—Beijing, Shanghai, Guangzhou, and Shenzhen—were more than two trillion RMB, surpassing the prosperous Hong Kong.[3]

---

[2]China's construction aid to developing countries is a different discourse. The data of China-built theater projects in overseas is collected by the authors. See Ding and Xue (2015).

[3]See news "Jingji wuqiangshi chongqing huo jiluo tianjin" (Five strong cities in economy, Chongqing may replace Tianjin), *Ta Kung Pao*, Hong Kong, January 22, 2018, A6. Shenzhen's GDP in 2018 was 2.4 trillion RMB, *Ta Kung Pao*, Hong Kong, January 20, 2019, A5.

As the provincial and municipal officials were rewarded with the growth of local economy from building new infrastructure and cultural facilities, they aggressively wanted to build more for uplifting the city's status in a region and in the nation, or even in the world. When planning new town or new zone, the city usually develops many different types of building, for example, museum, library, stock exchange center, office tower, shopping mall, and mass transportation terminal. Among them, grand theater often is the most impressive project with distinct design, state-of-the-art technology, and expensively built (Rowe 2005). It is considered as jewel in the crown by the general public and associates with "high culture"—European classical performing arts, which are totally different from traditional Chinese folk plays in teahouses or community stages (Fig. 1).

In particular, such massive and extensive construction of grand theaters is a special phenomenon of urban development which demonstrates four characteristics:

(1) Urbanization and city advancement;
(2) Globalization and competition;
(3) Consumerism in cities; and
(4) The role of foreign architects.

Urbanization physically is a large-scale development that demands and constructs many new buildings and new urban fabrics in the city. Globalization creates the inter-city competition that pushes cities individually looking for fame and status in order to have a leading position, while consumerism prepares the market of

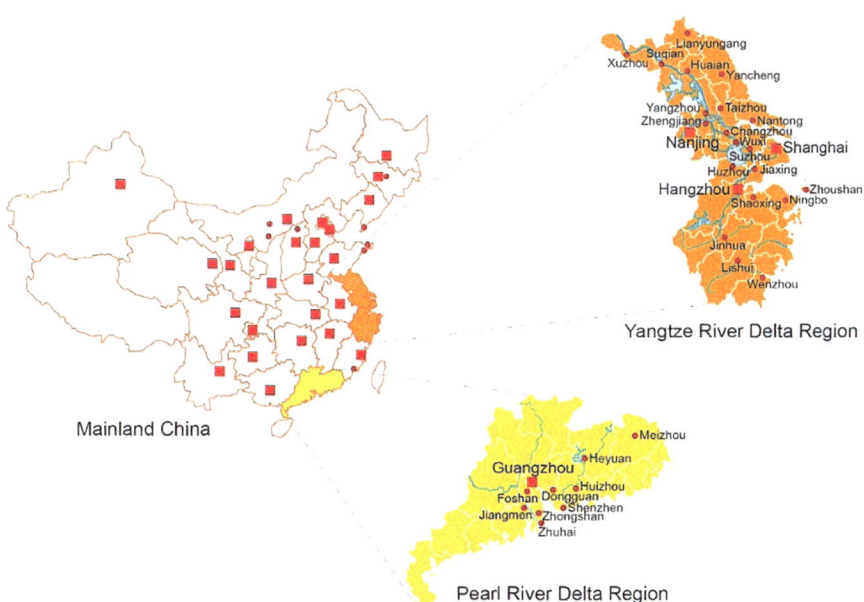

Fig. 1 Dot distribution map of grand theaters newly built in China 1998–2017 (by Sun Cong)

cultural productions for both theater operators and goers. Finally, globalization enables international architects, new technologies, top-class facilities, and performing events entering China. All these characteristics contribute to China's modernization and international participation. The following sessions provide more in-depth analysis of the four factors.

Urbanization and City Advancement: Urban Design of Cultural Centers

In the mid-twentieth century, China was still an agricultural society. Chairman Mao Zedong (1893–1976) and the communist government had attempted to realize a strong industrial economy, but new factories mostly were located in remote mountain areas for the purpose of national defense, so this early industrialization program had little impact on cities. When China launched the "reform and open-door" policy in 1978, the urbanisation ratio was only 18%, but later it jumped to 47% in 2009 and reached 57% in 2016. Almost one billion Chinese people will live in urban area in the near future. One of the most stunning statistics able to illustrate this singular urbanization is the consumption of cement. According to statistics from the United States Geological Survey (USGS), from 2011 to 2013, the three-year usage of concrete (6.6 gigatons) in China was more than the total usage of concrete (4.5 gigatons) in the USA during the entire twentieth century.[4]

Building the city for integrating global economy is the ultimate goal of Chinese urbanisation, so new urban designs should not only accommodate the population explosion in the city, but also improve the living and working environment. Many old towns with mono-multi-story residential buildings are incapable of providing sufficient spaces and compatible facilities for modern lifestyle and business. Today high-rise housing estates, office and commercial zones, shopping and entertainment centers are seen everywhere either in new town or old city. For example, in 2018, among the 143 newly built towers over 200 m tall worldwide, there were 88 towers completed in the burgeoning Chinese cities, this accounts for 61.5% of total number. Shenzhen was No. 1 in building largest number of 200-meter-plus skyscrapers consecutively from 2016 to 2018. The city recorded 14 completions in 2018.[5]

---

[4]See Bill Gates, "Have You Hugged a Concrete Pillar Today?" *Gatesnotes: The Blog of Bill Gates*, Available Online, https://www.gatesnotes.com/Books/Making-the-Modern-World, June 12, 2014; also Vaclav Smil, *Making the Modern World: Materials and Dematerialization* London: John Wiley & Sons, Ltd., 2014.

[5]Christopher DeWolf gives the number of 2016, in "Construction in China's Skyscraper Capital Shows Little Sign of Slowing," *CNN*, July 24, 2017.
    http://www.cnn.com/2017/07/23/architecture/shenzhen-skyscraper/index.html; figures of 2018 is from "CTBUH Year in Review: Tall Trends of 2018," http://www.skyscrapercenter.com/year-in-review/2018, accessed January 20, 2019.

When urban renewal in old districts faces bottlenecks, new town development becomes an effective option widely adopted by many cities. New towns or new zones are planned in almost every provincial capital city, with provisions of a new administrative center and a grand cultural center as the trend of urban design. The size of those new towns is ranged from 10 to 150 m², eroding huge amount of arable lands at the once suburban area.

In many cases, the cultural center is an essential element forming the civic heart of a new town, for example, at least one cultural complex associates with the civic core in Guangzhou, Shenzhen, Shunde, Dongguan, Hangzhou, Shanghai, Zhengzhou, Tianjin, and Taiyuan, just naming a few cities here.

Guangzhou built a museum, a theater, a library, and a children's palace at Huacheng Plaza of Zhujiang New Town. Shenzhen built a music hall, a library, a children's palace and a museum of modern art at the Civic Center of Futian New Zone. Shunde built a theater, a library, and a museum at Shunde New Town. Dongguan built a theater, a library, a convention hall, and an exhibition hall at the Central Plaza. Hangzhou built a theater and a convention center at the Civic Plaza of Qianjiang New Town. Shanghai built a science museum and the Oriental Art Center at Century Square of Pudong New District. Zhengzhou built the Henan Art Center and a convention center at the central park of Zhengdong New District. Tianjin built a big cultural center including a theater, a library, a museum, an art gallery, and a children's center, etc., at Hexi district …

The typical urban design of those cultural centers is an axial symmetrical layout with a central plaza surrounded by arts and cultural facilities, public buildings, or government complex. In Harbin and Ordos, the civic core with administrative complex, cultural facilities, and public transportation connections was built first as prior infrastructure and magnetic project during the development of the new zone, attracting potential investments, construction, and populations.

Globalization and Competition: Culture as Soft-Power

China was gradually influenced by Western civilization after losing the Opium War in 1860. The treaty-port cities along the coastal line were the first to witness modern lifestyle because of setting up foreign concessions and foreign trades. The reality of being defeated and colonized by Western powers had made many Chinese people begin to be skeptical about their traditional society and culture. They insisted that the old China was backward and should learn from the West in order to build a modern society technologically, economically, politically, and culturally (Xue 2006; Xue and Ding 2018). The social mainstream had always kept an eye on Western culture and ideology no matter democracy or socialism and communism were all imported from the West. We have no intension to discuss whether this is a right approach to modern China or not in this book. In fact, when the notion "globalization" was known to Chinese people in the early 1990s, it was accepted as a positive tendency and was converted into an attitude of "looking out to the West."

With the "open-door" policy launched in 1978, the mentality of Chinese people has been changed and freed, they tend to make reference to the advanced Western countries in fields of technology and management.

Globalization allows international trades and businesses to avoid obstacles as well as free circulation of capital, goods, and human resources. The impact of globalization on the city is assessed through that the "global city" as a distinctive type and an understanding of urbanization implements all city developments toward the globalized economy (Wu 2006, 2007; Jayne 2018). Building the city for global economy is the ultimate goal of urbanization. Under the circumstance of globalization, time and space are significantly shortened, greatly reducing the importance of geographical location and natural resources of a specific city. From this respect, almost every city has a potential to become an economic, political, or cultural hub, so each individual city is a potential competitor to other cities. Therefore, the competition between cities is inevitable. As a result, globalization has further increased the importance of establishing and promoting urban images. As John R. Short said, because of the fierce competition among cities, cities have to have positive new images to attract investment (Short 2004, 21–23). The globalization plays a vital role in shaping China's modernization.

There is an inseparable relationship between the use of space, city marketing, and image making. In fact, based on political and economic reasons, the construction of urban image, and then the promotion of cities (places) to other countries or regions are the central links for each authority to govern the city (Broudehoux 2004, 25). Advanced cultural spaces, such as libraries, museums, and opera houses, are indispensable for promoting city and "connecting with the international level." The government believes that when a city's hardware (infrastructure, cultural buildings, housing, etc.) is well prepared, investment and talents from home and abroad will naturally flow in and activate the economy. Therefore, the Chinese leaders at the central and provincial levels had an urgent imperative to "be connected with the international track"[6]; that is, building like an international city and behaving according to international norms. Hundreds of cities claimed to be becoming "international metropolises" by 2005 (Xue 2010). If the "international" dream is too far away, the achievement of neighbor provinces and cities is the best model to catch up. For example, if Cities A and B have opera houses, City C must have one.

When commercial activities have considerably enhanced their economic powers, cities begin to seek for uplifting their reputations by building grandiose cultural facilities—libraries, grand theaters, and museums—in order to get a chance to be indicated and noticed in the map of China and the world. Culture is the best manifesto of prosperities and the metropolitan glamor, and a means of "defining a rich, shared identity and thus engenders pride of place" (Landry 2008). When manufacturing declined in old industrial cities, culture was regarded as a remedy and savior. Cultural and economic development can be benefited from each other

---

[6]"Connecting to the international track" is a Chinese saying that means "be in line with the international practice." Before China joined World Trade Organization (WTO) in 2001, every trade of business was concerned with and hoped to be in line with the international norm.

and integrated—this has been proven by the world history in the past hundreds of years, as stated in a strategic paper for London, "culture is a strong force to promote understanding and forming the city's identities. It can transcend the obstacles and gather people from different background. Culture can stimulate inspiration, bring education, and create fortune and endless pleasures."[7]

In the 13th Five-year Plan of Shanghai's Economic and Social Development issued in 2016, "Enhancing Cultural Soft-power" stands as a chapter. Cultural soft-power is seen as an important means of enhancing a city's cohesion and "core" competitiveness. The important facilities, events, and leading master artists should be fully utilized for a better integration of culture, economy, and society. The aim is to build Shanghai as "an international cultural metropolis." Aligned with London, New York, Tokyo, and Paris, Shanghai launched and issued "cultural monitoring report" in 2011. More than 60 indicators are recorded the same time in these world cities. Number of performing art places and seats is one of them (Owens 2013).

To realize the plan of "international cultural metropolis," projects of cultural facilities are highly demanded in quantity and quality, and built at suitable locations. In addition to restore aged museums, grand theaters, theaters for indigenous operas, and libraries, Shanghai is planning and building the new annex buildings for municipal museums, libraries, and new opera house. Some are fitted in the old city center to consolidate existing cultural facilities, while more new projects are planned in Pudong and other new zones, so that the arts can serve and promote these brand new communities.

As a box for the performing arts, the grand theater should first meet the requirements of performing functions, such as number of audiences, comfortable sightline and acoustic effects, mechanical and automatic stage facilities, etc. Moreover, as a city icon, the grand theater represents hopes and dreams of the city and its people. It should symbolize the local identity, free ideas, and express a progressive gesture. In a news report on the proposal of Henan Art Center, local media claims that "cultural facilities are venues of carrying out cultural activity and enhancing people's cultural education. They are necessary for international cultural exchange and standing as important symbol of the city's cultural development and taste."[8] In the 1980s and the 1990s, local governments and decision-makers were more concerned about "improving environment for investment," but in the twenty-first century, they emphasized more on "facilitating the spiritual and cultural construction and activating people's daily life."[9]

To fulfill local citizens' specific imagination of the theater, architects frequently use a strategy of double skin—a shoe box concert hall to satisfy the acoustic requirements, and another skin wrapping the shoe box and forming the lobby space. The external skin is given plastic form so that it can easily be looked "like something." For example, in the national theater of Beijing, three auditoriums are

---

[7] From "London: Cultural Capital, the mayor's cultural strategies," February 2003.

[8] *Henan Yishu zhongxin jianyi shu* (Proposal of building Henan Art Center), Henan Government, 2004.

[9] Same as above.

with their own roof, while an oval titanium shell covers the opera hall, concert hall, and multi-functional theater. The shinning shell is lauded as "an opening curtain." The Oriental Art Center of Shanghai is designed as "five petals of magnolia" (Shanghai's city flower) to cover three performance spaces; Hangzhou grand theater as a "bright crescent moon playing jewel in West Lake"; Henan Art Center as "dinosaurs eggs and ancient musical instruments"; Guangzhou opera house as "two pebbles on the bank of the Pear River"; Chongqing theater as a "vessel ploughing the water"; Wuxi theater as a "butterfly"; Wuzhen theater as a "double lotus," etc. Most of these theaters stand at the waterfront where their reflections in water create awesome impressions. For example, the two latest theater projects—Zhuhai Grand Theater and Fuzhou Strait Culture and Art Center—both were built at the riverside (Fig. 2).

Because of the unusual form and extensive decoration, construction costs of these cultural buildings are expensive and sometimes beyond the cities' fiscal afford-ability. At the end of the 1980s, Shenzhen municipal government spent almost all of its budgets in building eight cultural facilities (see Chap. 4). In the beginning of the twenty-first century, Shanghai also faced financial stresses in building its grand theater (see Chap. 2). As these projects are treated as prior political tasks from the top of the city government, the construction of them is resolute and allocated with all available financial, material, and manpower resources.

Roy and Ong wrote about this Asian and Chinese phenomenon and policy: "Caught in the vectors of particular histories, national aspirations and flows of cultures, cities have always been the principal sites for launching world-conjuring projects. Urban dreams and schemes play with accelerating opportunities and accidents that circulate in ever-widening spirals. Emerging nations exercise their new power by assembling glass and steel towers to project particular visions of the world" (Roy and Ong 2011, 1). Skyscrapers, grand theaters, and other cultural buildings in the Chinese cities are just among these "world-conjuring projects." Roy and Ong (2011) further see this as an Asian only situation, "Urban-dwellers in Asia's big cities do not read spectacles as a generalized aesthetic effect of

(a)   **(b)**

Fig. 2 Two grand theaters in waterfront. **a** Zhuhai Grand Theater, designed by Chen Keshi and Peking University team, opened on January 1, 2017, locates at an island of the Pearl River estuary. The architecture depicts the form of "sea shells"; **b** Fuzhou Strait Culture and Art center, designed by PES Architects, opened on October 10, 2018, facing the Minjiang River. The design takes inspiration from the petals of a jasmine blossom, the city flower of Fuzhou

capitalism, but rather as symbols of their metropolis that invite inevitable comparison with rival cities."

Cultural industry, together with cultural accumulation (historic heritage), cultural management, cultural potential, and exchange are factors to assess a city's cultural competitiveness.[10] In the national ranking of Chinese cities in cultural competitiveness, Beijing, Shanghai, Guangzhou, Hangzhou, and Nanjing are listed as the top five. This is also compatible with their ranking in GDP per capita.

Consumerism in Chinese Cities—The Emerging Elite and Middle Class

Coincide with the economic development and shifting to post-industrial era, consumerism is seen as locomotive in the capitalist society (Featherstone 2007). Only when workers became consumers, they would spend money on purchasing large quantity of consumer goods and therefore stimulating capitalist productions. The consumerist behavior expresses people's desire, provides motivation for economy, and brings personal satisfaction. According to Pierre Bourdieu, consuming distinguishes a person's economic capital, and also his education, taste, living style, social status, identities, and differences. In the post-modern period, consuming is more seen as a symbolic activity instead of utility and money (Bourdieu 1986). The booming of shopping mall and commercial space development shows how consumerism has influenced urban design and architecture.

During Mao's era before 1978, a guideline of political correctness for Chinese people was "to work first, enjoy life later." There were shortages of housing in most cities, while decent performance space was extremely rare. However, the focus of government administration was shifted and translated to modernize China and to improve people's living standards in the 1990s. At the same time, civil servants, institutions, and big companies changed from six working days to five working days a week. Since then, the number of high-income urban elites has gradually increased and the middle class has emerged. They have a strong purchase power of high-end cultural activities and boosting the show and performance business. In 1996, the central government issued an instruction to build 50 or more cultural facilities nationwide, such as libraries, museums, and theaters "which are compatible to economic level and represent the image of the state and relevant cities."[11] Through going to concert, opera, Xiqu (folk opera), and other kinds of entertainment, audiences have shown their preference, choice, and taste in cultural and

---

[10] From "*Zhongguo chengshi wenhua jingzhengli yanjiu baogao*" (Report of cultural competitiveness of Chinese cities, 2016), Research Institute of Cultural Development, Communication University of China, August 2017.

[11] Ministry of Culture, *Wenhua shiye fazhan jiuwu jihua he 2010 nian yuanjing mubiao gangyao* (Development plan of cultural affairs and the vision of 2010), Beijing, Ministry of Culture, 2007.

leisure activities. "When cities are dominated by the service economy, aesthetics plays an important role in the use of space and lifestyles" (Zukin 1993).

In 2016, the box office turnover of various performances recorded RMB 47 billion yuan (US$7.5 billion) in China. There were 6.3 million audiences in concerts, 2.3 million in dancing, 3.2 million in drama, 3.2 million in Xiqu, 2.5 million in children's theater, and 1.2 million in acrobatic and folk art. Ticket prices range from US$10 to 3000, depending on different types and classes of performance and troupes.[12] According to the data, total theater audiences were equivalent to one-ninth of Chinese population in 2016. In the same year in the UK, there were 19 million theater audiences, close to 30% of her 65 million populations.[13] The GDP per capita in the UK is US$41,602 in 2016, five times higher than that of China.[14] Although China's GDP per capita is around US$8000, the distribution of wealth is unbalanced among cities. The Engel's Coefficient in China was once over 60% and dropped to 29% in 2017. In "rich" regions, cultural and entertainment expenditure of a family in average was about 11.4% of total household budget.[15] The tier-1 cities like Beijing, Shanghai, and Shenzhen have recorded the GDP per capita of $20,000–$30,000 USD and catch up the economic level of developed countries. People have extra money after food and clothing. Immense theater goers have created a strong demand on new spaces for the performing arts. Grand theaters are built with great expectations, especially from young parents with kids.

The above statistics just provide an average figure of how popular the performing arts in China. However, there is a great social disparity in the country, which is confirmed by the fluctuated level of GDP per capita among different provinces and cities. For example, in the four tier-1 cities (Beijing, Shanghai, Guangzhou, and Shenzhen), a theater can schedule 300–400 events annually, but in certain cities, a theater can hardly organize a couple of events in a month.[16]

---

[12] Annual Report of China's Performing Art Market, 2016. Ministry of Culture, 2017.

[13] The number of audience in the UK is from "There is no business like show business," BBC 4, Saturday, July 29, 2017. http://www.bbc.co.uk/programmes/b08yqb9r. The population of the UK is from Office of National Statistics, "UK Population 2017," https://www.ons.gov.uk/aboutus/transparencyandgovernance/freedomofinformationfoi/ukpopulation2017. Accessed on February 8, 2018. The statistics of audience counts the number of tickets. Some people, for example a musical teacher, may attend concert for 5 times a year. The number could not perfectly reflect how many people really entering theaters.

[14] The GDP per capital of the UK is from "Trading Economics," https://tradingeconomics.com/united-kingdom/gdp-per-capita; the GDP per capita of China is from Xinhua News Agency, April 20, 2017, http://www.xinhuanet.com/fortune/2017-04/20/c_129556927.htm. Accessed on February 8, 2018.

[15] "Quanqiu 22 guo enggeer xishu yilan: zhongguo yicheng fuyu guojia" (Engel's Coefficient in 22 countries: China becomes rich country), March 13, 2013. http://money.163.com/13/0313/16/8PS3DI2200253G87.html, Accessed on March 28, 2018. National Development and Reform Commission, "2017nian zhongguo jumin xiaofei fazhan baogao" (2017 Report of Chinese residents' consuming development), Beijing: People's Press, 2018.

[16] The number of performance was counted through Web sites of various theaters or from annual report of theaters by the author's research team.

For hundreds of newly built theaters, are there so many performances to fill in? China's theaters are mainly managed by two groups, one state-owned and another with government background. As mentioned in the following chapters, the Poly Theater Management Co. Ltd. (with government and military background) manages 63 theaters in 55 cities. The group organizes art performances, programming and sends them itinerating in various cities. For example, a foreign symphony orchestra may travel to 15 cities in the Christmas and New Year season from north to south. Poly Group built some theaters and also invested some programmes, but not many. Vernacular opera (like Peking opera or Cantonese opera, with less young fans) or indigenous performing art troupes could hardly afford to rent luxurious grand theaters. Their activities are limited in old small neighborhood auditoriums run by state-owned companies (see Chaps. 1 and 7).

Foreign Design and Urban Mirage

Since fourteenth century, the royal performing arts had declined inside the palace of Beijing, while folk music, dances, and plays were exuberant and public or commercial performances took place at outdoor spaces, or at simple roofed stages with outdoor sittings, or inside teahouses. The theater with indoor stage and auditorium was not a conventional building type in China, until the late nineteenth century when folk operas were popular. The first modern theater in Western style, Teatro D. Pedro V, was built in Macau in 1860. In the early twentieth century, movie theaters were spread over China along with the incoming of foreign especially American movies and the establishment of Chinese film industry. At the same time, large-scale modern auditoriums for assembly, meeting, and performance began to exist. The best example was the renowned Dr. Sun Yat-san Memorial Hall, built in Guangzhou in 1934. This milestone project with a 4000-seat auditorium was designed by Lu Yanzhi, a representative of the first generation of foreign-trained Chinese architects (see Chap. 3).

In the past, professional theaters and concert halls were hardly constructed in China, except Beijing, Shanghai, and Guangzhou. As the national capital and political center, Beijing in 1954 built the Capital Theater which was exclusively used for dramas, and converted a movie theater into the Beijing Concert Hall in 1960. As the biggest metropolis in China, Shanghai had formed an excellent philharmonic orchestra since the concession era, the Shanghai Concert Hall formally the Nanking Theater opened in 1959. As the host city of the annual China Import and Export Fair since 1957, Guangzhou built the Friendship Theater in 1965, it was considered as a top-class multi-functional hall for the performance of music, ballet, and other productions, and its design was included in the architectural textbook at the time.

However, assembly halls of various sizes, primarily used as venues of conducting Communist Party conferences and political meetings, were once widely built all over the country by different organizations including municipal governments at all levels,

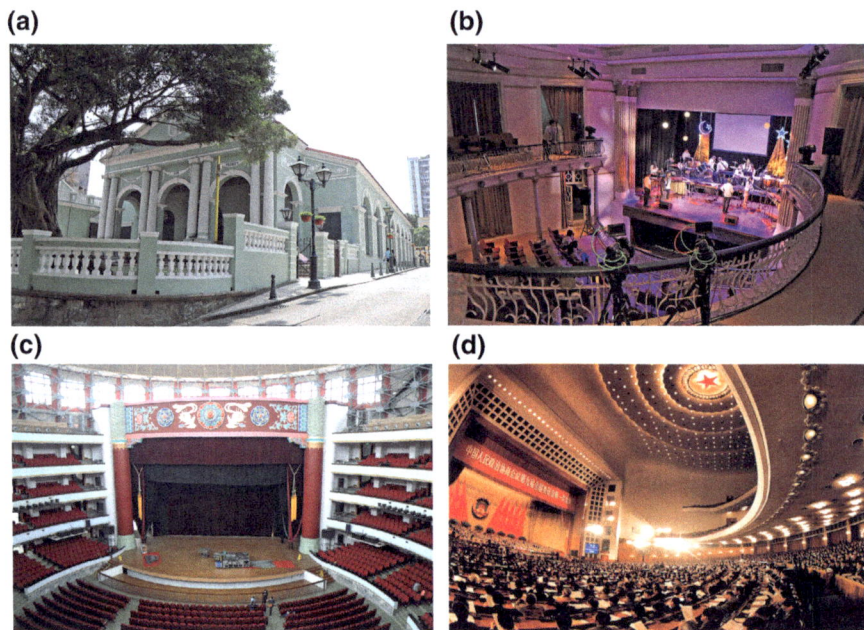

Fig. 3 Theaters in history. **a** and **b** Teatro D. Pedro V, Macau, 1860; **c** Great Hall of People, Chongqing, 1954; **d** Auditorium for 10,000 people, the Great Hall of the People, Beijing, 1959

large government agencies and state-owned enterprises, or headquarters of military bases after 1949. The architecture of those halls was similar to a theater with a stage and a big auditorium, but the basic function of the stage was to set up seats and tables for the party cadres making speeches, and the auditorium was a sitting area for the delegates, so there was little acoustic design because to run meetings was the main purpose (Lu 2009). However, the assembly hall was also used for major performing and entertainment events during the socialist period (Fig. 3).

Key constructions of this type are exemplified by two projects of the Great Hall of People. The Great Hall of People in Chongqing completed in 1954 is a municipal building and exhibits the style of traditional Chinese architecture, whereas the Great Hall of People in Beijing completed in 1959 is a state building for national legislative and ceremonial activities such as meetings of the National People's Congress, the Chinese People's Political Consultative Conference, and the National Congress of the Communist Party. Its design shows the influence of the Soviet Union architecture. Both halls stand for the government authority and as political symbols, but at different levels. The Great Hall of People in Beijing with a 10,000-seat auditorium was also used for special events, for example, during the evening of October 2, 1964, it was the venue for the premiere of the "Red" epic *Dong Fang Hong* (The East is Red), a monumental musical production regarding the history of Chinese Communist revolution. During the "Cultural Revolution" period (1966–1976), performances and repertoires were extremely rare. Apart from the dominant and frequent political meetings, eight major "Revolutionary Modern Model Plays" (including five new productions of Peking Opera, two new productions of ballet and a new composition of symphonic poem) were those limited lists that could be staged in assembly halls occasionally (Cheng 2015).

After the devastating "Cultural Revolution" (1966–1976), every trade of business in China was eager to resurge. Chinese people have worked hard at improving economy, civic infrastructure, and living standard in many respects including education, arts, and cultural developments. In the early 1980s, the Ministry of Construction announced a national design competition of medium and small size theater/cinema to call for feasible and affordable schemes that could be built in small cities and towns with available construction technology. At the time, China started to invite foreign design firms, and the overseas design was trickling into Chinese cities. Through star hotel and office edifice, architects from Japan, the USA, and Europe set up benchmark of high design/technology and classy living quality. Furthermore, China began to follow the international norm in the development of new arts and cultural projects by organizing architecture competitions opened to international architects.

On one hand, "to learn from foreign advance technology and experience" as a social understanding accompanied by the yearning of Western culture was the background to invite foreign architects and specialists participating in the design of arts and cultural facilities such as opera house and concert hall. Local architects had little knowledge at such types of buildings and especially were unfamiliar with the design and technology of large auditorium acoustics and the mechanized back stage, which formed the most important parts of theater. Foreign design firms had shown unparalleled advantages and skills in terms of experience and technical expertise.

On the other hand, the urge to improve and upgrade the city image, the motivation to promote the city as an international metropolis, the ambitions to build world-class cultural facilities in comparison with other existing landmarks, the chasing of extraordinary looks and striking form to attract public attentions, were decisive factors and justifications to mobilize the city including its officials and people investing huge money on the development of a grand theater. People were somehow quite obsessed with foreign famous architects or "Starchitects" not just based on their talents and success, but also on a perception or a prediction that once the design of a Starchitect gets built, the city would be recognized as an international city and notable to the world. They believed that the work of a foreign master certainly was what the city deserved to have in the twenty-first century and a representation of the city's achievement in becoming classy, tasteful, and cultivated, apart from pursuing and building wealth.

These mirage-like buildings are also glorious achievements of "capable" municipal officials during their tenure and will help these officials to ascend in career ladder. With the wave of urban renewal and new town construction, cultural district with fabulous museums, theaters, and libraries were tabled in provincial and municipal government, and got resolute support. In the trend of appealing for new mirage, local architects are generally regarded less competent of undertaking the task. Well-known foreign architects were sought after and eagerly welcomed for bringing new ideas.

Indeed, the large-scale, multi-functional grand theater project that funded with ample budget, located at a prominent site, asked for design of high-profile and bold statement, has challenged and attracted some reputable, talented foreign architects and well-established, leading international firms to submit high-quality and fresh competition entries. In terms of creativity, originality, innovative idea, and integration of state-of-the-art technology and building systems, facilities, and equipment, international teams often have the edge over local architects in winning competitions.

International design competitions were held and celebrity design firms of Japan, Europe, and America were invited. Some design competitions saw at least five shortlisted firms, some might be 40, like national theater design competition in Beijing in 1998. However, in the first five years of the twenty-first century, only several design firms were able to win projects in China—Paul Andreu (Aéroports de Paris Ingénierie or ADPi, three grand theaters), Jean Marie Charpentier of France (two), gmp of Germany (four) and Carlos Ott from Canada (four). The list above shows an interesting phenomenon that some architects repeatedly were chosen to design grand theaters by either winning competitions or invitations. Moreover, they are/were all internationally renowned, well-established, brilliant, and accomplished architects and firms. Their artistic talents, creative minds, architectural insights, professional knowledge, and practical experiences were fully exemplified by those compelling theaters that they designed. Some design firms upheld their consistent design rationales and approaches, and some only managed to please the Chinese decision-makers. The innovation in telecommunication technologies has liberated architectural production from territorial domains, as graphic drawings can be transferred instantly between design centers and construction sites across the globe (Ren 2011). Among all theaters of overseas design, although there were a few controversial projects, many stood for outstanding designs.

In addition to skillfully handle the issue of creating a tremendous, spectacular, and alluring theater space with a hi-tech building structure and elegant building materials, foreign design solutions tend to define sensible, inviting, inclusive, and liberal public spaces and public images better than local proposals. This is particular helpful to cities aimed at promoting city pride, by launching grand theater projects. In fact, news and reviews of the completion of a grand theater often mention how the project enhances the city, e.g., regarding the Guangzhou Opera House, (it) "has been the catalyst for the development of cultural facilities in the city including new museums, library and archive. The Opera House design is the latest realization of Zaha Hadid Architects' unique exploration of contextual urban relationships, combining the cultural traditions that have shaped Guangzhou's history, with the ambition and optimism that will create its future."[17] For the latest Fuzhou Strait Art and Culture Center designed by Pekka Salminen just opened on October 10, 2018,

---

[17]Guangzhou Opera House, from https://www.archdaily.com/115949/guangzhou-opera-house-zaha-hadid-architects, accessed October 17, 2018.

Fig. 4 Grand Theaters designed by DDB Architects Shanghai led by Xiang Bingren. **a** Hefei Grand Theater, 2009; **b** and **c** Datang Cultural District including concert hall, cinema city and art museum, 2009, and grand theater, 2017. Courtesy of Teng Luying

Fig. 5 Harbin Grand Theater, designed by MAD, 2016. Photograph by Sun Cong

Fuzhou Daily regards it as a new cultural landmark of the city, "with significant meanings in the field of expressing cultural confidence, building the city image, elevating soft-power, improving civic facilities, enhancing the competitiveness and the status of Fuzhou, promoting a balanced development of economy and society."[18]

---

[18] Opening of Fuzhou Strait Art and Culture Center, from *Fuzhou Daily*, http://fj.leju.com/news/2018-10-11/09246455961074029362811.shtml, accessed October 17, 2018.

Fig. 6 Nelum Pokuna—national theater of Sri Lanka, 2012

Through collaboration and Chinese peers' observation in near distance, this overseas impact positively fosters the upgrading and progress of general design standard in China. Chinese architects grew up through learning and started to grab the design of grand theaters in some cities, for example, in Hefei, Xi'an, Harbin, and Nanjing after 2010. This building type also becomes "gift," designed by Chinese design institutes and donated to foreign countries, for example, national theaters in Senegal (2011), Sri Lanka (2012), and Algeria (2016) (Figs. 4, 5 and 6).

Methodology and Structures of this Book

The intension of this book is to discuss the relationship between grand theater developments and urbanization in China, with a focus on foreign designs due to the leading role of international architects in building venues for the performing arts. We examine theater projects beyond architecture, functions, and construction technology, and put them in the context of urban development.[19] As outlined above, the grand theater as a key project undoubtedly is included into the city's master planning, together with other cultural facilities forming a new urban center as the catalyst for new town development. Therefore, we tentatively entitle this study "Grand Theater Urbanism." There are plenty of articles and books discussing urbanism and theater design, but almost none specifically links this building type with urban design. We aim to fill this academic gap.

What is urbanism? According to *Oxford English Dictionary*, it is the way of life characteristic of cities and towns, and the development and planning of cities and towns.[20] In observing the construction movement of cultural buildings, we have

---

[19]Although this book does not go further into the theater design technology, we have generally scanned literature on theater design, for example, Izenour (1996a, b), Hammond (2006), Kronenburg (2012), and Short et al. (2011).

[20] The definition of urbanism is from https://en.oxforddictionaries.com/definition/urbanism, accessed February 25, 2018.

noticed that the municipal government always takes a leading role in initiating and planning cultural buildings and the grand theater, which usually locate in a prominent site of new towns. Although the realization of grand theaters is inseparable from sophisticated technologies, we are not going to assess this dimension, but contextual urban relationships, "the way of life characteristic" and "the development and planning of towns."

China is a big country of many cities which compete for keeping ahead in economic and cultural developments among them in order to achieve regional, national, or even international recognitions. They have individual approaches and strategies to promote and build the cities subject to their own specific size, location, and executive grade (or position in the city-tier system), providing us the ground of methodology. In this book, we look at ten selected cities, which represent the rapid development and the ever-changing dynamic of Chinese cities in the twenty-first century. They range from large to medium size, from tier-1 to tier-2 and tier-3, from state capital, directly administered city (under the central government) to provincial capital and prefecture-level city, from north to south, east to west, and from mainland to outlying island. The ten cities are paired up based on their similarities for easy comparison:

- Beijing (capital, political center, tier-1, northern region), Shanghai (directly administered, financial center, tier-1, eastern region);
- Guangzhou (provincial-level, tier-1), Shenzhen (former Economic Special Zone, tier-1), both are metropolises of southern region, pioneers of the "reform and open-up" policy;
- Chongqing (directly administered, tier-2, southwestern region), Zhengzhou (provincial-level, tire-2, middle west region);
- Taiyuan (provincial-level, tier-2, northwestern region), Wuxi (prefecture-level, tier-3, southeast region);
- Taichung, Hong Kong (both are cities of outlying island, with different lifestyles and political systems from the mainland).

These cities have diverse evolving trajectories and stories of cultural buildings in the past hundred years, but all concluded by recently built grand theaters designed by foreign architects. It could be a fashionable or normal way in the age of globalization, since international design competition was the common practice in the development of public especially cultural projects. We hope to present a diverse range of projects with distinct urban contexts, design approaches, and technical methods (Fig. 7).

Whereas Taichung and Hong Kong are under different political and administrative systems from the Chinese mainland, the reason or decision to build a new cultural complex may not be exactly the same as other mainland cities, due to different planning policies and urban development strategies. In addition to the public demand and practical needs for new performance space, both cities are also facing challenges from East and Southeast Asian cities, if not directly from China mainland, in the context of globalization. It is interesting to see how different Taichung and Hong Kong develop theater projects from their mainland peers.

Fig. 7 Map showing locations of the ten selected cities (by Zhang Lujia)

Each chapter of this book is a case study on a selected city, with the focus on key projects of either one or two theaters. The authors had conducted on-site investigations. With primary information and materials, they analyzed grand theaters from different perspectives, i.e., planning, design, construction, operation, and management, and viewed theater developments against historical and social backgrounds of the city. Most of the authors were born, studied, or work in the selected cities. They have witnessed the cities' growth and how cultural buildings have contributed to people's quality of life. Therefore, they are resourceful about the areas and cases.

Chapter 1 delineates the development of Beijing from late Qing Dynasty (1644–1911) to the People's Republic after 1949. No matter in the feudalist society, the capitalist or communist rule, two sets of performance space co-existed. One is the formal theaters and cinemas open to the public, another is internally used by official or royal families. In the 1950s when socialist movements replaced the private business, state-owned companies, government departments, or institutions run their own small working and living world—"danwei" (unit). Hundreds of multi-purpose convention halls were built within such small world. This may be called workers' club in the Soviet Union or cultural hall in Europe. Lu investigates these two systems of performing art space. His narrative of the National Center of Performing Art from 1958 to the twenty-first century describes an intricate interaction of state leaders' will, old city renovation, design institute, designers, technical evolution, and global influences in a 40+ years' period. The chapter traces the origin of prevailing three-hall method in a newly built theater. Lu himself is part of the design team of national theater; therefore, his analysis is engaged with personal experiences.

After the political and power center of Beijing, Shanghai is the most important economic and financial metropolis in the Chinese mainland. The city has long been a splendid cultural star in Asia. However, it was lag behind after the devastation of Communist rule. Chapter 2 describes how Shanghai rise culturally in the open-door policy through case studies of five grand theaters. These theaters, all designed by the international architects either through design competition or invitation, well punctuate the different transition periods and the urban mission they undertook. Amazing at the tremendous achievements of Shanghai in cultural building, Xue sharply interrogates the proper use of theater public space which the member of public should deserve.

In Chap. 3, Ding further comments that gated nature is the product of the dialectical articulation between politics and experimentation in the Chinese political and cultural context. Chapter 3 links several performance spaces in Guangzhou in southern China from the national government, communist government, open-door period to the global economic competition of the twenty-first century. Hadid's design of Guangzhou Opera House was highly respected, expected, and built as a turning point for the city's new economic and cultural center.

If Guangzhou is benefited from free "southern wind," Shenzhen started its journey from a fishing town to metropolis of high-tech merely by bordering the capitalist Hong Kong in 1980. In Chap. 4, Sun traces the birth of the first "grand theater" in China when Shenzhen municipal government bravely threw half of its public expenditure to build eight cultural facilities in the mid-1980s. Shenzhen set up an example of urban design by planning its central axis in Futian area when American and Japanese architects were involved in planning and landmark building design in the 1990s. When districts and residents in Shenzhen become affluent in the twenty-first century, grand cultural mega-structures were built in several sub-centers. Shenzhen gives an example of fast-growing and resolute determination.

The development of China is uneven, and disparity between cities is obvious. Traditionally, the eastern and coastal cities enjoy higher developing rate and economic fruits. Therefore, cultural facilities are densely spread in these cities. On the contrary, cities in the western China are relatively backward. Chongqing is a city in the "west," although it is still geographically located in the east side if drawing a line in the middle of Chinese territory. In Chap. 5, Chu and Xue delineate the performance space and city's space from 1940 up to now. Chongqing Grand Theater and Guotai Arts Center typify two types of design, the former from international design competition, and the latter from domestic one. Chongqing Grand Theater lonely perches on the tip of northern bank of Yangtze River, its masculine "tank" image dialogues with the CBD in Yuzhong peninsula crossing the water. However, its heroic gesture does not provide physical comfort for pedestrians who approach it. Guotai, located in the old city center, is destined to inherit its tradition from the national government and act as transition spot from city center to the riverside. Through these cultural facilities, Chongqing sends strong statement from the upstream of Yangtze River—it is both vernacular and international.

Compared to Chongqing, Zhengzhou and Henan Province have longer history of more than two thousand years and once nurtured the ancient Chinese civilization. However, it was lag behind in the modern era. In Chap. 6, Zhang looks at Zhengzhou, capital city of Henan, and its rising from a chaotic insignificant industrial town to locomotive of Central China. The driving force comes from the Zhengdong new district, next to the old town, planned by Japanese master Kisho Kurokawa. Zhengdong new district uses its own grid, regardless the fabric of old town. Its audacious design includes auspicious form of land division and artificial lake, where the Henan Arts Center is perched. The functions of performance and exhibition supplement each other and form festive atmosphere in the central park. After ten years, the rising housing price near the park partly reflects the increasing quality of life. The once called "ghost city" is enthusiastically embraced by Henan people.

Further north, Taiyuan is known as capital of coal mine. The city is usually associated with bad air quality and wicked bosses of "bloody coal mine," where black gold is dug at the toll of numerous workers' lives. Chapter 7 describes the development of local opera and its performing venues, similar as those in Beijing in the early twentieth century. Xiao and Ni investigate the building of cultural center in Taiyuan and how these cultural buildings change the image of the city. Through international competition, French ideas (from Paris) and design serve the goals and ambition of Central Chinese city. The authors show that cultural buildings and mayor's lofty idea can bring the shift of industry and restore city's glorious past and confidence.

If the provincial cities just discussed have clearly deserved large-scale cultural structures, Wuxi, a city located in southern Jiangsu Province, would seem to have had less reason to follow suit. In Chap. 8, Li discusses the lakeshore grand theater designed by the Finnish architect PES in terms of its world-class architecture and facility in contrast to few performance events after completion. Wuxi is simply lack of a cultural atmosphere to sustain a grand theater normally built for classical performing arts. The grand theater project that proposed by the city government is a trend-goer more than a response to the current demand for new performance space. However, we would like to view this kind of projects optimistically as development-in-advance, but how to improve the low-usage-rate of the theater after its completion is a big challenge for the city. Indeed, most second- and third-tier cities face a similar embarrassing problem.

Although different in ideology, governments in both sides of Taiwan Strait are aware of the importance of landmark cultural building. Taipei has been building performing arts center in its busy old city area since 2012. The building designed by

Rem Koolhaas triggered debates and encountered difficulties in construction. Kaohsiung has built Weiwuying National Kaohsiung Center for the Arts, designed by Netherlands firm Mecanoo. The Center with opera, concert hall, play theater, chamber theater, and outdoor amphitheater opened in 2018. Before Taipei and Kaohsiung, Taichung was the early city engaging with global architectural design. Mayor Hu was known as "cultural mayor." City council hall and plaza were rebuilt and designed by international architects (through competition) during his office. Chapter 9 checks out the landmark building—National Taichung Theater designed by Japanese architect Toyo Ito—whose scheme defeated many competitors including Zaha Hadid's elaborated work. Xiao dates back the city's history from Japanese colony, the United Nations-aid to the globalization era. He depicts the up and down of the project, and how it stood up after overcoming numerous technical challenges. Although the theater perfects itself by space and technology, the conceived "central park" is at the mercy of surrounding luxurious residential towers. The theater consolidates the city's status as a habitable city in Taiwan Island.

Compared with the rapid development of Chinese mainland, Hong Kong, once "Asian dragon," looks shabby in cultural facilities. The territory receives top-class performing troupes from all over the world. However, its most "advanced" venue is Cultural Center built in 1989. The colonial government's main concern was to solve more urgent social problems like refugee and potable water. After the sovereignty handover in 1997, Hong Kong has embarked on democratic road, which made development pace even slower. Xue demonstrates the evolution of public buildings in Hong Kong in Chap. 10. The busy engagement with members of public in cultural buildings presents a sharp contrast with the scenario in the other Chinese cities.

Ten chapters may not fully reflect the panorama of "grand theater heat" in so many Chinese cities. Appendix I gives a database of design and construction of grand theaters in China. According to our definition of "grand," that is an auditorium larger than 1,200 seats, almost 200 such grand theaters were completed in the first 18 years of the twenty-first century. Appendix II selects typical theaters in six cities to demonstrate how frequently and in what ways these theaters are used. They reflect the popularity of performance space in different cities, effectiveness and efficiency of cultural buildings.

Through reading this book, one can see the fast pace, decision-makings, motivations, ambitions, and phenomena of Chinese urbanization in the twenty-first century, which continuously boosts urban developments and promotes economic performance in China. Urbanization has changed the life of Chinese people and has formulated a development pattern with both positive and negative impacts on the society. The building of cultural mega-structures and progress in globalization and urbanization are eventually driven by the individual instinct and collective desire of recognition.[21]

At the end of each chapter, authors give a short piece of their personal encounter about the city and their experiences in cinema/theater. Performing art buildings

---

[21] Here we use the definition of Francis Fukuyama, see Fukuyama (2018).

eventually serve people, the individual feeling gives a vivid scenario of Chinese cities and everyday life. If the Chinese Grand Theater Urbanism is specific, can we learn from their experimentations and experiences for a more reasonable and sustainable way in the development of cultural complex?

Charlie Qiuli Xue
Lin Li

References

Blundell-Jones, P. (2016). *Architecture and ritual: how buildings shape society*. London: Bloomsbury Academic.

Bourdieu, P. (1986). *Distinction: a social critique of the judgement of taste*. London: Routledge.

Broudehoux, A. (2004). *The making and selling of post-mao beijing*. New York: Routledge.

Cheng, Y. (2015). *Contemporary performing arts architecture in the multidimensional perspective*. Beijing: China Architecture and Building Press. 程翌 (2015). 多维视角下的当代演艺建筑. 北京: 中国建筑工业出版社.

Cupers, K. (2015). The cultural center: architecture as cultural policy in postwar Europe. *Journal of the Society of Architectural Historians, 74*(4), 464–484.

Ding, G., & Xue, C. Q. L. (2015). China's architectural aid: exporting a transformational modernism. *Habitat International, 47*(1), 136–147.

Featherstone, M. (2007). *Consumer culture and postmodernism*. London: Sage Publications.

Fukuyama, F. (2018). *Identity: the demand for dignity and the politics of resentment*. New York: Farrar, Straus and Giroux.

Grenfell, M. (2004). *Pierre Bourdieu: agent provocateur*. London: Continuum.

Hammond, M. (2006). *Performing architecture: opera houses, theatres and concert halls for the twenty-first century*, London and New York: Merrell Publishers Limited.

Izenour, G. C. (1996a). *Theater design*. New Haven: Yale University Press.

Izenour, G. C. (1996b). *Theater technology*. New Haven: Yale University Press.

Jayne, M. (Ed.). (2018). *Chinese urbanism—critical perspective*. London and New York: Routledge.

Kong, L., Ching, C., & Chou, T. (2015). *Arts, culture and the making of global cities—creating new urban landscape in Asia*. Cheltenham: Edward Elgar.

Kronenburg, R. (2012). *Live architecture—venues, stages and arenas for popular music*. London and New York: Routledge.

Landry, C. (2008). *The creative city: a toolkit for urban renovators*. London: Earthscan.

Li, L., & Xue, Q. L. (Eds.). (2017). *Chinese urbanism in the 21st century*. Beijing: China Architecture and Building Press. 李璘、薛求理主编 (2017). *21世纪中国城市主义*. 北京: 中国建筑工业出版社.

Lu, X. (2009). *On the Evolution of Modern Theaters in China*. Beijing: China Architecture and Building Press, 2009. 卢向东 (2009). 中国现代剧场的演进. 北京:中国建筑工业出版社.

Murray, P. (2004). *The saga of the Sydney Opera House: the dramatic story of the design and construction of the icon of modern Australia*. New York and London: Spon Press.

Owens, P. (2013). *World cities cultural report*. Shanghai: Tongji University Press.

Rowe, P. (2005). *East Asia modern: shaping the contemporary city*. London: Reaktion.

Ren, X. (2011). *Building globalization: transnational architecture production in urban China*. Chicago and London: The University of Chicago Press.

Roy, A., & Ong, A. (Eds.) (2011). *Worlding cities: Asian experiments and the art of being global*. Malden, MA: Wiley-Blackwell.

Short, C. A., Barrett, P., & Fair, A. (2011). *Geometry and atmosphere—theatre buildings from vision to reality*. London: Ashgate Publishing Ltd.

Short, J. R. (2004). *Global metropolitan: globalizing cities in a capitalist world*. London and New York: Routledge.

Wu, F. (Ed.). (2006). *Globalization and the Chinese city*. London and New York: Routledge.

Wu, F. (Ed.). (2007). *China's emerging cities: the making of new urbanism*. London and New York: Routlege.

Xue, C. Q. L. (2006). *Building a revolution: Chinese architecture since 1980*. Hong Kong: Hong Kong University Press.

Xue, C. Q. L. (2010). *World architecture in China*. Hong Kong: Joint Publishing Ltd.

Xue, C. Q. L., & Ding, G. (2018). *A history of design institutes in China: from Mao to Market*. London and New York: Routledge.

Zukin, S. (1993). *Landscapes of power: from Detroit to Disney World*. Berkeley, CA: University of California Press.

Contents

Editor and Contributors

About the Editor

Charlie Qiuli Xue has taught architecture at Shanghai Jiao Tong University; the University of Texas, USA; and City University of Hong Kong. An award-winning architect and writer, he has published 12 books, including *Building a Revolution: Chinese Architecture since 1980* (HKU Press, 2006), *Hong Kong Architecture 1945–2015: From Colonial to Global* (Springer, 2016), and *A History of Design Institutes in China* (with Guanghui Ding, Routledge, 2018), and research papers in international refereed journals such as the *Journal of Architecture, Urban Design International, Habitat International,* and *Cities.* His book "Hong Kong Architecture 1945–2015" was awarded by the International Committee of Architectural Critics (CICA) chaired by Sir Joseph Rykwert in 2007. Xue's research focuses on architecture in China and design strategies for high-density environments.

Contributors

Dongzhu Chu is the deputy dean and Ph.D. supervisor of the School of Architecture and Urban Planning, Chongqing University. Chu was previously a visiting scholar at the University of Toronto and Delft University of Technology, and worked at Rotterdam and KPMB in Toronto. Chu has published five academic monographs and more than fifty academic papers, including *Integrated Mechanism of Generation—Evaluation in Sustainable Building Design Process* (2015), *Enigmatic Code of the Netherlands: Cities Architecture and Design through an Architect's Vision* (2012), and *Starting Design on Architecture* (2011). Chu is now engaged in research, education, and design in the field of sustainable design, fine urban design, integration of architecture and traffic, and urban design for important locations.

Guanghui Ding teaches architecture at Beijing University of Civil Engineering and Architecture, China. His books *Constructing a Place of Critical Architecture in China* (2016) and *A History of Design Institutes in China* (with Charlie Xue, 2018) were published by Routledge. His articles have been published by *Architectural Research Quarterly*, *Habitat International*, and *Journal of the Society of Architectural Historians*. His research focuses on the history, theory, and criticism of modern Chinese architecture. Based in Beijing, he practices architecture both independently and collaboratively.

Lin Li a Hong Kong-based architect, has been involved in the design of numerous building projects in China since 1995. He is also the author or editor of numerous academic studies and publications in the field of Chinese architecture, landscape gardens, urban development, and heritage preservation, including his latest book *Chinese Urbanism in the 21st Century* (with Charlie Xue, China Architecture & Building Press, 2017). Li received architectural training at Pratt Institute and Columbia University in the City of New York.

Xiangdong Lu obtained a master's degree from Harvard GSD in 2001, and a Ph.D. from Tsinghua University in 2005. He teaches architecture at the School of Architecture at Tsinghua University. His research focuses on the history of modern theater in China under the influence of culture, politics, technology, and business, against the background of the modernization movement in China beginning in the twentieth century. His book *On the Evolution of Modern Theaters in China: A History from Grand Stage to Grand Theater* (in Chinese) was published in 2009 (Chinese Architecture and Building Press, CABP). He is also an active architect, and his experience in theater design in China has helped him to understand the dilemma of modern theater in Chinese over the past three decades.

Min Ni is an instructional assistant in Tourism Department of Normal College, Shenzhen University. In 2017, she became the first holder of master's degree in Piano Performance from Shenzhen University. As a Shenzhen-based pianist and piano teacher, she has received 55 awards of piano competitions and prominent teacher, including 15 international awards. Her piano students won several prizes from the domestic and international piano competition. She has also accumulated a wealth of experience during the concerts where she appeared as pianist and performance consultant.

Cong Sun is currently a Ph.D. candidate and works as a research assistant at the City University of Hong Kong, with interests in the linkage of cultural facility distribution and urban expansion, and the tension between urban policy and architectural practice. She holds a master's degree in Urban Design from the University of Hong Kong and a bachelor's degree in Architecture from Shenzhen University, where her graduation design received an award of excellence. Before joining CityU, she worked in a global architecture firm (Aedas) for more than three years and was involved in many large projects in Hong Kong and Mainland China, such as West Kowloon Terminus, Zhuhai Hengqin IFC Tower, and Retail Mall of Chengdu ICC.

Jing Xiao received his Ph.D. from the University of Nottingham, UK, in 2013. He has held the position of assistant professor of architecture at Shenzhen University, China, since 2016. He has received research funding from both international and domestic bodies, including the Getty Foundation, Universitas 21, and Guangdong Planning Office of Philosophy and Social Science. He has published research articles in many international refereed journals such as *Habitat International*, *Studies in the History of Gardens and Designed Landscapes*, *IDEA Journal*, and *Architecture Journal* (Chinese).

Yingbo Xiao (Raibbie) is a Ph.D. candidate with a particular interest in the development of architectural design firms before and after the Chinese Economic Reform. Before enrolling at the City University of Hong Kong, he worked for two years as an intern architect in Shanghai Xian Dai Architectural Design Group and the Shenzhen Municipality Public Works Bureau. He holds a master's degree in architecture from Tsinghua University and a bachelor's degree in architecture from Shenzhen University. For the 2016–2017 academic year, he was a research assistant at the City University of Hong Kong. He lives in Shenzhen and Hong Kong.

Kai Xue is master's degree student of School of Architecture and Urban Planning, Chongqing University.

Lujia Zhang is a Ph.D. candidate at the City University of Hong Kong. She obtained her master's degree in architecture from the South China University of Technology in 2016 and bachelor's degree of architecture from Zhengzhou University in 2013. She is interested in contemporary Chinese architecture practice and criticism. She participated in several design practices and research projects during her study periods in Guangzhou and Hong Kong.

Chapter 1
Development of Theaters and the City in Beijing: The 1950s and Post-1980s

Xiangdong Lu

1.1 Theaters and the City of Beijing

Theaters and the city of Beijing are two meaningful architecture and urbanism concepts, respectively. Theaters are an important type of building in Beijing, which as the capital of both the Ming and Qing Dynasties has developed a special urban spatial structure. The city has continuously changed since becoming the capital of the People's Republic of China in 1949. Across different periods, a series of intriguing changes in the relationship between theaters and the urban space of Beijing has emerged due to the development of theaters and the city itself. In this chapter, we mainly discuss the changes occurring after 1949.

Before our discussion, we must explain some basic information on Beijing and theaters before 1949—specifically, at the end of the Qing Dynasty (A.D. 1644–1911) and in the early years of the Republic of China (A.D. 1911–1949). This information serves as a basis for our later discussion.

Here we summarize essential information on the theaters in Beijing at the end of the Qing Dynasty and in the early years of the Republic of China (Xue 2009; Hou 1999) (Fig. 1.1). Several kinds of theaters existed at the end of the Qing Dynasty: royal stages, stages in bureaucratic mansions, folk tea garden theaters, folk opera gardens in guild halls and stages in temples. These different kinds of theaters were located in different areas of Beijing. Royal theaters were mainly located in the Forbidden City. However, the Summer Palace outside of the Forbidden City also had its own royal theater. Government-funded opera gardens were mainly located in the mansions of various aristocrats and bureaucrats in the Inner City of Beijing, such as the famous garden at Prince Kung's mansion. Opera gardens in guild halls were mainly located in the Outer City of old Beijing, supported by thanes, mer-

X. Lu (✉)
School of Architecture, Tsinghua University, Beijing, China
e-mail: lu-xd@mail.tsinghua.edu.cn

© Springer Nature Singapore Pte Ltd. 2019
C. Q. Xue (ed.), *Grand Theater Urbanism*,
https://doi.org/10.1007/978-981-13-7868-3_1

1

chants and some officials. Commercial tea garden theaters were also mainly found in the Outer City and later expanded gradually into the Inner City (Fig. 1.2).

Influenced by the style of occidental theaters, large-stage theaters began to appear among commercial theaters at the end of the 19th century. Later in the 1920s, the early years of the Republic of China, Western theaters were first opened in Beijing, such as Zhenguang (true light) Theater (currently the China National Theater for Children) in Wangfujing and Kaiming Theater in Zhushikou. The city of Beijing maintained its urban spatial structure and scope until the early years of the Republic of China. Its main streets were mostly situated within an area that resembled a "凸" shape on the map (constituting the districts in the current Second Ring Road of Beijing) and its urban spatial structure consisted primarily of the Inner City, the Outer City, the Imperial City and the Forbidden City with a clear central axis (Hou 1988).

Early in the Qing Dynasty, almost all folk theaters were clustered in the south of Beijing. However, at the end of the Qing Dynasty, they were finally able to start their gradual expansion into the Inner City (Li 1998). The folk theaters in the city had several major gathering areas. All of these areas were commercial districts, implying a connection between commercial theaters and urban business areas. Thus, commercial theaters ultimately became the dominant theater type in Beijing (Figs. 1.3, 1.4, 1.5 and 1.6).

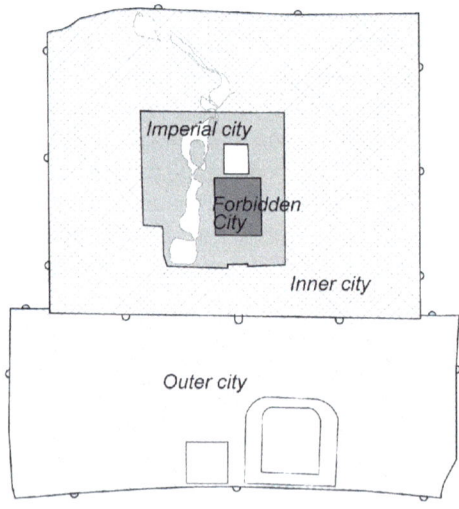

Fig. 1.1 Left: Map of Beijing in 1914 (the early years of the Republic of China). Right: Spatial structure of Beijing City during the Qing Dynasty (Forbidden City, Imperial City, Inner City and Outer City)

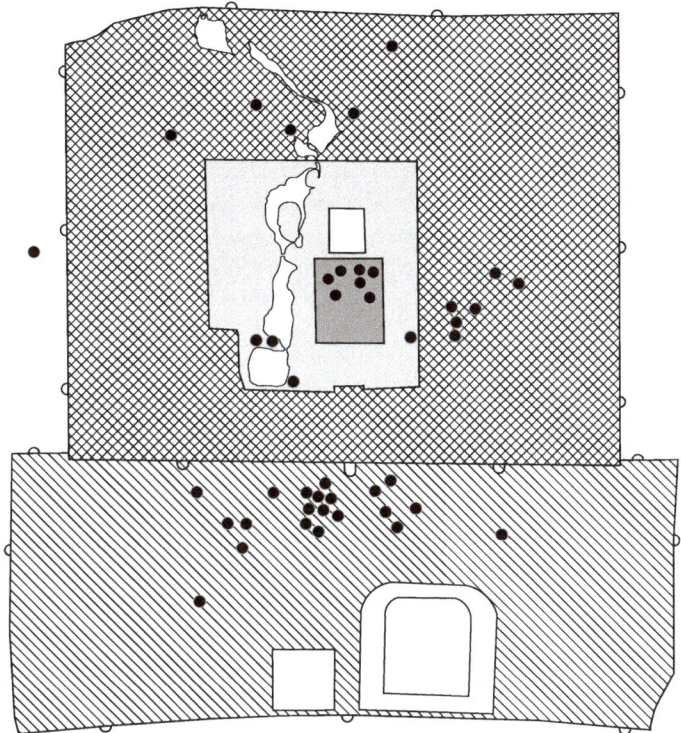

Fig. 1.2 Distribution of Beijing's major theaters during the Qing Dynasty. *Source* Li (1998)

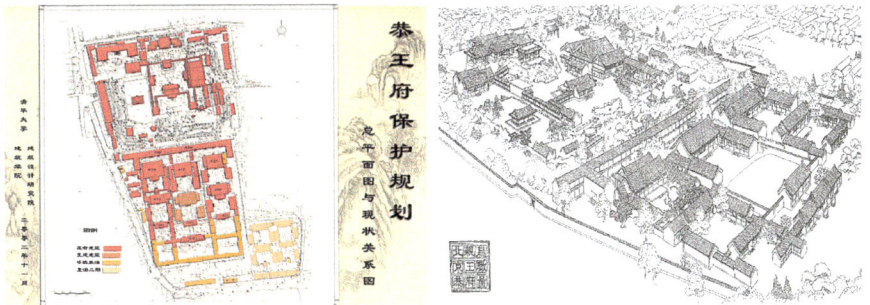

Fig. 1.3 Left: Planar view of Prince Kung's Mansion. Right: Aerial view of Prince Kung's Mansion (the theater is located in the backyard garden)

Fig. 1.4 Elevation view of
Beijing's Huguang Guild Hall

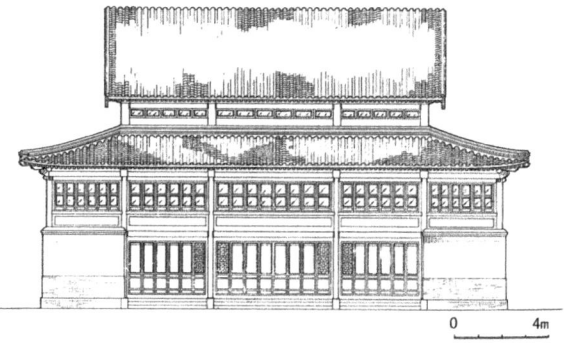

Fig. 1.5 Private commercial
theater from the Qing Dynasty

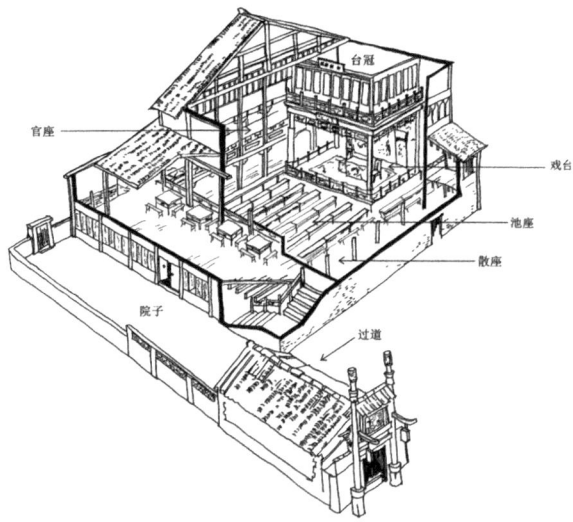

After the Republic of China was established, the Forbidden City was no longer
the municipal center of politics but a historical legacy and cultural symbol. The
administrative area of the city expanded across the Inner City. In spite of the
political areas, the urban spatial distribution of commercial theaters was maintained.

1.2   Two Types of Theaters in the 1950s

After the People's Republic of China was established in 1949, the new regime
enhanced the status of the performing arts to an unprecedented level. As the state's
capital, Beijing embarked on a process of continual historical change. An important
architectural type, theaters gained a new role in the development of Beijing. This
stemmed from the changes in the political system after 1949, which led to the end

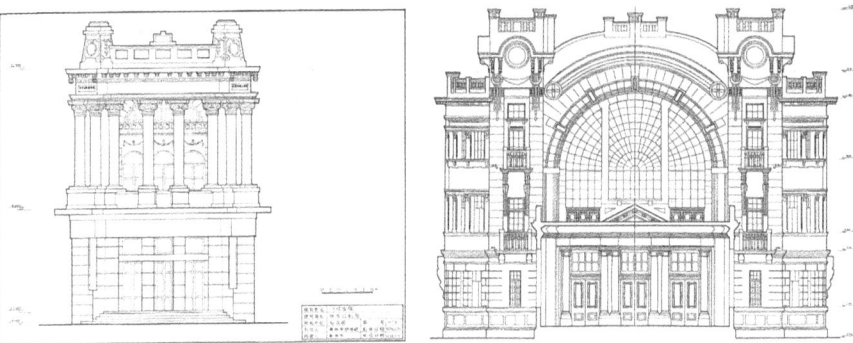

Fig. 1.6 Two theaters of the early 20th century. Left: Beijing Kaiming Theater. Right: Zhenguang Theater (China National Theater for Children)

of commercial theaters and the emergence of state-owned theaters dominated by political factors. Theaters were transformed from commercial buildings used for entertainment to venues used for arts and publicity serving political needs. The previous folk and entertainment attributes of theaters were completely altered. Furthermore, theaters gradually became an important place for the government. The scale, form and spatial location of theaters all completely rid themselves of their past folk label. Theaters occupied a major urban space and became one of Beijing's main architectural forms.

Throughout the 1950s, the development of theaters in Beijing City experienced a historical short-lived construction climax. As the capital of the new regime, the construction of theaters began immediately after its establishment. The driving forces for the development of theaters at the time, in addition to the needs of the performing arts, were more related to the political publicity of arts and the functional needs of a new social managerial space model. Two kinds of theaters existed in the 1950s: (1) professional and urban public theaters and (2) multifunctional enterprises and institution-owned auditoriums or clubs (Table 1.1). For urban theaters, the opera gardens of the past (mainly intended for opera performances) could not satisfy the needs of the newly formed performing arts, such as singing, dancing and drama. Moreover, as a means of publicity, the performing arts required more and bigger theaters. At the same time, social changes introduced a new unit space for the working and living compounds of enterprises and institutions in the country, which required appropriate theaters for conferences, assemblies and entertainment. The differences in the spatial distribution and identity of these two types of theater include their form, scale, level of investment, technology and equipment.

Traditional opera gardens stagnated, without any further development. The new theaters that emerged during this period were mainly proscenium theaters. A strong desire and demand for the modern equipment of theatrical stages and technology arose. This was especially true for urban public theaters. The changes in theatrical

Table 1.1 Two theater types in Beijing City in the 1950s

	Urban public theaters	Theaters in the living compounds of enterprises and institutions of the country (e.g., auditoriums and clubs)
Space distribution	Urban public space	In the living compounds of enterprises and institutions of the country
Form	Formal	Informal
Scale	Comparatively large	Suitable for its actual situation
Function	Mainly for professional performances	Multifunction
Owner/user	Performing art troupes	The Communist Party, Central Government and Central Army Forces, enterprises and institutions of the country
Audience	Folks	Internal members of enterprises and institutions of the country; rarely open to the public
Amount of investment	Huge	Small
Technology	Cutting-edge	Low-end
Equipment	Fully equipped	Inadequate

architecture paralleled the changes in Beijing's urban space. The forms, scales and locations of theaters underwent great change. Beijing's urban space continued to change as well. Such changes, from the old blocks, gradually expanded outward and remain present.

1.3   Urban Theaters, Auditoriums and Beijing City

In the 1950s, Beijing experienced a boom in theater construction (Table 1.2). With the incoming regime, one of the motivations for heavily increasing theater construction was to meet the needs of a number of performing art troupes and arts academies in Beijing. After the introduction of Soviet theaters with performing art troupes, the demand for theater construction seemed more reasonable. The second motivation was to fulfill the needs of foreign art troupes that might perform in Beijing and to be able to host special receptions (Table 1.3). A final reason was to be able to host the conferences of important government departments.

Several theaters were built as a result of such demand. One example is Capital Theater, which was owned by the Beijing People's Art Theater. A second example is Tianqiao Theater, which was built to meet the performance needs of Soviet art troupes or Beijing Friendship Hotel, which undertook foreign guest receptions, and its associated theaters. A third example is the CPPCC auditoriums built to hold the CPPCC National Conference and related performances (Fig. 1.7).

Table 1.2 Newly built theaters in Beijing City in the 1950s

	Theater	Completion year	Address	Status
1.	The Central Academy of Drama Xiaojingchang Theater	1950	West Xiaojingchang Hutong, west of the Xicheng Gate Intersection, Dongcheng District	Ruined
2.	The Rehearsal Field in the General Political Department of the PLA	1953	Deshengmen South, North Second Round Road, Xicheng District	Rebuilt into the PLA Opera House
3.	Tianqiao Theater	1953	Tianqiao, Xuanwu District	Rebuilt
4.	Beijing Exhibition Theater	Rebuilt in 1954 1959	North of Xizhimenwai Street, Xicheng District	Still in use
5.	Beijing Friendship Hotel Theater	1954	West of Zhongguancun South Street, Haidian District	Still in use
6.	People's Theater	1955	Huguo Temple Road South, Xicheng District	Still in use
7.	Beijing Workers Club	1956	Southwest of the Crossroads of Hufang Bridge, Xuanwu District	Still in use
8.	CPPCC Auditorium	1956	South side of Baita Temple Street, Fucheng Gate, Xicheng District	Still in use
9.	Capital Theater	1956	East of Wangfujing Street, Dongcheng District	Still in use
10.	The Rehearsal Field at the National Academy of Chinese Theater Arts	1957	National Academy of Chinese Theater Arts in Liren Street, Xuanwu District	Demolished and rebuilt
11.	Great Hall of the People	1958	West side of Tiananmen Square	Still in use
12.	Cultural Palace of Nationalities	1959	North of Fuxingmennei Street, Xicheng District	Still in use
13.	Wudaokou Workers Club	1959	North of Chengfu Road, Wudaokou, Haidian District	Still in use
14.	Central Conservatory of Music	1960	Central Conservatory of Music, Xicheng District	Remodeled and in use.
15.	February 7 Theater	1962	North of Fuxingmenwai Street, Xicheng District	Demolished and rebuilt

No special layout was defined for the distribution of these theaters in Beijing. It was mainly determined by the districts of the institutions to which the theaters belonged. As the former Imperial City districts were occupied by important government departments, new urban theaters could not be built there. Therefore, the Inner City and Outer City districts became the primary choices for the construction of urban theaters. In light of this, the old business district in the old blocks became

Table 1.3 Theaters for the residing performing art troupes in the 1950s

	Theater	Resident troupe	Remarks
1.	Tianqiao Theater	Experimental Songs & Dances Theater of China (currently the Ballet of China)	Built in the 1950s
2.	People's Theater	China Peking Opera Theater	
3.	Capital Theater	Beijing People's Art Theater	
4.	February 7 Theater	Ministry of Railways Art Troupe	
5.	Youth Palace Theater	China Youth Art Theater	
6.	Beijing Workers Club	Beijing Peking Opera Theater	
7	Folk Theater (the original site of Tianleyuan)	China Pingju Opera Theater	Built before 1949
8	Xidan Theater (the original site of Haerfei Theater)	Northern Kunqu Opera Theater	
9.	Beijing Theater (Zhenguang Theater)	China National Theater for Children	
10.	Qingle Theater	Beijing Acrobatic Troupe	

Fig. 1.7 Two theaters in the 1950s. Left: Tianqiao Theater in 1954 (*Source* Reference Library of School of Architecture, Tsinghua University). Right: CPPCC Auditorium in 1956

the primary area of construction for Tianqiao Theater, Capital Theater and the People's Theater. This choice formed a trend in the construction of Beijing's theaters. Yet, urban administrative districts gradually became popular areas of construction for subsequent urban theaters. This issue is discussed later.

Due to inadequate space in the old street blocks, the construction of new urban theaters began in districts close to but outside of them, with convenient traffic. At this time, the west side of the old blocks became the construction area of many government agencies, such as the districts of Sanli River and Baiwanzhuang. The government's administrative districts in the old blocks mainly occupied the former Imperial City, the later Tiananmen Square and Chang'an Street, forming a line. The expansion of urban theaters outside of the old blocks of Beijing is clearly consistent with that of the new regime districts.

Although the scales of these urban theaters were not comparable to that of the unfinished National Center for the Performing Arts, they far exceeded the scales of

Fig. 1.8 Layout of Beijing's major theaters, Auditoriums and cultural palaces in the 1950s. Red dot: theaters; blue dot: auditoriums and cultural halls

the pre-1949 folk commercial theaters (Fig. 1.8). Moreover, most urban theaters were independent and maintained a certain distance from the surrounding buildings. They were entirely different from the previous commercial theaters and were completely unrelated to commerciality.

Theater complexes appeared in the 1950s. The designs of the Beijing Exhibition Theater, the Beijing Friendship Hotel Theater and the Cultural Palace of Nationalities integrated the features of theaters, hotels and exhibitions. These complexes were government-dominant instead of private. Theaters were incorporated and hidden in these complexes. Being of large scale and great significance, these complexes were recognized as regional landmark buildings in Beijing.

Auditoriums and halls are another type of theater. They exist in large numbers in enterprises, government departments/institutions and military compounds in Beijing. The number of such theaters is estimated to be at least 20% more than that of professional theaters. Due to their relative separation from the public space of the city, many auditoriums have become hidden theaters in Beijing.

After 1949, a type of residential space called "unit compounds" (*danwei dayuan*) came into existence in Beijing (Lian 2015). Such compounds were the units of the Party, the central government and the Central Army Forces and occupied the urban space of Beijing in such mode. A number of compound complexes emerged in Beijing City. Such space colony units once dominated the urban space of Beijing for a long time. Compounds were initially distributed mainly in the districts near the periphery of the Imperial City. Once entering these places, people might have felt as though they were independent towns, usually within enclosed courtyard walls with layouts of living, working, entertainment and other building facilities. There were several types of compounds: those of government agencies, Army Forces, factories and schools. In these compounds, the closure of the space by a wall was obvious and clearly indicated domain boundaries. Compounds became a major spatial unit of Beijing City. However, they contributed little to the city's public space. In such

Fig. 1.9 State Administration of Radio Television Auditorium. Left: Building in 1954. Right: Satellite View in 2018

Fig. 1.10 Distribution of the major auditoriums in the district of Sanli River. Right: Red Tower Auditorium (State Planning Commission Auditorium)

compounds, auditoriums often became major buildings. They were a special type of theater and were combined with the compounds. Of course, the auditoriums in compounds usually had quite inadequate equipment. In addition to conferences, they were often used for the performing arts and playing movies (Figs. 1.9, 1.10).

Auditoriums sometimes open to the public include the Geological Department Auditorium, the Materials Department Auditorium, the CPPCC Auditorium and the State Planning Commission Auditorium.

As mentioned, the State Planning Commission Auditorium in Sanli River Block is also known as the Red Tower Auditorium. This auditorium is one of the many buildings in the compounds of the State Planning Commission. It was designed in 1953 in accordance with Soviet drawings. Auditoriums were typically situated in office, residence and entertainment buildings and in other similar venues. In the early days of the reform and opening up, the Red Tower Auditorium was used for the visiting performances of the famous Japanese conductor Seiji Ozawa and Boston Symphony Orchestra. It had good acoustic quality and was once famous for holding such performances in Beijing.

The construction climax of auditoriums began in the 1950s as a result of the different departments of the new regime occupying different districts of Beijing. First, the most important departments of the Party, government and Army Forces divided their respective grounds across the space of the Imperial City and the Inner City. Yet, the establishment of some government departments and agencies was not possible. Therefore, new administrative districts were established outside of the city. The areas along the west side of the Inner City, such as Sanli River, Baiwanzhuang and Shatan, were also important administrative areas of Beijing. These places were even referred to as the invisible centers of Beijing. They were home to many important government ministries, such as the State Planning Commission, the Ministry of Geology, the Ministry of Heavy Industry, the First Ministry of Machinery Industry and the Second Ministry of Machinery Industry.

The auditoriums of such compounds were usually built inside each compound for its own use. Although some auditoriums were hidden within compounds, some were located in the suburbs of the city. As such, it was difficult to see such theaters on the streets of the city. Some of these theaters were in urban public spaces and were even open to the public as urban public facilities, such as the Wudaokou Workers Club, which was a major theater in Haidian District at the time that originally belonged to the Beijing Municipal Trade Union. After several renovations, it remains in use today.

Throughout the 1950s, the number of theaters in Beijing was incredibly high (Wang 1959). However, there were few specialized theaters and, according to scholarly statistics, more than 200 auditorium buildings. Some buildings in factories were generally referred to as clubs (i.e., instead of auditoriums).

The combination of the auditorium and the compound became a spatial model for almost all social institutions. This model was adopted by almost all government ministries, factories, schools and research institutes. Some people even criticized that it was the auditorium culture that developed theaters in Beijing during that period. Auditoriums combined with compounds are still present in some universities and military colleges in Beijing. After 1980, with the economic reform and opening up, the spaces of those compounds in Beijing began to disintegrate. With urban renewal and real estate development, many original compounds were gradually opened to the public and were prepared for reintegration into the city. Numerous auditorium buildings built in the 1950s also changed dramatically in this process. Although some were demolished and some were rebuilt, many of them remain in use today. In Beijing City, the term "auditorium" once referred to a special public building during the era of compounds. It is now used to describe a special theater history in Beijing (Table 1.4).

Table 1.4 Famous auditoriums run by state-owned companies or governmental departments in Beijing in the 1950s

	Theater	Number of seats
1.	Tong County Workers Club	947
2.	White Paper Workshop Auditorium	1852
3.	211 Factory Workers Theater (in the Ministry of Astronautics Industry)	3800
4.	Fengtai Bridge Factory Auditorium	1197
5.	27 Workers Palace of Culture	1600
6.	Yongding Club	1300
7.	Beijing Power Plant Club	1475
8.	Chinese Academy of Sciences Auditorium in Zhongguancun	1800
9.	Nanhu Canal Bricks Plant Auditorium	1018
10.	51 Theater of Shougang Group	1642
11.	Tuqiao Bricks and Tiles Plant Auditorium	930
12.	Mentougou Workers Club	1050
13.	Hongxia Theater (738 Factory)	1500
14.	Dongtieying Club & Workers Palace of Culture	1361
15.	Xinjiekou Club	880
16.	Dongcheng Workers Club	1361
17.	Beijing Coking Plant Theater	1800
18.	Electronic Tube Factory Theater	1600
19.	The 5th Workers Club in Hepingli	1600
20.	Labor Theater of All-China Federation of Trade Unions	3500
21.	Ministry of Geology and Mineral Resources Auditorium	1030

1.4 Unbuilt National Center for the Performing Arts in the 1950s

The National Center for the Performing Arts was Beijing's largest urban theater under planning in the 1950s. Being a national theater, it differed from other urban theaters in many ways.

The National Center for the Performing Arts was initiated in 1958. It was one of the projects planned for the 10th anniversary of the People's Republic of China. At the same time, the Great Leap Forward Movement (1958–1960) was occurring in China. Furthermore, China joined the Soviet-led socialist camp. As such, the main recommendations of the Soviet planning experts program were adopted in Beijing's urban construction planning. In light of this, a new form of urban planning in Beijing emerged. The main task of this planning was to update and renovate the old blocks based on their location. The planning determined the next administrative and cultural districts, including the construction of Beijing's central districts, such as the planning of Tiananmen Square and Chang'an Street (Zhao 1959a). Fortunately, the National Center for the Performing Arts was honored to be on the project list of the main building construction in Beijing's central districts.

In this urban planning, the National Center for the Performing Arts was placed in the vicinity of Tiananmen Square, which represents the highest authority of China and is adjoined to the Great Hall of the People, forming a center for both political and cultural buildings. This construction program was approved by the highest leaders of China at the time. Outside of the Forbidden City, Beijing's new urban center was launched, gradually becoming a model of the city center (Fig. 1.11).

After the 1990s, this model was widely imitated in many cities across China. It ultimately became the officially designated and most-used urban space model. Nowadays, it is said that this urban center model is "three dishes and one soup" or "four dishes and one soup." The so-called "soup" refers to the square and the so-called "dishes" refer to the buildings around the square, such as government buildings, theaters, museums, libraries and memorials.

In 1958, the National Center for the Performing Arts project began on the west side of the Great Hall of the People. It was adjacent to Chang'an Street and originally a political district of both the Ming and Qing Dynasties in the south of the Forbidden City. During the planning of the new Beijing City, many old blocks were demolished. All of the main buildings in this place, such as the Great Hall of the People, the National Museum of China and Tiananmen Square, were newly built after the demolition of the old buildings in the original Imperial City (Figs. 1.12, 1.13). The National Center for the Performing Arts project was involved in the urban renewal. However, compared to the Great Hall of the People, it was subordinate. The large-scale buildings were quite different from the traditional courtyard buildings and palaces of the past. Such disparity in both form and space became a symbol of the new era.

Fig. 1.11 Model of the National Center for the Performing Arts in 1958 (the fifth person on the right is Jiang Nanxiang, the president of Tsinghua University). *Source* Reference Library of School of Architecture, Tsinghua University

Fig. 1.12 Aerial photograph of Tiananmen Square in 1959 (with the National Center for the Performing Arts on the top left corner). *Source* Reference Library of School of Architecture, Tsinghua University

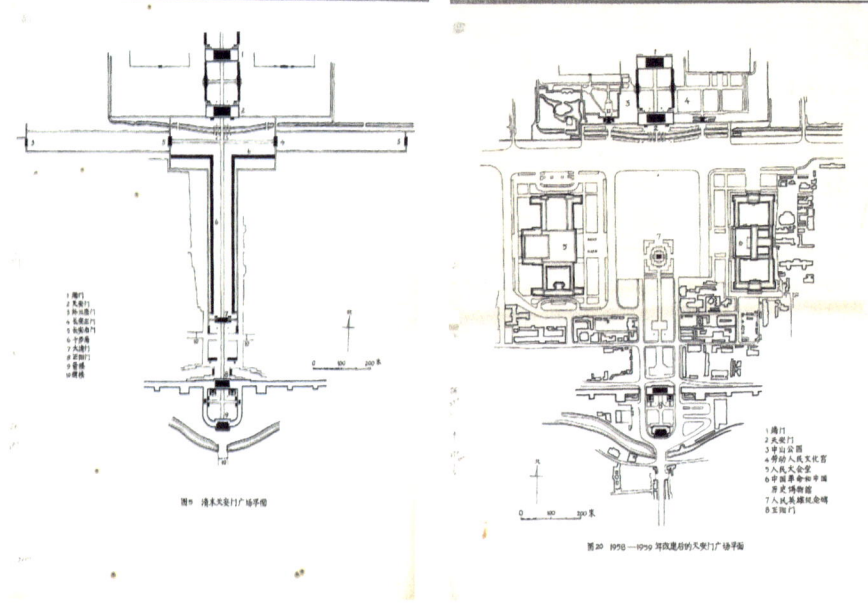

Fig. 1.13 Left: Tiananmen Square during the Qing Dynasty. Right: Plan of Tiananmen Square in the 1950s. *Source* Reference Library of School of Architecture, Tsinghua University

One person famous for advocating the protection of the old blocks of Beijing was Liang Sicheng (1901–1972). He opposed the demolition of the city walls, gates, archways and streets. Some of his arguments were perceived as outdated and were even heavily criticized as bourgeois academic views. His awkward situation made him a famous architect who was not involved in the design of grand national projects, but just as a design consultant. Liang was the founder of the Department of Architecture at Tsinghua University and was the dean of the department at that time. Ironically, there was no place for him on the Tsinghua University design team for the National Center for the Performing Arts. The team leader was one of his former students, Li Daozeng, a young teacher of 27 years old who was followed by a group of young teachers and students. Encouraged by the Great Leap Forward Movement, these young people were enthusiastic and completed the National Center for the Performing Arts design in a very short time, which was recognized by the official government (Li 2011) (Fig. 1.14).

The main source of inspiration was Anhaltisches Theater in East Germany. In 1957, an art troupe sent by the Chinese government toured the socialist countries of the Soviet Union and Eastern Europe and visited this theater. The design of theater was recorded by a young stage-art designer, Li Chang, and his colleagues and was introduced into China. Anhaltisches Theater had extensive stage space and owned advanced stage equipment that Chinese entertainers had never seen before. It was considered to be representative of advanced theaters and was highly recognized by the officials of the Chinese Ministry of Culture. Today, it is well-known that German and European theaters and their architecture serve the upper class. They are quite different from the commercial theaters of Broadway in New York and the West End in London, whether in the scale, form or planning of the city as to the building (Fig. 1.15).

The East German Theater sought by the National Center for the Performing Arts was a typical independent European opera house. In this design, the architecture of

Fig. 1.14 Design team of Tsinghua University with the Tiananmen Square Model in 1958. *Source* Reference Library of School of Architecture, Tsinghua University

Fig. 1.15 Anhaltisches Theater, Dessau, East Germany (role model for the National Center for the Performing Arts)

such a European opera house and its spatial relationship with the city were introduced together for the first time to Beijing (China). This site selection was neither based on commercial factors nor a technical factor in urban design or urban planning, but was mainly governed by political motivations.

What was the logic beyond this juxtaposition of theaters with the political parliament building (which represents the institution's highest authority—the Great Hall of the People) in the center of the city? Explaining such a city center model, which is currently prevalent in cities across China, may require addressing the relationship between the attributes of theaters and urban space. The attributes of a theater cannot be separated from the functions it carries—that is, as a venue for the performing arts, such as operas or dramas. In the traditional ideas of Chinese people, the purpose of orthodox drama is not entertainment but education. Ordinary people must be educated through arts and drama. During the May 4th Movement, this concept was once again amplified by many educated intelligentsias. Chen Duxiu (1879–1942), a politician and thinker, said theaters could become a classroom for educating the masses. This concept was actually inherited by the later ruling Party. Chairman Mao once expressed many opinions about the function of literature and arts. Central to his thinking was that literature and arts should be used for publicity in society and to educate people. The theater is of course the camp of the performing arts to educate people (Fig. 1.16).

Another kind of entertainment-oriented theater in China's history was the folk commercial theater, which had a binary relationship with the theater attributes mentioned above. Entertainment and education, or business and politics, are dual attributes that have led to two distinct phenomena of the relationship whether in the

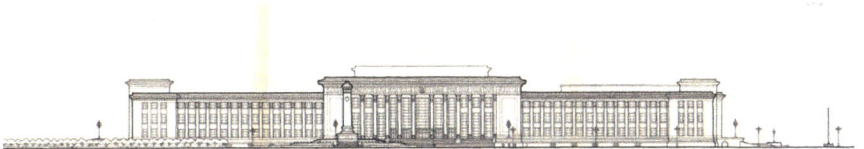

Fig. 1.16 Elevation of the Great Hall of the People. *Source* Su (1964). Reference Library of School of Architecture, Tsinghua University

form of theater architecture or its urban space. As discussed above, Beijing has two kinds of theaters with different urban spatial relationships. One is that the political center forms the core space of the city and the other is that the commercial center forms the core space of the city.

In the history of Beijing's urban development, the first instance of implementing this model and enhancing the political status of theaters to an unprecedented level was no other than the site selection of the National Center for the Performing Arts. Adjacent to the previous political center, the Forbidden City, the central district of Beijing City was combined with the new political center, the Great Hall of the People and Tiananmen Square.

During the Qing Dynasty, there were no specialized stages in the Forbidden City. Small venues for the Emperor's entertainment did exist, but they were informal theater buildings that were hidden in the solemn sequence space of the Forbidden City. The Royal Grand Theater was in the Summer Palace. Although there was some space for the Emperors' office there, it was not a formal political building.

Here we examine the analysis of the theater form in the 1958 program of the National Center for the Performing Arts. It took some forms of occidental classical architecture and was clearly consistent with the architectural style advocated by the Soviet architectural community at the time. The so-called socialist content of architecture has also been discussed in academic Chinese architectural journals (Zhao 1959b).

Under the influence of domestic politics in the 1950s, the Chinese architectural community was in wandering with a series of official guidelines on architectural art. These official architectural art guidelines were not always consistent. In a word, Western modernist architecture was criticized by the authority as being a product of capitalism. In the early 1950s, Liang Sicheng, who advocated traditional architectural forms, was also criticized for wasting money and materials. He was perceived as a representative of the old era. Surprisingly, in celebration of the 10th anniversary of National Day in 1958, the Chinese traditional architectural style and occidental classical architectural style were upheld. Such buildings were regarded as having architectural styles of socialism and national forms (The Theater of The Palace of Nationalities and the National Art Museum of China adopted traditional architectural forms). The architectural style of the National Center for the Performing Arts was consistent with that of the Great Hall of the People and the

National Museum of China, all using Western classical forms. Liang Sicheng, who objected the design proposal, was once again criticized by the authority.

In 1958, the National Center for the Performing Arts project proposed by the Tsinghua University design team implied a number of fade designs, all in the form of classic occidental architecture (Fig. 1.17).

This was mainly the result of official-oriented politics. Moreover, the highest leaders were directly involved with the guidance of the design. There were some memories and narratives about the design history of the National Center for the Performing Arts and how the then Premier Zhou Enlai (1898–1976) guided the design. For example, for the project of the National Center for the Performing Arts designed by the Tsinghua design team, through the report Premier Zhou Enlai provided specific guidance on many occasions. He recommended decorating the facade of the theater fly tower on the colonnade and designed the interior space of the auditorium. Premier Zhou Enlai even invited North Korea's highest leader, Kim Il Sung, who visited China to take a look at the program of the National Center for the Performing Arts and told him smugly that it was designed under his guidance. In fact, the renovation of all of Beijing City and the design of the main buildings were approved by the highest leaders (Fig. 1.18).

The Great Leap Forward Movement in 1958 led to an unforgettable disaster that directly halted the project of the National Center for the Performing Arts. At the time, construction had begun and a large amount of earth had been excavated. This left a huge foundation pit, which was maintained for approximately 40 years. Its wall blocked this place, forming an interface for Chang'an Street for a long time. The Great Hall of the People is the symbol of the supreme authority and its Great Hall of Ten Thousand, as well as other auditoriums, serves both as a lecture hall and a performing theater. In fact, it has become the highest-status performance venue.

In other considerations of Chang'an Street thereafter, such as the planning of 1964, the National Center for the Performing Arts was once located on the west side of the street, far away from the Great Hall of the People. However, such planning was not implemented (Fig. 1.19).

北京   3000观众剧院设计方案   正面透视图

Fig. 1.17 Design scheme of the National Center for the Performing Arts in 1958

Fig. 1.18 Left: Tsinghua design team presenting the National Day Projects Design Scheme to Premier Zhou Enlai. Right: Zhou Enlai and Kim Il Sung visiting the model of National Center for the Performing Arts. *Source* Reference Library of School of Architecture, Tsinghua University

Fig. 1.19 Left: Scheme of Chang'an Avenue proposed by the Tsinghua University design team in 1964 (the Cultural Palace of Nationalities and its theaters). Right: Scheme of Chang'an Avenue proposed by Tsinghua University in 1964 (Tiananmen Square)

1.5 Upsurge in Theaters in Beijing Post-1980s

In 1978, China began to implement the reform and opening up policy. The construction of Beijing's theaters ushered in another climax after the early 1980s (Zhao 1989). A large number of modern theaters were built during this period and both the theater scale and investment far exceeded those of the past. Urban expansion and old city transformation provided an opportunity for the new development of theaters (Urban Planning Teaching and Research Division of School of Architecture 1980). Meanwhile, the reform and opening up policy contributed to the import of foreign capital, technology, art and ideas. Land policy adjustment and real estate development also greatly promoted theater construction.

With Haidian District and Chaoyang District in the northern part of Beijing having gradually become the key areas for urban expansion, the development of theaters clearly kept pace with the construction of these emerging regions. For example, Poly Theater was constructed in the Dongsi Shitiao Embassy District, Century Theater was constructed in the Yansha Business Circle, Beijing Theater was constructed in the Asian Games Village and Haidian Theater was constructed in the Zhongguancun Business District (Lv 2006).

After the 1980s, theater development in Beijing demonstrated new features. Theaters were no longer greatly involved in serving political purposes and partly resumed their commercial nature. In spite of this, the commercial nature in this period was quite different from a large number of private commercial theaters in Beijing before 1949. In the 1980s, the main body of theater construction still consisted of government-administered institutions rather than private institutions. Such government-administered institutions had more funds and land. Another kind of theater that was combined with commercial buildings appeared, namely a combination of theaters and hotels or office buildings. It should be noted that theater complexes appeared early in the 1950s. The Cultural Palace Theater and the Beijing Friendship Hotel Theater are both of such kind. All such theater complexes were government-dominant non-commercial buildings.

This type of theater model emerged because in the process of urban renewal and expansion, social capital and previous unit compound land were integrated into real estate speculations to achieve higher profits. This reflects the disintegration of the spatial pattern of the unit compounds in Beijing, especially the art troupe units originally allocated in the old quarter after the reform and opening up. The land value of art troupe units rapidly increased, resulting in greedy land and real estate property speculations. Another type of commercial operation—building a theater to increase attractiveness—also led to the emergence of commercial theater complexes. Such incorporation of theaters and commercial buildings into complexes is similar to the many casino complexes in Las Vegas. Due to the intensity of land exploitation and pursuit of commercial value, this type of theater complex is often large in scale, occupies a prominent location and becomes a prominent landmark. However, the conspicuous part of this type of theater complex is the commercial high-rise building, with the theater formally attached to or even hidden inside of the building. As for the architecture form, such a theater is completely different from government-led independent theaters.

After the reform and opening up, Beijing's first project combining theaters and commercial buildings was the Oriental Singing and Dancing Troupe Theater. This project ultimately failed to combine a commercial building and theater. In terms of its implementation, it was originally a theater project for the Oriental Singing and Dancing Troupe. Then, due to capital investment from Hong Kong, a high-rise Hilton Hotel building was added. However, after construction was completed, the investor hoped that the theater could be changed into a nightclub as an entertainment facility for the hotel. This led to the theater being shut down after conflict with government administration. Several years later, the theater was changed into an office building. Finally, the capital achieved victory.

Poly Theater and Meilanfang Theater are two successful cases. The two projects incorporating a theater and hotel constitute another type of theater model based on commercial property. Other similar cases include Chang'an Grand Theater (Fig. 1.20).

Fig. 1.20 Left: Rendering of the Hilton Hotel and the unfinished Oriental Singing and Dancing Troupe Theater. Middle: Poly Theater. Right: Meilanfang Theater

Another theater case incorporating a high-rise office building is Century Theater in the Sino-Japan Exchange Center, a project sponsored by the Japanese government in the 1980s. Japanese architect Kurokawa Kisho designed this theater. The complex model used was similar to that mentioned before that combined a high-rise hotel and theater. However, this project was not a product of commercial development.

The theater renovation project was another event that occurred during this period. Specifically, some old theaters retained their facades but transformed all of their other parts, such as Children's Theater, whereas other original theaters were completely demolished and rebuilt in situ, such as Tianqiao Theater. These constitute another kind of Beijing theater.

As for the auditorium buildings of unit compounds, great changes took place during the process of reform and opening up. The fate of various unit compounds was quite different. In general, the unit compound space model disintegrated and most auditoriums declined. Some were demolished and some were used for other purposes. Some were completely turned into urban theaters. However, not all unit compounds were transformed. The unit compound model on university campuses remains intact. Furthermore, new progress was made in theater construction. Two famous university theaters are Peking University's Centennial Hall and Tsinghua University's New Tsinghua Auditorium. Both are large theaters open to the public with over 2000 seats and good facilities. Each has become the center of its respective campus (Fig. 1.21).

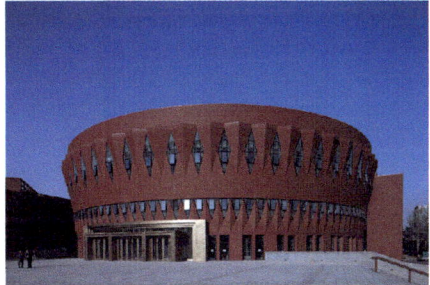

Fig. 1.21 Left: Peking University Centennial Hall. Right: New Tsinghua Auditorium

In addition, some military compounds have been preserved and more theaters have been built. Some of them have even become urban theaters that are completely open to the public, such as the PLA Opera House and Chinese Theater.

1.6 National Center for the Performing Arts

More than 20 years after its stagnation in 1958, the Ministry of Culture resumed preparation for the National Center for the Performing Arts project in 1986. Due to the length of time that passed, the government had to re-examine the project's feasibility. By then, the development of theaters in Western countries had greatly changed and new famous theaters had been built. Since China's reform and opening up in 1978, learning from the West had become a government-dominated policy, quite different from learning from the Soviet Union in the 1950s. Learning from Western modern architecture became a new trend. Around 1988, a special group of the Ministry of Culture visited a number of theaters in Canada, the United States, the United Kingdom, France, Italy, Japan and other countries and collected many theater design materials (Lu 2009). Finally, the group chose the Kennedy Performing Arts Center of the United States as its learning model. This model, which originated from German theaters, reflected the Beijing government's vision. As such, the construction of the National Center for the Performing Arts followed the German theater model (Fig. 1.22).

Around 1990, the Ministry of Culture also commissioned a number of design and research institutes for the feasibility schemes of the National Center for the Performing Arts. Of the schemes, that of Professor Li Daozeng's team is worth mentioning. Li Daozeng was the main designer of the National Center for the Performing Arts in 1958. The plane of this scheme was similar to that of the Kennedy Center for Performing Arts. That is, it had three main juxtaposed theaters. In the scheme of Professor Li, the main entrances of the three theaters face toward the north and south. This arrangement highlights the north and south facade design and the accessibility of the building. Specifically, the north and south orientation of the main entrances helped establish a closer connection with the urban space. Another aspect of Li's scheme that is worth mentioning is that the facade design still followed the idea of the 1950s, adopting the architectural style similar to that of the Great Hall of the People (Figs. 1.23, 1.24). In 1997, official domestic design tendering for the National Center for the Performing Arts began. Professor Li also participated and again proposed a similar scheme. However, under the background of the reform and opening up, learning from the West had become popular. This completely changed the architectural style of the National Center for the Performing Arts near Tiananmen Square.

The international design competition was officially held in 1998. In this project, the design scheme of the National Center for the Performing Arts focused much attention on the introduction of theater styles, such as opera houses, concert halls

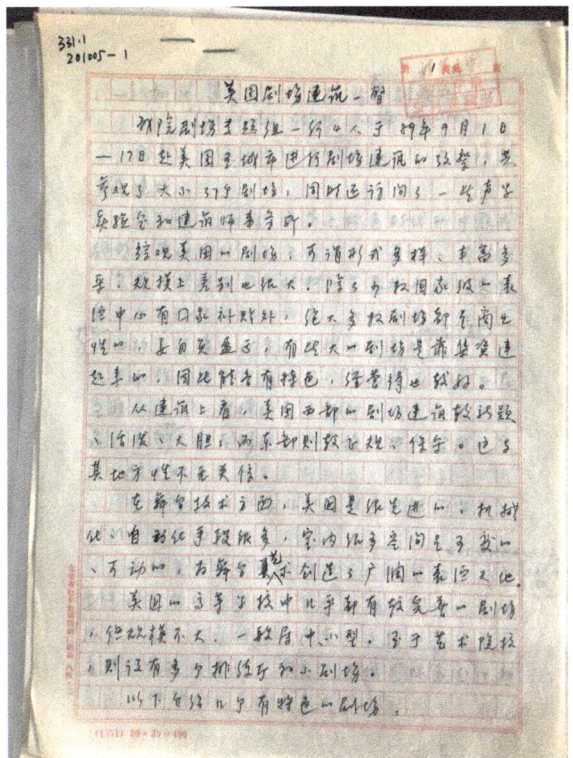

Fig. 1.22 Manuscript of Wei Dazhong, famous architect and theater researcher, while visiting American theaters in 1989

and experimental theaters originating from Europe. In the design of French architect Paul Andreu that was ultimately adopted, the plane layout follows that of the Kennedy Center for Performing Arts in the United States and the form follows the

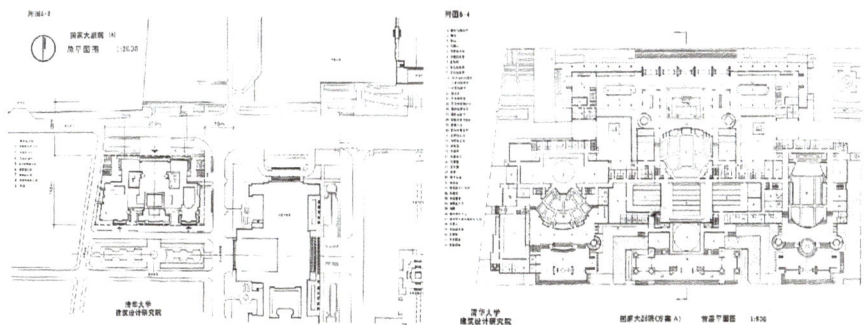

Fig. 1.23 Left: Feasible site plan of the National Center for the Performing Arts. Right: Planar graph of the first floor in the 1993 scheme

Fig. 1.24 Professor Li Daozeng's schemes. Left: 1993. Right: 1997

style of the Sydney Opera House, which separates its form and function with three theaters covered by a huge metal shell. This is indeed a wonderful combination.

During the design competition of the National Center for the Performing Arts, the site expansion considerably changed the design proposals. The range of the site continued to expand southward, giving the theater more outdoor space such that the relationship between the theater and the surrounding environment changed significantly. At first, the theater faced the street. This gradually changed into the theater being on the northern side of the square. Finally, the theater was surrounded by open space and formed an east-west axis relationship with the Great Hall of the People. The design of the National Center for the Performing Arts not only strengthens its own position as an independent building, but also intensifies its connection with the Great Hall of the People. This result is in full compliance with the official position of the National Center for the Performing Arts that the building be a venue for both the performing arts and politics. It also satisfies the educational function of theaters in traditional Chinese culture.

Notably, Paul Andreu (1938–2018) boldly placed the theater on the east-west axis, which was opposite the western facade of the Great Hall of the People, aligning the axis of the two buildings. Therefore, the client decided to expand the site boundary toward the south and demolished more old buildings on the southern side of the original site (Figs. 1.25, 1.26 and 1.27).

The architectural approach of Andreu's scheme once caused great controversy (Zhou 2009). Using a huge outer shell to cover three theaters emphasizes the great uniqueness of the scale and form of the theater. Compared with other significant previously constructed buildings nearby, such as the Forbidden City and the Great Hall of the People, there are huge differences in scale and form. Accepting this futuristic Western modern architecture may reflect the official mind-set of opening up. The separation of the huge outer shell from the inner theater actually represents the different value objectives of this building's form and functions. In terms of architectural form, the huge outer shell makes the theater one of Beijing's landmarks. Due to its strong contrast with the Forbidden City, the Great Hall of the People, Hutong and courtyards in terms of scale, material, color and geometry, the

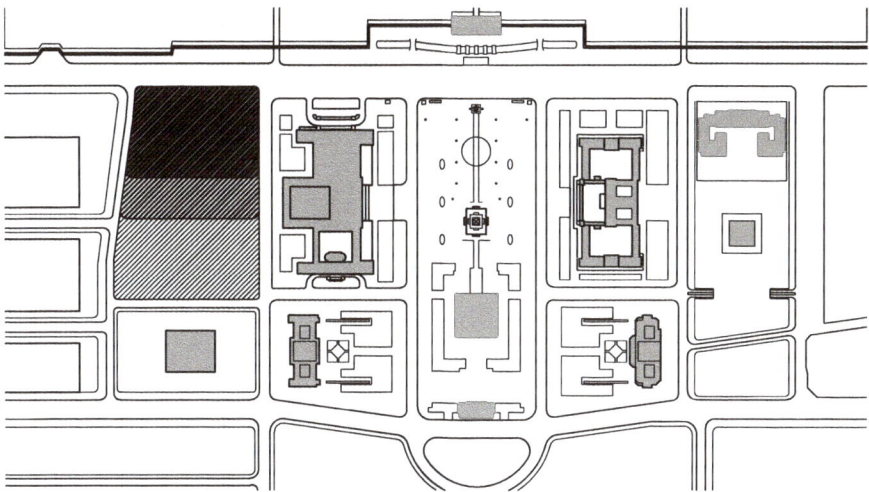

Fig. 1.25 Site changes of the National Center for the Performing Arts

Fig. 1.26 The Tsinghua design team and the Andreu design team at Aéroports de Paris in 1999 (the author is the first person seated on the left)

National Center for the Performing Arts represents another epochal symbol of Beijing's urban transformation. In terms of architectural functions, the design of the National Center for the Performing Arts, which adopts the American performing arts center model, incorporates different professional theater types into a comprehensive complex, which is consistent with the ideas of modernization and "advanced culture" advocated by the government after the reform and opening up. The Kennedy Center for Performing Arts is considered to represent an advanced theater

Fig. 1.27 National Center for the Performing Arts **a** from Xirongxian Hutong. **b** The main elevation; **c** opera house; **d** lobby. **b–d** courtesy of Fu Xing

concept, one that is the direct cause of the large scale of the National Center for the Performing Arts. The National Center for the Performing Arts has become the largest theater building in Beijing (and even in China) and has changed the urban fabric of this region.

Furthermore, the urban design of the National Center for the Performing Arts has become the design pattern of China's urban centers, popularized and imitated by many cities across China. Many cities have tried to combine performing arts buildings with other types of cultural buildings, government buildings and city squares to form the central parts of cities. This model has permeated many cities around the world, especially in China, where people prefer to follow the example of superiors. This results in a number of urban core areas with cultural and art centers adjacent to the administrative center. In short, this model has had a major impact on the design of the urban centers of Chinese cities.

1.7 Conclusion

In the 1950s, the era of Beijing's commercial theater ended and a completely different theater era started. At the time, political factors dominated the construction of theaters. The spatial layout of Beijing's theaters was in accordance with the spatial distribution of administrative power. The top National Center for the

Performing Arts located near Tiananmen Square and many theaters of art troupes situated in the inner and western parts of Beijing City reflected this feature, with building distributions basically independent of commercial nature. The spatial distribution of auditoriums of unit compounds also followed this principle. The land of different locations was allocated according to a unit's level and scale. This became the basis for the distribution of the hidden auditoriums in Beijing.

Western-style theaters became the leading theaters in Beijing and were significantly larger in scale than the traditional ones. Most newly built theaters in Beijing existed as independent theaters, indicating that theaters assumed a more important position in urban life.

To study theaters in Beijing after the 1980s, the reform and opening up must be considered. The transformation of Beijing's old city and the rapid city expansion (Zuo et al. 1996) facilitated the development of theaters. With the intervention of real estate development and external capital, the originally solidified unit compound began to collapse. Some old auditoriums of unit compounds gradually declined, but the unit compound model of the military and colleges still exists and new theaters have been built. Some art institutes have tried to adopt integrated utilization of the land of unit compounds and the external capital to build commercial theater complexes. There has also been a moderately strong tendency to re-commercialize theaters. However, when beginning to recognize the commercial value brought about by theaters, investors actively set up theaters in commercial buildings to increase their commercial appeal and value, such that a series of large urban theater complexes emerged.

The National Center for the Performing Arts reflects the government's recognition of the value of theaters. It is the highest-level combination of national culture, art and politics, with such recognition implemented in the urban space design. It has become part of a city centerpiece that also consists of Tiananmen Square, the Great Hall of the People, the Chinese History Museum, the Chairman Mao Memorial Hall and the Monument to the People's Heroes. It is a typical example of politically dominant theaters and represents official theater values. Furthermore, it facilitated the complete construction of the unrealized Beijing City center in the late 1950s. Ultimately, it has helped form a core urban model that combines performing arts architecture and political centers, which has greatly affected other cities in China.

In recent years, based on cultural tourism and real estate development, the local governments of different areas of Beijing have also promoted their own cultural construction. For example, in Chongwen District and Xicheng District, plans have been made to build a new Tianqiao and Tiantan Performing Arts Zone in the Tianqiao area and to establish a large number of theater communities. This would revitalize the previously famous Beijing Opera City Park and ultimately develop a theater gathering area similar to Broadway or the West End. Other administrative districts in Beijing also have similar plans to set up theaters. These new trends are expected to once again change the relationship between Beijing's theaters and urban space (Ai et al. 2008) (Figs. 1.28, 1.29).

28

X. Lu

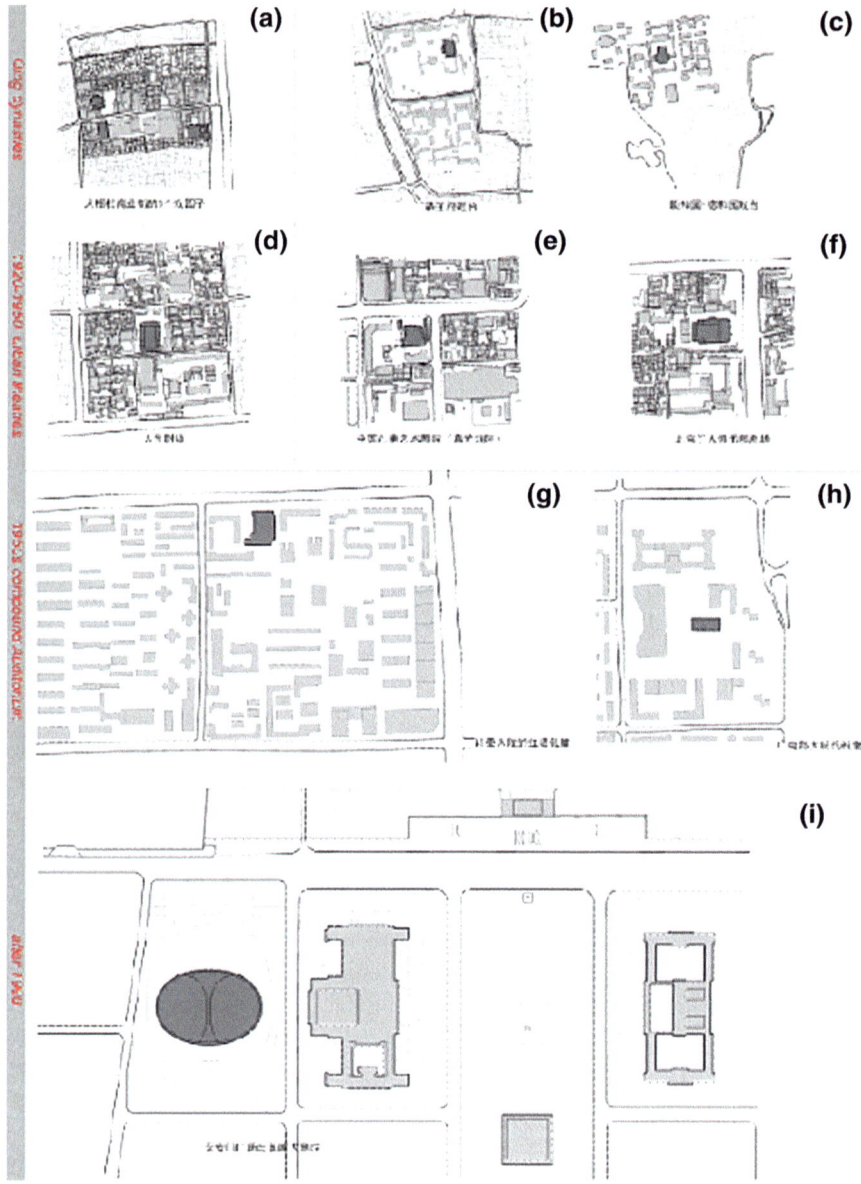

Fig. 1.28 Several theaters and their surroundings in Beijing City in different periods (drawn in the same scale). **a** Three tea garden theaters on Dashilan Commercial Street. **b** The theater in Prince Kung's Mansion. **c** Dehe Yuan Theater in Summer Palace. **d** People's Theater. **e** China National Theater Children (Zhen'guang Theater). **f** Beijing Workers Club. **g** The State Planning Commission Auditorium (Red Tower Auditorium) in Sanli River Block. **h** The State Administration of the Radio Television Auditorium. **i** Tian'anmen Square and the National Center for the Performing Arts

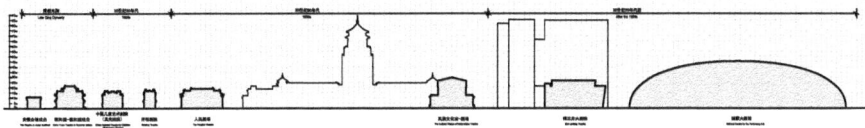

Fig. 1.29   Comparison of the elevation scales of major theaters in Beijing during different periods

Acknowledgements   The author thanks Lily Wang and Cong Guo for their drafts and gives special thanks to Zonglie Sun, Fuhe Zhang and Chunmei Li for providing very important materials. Without their help, the author could not have completed this chapter.

In 1984, I became an architectural student at Tsinghua University. I came from Guiyang in Southwest China to Beijing for the first time during the early years of the open-door policy. The first time I saw a theatre in Beijing was the auditorium designed by American architect Henry Murphy in the 1920s on the Tsinghua campus. Outside the south gate of Tsinghua was a vegetable field. Wudaokou, a prosperous sub-centre today, was a generic and narrow street then, flanked by shanty shops. Crossing the railway, there was the Wudaokou Workers' Club, a theatre/cinema built in the 1950s. Occasionally, we students came to see films here for a temporary break from busy school life.

During my five-year undergraduate period, I explored old Beijing by bicycle numerous times. Many places in Beijing were peaceful then. In famous Wangfujing, I saw the Capital Theatre, a Soviet-style theatre built in the 1950s. As a student, I could not afford to see performances by the famous People's Art Theatre (the resident troupe theatre), however, and the theatre was far from the Tsinghua campus. In the southern part of the city, there is Dashanlan Commercial Street. Several 'drama gardens' from the Qing Dynasty remained but were sadly derelict. At the Summer Palace, I visited the Royal Deheyuan theatre building from the Qing Dynasty. These were my early impressions of Beijing's theatres. Many state-owned enterprises and government departments had their own auditoriums, but I did not know this at the time.

In 1993, when I was a Master's degree student, I participated in the renovation of Tianqiao Theatre. The renovation was led by Professor Li Daozeng, a famous scholar of theatre architecture. This theatre in southern Beijing, which was used for ballet performances, was built in the 1950s, when China and Beijing were undergoing rapid expansion and urban construction. Many skyscrapers were being built, and theatre construction proliferated. Outside East Third Ring Road is the Century Theatre, designed by Japanese architect Kisho Kurokawa; it is among the most advanced in Beijing. As I explored the basement of the stage and the catwalks of theatre, I was amazed by its mechanical facilities. At the Poly Theatre of East Second Ring Road, the stage and mechanical facilities are even more perfect. These theatres represent a trend that reached a climax in the opening of the National Theatre in 2007.

Over the 30 years of theatre construction in Beijing, I have been fortunate to experience a number of important events. I was a member of the Tsinghua design team and collaborated with Paul Andreu of France. I witnessed the early scheme designed by Andreu and listened to his introduction in Paris. Seeing his giant egg near Tiananmen Square, I felt the drastic and unresolved conflicts between time and space, past and future and West and East. However, this is not the full story of Beijing. Today, privately run commercial theatres are emerging throughout Beijing's hutongs, commercial complexes and old factories, satisfying the different demands of many audiences. This development of theatres is quietly changing the map of Beijing.

References

Ai, W., Zhuang, D., & Liu, Y. (2008). The variation of urban land use in Beijing in the last one hundred years. *Geo-information Science, 10*, 489–494. 艾伟、庄大方、刘友兆 (2008). 北京市城市用地百年变迁分析. 地球信息科学，*10*, 489–494.

Hou, R. (1988). *Map collections of Beijing across the history*. Beijing: Beijing Publishing Group. 侯仁之 (1988). 北京历史地图集. 北京: 北京出版社..

Hou, X. (1999). *The traditional theater of Beijing*. Beijing: China City Press. 侯希三 (1999). 北京老戏园子. 北京: 中国城市出版社.

Li, C. (1998). *Theaters in Beijing since Qing Dynasty*. Beijing: Beijing Yanshan Press. 李畅 (1998). 清代以来的北京剧场. 北京: 燕山出版社.

Li, D. (2011). *Selected works of Li Daozeng*. Beijing: Tsinghua University Press. 李道增 (2011). 李道增选集. 北京: 清华大学出版社.

Lian, X. (2015). *Unit compound: On residential space in modern and contemporary Beijing* (Master dissertation). Tsinghua University. 连晓刚 (2015). 单位大院: 近当代北京居住空间演变[硕士学位论文]. 北京: 清华大学建筑学院.

Lu, X. (2009). *The evolution of modern theater in China*. Beijing: China Architecture & Building Press. 卢向东 (2009). 中国现代剧场的演进. 北京: 中国建筑工业出版社.

Lv, X. (2006). *Study on the space changes of theaters in Beijing* (Master dissertation). Tsinghua University. 吕僡 (2006). 清末以来剧场在北京城市空间的变迁研究[硕士学位论文]. 北京: 清华大学建筑学院.

Su, Z. (1964). *Discussion of the reconstruction and planning of Tian'anmen Square* (Master dissertation). Tsinghua University. 苏则民 (1964). 天安门广场改建和规划的经验探讨[硕士学位论文]. 北京: 清华大学建筑学院.

Urban Planning Teaching and Research Division of School of Architecture. (1980). Thoughts on urban planning of Beijing. *Architectural Journal, 5*, 6–15. 清华大学建筑系城市规划教研室 (1980). 对北京城市规划的几点设想. 建筑学报, *5*, 6–15.

Wang, D. (1959). The architecture of Beijing from 1949 to 1959. *Architectural Journal, Z1*, 13–17. 王栋岑(1959). 北京建筑十年. 建筑学报, *Z1*, 13–17.

Xue, L. (2009). *Chinese traditional theater buildings*. Beijing: China Architecture & Building Press. 薛林平 (2009). 中国传统剧场建筑. 北京: 中国建筑工业出版社.

Zhao, D. (1959a). Tian'anmen Square. *Architectural Journal, Z1*, 18–22. 赵冬日(1959). 天安门广场. 建筑学报, *Z1*, 18–22.

Zhao, S. (1959b). Create architectures with Chinese socialism style. *Architectural Journal, 7*, 4–6. 赵深(1959). 创造中国的社会主义的建筑风格. 建筑学报, *7*, 4–6.

Zhao, D. (1989). The contemporary architecture of Beijing. *Architectural Journal, 10*, 2–6. 赵冬日(1989). 北京的当代建筑. 建筑学报, *10*, 2–6.

Zhou, Q. (2009). Survived through disputes—Project of the National Center for the Performing Arts. *Architectural Journal, 1*, 21–25. 周庆琳(2009). 在争论中生存——国家大剧院工程. 建筑学报, *1*, 21–25.

Zuo, C., Zheng, G., Zhao, B., & Hu, S. (1996). *Collections of papers on Beijing City Planning*. Beijing: China Architecture & Building Press. 左川、郑光中、赵炳时、胡绍学 (1996). 北京城市规划研究论文集. 北京: 中国建筑工业出版社.

Chapter 2
To Be Cultural Capital: Grand Theaters in Shanghai

Charlie Qiuli Xue

Why and how have so many grand theaters been built so quickly in China? How were those designs selected in the process of decision making? How do these theaters influence the ambience of a city, and how do they provide public space and amenities for a vibrant civic life? What is the design language of the grand theaters?

This chapter attempts to answer these questions using Shanghai as an example. The author hopes to examine how a grand theater is built with a particular mission in urban renewal and new town construction and how they reflect the ambition of the city and its people in the tide of globalisation. The first section reviews the glorious past of Shanghai. The chapter uses five theaters in Shanghai to align with the salient phenomenon in China's urban construction in the late 20th century and early 21st century and reveal the development trajectory of Chinese cities. The phenomenon includes Chinese cities' busily employing international architects to create or enhance their brands, eagerness of expressing features of the time and addressing imminent urban problems.

These five theaters are most expensive, appealing, noticeable and can represent the trends emerging in this century. The process of building performance spaces in Shanghai fits well into the historic process and framework of modern China, as illustrated in the following sections, followed by our query and conclusions. Individual theater was built with special mission and conditions, which together make a jigsaw of Chinese society and architecture in the 21st century. The proper use of tax-payers' money in public buildings is discussed. This chapter aims to shed light on the rapid development of Asian cities and reveal the problems attached to these prominent cultural landmark buildings.

C. Q. Xue (✉)
Department of Architecture and Civil Engineering, City University of Hong Kong,
Kowloon, Hong Kong
e-mail: bscqx@cityu.edu.hk

© Springer Nature Singapore Pte Ltd. 2019
C. Q. Xue (ed.), *Grand Theater Urbanism*,
https://doi.org/10.1007/978-981-13-7868-3_2

2.1 Restoring the Old Glamour

As an early "global" city in the eastern China, Shanghai was exposed to Western civilization in the late 19th and early 20th centuries. With the opening of the port, parts of the city were leased to the United Kingdom, the United States, France and Japan as concession areas. Western management and materialistic advancement transformed the city into a modern society, which attracted millions of people from nearby provinces and foreign countries. Between the two World Wars, Shanghai was under the spotlight in the Far East and was nicknamed the "Oriental Paris": its ports, factories, garden houses, department stores, hotels and apartment buildings were a physical manifesto (Lee 1999). Before the burst of the Pacific War, Japanese troops had occupied many provinces and Greater Shanghai, but the foreign concessions remained untouched. This extended and enhanced prosperity in this "isolated island" from 1938 to 1941. Intellectuals, writers and artists gathered in Shanghai, particularly in the concession areas because of their effective management and safe and clean environment. The city became an early center of film production, symphonies, plays and Chinese opera in the 1920s.

In its heyday, performance halls and cinemas were constructed in the concession areas. For example, Nanking Theater (1929), designed by Zhao Shen and Robert Fan, could accommodate musical performances, including those of symphony orchestras. Majestic Cinema (1939), Cathy Theater (1934) and Grand Theater (1931), designed by Chinese and foreign architects, all adopted Art Deco design features in tandem with their counterparts in Europe and the US. These cultural facilities, together with dancing halls, luxurious hotels and apartment stores, splendidly gilded the city center (Fig. 2.1).

During the Pacific War, Japanese troops entered the concession areas and dragged the city into war. After the Communist Party took power in 1949, Shanghai was planned as an industrial base. Sporadic cultural pavilions and cinemas were built together with workers' residential areas at the city's periphery. In 1959, the central government built ten "grand buildings" in Beijing to celebrate the ten year anniversary of the People's Republic of China, at the expense of great famine in other provinces. In the wave of building grand projects to symbolise the strong socialist dictatorship, Shanghai once prepared blueprints for an opera house that could seat an audience of 3000, but the project had to be shelved because of economic difficulties in the early 1960s (Fig. 2.2).

In 1978, China embarked on its open-door policy and began to eagerly learn Western technology and management (Xue 2006). At the time, Shanghai was embarrassingly dilapidated, and its only remaining glamour came from its old 1930s foreign concession legacies, a source of pride for Shanghainese. However, in the early years of the open-door policy, Shanghai was busy housing its residents and building hotels and offices for the burgeoning market business after decades of delay. The city took off again when Pudong, the east bank of the Huangpu River, was

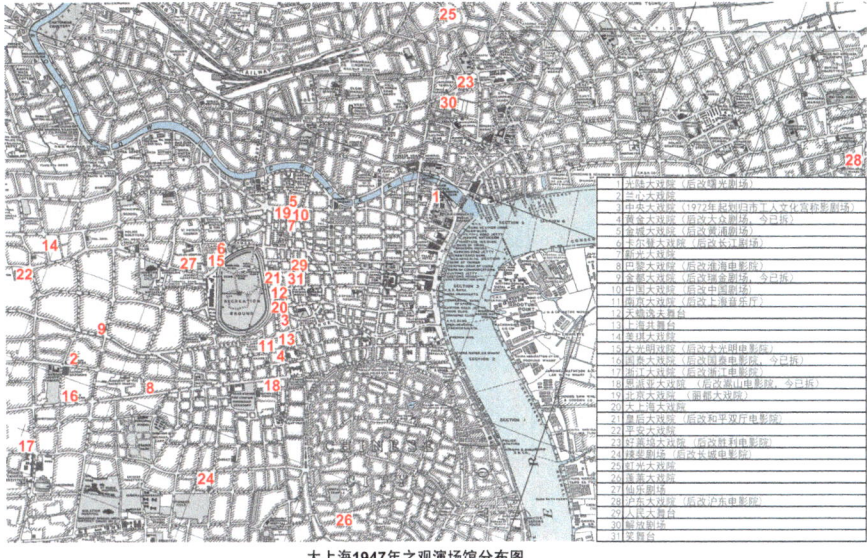

Fig. 2.1 Distribution of main theaters and cinemas in Shanghai in the 1930s. The number represents various cinemas and theaters (drawn by Sun Cong)

Fig. 2.2 Shanghai concert hall (Nanking Theater), designed by Zhao Shen and Robert Fan, 1929; renovated in 2004

developed in 1990. In 1993, the GDP of Shanghai was US$1500 per capita.[1] Although the city was still in the lower-middle income stage, the construction of cultural buildings was tabled in the government's agenda because "Shanghai was

---

[1]The figure of Shanghai's GDP is from *Shanghai Statistic Annual Report*, 2012.

seeking to reclaim its pre-communist role as China's world city"(Rennie-Short 2004, 21). In this process, performing art space was used as means of reclaiming world status as specified in the following five cases.

2.2   Case 1: Shanghai Grand Theater, 1998

When the open-door policy was adopted in 1978, an early experiment with a market economy occurred in southern China, where Shenzhen, the rural custom town adjacent to capitalist Hong Kong, was designated a Special Economic Zone. Shenzhen was synonymous with the "open-door" (to the capitalist world) in the 1980s. The term "grand theater" was coined in Shenzhen when eight cultural projects were proposed in 1984. Five years later, the Shenzhen Grand Theater was constructed on the north side of Shennan Zhong Road, an East–West thoroughfare of the city proper. The grand theater consists of an opera house and concert hall under the same roof, sharing an entrance concourse and an outdoor sunken garden. The grand theater, together with a nearby library and science museum, brilliantly promoted the image of Shenzhen as the engine of economic development and new culture in the period of the open-door policy (Sun and Xue 2017) (see Chap. 4).

When Shenzhen was rising, Shanghai, once the "Oriental Paris", dimmed. The development of Pudong gave Shanghai the impetus to march forward with bigger steps and lead the trend. In early 1994, violinist Itzhak Perlman and the Israel Philharmonic Orchestra toured Shanghai, but the city lacked a qualified professional concert hall, which left Perlman disappointed. The highest-class performing facility was the conference hall of the municipal government, a temporary pavilion remodelled from an old building in the 1950s. The event shocked the government. Huang Ju, the mayor, pointed out that cultural construction must be achieved in tandem with economic construction. The government planned to build a grand theater, "lifting the face for Shanghai people, and being responsible for the future generations" (Yu 2014). The grand theater transcended a cultural performance building to become a symbol of political statement and a power gesture of the "open door".

Vice-mayors Gong Xueping and Chen Zhili selected a site next to the municipal government, facing the People's Square. In the socialist period, the capital city, Beijing, built Tiananmen Square, which could accommodate a million people for political gatherings, demonstrations, and festival parades. The other cities followed this model and built their own political centers. People's Square in Shanghai exactly parallels the function of Tiananmen Square in Beijing. The municipal government occupied the old Hong Kong and Shanghai Bank building in the Bund in the 1950s–1980s. In the years of the open-door policy, the municipal government returned the building to the banking industry, and the new building was set at the central axis, north of the People's Square. On the opposite side is Shanghai Museum. Both buildings were designed by the Shanghai Civil Architectural Design Institute and completed in the early 1990s. The grand theater stands to the west of the government building, and the Shanghai Planning Exhibition Pavilion is on the east. The siting strategies of the grand theater and museum show the government's determination to govern the city with soft and cultural power. Grand theaters and museums are given sacred status by placing them in the city's heart (Yang 2016).

Through the invited consultation for Lujiazui CBD planning in 1992, Shanghai municipal government enjoyed fruitful new ideas of international consultants. For the high class Shanghai grand theater, a good way of obtaining first class design is through design competition. An international design competition was held in early 1994, and the French firm Arte Charpentier Architectes won. Charpentier's design featured a reverse flying roof supported by a truss, with a crystalized white glass box inserted under the roof (Fig. 2.3). The rear of the site is against the old Jockey Club (which was the city library at the time), so the length is limited. The grand theater consists of a lyric theater of 1631 seats, a drama theater of 575 seats, and a studio theater of 220 seats. The front lobby links only to the lyric theater. The other two small theaters take the back and leftover space. Their entrances are on the side, without a spacious lobby. Therefore, only the lyric theater can cater to all major performances. Under its thick roof are restaurants and cafés. The reverse flying roof resembles a sacred palm gesture toward the sky. As an echo, the Shanghai Planning Exhibition Pavilion, constructed later on the other side of the municipal government, also shows a large frame wing cantilevering 15 m out. After three years of intensive construction, the grand theater officially opened in August 1998 (Fig. 2.4).

The grand theater in Shenzhen was designed by a local firm in Guangzhou, and the design method is a natural extension of Chinese architecture from the 1980s. However, the Shanghai Grand Theater was selected from an international design competition, and the design stood out from the Chinese architecture at the time. This was the first international design competition of cultural building in China and set an example for other cities. Arte Charpentier Architectes is not an avant-garde

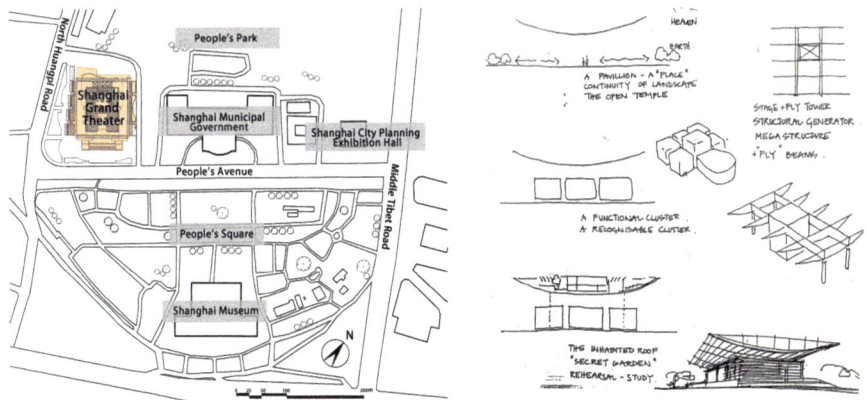

Fig. 2.3 Master plan and sketch of Shanghai Grand Theater by Arte Charpentier Architectes (left picture drawn by Chang Wei, the right picture, courtesy of Charpentier Architectes)

Fig. 2.4 Shanghai Grand Theater: elevation, lobby and auditorium

firm in France, but good at understanding the needs of clients. The designer Andrew Hobson's concept of "sky" and "earth" soon captured the heart of Shanghai's decision makers. These municipal leaders in the 1990 respected French as "high art creator", and they also liked gesture of "symbolizing" the Chinese culture. The design elaborated the facade facing the People's Square.

As the client hoped to have more functions with limited budget and space, only lyric theater has a natural and logic connection with the magnificent lobby. The drama and studio theaters are packed in the leftover space, with little publicity. The box office is at the ground floor of the west side. When a person buys a ticket, he or she should go out to walk up from the big steps to enter the lobby at first floor, instead of directly sneaking into the lobby. Under the lobby is the ground floor with coffee, book shops and exhibition. The remodeling in 2014 addressed this problem by making openings between ground and first floors. People from box office can enter the ground floor and go up to the first floor lobby.

The glass curtain was imported from Germany and the white stone-clad columns were brought from Greece. The crystallised glass and white lobby create a noble temperament. The completion of Shanghai's grand theater began decades of construction of similar grand theaters in other cities, particularly the fiercely debated national theater in Beijing. A year later, the international design competition for the national theater in Beijing was run in three rounds (Xue et al. 2010) (see Chap. 1).

The Shanghai Grand Theater, which opened in 1998, was associated with the Grand Theater in Nanjing Road, a cinema from 1931 designed by Hungarian architect Ladislav Hudec (1893–1958). Separated by almost 60 years, both buildings reached the international standards of their times and lifted Shanghai to a glamorous state. The latter is a reincarnation of the former, an important symbol of Shanghai's reinstated role in the globalisation era.

Vice-mayor Gong was nicknamed the "cultural mayor" because he set up a visual arts college and many cultural projects during his tenure in the 1990s. When the grand theater project was being constructed in 1996, the city was hit by the economic recession. Many projects were suspended. The grand theater faced cash flow problems. Gong suggested that the Shanghai Bureau of Broadcast and Television take the main stock and further finance it. Gong also decided many important building details. For example, Ding Shaoguang, a Chinese-American artist, hoped to donate a large painting, but the client found that there was no proper wall space on which to hang the painting. Gong and colleagues finally decided to demolish a piece of the secondary floor balcony, and the wall set off Ding's painting in a grand way. The painting was later replaced by Chu Teh-Chun (1920–2014, Chinese-French artist)'s work. Gong's colleague Chen Zhili assisted him and was later promoted to the central government as vice-premier.

The grand theater is a notable achievement.[2] The Shanghai Grand Theater opened in August 1998 and has accommodated many impressive performances from around the world, including the musicals *Les Miserables*, *Cats*, *The Lion King*, *Sound of Music*, and *The Phantom of the Opera*. The once-angry violinist Itzhak Perlman and the Israel Philharmonic Orchestra returned to perform, as did the Berlin Philharmonic Orchestra and many other artists and musical troupes. The theater stages an average of two performances every three days. The vacant day is used for installing and breaking down setting and for rehearsal. In terms of income, the theater receives a yearly government subsidy that accounts for around 8% of its funding. Approximately 70% of its income comes from box office receipts and the rest from site rental and sponsors, such as Buick. Its annual income of nearly RMB70 million (around US$11.5 million) is spent on operation, including performances, staff salaries and maintenance fees.[3]

2.3 Case 2: Oriental Art Center, 2005

In the ten years since its inception in Pudong, Shanghai has regained the reins of China's economy. The thrust is from Pudong, the east bank of Huangpu River. The new central business district (CBD) is located in Lujiazui. A tip of Pudong and Central Avenue, 100 m wide, connects the East–West axis of the city across the river and extends eastwards. The Pudong area is even larger than the city proper on

---

[2]The construction history of Shanghai Grand Theater is mainly referenced from Yu (2014). Some situations and facts are taken from the authors' on-site investigation.

[3]The operation fee of Shanghai Grand Theater is from its annual report of 2015 and from the interview of general manager Ms Zhang Xiaoding, engineer Wu Zhihua and executive officer Pan Lan on July 2, 2017.

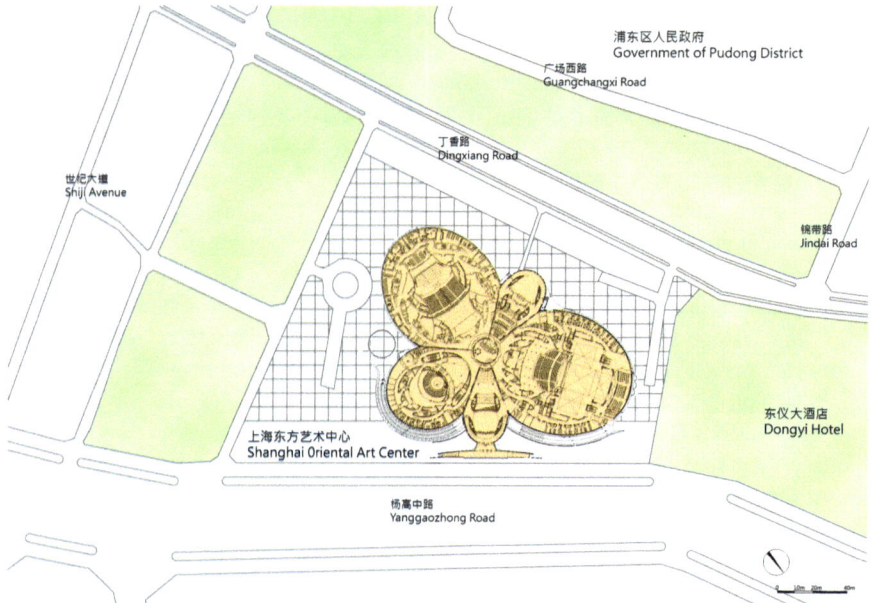

Fig. 2.5 Master plan of Oriental Art Center (drawn by Zhang Lujia)

the west bank. High-class apartments, Class A office buildings, and technological parks were constructed in the area. When the Shanghai Grand Theater was planned in 1994, it was assigned the performance types of opera and ballet. An Oriental concert hall designed by Japanese architects was planned in Lujiazui of Pudong. The site was found to be too small, and the oriental concert hall was moved to the administrative district of Pudong. By taking this opportunity, the Pudong government hoped to make it more than merely a concert hall (Fig. 2.5).

The original concert hall was expanded to three performing spaces under one roof and named the Oriental Art Center. Its ground-breaking ceremony was held in March 2002 and was completed in early 2005. It was designed by French architect Paul Andreu (1938–2018), who had already designed the Shanghai Pudong Airport terminal in 1997 and the National Grand Theater in Beijing in 1999. Andreu is fond of symbolic and particularly circular shapes, which the decision makers in China also enjoy. In the Oriental Art Center, Andreu designed a shape of five-petal magnolia, the city flower of Shanghai. The three large hemispheric petals are the concert hall (2000 seats), opera house (1100 seats) and recital hall (300 seats), and the two small ones are the entrance and exhibition hall. The three performance halls are relatively enclosed, and the leftover space is for public use. In other words, the indoor public space serves three performing spaces. This is better than the treatment of Shanghai Grand Theater, where lobby only serves main lyric theater. The performance space is enclosed by a thick concrete wall, from which steel rods support the external curvilinear curtain wall. The external wall is made of bulging glass curtain, and all internal walls are decorated with warm-coloured porcelain panels. A total of 880 embedded lighting fixtures are installed on the rooftop. In the evening, when the sound of music bursts, the bulbs blink like twinkling stars in the sky. Compared to Shanghai Grand Theatre, Oriental Art Centre has stronger iconic effect, which is good for promoting new district.

Almost every important music troupe in the world has performed at the Oriental Art Center. Many high-income white-collar workers live near the CBD. According to a statistical investigation commissioned by the art center, many audience members come from the western side of the Huangpu River, crossing the Yangpu and Nanpu Bridges.[4] The high-class performance center, plus the library, sport hall and other facilities, make the area appealing to high-end global residents. The completion of the Oriental Art Center greatly boosted the confidence of the Pudong government. It is a cultural landmark of the city, particularly the Pudong of Shanghai (Fig. 2.6).

The Shanghai Grand Theater is located in the old city center, facing the People's Square and supported by the transportation network. In contrast, as part of the Pudong district government facilities, the Oriental Art Center was planned on vacant land and surrounded by parks and wide roads. The government office building and Science Museum are also in the area. They were beautifully drawn, like independent sculptures, in the master plan, but were not designed for the

Fig. 2.6 Oriental Art Center, building, lobby and halls (first picture, courtesy of Fu Xing)

---

[4]The situation of Oriental Art Center was established in an interview with Ms Li Yan, deputy manager of the Center, on July 4, 2017; and from the authors' on-site investigation.

convenience of pedestrians. The main public transportation is the metro line, whose exit is around 500 m away, and pedestrians are exposed the elements. There are no restaurants or food courts within walking distance, so audience members must eat in other places and then travel to the center. As it is away from the city center and the west bank of Huangpu River, where most residents are concentrated, audiences must rush to catch the last train back home, and thus they must usually leave the theater before the curtain call.

The Oriental Art Center is managed by Poly Theater Management Co Ltd, which manages 63 theaters in 55 cities. The income and expenditures of the Oriental Art Center are similar to those of Shanghai Grand Theater. The difference is that the Oriental Art Center does not receive a government subsidy. All of its money comes from box office receipts, sponsorships and occasional government grants for special project applications.[5]

2.4   Case 3: Shanghai Cultural Square, 2011

The Shanghai Grand Theater is located in People's Square, once horseracing course in the British concession area. Shanghai's prosperity between the Wars was mostly exhibited through French concession, an enclave in the messy port city. Both British and French concessions were managed by Shanghai International Settlement. In the heart of French concession, a greyhound racecourse was built for entertainment in the 1920s. Hotel, dancing hall and cinema were rising up nearby.

After 1949 when the Communist took over the power, gambling was banned. The greyhound racecourse was converted to Cultural Square with a capacity of 15,000 people in 1954, a semi-open convention space for political assembling. From 1954 to 1966, over 600 conventions (mainly revolutionary brain washing) were held and they involved more than two million people. In the Cultural Revolution, the venue witnessed many cruel political struggles when the municipal leaders were humiliated. The Cultural Square was demolished by an accidental fire in 1969. To restore this important assembly venue, a new indoor structure covered with three-dimensional spatial truss was completed in 1973. The stage has a headroom of 19 m. It was hailed as advanced performance space in China. Revolutionary operas from China and North Korea were staged. In the years of open-door policy in the 1980s, large scale performance and revolutionary education were outdated. Cultural Square was used as stock exchange when the stock market in China was restored in 1988. After the stock exchange was moved to Pudong CBD, the venue was used as flower market, which took 70% of the market share.[6]

---

[5]The details of the operation of the Oriental Art Center were learnt in an interview with Li Yan, deputy manager, on July 4, 2017.

[6]The history of Cultural Square is partly from the author's experiences, and partly from website, https://baike.baidu.com/item/%E4%B8%8A%E6%B5%B7%E6%96%87%E5%8C%96%E5%B9%BF%E5%9C%BA, Accessed on July 22, 2018.

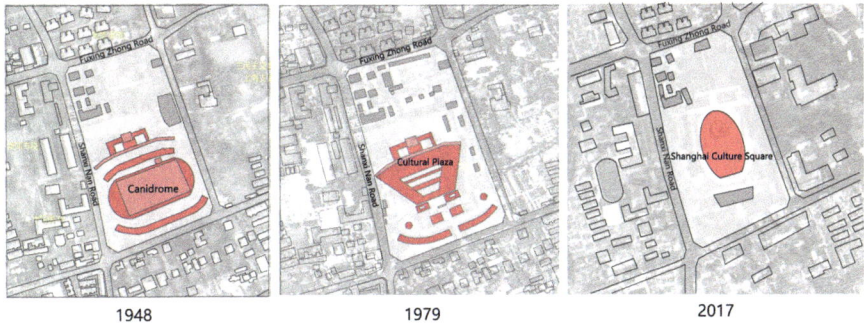

Fig. 2.7 Site of Cultural Square: a changing history (drawn by Zhang Lujia)

When Shanghai Grand Theater was open in 1998, it soon found that a more specialized auditorium for musical might be needed. The municipal government eyed on Cultural Square again. As the site is located in the old French concession and scenery Ruijin Garden, the management hoped that a new theater could give more space to greenery, so as to achieve "green culture". In an international design competition held in 2005, Beyer Blinder Belle (BBB) from New York City together with Xian Dai Group of Shanghai won the design (Fig. 2.7).

Not to disturb the traditional French concession neighborhood, the winning scheme keeps low profile in the vast garden and sinks the main part of building to subterrane. The part above the ground is no more than 10 m, another part of 24 m deep is in underground. An audience member enters the lobby level (±0.00 m), and can directly walk to the third floor balcony. The atrium lobby and entrance to main auditorium of 2000 seats are at the level of −7.5 m. Therefore, audience members mostly go down through grand stairs when entering the big lobby. The most striking design is a huge glass funnel in the center of lobby, where lighting, water and air converge, against the color glass mural on the wall. The theater is surrounded by emergency vehicular access (EVA), ramping down from the streets, they form a sunken plaza, where audience members can enter and exit. Because of its sunken strategies, the building complex with a GFA of 50,000 m². modestly lies prone in a lush garden, which was converted from a site of old lane house. People in the nearby streets do not feel any building block, but a green garden. The old spatial truss is partly kept at back side to form an open amphitheater for people's leisure, amusement and performance.[7]

The Cultural Square supplements Shanghai Grand Theater, especially in musical. Broadway musicals were staged frequently, for example *Cinderella*, *Rent* and

---

[7]The design of Shanghai Cultural Square is partly from Liu Xin, "Shanghai zuishen de dixia juchang—Shanghai wenhua juchang sheji" (The deepest underground theater in Shanghai—Cultural Square), *Shanghai jianshe keji* (Shanghai Construction Science), No. 6, 2010, pp. 1–4, and the website of BBB, http://www.beyerblinderbelle.com/projects/119_shanghai_cultural_plaza?ss=performing_arts, Accessed on July 21, 2018.

Fig. 2.8 Cultural Square: a strategy of low profile in garden

Kinky Boots. To help the theater financially, Shanghai Automobile Company became the title sponsor in 2016. The garden and theater continue the city's cultural glory originated from the 1920s. The site's changing history reflects the city's political and economic agenda in the past hundred years (Fig. 2.8).

2.5 Case 4: Concert Hall, Shanghai Symphony Orchestra, 2013

Shanghai established the earliest philharmonic orchestra in China, by the International Settlement in 1922. Before the orchestra had its own concert hall, the musicians packed into a small house to practice, where noise from street and next door was inevitable. When music was recorded, even in the summer, the air-conditioning had to be shut down. In 2009, Shanghai government gave the old Shanghai diving pool to the orchestra to build its concert hall. The site is in the city center, where Metro Line 10 passes underground. The client first found the acoustic consultant Yasuhisa Toyota from Japan, who had designed concert halls for Suntory in Tokyo and Disney in Los Angeles. An architectural design by Japanese architect Isozaki Arata was selected from four competitors, and Tongji University design institute assisted as the local architect.

A 2000-seat concert hall and a 300-person recital hall (also a recording studio) are arranged longitudinally in a box along the road. The long lobby serves the two

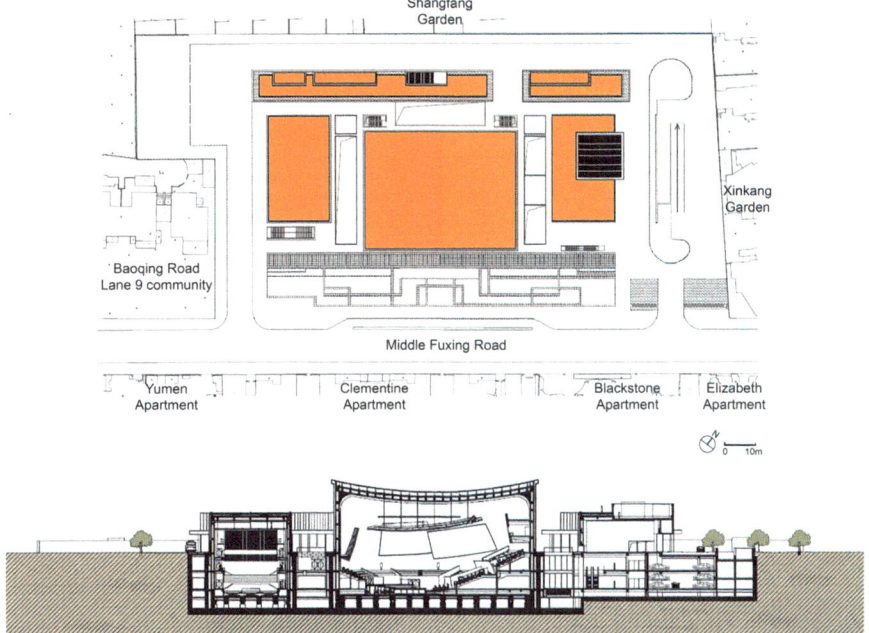

Fig. 2.9 Master plan of symphony orchestra concert hall

halls and links them to a sunken garden. The auditorium in the concert hall is designed in a vineyard pattern, with the terraces warmly cascading to the stage. To prevent noise, double concrete walls, each 250 mm thick and 400 mm apart, were poured. As mentioned above, Metro Line 10 passes under the site. To isolate the concert hall from the train noise, 168 short concrete posts were built from the foundation, upon which were installed dampers produced in Germany. The floor and the building are actually suspended atop a raft of springs and thus will not shake when a train speeds through beneath. To revitalize the old city of high density, design must be carried out like surgeon operation (Fig. 2.9).

The Shanghai Symphony Orchestra moved into its new home in 2013. The venue is near the Conservatory of Music, so the art teaching/learning and performing can include more interactive communication in walking distance. Not only does the orchestra rehearse and perform in the concert hall, but it also hosts touring international music troupes. The building enhances the status of Shanghai's symphony orchestra, which is able to attract better musicians and more sponsorships[8] (Fig. 2.10).

---

[8]The facts of Concert Hall, Shanghai Symphony Orchestra are from I. Arata, 'Shanghai Symphony Orchestra Concert Hall', *id + c* (interior design + construction), Feb 2015, 94–100; F. Xu, X. Hou, C. Ma and X. Lv, 'The Urban Box—design of the Shanghai symphony hall', *Time + Architecture*, 31(1), 2015, 106–113.

Fig. 2.10 Symphony orchestra concert hall, building and lobby

Designer Isozaki Arata has been famous for his changing face/method since the 1970s and is categorised among the "post-modernists". He has been active in China since the 1990s. In 2001, he won the first job in China—Shenzhen Cultural Center, consisting of a library and a concert hall. He designed the art gallery for the Central Academy of Fine Arts in Beijing (2008), Himalaya Center in Shanghai (2011) and Harbin Concert Hall (2016), and most of these works were implemented from his Shanghai studio organised by his partner Hu Qian. His postmodernist method appeals to the clients' eagerness to create a new image. The concert hall possesses high-quality acoustics and architecture and is intimate for people and pedestrians.

2.6   Case 5: Poly Theater, Jiading, 2014

While the city proper was busily building subways, skyscrapers and cultural buildings, the suburban towns were making their own way towards modernisation. Dr. Sun Jiwei, graduated from Tongji University, was responsible for the town planning and construction in Qingpu and Jiading, both old rural towns in Shanghai, in the 21st century. He believes that excellent architecture can light up the old city. During his time in Qingpu, he created many opportunities for elite architects to build experimental architecture in his district. The rural towns have more land than the crowded city and thus more freedom for designers' creativity. When he moved to Jiading, he planned a new CBD, parks and landscapes for the district and invited famous architects from home and abroad to design public buildings. When the land for a theater was leased to the Poly Group, the Group committed a design. However, as a district planner, Sun hoped to have a world class architect who could 'light up the area'. With this thinking, he and the client invited Japanese architect Tadao Ando, who was said "to understand China's construction conditions and be flexible enough" (Ma 2015) (Fig. 2.11).

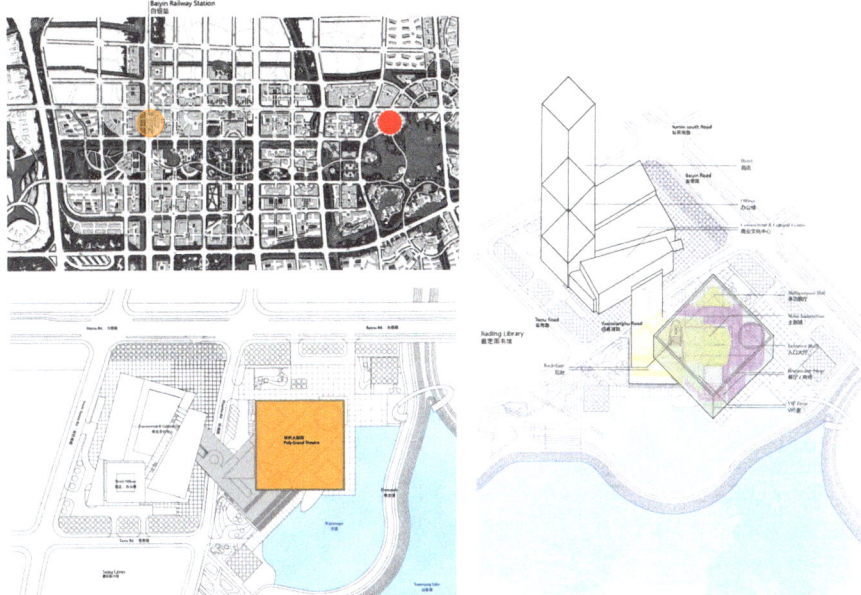

Fig. 2.11 Master plan of Poly Theater

Tadao Ando began his China venture in 2004 and has designed nearly 20 projects in various cities. He is highly esteemed and eagerly sought after, and his designs have won enthusiastic applause from municipal leaders and clients. The Poly Theater is located at the end of a road axis facing a large park and lake. The basic building form is a square 100 m on each side. A 1575-seat theater lies diagonally in a 34-m-high square box. The central axis of the auditorium extends to the main entrance in the corner. Four groups of cylinders, 18 m in diameter, are inserted into the box. They interconnect and form a complicated interior space and are reflected on the external wall. Through the dramatic holes on the external wall, people from the park can peep into the internal space, like a "cultural kaleidoscope". The lake is extended to the theater, and an open stage projects into the water. The huge double-curved surface is cladded with aluminium strips, which have a timber-like texture after heat treatment. According to Ando, wind and light in these complicated spaces are making another play.[9] The fare-faced concrete wall is veneered by a second skin curtain wall, which soften the external wall in daytime and lighten up by flooding light in the evening. He continues his design language of

---

[9] About the design of Poly Theater, see T. Ando, 'The challenges of creating a cathedral to culture', *A + U*, Special Issue on Poly Grand Theater, 3, 2015, 24–27; and also J. Chen, X. Qi and J. Chen, 'Multi-collisions in the kaleidoscope—a review of Shanghai Jiading Poly grand theater', *Time + Architecture*, 1, 2015, 120–125.

Fig. 2.12 Poly Theater, building and lobby

fair-faced concrete and curtain wall. Ando's design may look too strong in a city environment, but displays a sculptural effect in a big park of suburban town.

Many world cities will welcome designs from such a Pritzker Architectural Award laureate. An old rural town between Shanghai and Jiangsu Province, Jiading has hosted a Volkswagen production line, "German Town", a Formula One race-course and some ancient heritage.[10] The Jiading New Town is one of the three new towns planned to upgrade suburban Shanghai, and it will house up to one million residents. During its rapid development, it has had Tadao Ando's name to lift its face. Tadao Ando had not previously designed a grand theater and grasped the opportunity to make this statement and add to his already brilliant portfolio. Although far (28 km) from the city center, Poly Theater has served residents with its own performing niche in the nearby areas since its opening in 2014. One business of Poly Group is real estate. Many of Poly's residential estates were built around the theater. Residents and office workers can enjoy the nice environment of the park, theater and CBD. Together with the library designed by Mada Spam, Poly Theater will assume a greater role as a landmark in the Jiading new town. Another business of Poly Group is theater management. Through its network of show planning, performing troupes in China and abroad can circulate among various cities, including the suburban location of Jiading (Fig. 2.12).

---

[10]"German Town" is one of the "One City Nine Towns" launched by Shanghai government in 2001. Along with German Town designed by German architects, the other towns are Thames Town designed by British architects, Italian Town, Holland Town, Scandinavian Town and etc. See Xue and Zhou (2007).

2.7 Whose Theater?

In less than 20 years, Shanghai has restored the old concert hall and built nearly ten grand theaters, a dance theater, a play house, a concert hall and a circus city. The north part of Suzhou Creek was traditionally a poor area, and the classy theaters and cinemas were concentrated on the south part. In 2014, Daning Theater opened in the old industrial district of Zhabei. Not far from the symphony orchestra, an opera house of the Shanghai Conservatory of Music is under construction. The Shanghai Grand Opera House, initiated in 1958, is located on the waterfront of the World Expo 2010 site. Snøhetta, the designer of the Oslo opera house, is committed to the design. As said above, the performance spaces were mostly in the south bank of Suzhou Creek. With the city's gravity moving to the east bank of Huangpu River, more grand theaters crossed the river and settled in Pudong. Districts are actively planning their own theaters and cultural facilities. The number of performing art facilities and total seats are well over those of Hong Kong, whose GDP per capita is twice that of Shanghai[11] (Fig. 2.13).

Four of the five theaters mentioned above were the result of direct investment by government, either municipal or district. Poly was built by the Poly Group, a private corporation with a government and military background, and the land was provided by the government. In return, Poly gained a concession price of land in nearby sites to construct office and housing blocks. The five theaters, like most grand theaters built in China, were directly or indirectly funded by government. It is true that taxpayers' money should benefit more people. However, most of these theaters shut their doors during the daytime and are only open to ticket holders in the evening. The management does not fully use the possibility of publicity given in the design stage.

The Shanghai Grand Theater faces the People's Square. An iron fence surrounds the outdoor grassland. Passers-by can only appreciate the crystalline sculpture-like theater at a distance. Many residents in the surrounding areas never have a chance to enter the theater. The management has explained that there are too many people in the square. If the theater removes the fence, tourist buses will park in front and damage the pavement. Opening the lobby to the public is unthinkable.[12] In the Oriental Art Center, people can enter the box office only after passing through security guards and an X-ray bag check. After buying tickets, people are allowed to enter the lobby, which connects to the three performing spaces. As it is far from the city and the Metro line, and because of the strict entrance security check, very few people will be in the mood to stroll through the lobby during the day.

---

[11]According to authors' preliminary statistics, Shanghai has more than 18,000 theater seats, and Hong Kong has more than 15,000. The GDP per capita of Hong Kong was US$43,600 in 2016. See *Gross Domestic Products*, Census and Statistics Department, Hong Kong Government, 2016.

[12]The management situation is taken from the interview of general manager Ms Zhang Xiaoding, engineer Wu Zhihua and executive officer Pan Lan on July 3, 2017.

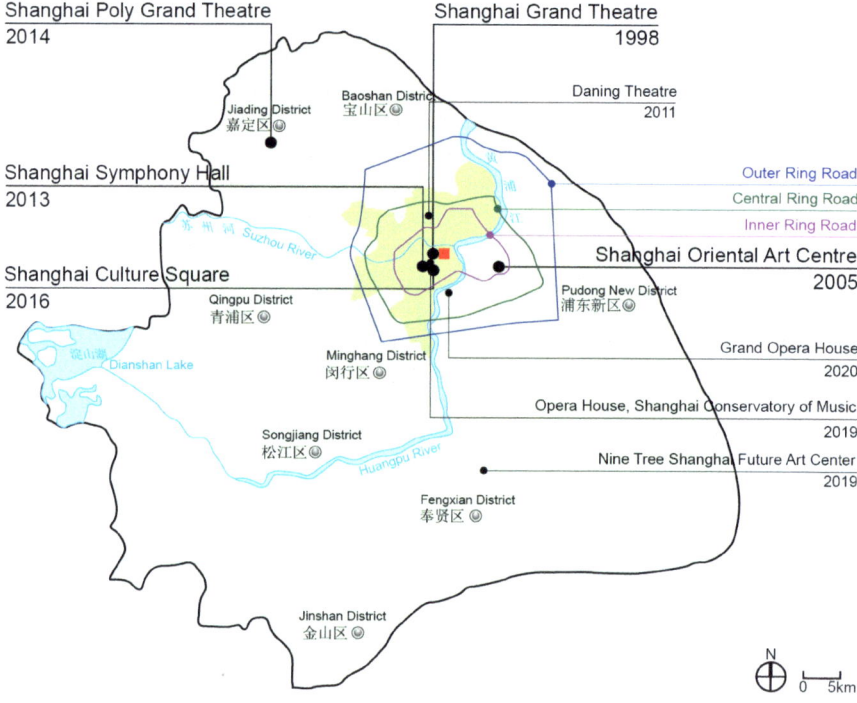

Fig. 2.13 Distribution of major performing space in Shanghai (drawn by Sun Cong)

The garden surrounding the Cultural Square is lovely and open to the public, however, the theater is open to the ticket holders only 45 min before the show. The situation is similar with the Poly Theater. The lobby opens to the public on the second Sunday every month, but only for four hours. The concert hall of the symphony orchestra is aligned with other buildings in the street of the old French concession area. It is among the very few theaters that open to the public their lobby and exhibition gallery, where musical instruments and interactive sound devices are displayed. Because it partly sinks into the underground, pedestrians can hardly find its full face in the tree-lined road. Both Cultural Square and the symphony orchestra concert hall are modest and intimate and not as glamorous as the other grand theaters.

In these theaters, a ticket is usually priced RMB80 (US$13) to RMB1800 (US $300), according to the location and the class of performance. The average admission ticket at Shanghai Grand Theater is RMB207 (US$34.50) in 2015.[13] Although the theaters make every effort to obtain sponsorship funding to reduce prices, a ticket is still expensive for most working class residents, whose monthly

---

[13]The average price of Shanghai Grand Theater is from its 2015–16 Annual Report. The other prices are taken from the authors' record of theaters' online ticket sales from 2014 to 2017.

salary is around RMB5000 to RMB10,000 (US$833 to US$1666).[14] Compared to the state-run museums and libraries, which are freely open to the public, the theaters can serve only a handful of middle- and upper-class people. If the indoor and outdoor public space can be open to the public free of charge, the theaters will display better social functions and enliven civic life.

2.8   Conclusion: Quest for City and People

This chapter briefly reviews the production of five theaters in Shanghai in the past twenty years. By discussing the various theaters' situations, we can answer the questions raised in the beginning.

Many grand theaters were initiated and built, mainly for the city's imperatives of enhancing their domestic and international status, producing an ideal environment for (foreign) investment and providing a venue for high art (Sassen 2001). After the major theaters, other cultural buildings and the subway network (580 km long) are completed, Shanghai plans to jump from an "international metropolis" by 2020 to a "global city" by 2040 that possesses a configuration of international resources, influence and high competitiveness (Shen et al. 2016). Such cultural venues are indispensable for a city with this global ambition. In terms of per-capita GDP, China is still a developing country.[15] However, first-tier cities like Shanghai, Beijing, Guangzhou and Shenzhen are catching up with Hong Kong, Singapore and Tokyo.[16] They have sufficient resources to build cultural facilities, which are regarded as the city's calling cards in the official and mass media.

Rapid urbanisation promotes economic growth and gathers more people into the city. More and more of these people become affluent each year, and they demand cultural vitality.[17] The conceptual cultural buildings are constructed to substantiate the city's claims to global significance. The increasingly strong wave of post-industrial consumerism supports the operation of cultural spots and allows them to thrive. These changes are similar to the gentrification process described by Zukin (1993). However in China, they are the results of government-led gentrification. The author's team has investigated more than 10 Chinese cities, and observed averagely 80% theatre occupancy.

In Unitarian China, there is one more characteristic in addition to the cultural building production and consumption in capitalist cities. The central government

---

[14]The salary level is taken from *Shanghai Statistic Annual Book*, 2016.

[15]*China Statistic Annual Report*, 2015.

[16]In 2015, Shanghai's GDP per capita was over RMB100,000, that was around US$16,600, according to *Jiefang Ribao* (Liberation Daily), March 1, 2016. http://newspaper.jfdaily.com/jfrb/html/2016-03/01/content_176914.htm, accessed Aug 23, 2017.

[17]In 2016, per capita annual disposable income of China's urban residents was US$5054, with an Engel coefficient of 30.1%, which declines by 0.5% from 2015 and approaches the 20–30% standard of affluence specified by the United Nations. *China Statistic Annual Report*, 2017.

hopes to maintain the strong momentum of economic development and the local governments compete for resources. "Global cities" and "perfect urban and cultural facilities" are important indexes to win in the competition among cities. With the leadership of the Communist Party, decisions are made from the top down with little opposition at the civic level, which makes site selection, excavation, preparation, design and construction relatively smoother than in the "democratic" societies, whose public expenditures are scrutinised by a voter-elected council or congress. Even in difficult financial circumstances (as in the case of Shanghai Grand Theater and Cultural Square), the government can motivate social forces (mainly state-owned corporations) to solve the problem. Social watchdogs, public opinion and financial procedures are bypassed. The grand theaters are new spectacles in Chinese cities, wrought by absolute ambition, power and money, as David Havey pointed out: "it is a right to change and reinvent the city more after our hearts' desire… when people are remaking the city, they are indirectly remaking themselves as well" (Havey 2012, 3–5). When the provincial or municipal leaders decide a direction, they can make it.

This Chinese characteristic is making miracles and mirages. The Sydney Opera House took 17 years to complete. The West Kowloon Cultural District of Hong Kong has been discussed for 20 years and has gone through several rounds of planning and Legislative Council debate. The first building, Xiqu Theater, took six years for construction (Xue 2016). In contrast, the grand theaters in Shanghai and other Chinese cities were usually completed in 3–4 years. The implementation ability of the Chinese government and developers are unchallengeable.[18] Some may be rough in construction, but most theaters reach international standards and are praised by the international artists, musical troupes and architects.[19]

In our case studies, three theaters' designs were acquired through design competition. French and American architects won for their innovative design, especially in the building image and association with romantic symbols. With these international design competitions, Shanghai acquired designs whose forms graced the city. The Shanghai Grand Theater was the first of more than 100 grand theaters constructed in China in the 21st century. The concert hall of the symphony orchestra was committed to a Japanese acoustic expert because of his track record in designing concert halls. Poly Theater invited a world-class architect, and both the client and the government felt fortunate to have such a big name and extraordinary work. The design adds colour to the theater and the area. Regardless of whether a design competition is held, the selection of a design emphasises unique qualities in a particular location and the long-term impact of the building. The traditional shoebox form was wrapped with post-modern and post-industrial cloth, which is expected to express the client's pride and the government's achievement and

---

[18]This statement is true not only in China, but also in China's aid building projects in Asia and Africa, see L. Beeckmans, 'The Architecture of nation-building in Africa as a development aid project: Designing the capitols of Kinshasa (Congo) and Dodoma (Tanzania) in the post-independence years', *Progress in Planning*, online May 10, 2017.

[19]See Yu (2014), and the websites of the relevant theaters.

vitalising the city or suburban area. It has partly accomplished these goals. In an assessment of the image of Shanghai's cultural space, Shanghai Grand Theater was rated No. 6 and the Oriental Arts Center No. 8.[20]

With the completion of these theaters, Shanghai has hosted more domestic and international art exchanges and performances, and local artists, students and musical troupes have ample opportunity to practice and exercise their roles for an audience. Shanghai Grand Theater alone hosted 367,000 people to see performances during fiscal year 2015–16.[21] Although the design schemes considered public use and accessibility, most theaters' social function extends only a couple of hours before the show, as the lobby opens at 6.30 or 6.45 P.M. for the audiences. The theaters run open days and other outreach activities once or twice per month. More people can attend the seminars and view exhibitions on those days. Compared to the huge investment they require, the magnificent space and prominent status they present in the city, and the citizens' high expectations, theaters' social functions need to be better and more fully displayed.

A relatively good example may be the concert hall of the symphony orchestra. The building is located in the old city area, instead of an isolated sculpture on vacant land. It is a natural extension of the street facade, and pedestrians can easily enter the courtyard and lobby during the day. The building consolidates the original street function of continuity and encourages pleasant civic and street life.

Table 2.1 summarises the public space and design language of the five grand theaters in Shanghai. The five prominent theaters were all designed by international architects and firms, which is more expensive than using local architects.[22] This shows the city's determination to join the global cultural exchange and acts as a gesture of mind-opening. The design and building quality of the five theaters is completely different from the trajectory of Chinese architecture. They set trends and examples for Chinese architects in the design of cultural buildings. Each, both, or all can be aligned with phenomena in Chinese architecture; for example, a symbolic form with a story, the use of a cultural building to vitalize an area, respecting the old neighborhood, form determined by technology and the use of star architects to promote a remote area. The aspiration of being "global" is partly realised through the concerted efforts of government, developers, designers, theater managers and audiences in a consumerist society. Shanghai's path of building cultural buildings realizes its dream of "Oriental Pearl" and represents the development trajectory of Chinese cities. However, Chinese cities and their people also deserve more

---

[20]This is taken from an investigation made by Shanghai Investment Consultancy Ltd. in 2014. From Shen et al. 2016. No. 1–5 of impressive cultural spaces are Oriental Pearl (TV tower), The Bund, Yu Garden, Shanghai Museum, China Arts Palace (China Pavilion in the World Expo).

[21]The data are taken from the 2015–16 Annual Report of Shanghai Grand Theater.

[22]It is estimated that the design fees of international architects are around four times higher than those of local architects. Organising an international design competition involves compensation fees for the shortlisted firms, logistics for meetings and a jury panel. See Xue (2010).

Table 2.1 Summary of the five theaters in Shanghai

	Urban and public space	Theater and design language	Phenomenon or significance in urban architecture
Shanghai grand theater	Limited by the site, the lobby is short. Little consideration of outdoor public space in the design. The side garden is open to the public, but the front square is fenced. It is part of a space of power in the city	The theme is embracing 'Heaven and earth'. A light-white sculpture sits on the lawn. The stage and audience have excellent sight-lines and acoustics. The lobby is elegantly decorated. It is noble and beautiful but keeps a distance from ordinary people	The first grand theater in China, whose design was acquired through an international design competition. One hall satisfies multiple functions of concert and opera. Expression of the Chinese characteristics
Oriental art center	There is no consideration of outdoor space. The lobby connects to three theaters and is lively in the evening before the show	The theme is magnolia petals—the city's flower. The shape can be best appreciated from sky, not from ground level	Symbolic form 'to be like something' to please the decision maker. Cultural building is used to vitalise the new district
Shanghai cultural square	Big garden in the old French concession open to the public. Beautiful lobby only opens to the ticket holders	Curvilinear form with funnel. Partly radical and iconic	Respecting the traditional neighborhood. Prioritizing the greenery coverage and providing park for the crowded city center
Symphony orchestra concert hall	The entrance courtyard, lobby and exhibition gallery are open to the public during the day	The roof is curved. The vineyard-patterned concert hall achieves good acoustic effects	Technology dominates the building design. Building fits into the old fabric of the city
Poly grand theater	The building enjoys a superb park landscape. There are many views of the forest and lake from the building. However, the theater does not open to the public outside of show times	The huge tubes and their intersection create abundant spatial effect. The theatrical treatment of building volume plays with lake	Star architects and their imagination to boost the remote area by cultural buildings

enjoyment and sharing of cultural facilities and their affiliated public space. In the end, governments should be held accountable for the use of taxpayers' money, a public building should serve people and a city should make people's lives better.

Acknowledgements This chapter is part of a study supported by Research Grant Council, Hong Kong government, project No. CityU 11658816. The author heartily thanks Huang Wenfu and Li Shuan for their referring of Shanghai Grand Theater; the introduction and leading visit of Zhang Xiaoding, Pan Lan and Engineer Wu from Shanghai Grand Theater and Li Yan from Shanghai Oriental Art Center. Thanks to Professor Zhang Liang for his advice on the Shanghai Grand Theater.

During the Cultural Revolution (1966–1976), Shanghai and the other Chinese cities were engulfed by political turbulence. Cinemas remained open, but were filled mainly with documentary films such as "Chairman Mao meeting foreign guests" or dull, formulaic feature films about the revolution. Foreign movies with exotic flavour were admired, but these were imported only from China's comrades, North Korea, Romania, Albania and Yugoslavia. As a primary school pupil, I went to see a film every month or two. No matter how banal the topic (from today's viewpoint), seeing a film was an event for me in those years. An admission ticket could excite kids for weeks. Most of the cinemas in Shanghai were built in the 1930s, some in the art deco style. During the turmoil of the Cultural Revolution, cinemas were maintained as organs of revolutionary propaganda. Before a film formally started, several slides were presented, with the last slide showing the word "Jing" (silence) with a full moon hung above still water. The ambient lighting was dimmed and your heart was haunted.

Factories and the countryside replaced school in the revolutionary years. In rural threshing grounds, a white cloth was suspended from two bamboo posts when the sky became dark. On his bicycle, an itinerant projectionist carrying old films brought happiness to the remote rural villages. The stories were old and known to everyone, but the films relieved the fatigue of intense rural labour.

When the Cultural Revolution ended and China returned to normal life, Chinese and foreign films/plays filled cinemas and theatres. As I entered the university and worked toward my professional goals, seeing films was one of my many pastimes and social activities. I had a chance to join a team to design theatres and film studios, and I studied this building type attentively. In Texas, I participated in the renovation of a large, old church with choir and musical functions. During the past 10 years, I have paid attention to China's newly built grand theatres and visited dozens of performing arts venues in more than 10 cities. In these palace-like grand theatres, I have viewed ballets, symphonies, dramas, musicals and quartets by both Chinese and foreign artists. A ticket can still arouse my excitement for weeks and even months. Walking into these theatres, the sacred feeling in my heart is no less than it was in childhood. The theatre is a noble palace indeed, and it elevates our life.

References

Havey, D. (2012). *Rebel cities: From the right to the city to the urban revolution.* New York: Verso.

Lee, L. O. F. (1999). *Shanghai modern: The flowering of new urban culture in China.* Cambridge, MI.: Harvard University Press.

Ma, W. (2015).'Interview with Sun Jiwei', *A + U*, Special Issue on Poly Grand Theater, *3*, July, 42–47.

Rennie-Short, J. (2004). *Global metropolitan: Globalizing cities in a capitalist world.* London and New York: Routledge.

Sassen, S. (2001). *The global city: New York, London, Tokyo* (2nd ed.). Princeton, NJ: Princeton University Press.

Shen, L., Lu, W., & Wang, B. (2016). Strategic thinking on the cultural spatial planning of Shanghai towards a global city. *Urban Planning Forum, 3*, 63–70.

Sun, C., & Xue, C. Q. L. (2017). The construction heat of cultural facilities in contemporary China —A case study of Shenzhen's performing space. In *East Asia Architectural Conference (EAAC)*, Tianjin, November.

Xue, C. Q. L. (2006). *Building a revolution: Chinese architecture since 1980*. Hong Kong: Hong Kong University Press.

Xue, C. Q. L. (2010). *World architecture in China*. Hong Kong: Joint Publishing Co., Ltd.

Xue, C. Q. L. (2016). *Hong Kong architecture 1945–2015: From colonial to global*. Singapore: Springer.

Xue, C. Q. L., Wang, Z., & Mitchenere, B. (2010). In search of identity: The development process of the national grand theater in Beijing, China. *The Journal of Architecture, 15*(4), 517–535.

Xue, C. Q. L., & Zhou, M. (2007). Importation and adaptation: Building "One City and Nine Towns" in Shanghai, a case study of Vittorio Gregotti's plan of Pujiang Town. *Urban Design International, 12*(1), 21–40.

Yang, Z. (2016). The 'political narration' of the grand theater and its shaping of the urban culture. *Henan shehui kexue (Social Science of Henan Province), 24*(3), 115–122. 扬子 (2016). 大剧院的政治叙事及对城市文化的塑形. 河南社会科学. 24(3), 115–122.

Yu, J. L. (2014). *Pobing zhilv—Shanghai dajuyuan xunli (Breaking the ice—Road of Shanghai Grand Theater)*. Shanghai: Shanghai Jiaotong University Press, 2014. 俞璟璐 (2014). 破冰之旅-上海大剧院巡礼. 上海:上海交通大学出版社.

Zukin, S. (1993). *Landscapes of power: From detroit to disney world* (p. 1993). Berkeley, CA: University of California Press.

Chapter 3
Guangzhou Opera House: Building a Gated Public Space

Guanghui Ding

3.1 Introduction

In 1931, the Sun Yat-sen Memorial Auditorium was erected in Guangzhou, the capital city of Guangdong Province in southern China. Nearly 80 years later, in the summer of 2010, the Guangzhou Opera House held its first performance—Italian composer Giacomo Puccini's classic opera *Turandot*, directed by American filmmaker Shahar Stroh. Designed by the Iraq-born, London-based architect Zaha Hadid, the Guangzhou Opera House was one of the highest-profile theater building projects in China at the time (Cheng 2010). Leading international newspapers, such as *The Guardian, Financial Times, The New York Times* and *The Telegraph*, reviewed the building (Glancey 2011; Heathcote 2011; Moore 2011; Ouroussoff 2011). Prominent architectural magazines such as the *Architectural Record* and *Domus* also reported on the completion of the project (Anonymous 2011a; Galilee 2010). Conceived as an urban catalyst for the new cultural district of Guangzhou, the project became a new representation of the city, showcasing both a commitment to cultural prosperity and a vision for global exchange.

In as much as the construction of the Guangzhou Opera House was closely associated with state-driven urban expansion, globally-based architectural creativity, domestically-initiated institutional reform and market-oriented cultural production, the project became a quintessential example able to illustrate the complexity of architectural practice under China's socialist market economy. The interplay of politics and experimentation in the Guangzhou Opera House gave rise to a "gated public space"—both a material space with the juxtaposition of inclusive public gatherings and exclusive commercial activities and an immaterial space of freedom yet controlled by the agents of the state and capital. The gated nature of

G. Ding (✉)
School of Architecture and Urban Planning, Beijing University of Civil
Engineering and Architecture, Beijing, China
e-mail: tin_tin0504@hotmail.com

© Springer Nature Singapore Pte Ltd. 2019
C. Q. Xue (ed.), *Grand Theater Urbanism*,
https://doi.org/10.1007/978-981-13-7868-3_3

this public realm was characterized by the tension between the decentralization of authority and the intervention of power, reflecting the intrinsic character of China's reform and opening-up process. The state intended to use the project as a spatial instrument to achieve economic development, political stability and cultural prosperity, struggling to address the "three goals" (growth, control and equality) in the course of China's modernization (Perry and Wong 1985).

3.2   Expansion of Urban Territory

Before the erection of the Guangzhou Opera House, the city possessed two main performing venues: the Sun Yat-sen Memorial Hall (Fig. 3.1) built in the 1930s, with a predominantly classical Chinese octagonal roof and structured for political gatherings to advocate Sun's revolutionary ideas by the Nationalist Party, and the Youyi (Friendship) Theater (Fig. 3.2) in the 1960s, a medium-sized, multi-purpose modern theater with merits of subtle interaction between architecture and nature and between audiences and artists (Lu 2004; Lin 1982). The two buildings have become popular venues for a variety of performances, holding more than 200 shows every year.

The level of cultural exchange increased after China's opening-up in the early 1980s, but various major international plays and operas that had been introduced could not be staged in Guangzhou, due to the layout of the two buildings (Lau 2010). The decision to build a grand theater for various performing arts was not made immediately, however, inasmuch as a number of internal and external factors were involved. In an effort to accommodate music performance and demonstrate cultural prosperity, the state-of-the-art Xinghai Concert Hall was built by local authorities in 1998.[1] The iconic part of the building is its roof, a hyperbolic paraboloid reinforced concrete shell with diagonal span to 67.88 m, under which a 1500-seat concert hall was designed with "vineyard terraces", an arrangement of orchestra initially appeared in Hans Scharoun's Berlin Philharmonic of 1963. At the turn of the twenty-first century, the Xinghai Concert Hall located on the Ersha Island in the Pearl River became the most representative destination of the city's cultural tourism (Fig. 3.3).

While visiting South China in 1992, Deng Xiaoping advocated the establishment of a socialist market economy that would enable China to be involved in global capitalism. He particularly encouraged local officials in Guangzhou to energetically develop the economy, urging that Guangzhou should catch up with the so-called Four Asian Dragons within 20 years' rapid development (Vogel 1991). The priorities for the mayor Li Ziliu were, by following Hong Kong, to construct both a

---

[1]This concert hall was designed by the architect Lin Yongxiang and his colleagues from the South China University of Technology Architectural Design and Research Institute, in collaboration with leading acoustics consultant like Xiang Ruiqi from Beijing Institute of Architectural Design.

Fig. 3.1 Lu Yanzhi, Sun Yat-sen Memorial Auditorium, Guangzhou, 1931. Photo by Charlie Xue

Fig. 3.2 She Junnan, the Youyi (Friendship) Theater, 1965

commercial and financial center and a metro system, without which the city could not be called an "international metropolis" (*guojihua dadushi*) (Nanfang dush-ibao 2011). Building an underground rapid transit system requires huge investment, well beyond the financial means of the local authority. The booming property market of the time enabled Li to consider raising funds by planning a new town and selling land (Rithmire 2013). [2]

---

[2]In China, all land was state-owned (in urban areas) or collectively-owned (in rural areas).

Fig. 3.3 Xinghai Concert Hall, 1998. Photo by Zang Peng

The under-urbanized territory to the south of the Tianhe Sports Center was an ideal site, as the large area of farmland could be converted quickly to satisfy the expansion of urban life. In 1993, the Guangzhou Urban Planning Bureau invited three firms—Thomas Planning Service Inc. from Boston, USA, Leung Peddle Thorp Architects and Planners Ltd. from Hong Kong and the local Guangzhou Urban Planning and Design Survey Research Institute—to deliver planning proposals for the Zhujiang (Pearl River) New Town. The final master plan with a hierarchical structure was based on the proposal by American planner, Carol J. Thomas (Huang 2005). A noticeable urban axis linking the Tianhe Sports Center in the north with the Pearl River in the south dominated the plan. This 128 m wide landscape axis divided the town into two primary areas, which included 440 residential (east) and commercial (west) blocks, together with a number of cultural facilities such as theater and museum. Small-scale blocks and high-density developments enabled land to be easily sold to private developers for speculation.

The financial crisis that struck many Asian countries in late 1997 however led to a significant drop in property prices, affecting real estate development in Guangzhou. The local authority reviewed the new town's sluggish development and decided to promote the new town as the Guangzhou Central Business District of the Twenty-first Century (GCBD21). Piper Gaubatz has argued that one of the most common strategies municipal planners use to transform locally oriented cities into internationally oriented cities is the designation of CBDs (Gaubatz 2005). The emergence of CBDs exemplified that the state tended to employ the production of urban space as an instrument to achieve capital accommodation (Gottdiener 1985). While preserving the central landscape axis, the revised plan consisted of 269 larger blocks and adjusted a number of the architectural programs (Fig. 3.4). More importantly, for the first time it was clearly stated that the Guangzhou Opera House should be built in the new town, suggesting that the previously planned convention and exhibition center, along with other administrative and legislative institutions, be

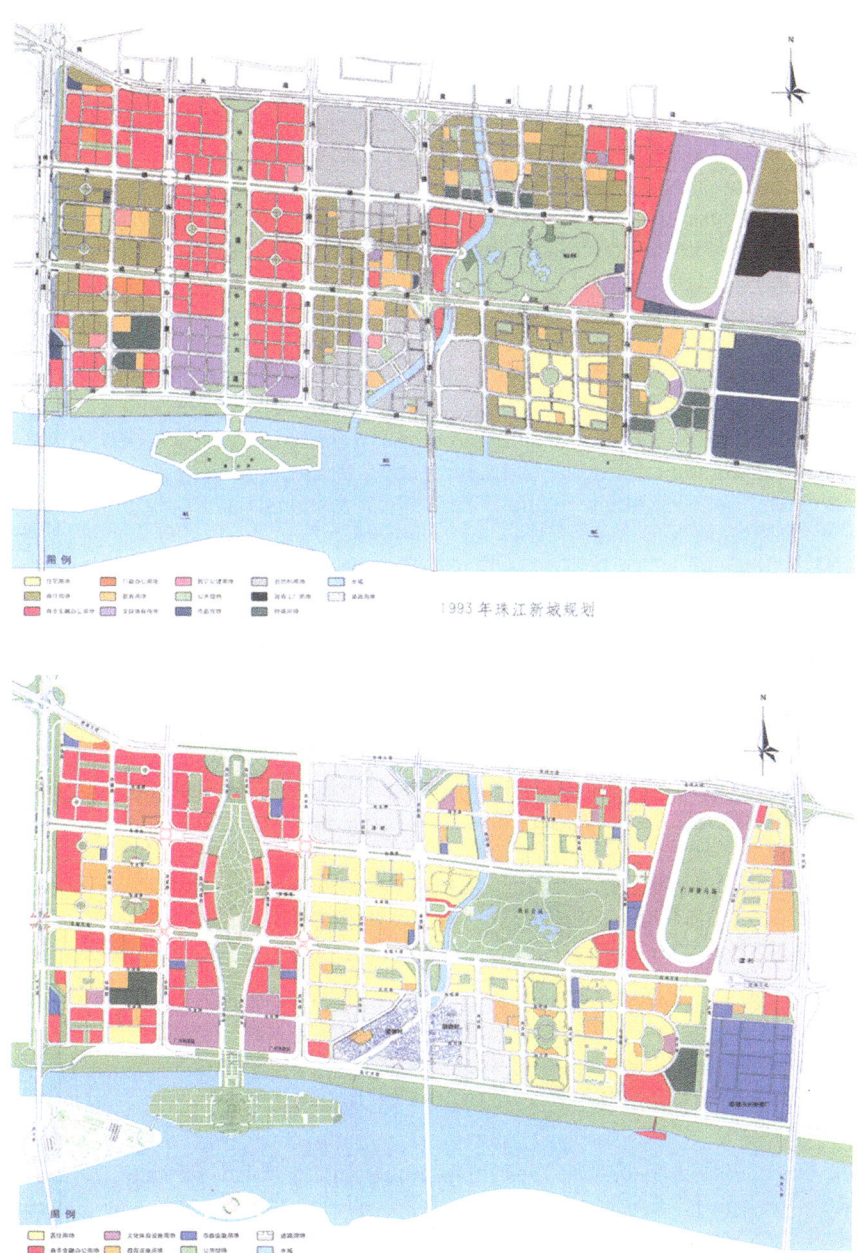

Fig. 3.4 The comparison between the 1993 Zhujiang New Town Plan (upper) and the 2001 Revised Plan (down)

relocated to the south of the Pearl River (Guangzhou Urban Planning and Design Survey Research Institute 2003).

The local authorities began to develop the new town more rapidly in the early 2000s, but it was four years until the revised plan was officially published. The construction of the Guangzhou Opera House was one of the most important steps and became a catalyst for surrounding development. To help understand this bold decision, it is useful to see it in the context of the public debate on theater building, particularly the heated discussion that had surrounded the National Grand Theater project in Beijing. At the turn of the millennium, the central government organized an international architecture competition to design the National Grand Theater. After two rounds of the competition, the proposal of French architect Paul Andreu, characterized by an ellipsoid dome of titanium and glass surrounded by an artificial lake, was selected for implementation (Xue et al. 2010). The project's location, to the west of the Great Hall of the People, was extremely politically sensitive, and its simple and futuristic form was in sharp contrast to the surrounding buildings, with their strong national ornamentation. The radical aesthetics and issues of structural safety led to national controversies and vigorous public debates.

The Shanghai Grand Theater, designed by French architect Jean-Marie Charpentier, also opened in 1998 (see Chap. 1), and hundreds of national and international performances had been staged there. Guangzhou is the third-largest city in China. To compete with its rivals Beijing and Shanghai, it needed a remarkably different image and a distinctive landmark. The opera house project included a public building with a 46,000 m^2 floor area, with seating for 1800 in the main theater, a 4000 m^2 lobby and lounge and 2500 m^2 rooms for ancillary and supporting facilities. The construction budget (excluding the land price) was RMB 850 million (about USD 120 million). The Guangzhou Urban Planning Bureau, the competition's organizer, hoped that the construction of the building would "promote socialist spiritual civilization, meet the growing cultural needs of the people, expand cultural exchanges, improve and perfect the city's functions and establish Guangzhou's central position in the Pearl River Delta and even in southern China (Anonymous 2002c)."

3.3   Experimenting with Opinion Space

The bureau decided to hold their high-profile international competition in July 2002. Previously the institution had followed the then-mayor Lin Shusen's instructions that proposals for significant public projects should be generated through design competitions. Yu Ying was appointed by the planning bureau's leader Wang Menghui to organize the competition for the opera house, due to his involvement in the previous competition for the Guangzhou International Convention and Exhibition Center, which was critically acclaimed by officials, experts and the public (Yu 2009). Yu's ambition was to create an eye-catching event, manifested in the way he successfully invited a number of internationally celebrated architects, such as Rem Koolhaas (Holland), Zaha Hadid (Britain), Coop Himmelb(l)au (Austria), Takamatsu Shin (Japan), Cox Architects (Australia), Gerkan, Marg and Partners (Germany), Gonzalez Hasbrouck Architects (USA) and prominent domestic design companies such as the Architectural Design Institute of the South China University of Technology and the Beijing Institute of Architectural Design. This line-up of invited architects was far more impressive than that of any other Chinese design competition.

The nine firms submitted their proposals by November 1, 2002, which were examined initially by the Technical Committee, which consisted of twelve experts from the fields of urban planning, architecture, structural engineering, acoustics, stage technology, equipment and cost management. They provided careful, comprehensive and detailed written opinions and professional technical advice. The Jury Committee consisting of leading architects and academics then voted on the nine entries to shortlist three excellent proposals. The voting process was observed by staff of the Guangzhou Notary Public Office.

From November 30 to December 16, 2002, the submitted proposals, including drawings and models, were exhibited in the Guangzhou Urban Planning Bureau's exhibition hall and posted on its official website. The bureau encouraged citizens to visit and vote for their favorite proposals; a democratic gesture allowing people to express their opinions on the city's construction. It was reported that 2802 people visited the exhibition, and a number of them voted for a particular scheme. Nearly 20,000 people voted through the website.

Alongside the voting, the competition proposals could be found on the Urban Planning Online website, where people also actively expressed their opinions. Regarding the Himmelb(l)au proposal, which was in the top three of both the physical and the online polls, the comment posted was that "from the point of view of renderings posted on the Internet, proposal No. 2 is extremely good-looking. It should be said that it is the most beautiful and unique building in the world and even the United States has not yet had such a project" (Anonymous 2002a). These comments revealed the aesthetic and ideological shock that the Himmelb(l)au proposal provoked in Chinese audiences. This public opinion also reflected the expectations of local people for a brand new structure, able to represent the city's forward-looking spirit.

The proposals, exhibited in the bureau's exhibition hall and on their official website, were also closely examined by architectural professionals and students from the Chinese architectural community. A short introduction appeared in the Shanghai Tongji University's journal *Shidai jianzhu* (Time + Architecture), and the 2002 event was also hotly debated in the ABBS (Architecture Bulletin Board Service), a prominent online forum founded in 1998 and dedicated to discussing various architectural issues.

The proposals submitted for the Guangzhou Opera House, particularly the Himmelb(l)au and the Hadid proposals, were in the main regarded as exceptionally high quality, in comparison with those for the controversial National Grand Theater competition. In part, this was evident in the positive responses from other architects. On January 28, 2003, the Guangzhou Urban Planning Bureau unveiled their three shortlisted proposals: Coop Himmelb(l)au (proposal No. 2), Zaha Hadid Architects (No. 4) and the Beijing Institute of Architectural Design (No. 5).

The Himmelb(l)au proposal, described as *jiqing huoyan* (vehement flame), consisted of two parts: a simple, cubic, volumetric form containing the stage, fly tower and auditorium and a visually splendid glass shell extending towards the artistic plaza (Fig. 3.5). The most striking and innovative aspect of the design was the large-scale glass structure, implying a gesture of openness that would resonate with the city's strong civic tradition. Under this shell, a series of artificial lakes, towers, pavilions, bridges, ramps, stairs and trees were organized organically, forming a dynamic urban realm. The building itself created a continuous spatial sequence with gradual transition from the public bustling city life to the semi-public artistic activities to the exclusive theatrical ambience. The jury commented that "this proposal was extraordinarily excellent, demonstrating both a conflict and a unity between rationality and emotion, between logic and intuition (Anonymous 2002b)."

Zaha Hadid's proposal, called *lengjun shuangli* (double pebbles) was highly praised by the jury as of brilliance in function, form and feasibility. It integrated two non-rectangular interlocking buildings sitting on an artificial, raising platform (Fig. 3.6). The larger "pebble" contained the lobby, main auditorium, proscenium stage and various workshops and supporting facilities, while the smaller housed a multipurpose performance space. The idea to separate the project into two parts was a continuation of Hadid's 1997 Luxembourg Philharmonic Hall proposal, and possibly influenced by Jørn Utzon's Sydney Opera House. The gentle slope created a multi-layer continuous public space, ideal for various cultural events and accessible to all. Like Hadid's winning, but never built, project for the Cardiff Bay Opera House, landscape played a crucial role. The Guangzhou proposal included plans to reshape the site by creating an artificially made landscape (Hadid 2013). More interestingly, the project's smooth envelope presented an extraordinary icon of

Fig. 3.5 Coop Himmelb(l)au's proposal for the Guangzhou Opera House, 2002. Courtesy of Coop Himmelb(l)au

Fig. 3.6 Zaha Hadid's proposal for the Guangzhou Opera House, 2002. Courtesy of Zaha Hadid Architects

theater building, in sharp contrast with the surrounding tall buildings. Literally and figuratively, its fluid forms were inspired by pebbles smoothed by erosion in the Pearl River, a compelling rhetoric that enabled the architects to persuasively explain their intentions and the client and the public to recognize the relevance of the design concept to the city and the location.

The shortlist was announced in January 2003, but it seemed that the jury had made a professional decision before the exhibition of the submitted proposals. To some extent, the exhibition became a deliberate test of public opinion and a demonstration of the authorities' democratic attitude. The competition did nonetheless become the subject of public discourse, increasing public interest in architecture and communicating architectural knowledge in a professional and social sense. The architects of the shortlisted proposals were then requested to revise their schemes following the Jury Committee's suggestions, before the final decision was made in June. The attitude of the local political elite would have a significant bearing on the final decision. The so-called "three combination" (*san jiehe*)—experts reviewing (*zhuanjia pingshen*), public voting (*qunzhong toupiao*), and leaders deciding (*lingdao jueding*)—describes the procedure used in the 2000s in China to select proposals for significant government-sponsored public projects.

The winner was not announced until December 28, 2003. It was not a surprise that the Hadid proposal was selected as the implementation scheme, as there were a few indications that it was favored by local officials. The competition director Yu had initially presented the proposals to the then-mayor Lin Shusen, before the jury's review. He was immediately impressed by the so-called "double pebbles" of Hadid Architects (Yu 2009). Interestingly, Lin's appreciation of the "double pebbles" proposal was also consistent with the jury's recommendation. This agreement helped Lin persuade his colleagues of the merits of the Hadid proposal. The final, formally approved and legal decision was made by the municipal committee, and on December 11, 2003, a local newspaper reported that the Hadid proposal had won the competition. Explaining why this proposal was special, the journalist cited the discourse of Zhao Boren—the chair of the competition's Technical Committee—who argued that the House should be unique and differentiates the Beijing and Shanghai Theaters (Ling 2003).

This comment clearly revealed that the distinctive form of the winning Hadid proposal was a crucial factor, as its form would establish a unique identity, eventually enhancing the image of Guangzhou's economy and culture nationally and internationally. The Hadid proposal was therefore accepted by local authorities and architectural professionals mainly owing to its spectacular forms, which maintained the potential to attract regional, national and global attention. Guy Debord argued that the spectacle is capital accumulation to the point where it becomes image (Debord 1995). This image, for the art historian Clark, is never securely and finally fixed in place; the spectacle is always an account of the world competing with others and meeting with resistance from different, and sometimes tenacious, forms of social practice (Clark 1999). The ability of an architectural spectacle to brand and transform a city had been exemplified by Frank Gehry's Bilbao Guggenheim Museum in Spain. Similarly, the city of Guangzhou needed a new image to compete with its rivals, a means of representation to market the city in the world and a radical form to project the future. Hadid's opera house is likely to be an appropriate instrument to showcase both political vision and cultural ambition.

3.4 Project Construction

The project's realization was an experiment with construction project management (*dai jian zhi*) in China. The municipal government commissioned the Guangzhou Municipal Construction Group, a leading state-owned company, in August 2004 as the agency responsible for the project's construction (Huang and Yan 2004). In October, the Guangzhou Municipal Construction Group and Zaha Hadid Architects selected the Guangzhou Pearl River Foreign Investment Architectural Design Institute as their local partner, as the institute had won and designed the Wuhan Qintai Grand Theater and was experienced in the design of theater buildings (Huang 2012). Zaha Hadid Architects took responsibility for the control of the project's total effect and schematic design (Fig. 3.8). The local architects were responsible for technical drawing and support and for coordinating the various engineering consultants (Zhang 2010). The contributions of various other design firms exemplified the new international divisions of labor and the direct influence on architecture and the built environment.

On January 18, 2005, the construction of the long-awaited Guangzhou Opera House began. Local political leaders, Cantonese opera master Hung Sin-nui, the

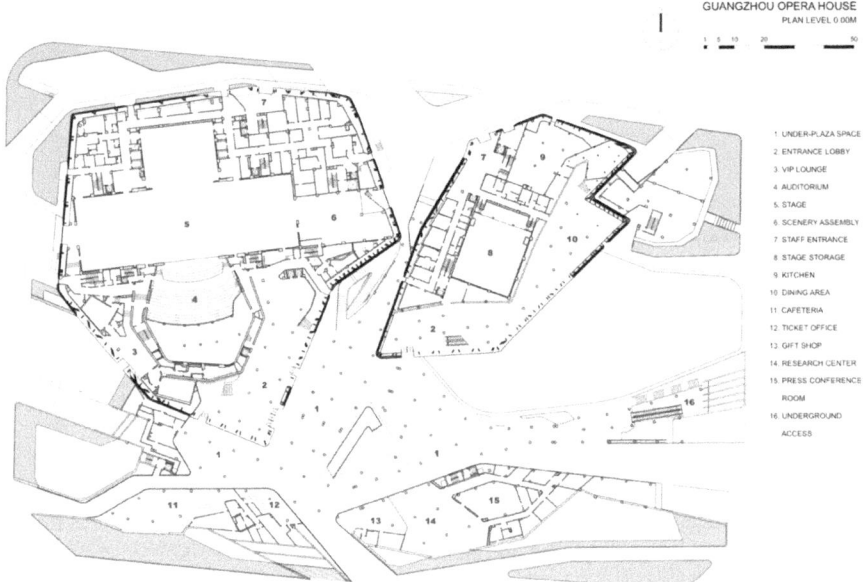

GUANGZHOU OPERA HOUSE
PLAN LEVEL 0.00M

1. UNDER-PLAZA SPACE
2. ENTRANCE LOBBY
3. VIP LOUNGE
4. AUDITORIUM
5. STAGE
6. SCENERY ASSEMBLY
7. STAFF ENTRANCE
8. STAGE STORAGE
9. KITCHEN
10. DINING AREA
11. CAFETERIA
12. TICKET OFFICE
13. GIFT SHOP
14. RESEARCH CENTER
15. PRESS CONFERENCE
     ROOM
16. UNDERGROUND
     ACCESS

Fig. 3.7 The ground plan of the Guangzhou Opera House. Courtesy of Zaha Hadid Architects

Guangzhou British Consulate general Chris Wood and Hadid's partner, Patrik Schumacher attended the ground-breaking ceremony. In his speech, Lin hailed the Guangzhou Opera House as a twenty-first century theater, maintaining that it will be recorded in the history of Guangzhou urban development (Fig. 3.7) (Lin 2005).

The selection in 2003 of Guangzhou to host the 2010 Asian Games should be noted as the context in which local officials offered enthusiastic support for the project. They used this event as a reason to speed up the construction of the opera house and the new town. With this kind of event-driven urban expansion, the Hu-Wen administration experimented with Keynesian economics, which empha- sizes heavy investment in infrastructure and the built environment supported by credit from state-owned banks (Warner 2015). The grand theaters built in many provincial cities, from Guangzhou to Hangzhou are tremendously ambitious pro- jects, and epitomize the possibilities and limits of Keynesian theories (Anonymous 2011b).[3] The authorities' endowments for cultural prosperity (including the building of performance venues), whether or not they operate properly in practice, may help engender a sense of solidarity and pride and accumulate political, eco- nomic and cultural capital, resonating with Keynes' advocacy of the state's role in supporting the arts (Keynes 1937). Authorities in second and third-tier cities such as Wenzhou, Wuxi, Yantai and Bengbu have sometimes, however, made imprudent

---

[3]The possibilities include the state's investment transformed urban landscape and stimulated economic growth, while the limits refer to the fact that the wasteful investment distorted resource allocation and retained domestic consumption.

decisions to build extravagant and inappropriate theaters (the so-called image projects, or, *xingxiang gongcheng*), in an attempt to construct a positive political image (Anonymous 2013).

The construction process of the Guangzhou Opera House also involved a level of experimentation, owing to the structure's unprecedented complexity. Before the pouring of the concrete, the construction company made a variety of experimental models such as a sloping wall, a sloping balustrade, an inclined column and a triangular groove, in an attempt to deal with the high demands placed on the fair-face concrete surfaces (Zhang 2010). The realization of the irregular envelope presented another major difficulty, which as the project's distinctive characteristic, was generated from the 3D software Rhino. The architects and structural engineers separated the envelope into two layers: an integrated single-layer lattice shell, structurally separated from the auditorium and consisting of various triangular and square units, and granite stone wall hanging.

It was reported that the architects were initially inclined to use metal or as-cast finish concrete to create the fluid forms, but local officials argued that as the proposal expressed a sense of pebbles eroded by water, using stone as the facade material would better convey this intention (Feng and Xu 2006). This made sense in its own right, but it overlooked the fact that stone is a fragile material and could not be processed into the desirable shapes as easily as metal or concrete. The officials possessed significant power in this government-funded project, so it was likely that the architects would bow to political pressure. In an effort to create this kind of smoothed aesthetic, one of the solutions was to tessellate the continuous surface into a large number of triangular and polygonal units (about 75,400 pieces) (Duo 2010) (Figs. 3.8, 3.9).

The local authorities requested that the pace of construction increase, so the closing ceremony of the Ninth China Art Festival could be held in the opera house on 25 May 2010, and to prepare for the Asian Games (Liu 2010). Like many major public projects in China, there was a slapdash approach to the construction of the opera house. The curved surfaces of the building's corners challenged the limits of stone and skills of the builders, and the roof of the office lobby leaked (Fig. 3.10). The inability to produce a perfect envelope was to some extent an illustration of the predicament of architectural practice when profoundly constrained by politics.

Compared with the flawed skin, the interior, particularly the splendid auditorium and its excellent acoustics, was widely commended. A critic commented that "seats are arranged in a slightly asymmetrical pattern, enveloping the stage on three sides, with undulant balconies cascading down in front of the stage" (Ouroussoff 2011) (Figure 3.11). The streamlined space, both in the lobby and the golden-hued auditorium, was clad with Corian (glass fiber reinforced gypsum panels), which can be modeled into different shapes. Local officials challenged criticism over the poor quality of construction, declaring that the project's structure was safe and that the appearance of cracks on the wall and ceiling was due to the local climate (Zeng 2010). The increase in the project cost to RMB 1.38 billion (about USD 200 million), but any coverage of criticism or suggestions of corruption was relentlessly censored (Huang 2009).

Fig. 3.8 The Guangzhou Opera House in construction, 2007. Courtesy of Raymond Wong

Fig. 3.9 The central axis of Zhujiang New Town. The Guangzhou Opera House is on the left hand side. The Guangdong Museum is opposite the opera house, 2008. Courtesy of Raymond Wong

Fig. 3.10 The flawed skin of the Guangzhou Opera House

Fig. 3.11 The main auditorium of the Guangzhou Opera House. Right photo by Charlie Xue and Zhang Lujia

3.5 Medium of Cultural Production

The Guangzhou Opera House is both a product of and an incubator for cultural production. The term "culture" refers to both the project's material and symbolic forms and the content and programs the building was designed to contain (King 1990). The building itself was derived from the state's ambition to construct, regardless of cost, a distinctive identity representing the city in the world. It also reflected local political and cultural elites' perception of the international climate of architecture. The many examples of global and national cities that built architectural spectacle for urban competitiveness undoubtedly helped motivate the client to erect something different. As a physical object, the opera house revealed the extent to which global, national design intelligence and local building craftsmanship could interact in a specific political and economic circumstance.

Occupying a crucial point in the city's new axis with overwhelming monumentality, the Guangzhou Opera House, with its fluid forms and theatrical spaces, compellingly demonstrated the flamboyance of architectural spectacle, a goal that politicians, cultural elites and architects, among others, collaboratively pursued. This flamboyance was widely disseminated through the publicizing of the project in international newspapers and professional magazines. In this sense, the state playing key role in directing the global flow of culture not only imported international design ideas but also employed the project as a tool to export the city's image to the world and to attract tourists, exemplifying the implication of globalization as an interactive, not a one way process of communication (King 1997).

The opera house is also a medium carrying out new approach of cultural management and a platform upon which national and global performing arts are staged, consumed and produced. For one thing, compared with many grand theaters that receive a state subsidy in China, the Guangzhou Opera House experimented with what they called "zero-establishment staffing and zero-subsidy (*ling bianzhi, ling butie*)." Clearly, this alternative mode of operation, based on market mechanism, saves a large amount of taxpayers' money every year. To recover maintenance costs, and even generate some profit, the opera house had to substantially increase ticket prices, which sometimes resulted in poor attendance and a waste of artistic resources (Chen and He 2011).

The paradox is that only the upper-middle classes who can afford the tickets are able to engage with the building and its performances. Though the opera house's management invited more than 800 representatives of the builders and professionals that contributed to the project to watch a trial performance before the first formal show, such kind of activities, which both pay tribute to the builders and offer an opportunity for low-income people to appreciate musical arts was still an exception, not the rule (Deng 2010). While consuming so-called high culture, emerging affluent people show their privileged status and have access to the city's artistic palace.

For another, the opera house's state-of-the-art facilities are able to stage performances of ballets, chamber music concerts, musicals, operas, spoken dramas and symphonies, remedying the previous situation in which large-scale opera or ballet, such as *Swan Lake,* cannot be performed in the city's other smaller theater stages. By attracting both international and national performing arts groups, the opera house provided local music enthusiasts with cultural feasts, representing the city's increasingly energetic and dynamic artistic scene.

3.6 Conclusion

Building a grand theater in contemporary China is first and foremost a political project, as the will of politics played a crucially important role in experimenting with new formal languages, competition organizing, project management and operation. In this circumstance, a grand theater is not only a performing venue but also a demonstration of political ideology, a catalyst for urban expansion and cultural exchange. The diversity of forces shaping the Guangzhou Opera House created a "gated public space," a juxtaposition of inclusion and exclusion, of freedom and restraint. Characterized by contradiction and tension, this gated public realm presented an array of cultural, social and political ramifications.

Through designing a landscaped platform, the architects redefined and transformed the featureless site in a cultural and commercial district into an accessible public plaza. The raised plaza can be used as an outside stage for artistic events, and is reached by a variety of approaches (Fig. 3.12). Under the platform, the architects slightly inclined conventionally perpendicular columns, creating spaces with a strong sense of motion (Fig. 3.13). These sheltered, open spaces provide local people with leisure facilities. Inside the foyer, however, the public could experience very limited spaces, mainly in the box office, souvenir and coffee shops (Fig. 3.14). While the opera house attempted to display its civic character, it also revealed the truth of class relations, representing spatially the social and political hierarchy and conveying a daunting feeling to the poor and unprivileged who had less chance to appreciate the performing arts, even though their taxes contributed to the building (Yu 2011).

Fig. 3.12 The outdoor platform of the Guangzhou Opera House. Photo by Charlie Xue

Fig. 3.13 The ground floor space under the platform

Fig. 3.14 The interior of the Guangzhou Opera House. Photo by Charlie Xue

Aside from physical level, this gated character was also embodied in immaterial dimensions. For one thing, the position that local government actively embraced international design intelligence demonstrated an open attitude during China's reform and opening process. Masked by the ideology of planning and design, the state's intervention into both urban expansion and architectural making exposed its intention to manipulate the production of space in such a way as to accumulate economic, political, and social capital. For another, by organizing both on-site and online exhibitions of submitted proposals for the theater, the local authorities encouraged ordinary citizens to express their ideas on project design, creating an increasingly democratic public realm to accommodate diverse opinions and debates. The state, however, maintained the power to control this opinion space and tended to influence the consequence of this space through political intervention. Similarly, the authorities also encouraged a variety of cultural production and experimentation within the opera house, yet still closely scrutinized those explorations and kept them in the politically correct track.

Situating the project of the Guangzhou Opera House within China's modernization process, it has become clear that the implementation of reform and opening-up was a dynamic process of adjusting the location of the "gate," or the physical, social, political and cultural boundary. Opening the door to the outside world helped implement domestic reform, while deeper reform would improve the degree of openness. The course of game was suffused with the decentralization of authority and the intervention of power. The former implies a decrease of the state's capacity to control social, cultural and aesthetic affairs; the latter refers to the state's inclination to use political power to maintain specific order. The Guangzhou Opera House in this regard illustrated explicitly that the creation of public space was meaningful and maintained a gated nature, controlled by the ruling class.

Acknowledgements This chapter is part of a study supported by Research Grant Council, Hong Kong government, project No. CityU 11658816 and by the Fundamental Research Funds for Beijing Universities, Project No. X18237.

My preoccupation with the Guangzhou Opera House originates less from my obsession with theater performance and its building type and more from my interest in the project's design competition. When I was studying at architectural school in the early 2000s, the debate on the National Theater of China in Beijing dominated the architectural community. To some extent, the French architect Paul Andreu's winning proposal ended the long-term debate over formal similarity (xing si) and spiritual similarity (shen si), both of which were related to attitudes towards tradition. While the debate over the National Theater was confined to professional periodicals and elite figures, the design competition for the Guangzhou Opera House transcended the public's perception of architecture in a number of ways. The proposals submitted by leading avant-garde architects from the West surpassed many people's imagination, and the report and discussion of these proposals online, such as the ABBS, profoundly increased its influence in the field and beyond. The commitment to creating quality urban public spaces transformed my attitude towards architecture and the city. Fifteen years after the competition and 10 years after its completion, the Guangzhou Opera House deserves critical scholarly evaluation for its singular position in the evolution of architecture in contemporary China and for its significant influence on my own understanding of architecture.

References

Anonymous. (2002a). *Gongzhong toupiao ji liuyan (The public voting and comments)*. The Guangzhou Urban Planning Bureau's digital archives. [Online] Available from http://www. upo.gov.cn/plan2007/ggjzsj/910_4.shtml. Accessed April 11, 2015. 匿名(2002). 公众投票及留言. 广州城市规划管理局数字档案. 网址 http://www.upo.gov.cn/plan2007/ggjzsj/910_4. shtml.

Anonymous. (2002b). *Gejuyuan yousheng fang'an ji qita fang'an jieshao (The introduction of the shortlisted and other proposals)*. The Guangzhou Urban Planning Bureau's digital archives. [Online] Available from www.upo.gov.cn/plan2007/ggjzsj/910_3.shtml. Accessed April 11, 2015. 匿名(2002). 歌剧院优胜方案及其他方案介绍. 广州城市规划管理局数字档案. 网址 www.upo.gov.cn/plan2007/ggjzsj/910_3.shtml.

Anonymous. (2002c). *Guangzhou gejuyuan guoji yaoqing jianzhu sheji jingsai (The inviting international architecture competition for the Guangzhou Opera House)*. The Guangzhou Urban Planning Bureau's digital archives. [Online] Available from http://www.upo.gov.cn/plan2007/ggjzsj/910.shtml. Accessed April 15, 2015. 匿名(2002). 广州歌剧院国际邀请建筑设计竞赛. 广州城市规划管理局数字档案. 网址 http://www.upo.gov.cn/plan2007/ggjzsj/910.shtml.

Anonymous. (2011a). AR Preview Pearl River Delta. *Architectural Record* (1), 73.

Anonymous. (2011b). Keynes versus Hayek in China. *The Economist*. November 17. [Online] Available from http://www.economist.com/node/21537010. Accessed April 13, 2015.

Anonymous (2013). Er san xian chengshi xian dajuyuan jianshe rechao, jianchenghou dabufen xianzhi (The Construction Boom of Grand Theaters Appeared in Second and Third Tier Cities, While the Majority of Them Built Were Unused). *Renmin ribao (People's Daily)*, March 14. 匿名(2013). 二三线城市现大剧院建设热潮.建成后大部分闲置. 人民日报, 3月14日.

Chen, W., & He, S. (2011). Dajuyuan huifou chengwei furen julebu (Will the Guangzhou Opera House Become Club for the Rich?). *Xinkuai bao (New Express Daily)*, June 6. (2011) 陈文, 何姗(2011). 大剧院会否成为富人俱乐部. 新快报, 6月6日.

Cheng, Y. (2010). *Dangdai yanyi jianzhu fazhan yanjiu (A study on the development of performing arts architecture, 1998–2008)* (Ph.D. dissertation). Tongji University. 程翌(2010). 当代演艺建筑发展研究, 1998–2009. 上海:同济大学博士论文.

Clark, T. J. (1999). *The painting of modern life: Paris in the art of Manet and his followers* (p. 36). London: Thames & Hudson.

Debord, G. (1995). *The society of the spectacle* (p. 24). New York: Zone Books.

Deng, Q. (2010). Guangzhou gejuyuan yaoqing babai ming jianzhu gongren guankan shouyan (The Guangzhou Opera House Invited 800 Builders to Watch Trial Performance). *Yangcheng wanbao (Yangcheng Evening News)*, April 9. 邓琼(2010). 广州歌剧院邀请800名建筑工人观看首演.羊城晚报, 4月9日.

Duo, N. (2010). Guangzhou gejuyuan: tashan zhi shi de yinyu jiqi shitihua guocheng (Guangzhou Opera House: The Metaphor of Stone and Its Realization Process). *Jianzhu xuebao (Architectural Journal)* (8), 71–75. 朵宁 (2010). 广州歌剧院:他山之石的隐喻及其实体化过程. 建筑学报. (08), 71–75.

Feng, J., & Xu, H. (2006). Conversation about two stones beside the Pearl River: On the technical design of Guangzhou Opera House. *Xin jianzhu (New Architecture)* (4), 42–44. 冯江, 徐好好(2006). 关于珠江边两块石头的对话:广州歌剧院设计深化访谈. 新建筑, (4), 42–44.

Galilee, B. (2010). Zaha Hadid in Guangzhou. *Domus Web*. 21 December. [Online] Available from http://www.domusweb.it/en/architecture/2010/12/21/zaha-hadid-in-guangzhou.html. Accessed April 11, 2015.

Gaubatz, P. (2005). Globalization and the development of new central business districts in Beijing, Shanghai, and Guangzhou. In F. Wu & L. Ma (Eds.), *Restructuring the Chinese city: Changing society, economy and space* (pp. 98–121). New York and Oxford: Routledge.

Glancey, J. (2011). Move over, Sydney: Zaha Hadid's Guangzhou Opera House. *The Guardian*. 28 February.

Gottdiener, M. (1985). *The social production of urban space*. Austin: University of Texas Press.

Guangzhou Urban Planning and Design Survey Research Institute. (2003). *Zhujiang xincheng guihua jiantao: guihua fang'an gongzhong zhanshi (Review on the development of Pearl River New Town: Public exhibition of planning proposal)*. 广州市城市规划勘察设计研究院 (2003). 珠江新城规划检讨: 规划方案公众展示.

Hadid, Z. (2013). *The complete Zaha Hadid*. London: Thames & Hudson Ltd.

Heathcote, E. (2011). Zaha Hadid's Guangzhou Opera House. *Financial Times*. March 11.

Huang, J. (2012). The artistic and natural expression: The innovation and practice of the Guangzhou Opera House. *Jianzhu jiyi (Architecture Technique)* (10), 88–93. 黄捷(2012). 艺术性与自然性的表达: 广州歌剧院设计创新与实践. 建筑技艺. (04): 88–93.

Huang, R. (2005). Guangzhou shi rongyu shimin kaluoer tuomasi furen (Ms. Carol J. Thomas, A Honorary Citizen of Guangzhou). In Guangzhou chengshi guihua fazhan huigu bianzhuan weiyuanhui (Ed.), *Guangzhou chengshi guihua fazhan huigu, 1949–2005, shangjuan (Review on Guangzhou urban planning and development, 1949–2005, I)* (pp. 233–235). Guangzhou: Guangdong People's Press. 黄润娟(2005). 广州市荣誉市民卡罗尔·托马斯夫人//广州城市规划发展回顾编撰委员会编, 广州城市规划发展回顾,1949–2005, 上卷. 广州:广东人民出版社,233–235.

Huang, S. (2009). Guangzhou gejuyuan jianshe beizhi you heimu (The construction of the Guangzhou Opera House alleged to have corruption). *Minzhu yu fazhi shibao (Democratic and Legal Times)*, March 23. 黄守洲 (2009). 广州歌剧院建设被指有黑幕. 民主与法制时报, 3月23日.

Huang, Y., & Yan L. (2004). Guangzhou gejuyuan niannei donggong xuanzhi zhujiang xinchengnan (The Guangzhou Opera House will be built this year and the site is in the south of Zhujiang New Town). *Nanfang ribao (Southern Daily)*, August 18. 黄影霞, 严丽君(2004). 广州歌剧院年内动工,选址珠江新城南. 南方日报. 8月18日.

King, A. D. (1990). Architecture, capital and the globalization of culture. In M. Featherstone (Ed.), *Global culture: Nationalism, globalization and modernity* (pp. 397–411). London: Sage Publication.

King, A. D. (1997). Preface to the Revised Edition. In A. D. King (Ed.), *Culture, globalization and the world-system: Contemporary conditions for the representation of identity* (pp. vii–xii). Minnesota: University of Minnesota Press.

Keynes, J. M. (1937). Art and the state. In C.Williams Ellis (Ed.), *Britain and the Beast* (pp. 1–7). London: J. M. Dent and Sons,

Lau, J. (2010). Arts playground sprouts in China. *The New York Times*. August 3.

Lin, K. (1982). Guangzhou zhongshan jiniantang (The Guangzhou Sun Yet-sen Memorial Auditorium). *Jianzhu xuebao (Architectural Journal)* (3), 33–41. 林克明(1982). 广州中山纪念堂, 建筑学报 (3), 33–41.

Lin, S. (2005). Speech delivered in the ground-breaking ceremony of the Guangzhou Opera House. *Guangzhou ribao (Guangzhou Daily)*, January 19. 林树森(2005). 歌剧院:广州新世纪新阶段标志性建筑——林树森在广州歌剧院奠基典礼上的讲话. 广州日报,1月19日.

Ling, H. (2003). Guangzhou gejuyuan sheji fang'an qiaoding, waixing si shamo mingnian donggong (The final proposal of the Guangzhou Opera House, the desert-shape building to be built next year). *Xinxi shibao (Information Times)*, December 11. 凌慧珊(2003). 广州歌剧院设计方案敲定,外形似沙漠明年动工. 信息时报,12月11日.

Liu, Y. (2010). Jiuyijie yinglai daojishi yibai tian (The 100-day countdown to the ninth China art festival). *Guangzhou ribao (Guangzhou Daily)*, February 1. 刘艳,蔡锦明(2010). 九艺节迎来倒计时100天, 广州日报,2月1日.

Lu, J. (2004). *Guangzhou zhongshan jiniantang goucheng (The history of Guangzhou Sun Yet-sen Memorial Auditorium)*. Guangzhou: Guangdong People's Press. 卢洁峰 (2004). 广州中山纪念堂钩沉. 广州:广东人民出版社.

Moore, M. (2011). Guangzhou Opera House Falling Apart. *The Telegraph*. July 8.

Nanfang dushibao. (2011). Interview with Li Ziliu. In T. Ren., H. Wei., & J. Wang (Eds.), *Chengbian: Guangzhou shinian chengjian qishilu (Urban transformations: The revelation of urban construction in Guangzhou, 2000–2010)* (75–87). Guangzhou: Guangdong People's Press. 南方都市报 (2011). 采访黎子流//城变: 广州十年城建启示录. 广州:广东人民出版社, 75–87.

Ouroussoff, N. (2011). Chinese gem that elevates its setting. *The New York Times.* July 6.

Perry, E. J., & Wong, C. (Eds.). (1985). *The political economy of reform in Post-Mao China* (pp. 21–22). Cambridge, Massachusetts: Council on East Asia Studies, Harvard University.

Rithmire, M. (2013). Land politics and local state capacities: The political economy of urban change in China. *The China Quarterly, 216,* 1–24.

Vogel, E. (1991). *The four little dragons: The spread of industrialization in east Asia.* Cambridge, Massachusetts: Harvard University Press.

Warner, M. (2015). Keynes and China: 'Keynesianism with Chinese characteristics'. *Asia Pacific Business Review, 21*(2), 251–263.

Xue, C. Q. L., Wang, Z., & Mitchenere, B. (2010). In search of identity: The development process of the national grand theater in Beijing, China. *The Journal of Architecture, 15*(4), 517–535.

Yu, Y. (2009). Hadide de Guangzhou gejuyuan (Hadid's Guangzhou Opera House). *Sina Blog.* Weblog [Online] Available from http://blog.sina.com.cn/s/blog_603442100100fwju.html. Accessed April 13, 2015] 余英 (2009). 哈迪德的广州歌剧院.新浪博客. http://blog.sina.com.cn/s/blog_603442100100fwju.html.

Yu, Y. (2011). Shengyin: Guangzhou dajuyuan buru gaiming wei Guangzhou 'gui' juyuan (Opinion: The Guangzhou expensive theater rather than the Guangzhou grand theater). *Nanfang dushibao (Southern Metropolis Daily),* June 10. 余以为 (2011). 声音:广州大剧院不如改名为广州"贵"剧院. 南方都市报,6月10日.

Zeng, N. (2010). Shijianwei: Guangzhou dajuyuan waiguan quexian bu yingxiang jiegou anquan (The flawed appearance of the Guangzhou Opera House does not influence structural safety). *Nanfang ribao (Nanfang Daily),* October 20. 曾妮, 史伟宗 (2010). 市建委: 广州大剧院外观缺陷不影响结构安全. 南方日报, 10月20日.

Zhang, G. (2010). Cong yihuo dao shixian: Guangzhou gejuyuan sheji shishi zhilu (From doubt to realization: The road of the design implementation of the Guangzhou Opera House). *Jianzhu xuebao (Architectural Journal)* (8), 68–70. 张桂玲 (2010). 从疑惑到实现: 广州歌剧院设计实施之路. 建筑学报, (8), 68–70.

Chapter 4
City and Cultural Center Shift—Performance Space in Shenzhen

Cong Sun

Shenzhen sets an example for rapid development of urban planning and construction. It was the starting point of the largest city-construction movement in contemporary China and also a miracle in the history of global urbanization. On August 26, 1980, Shenzhen became the first Chinese Special Economic Zone (SEZ) and was pushed to the forefront of the reform and opening-up of mainland China. In less than 40 years, Shenzhen has grown from a special economic zone with a total area of 327 km^2, a resident population of 310,000 and a GDP of 270 million yuan to a metropolis of 2465 km^2 (including Shenzhen-Shantou Special Cooperation Zone), over 12.52 million people, and a GDP of 2.2 trillion yuan.[1] Thus the area, resident population, and GDP have increased by more than 7, 40 and 8000 times, respectively. This rapid growth is embedded in the construction history that spans nearly 40 years, and in the representative buildings.

The interaction between urban development and spatial structure is important, and has long been a focus of planning researchers' investigations. The development history of the banded and clustered multi-center structural layout in Shenzhen provides an excellent study context for this subject.[2] By analyzing the development process of Shenzhen since the end of the 1970s, several key spatio-temporal nodes can be identified that represent the urban development centers in different periods of Shenzhen (Fig. 4.1). They are:

---

[1]Data sourced from Statistics Bureau of Shenzhen Municipality website, retrieved January 10, 2019 from http://www.sztj.gov.cn/. For more about the general development of Shenzhen, see Chung et al. (2001), International New Town Institute (2016), O'Donnell et al. (2017).

[2]For details on the value and significance of Shenzhen's planning practice and spatial structure, see Zou (2016, 112–115).

C. Sun (✉)
Department of Architecture and Civil Engineering, City
University of Hong Kong, Kowloon, Hong Kong
e-mail: sunconghk2011@126.com

© Springer Nature Singapore Pte Ltd. 2019
C. Q. Xue (ed.), *Grand Theater Urbanism*,
https://doi.org/10.1007/978-981-13-7868-3_4

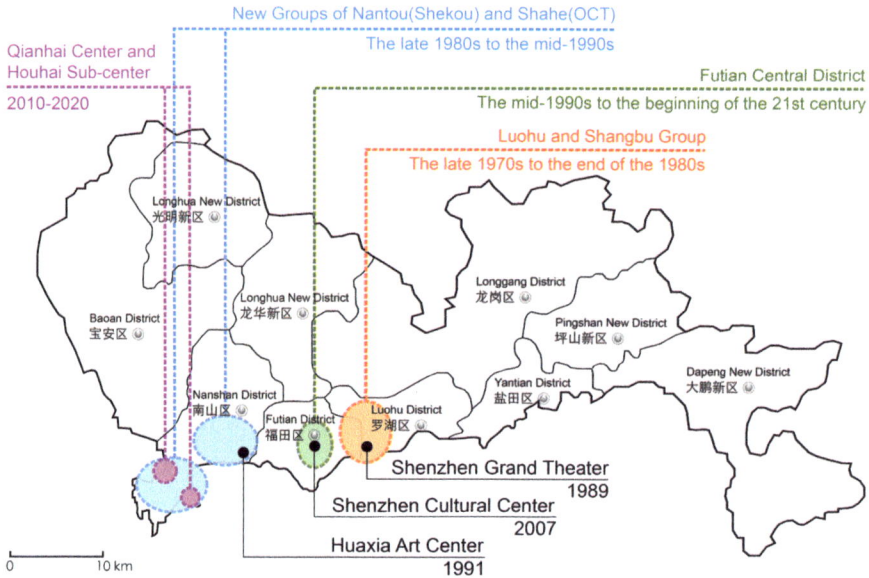

Fig. 4.1 Key areas for several construction booms of cultural facilities and distribution of main performance spaces in Shenzhen. Drawn by the author

(1) The beginning of the SEZ construction (from the late 1970s to the end of the 1980s)—the concentrated development of the Luohu and Shangbu groups (32 km^2);

(2) Expansion stage (from the late 1980s to the mid-1990s)—the construction of the new groups Nantou (Shekou) and Shahe (OCT);

(3) Development stage (from the mid-1990s to the early 2000s)—the construction of Futian Central District;

(4) Maturity stage (2010–2020)—development and construction of Qianhai Center.

By connecting these together, the transition process of spatial structure and the transfer path of the city center can be outlined. The key areas of several construction booms in which cultural facilities were developed in Shenzhen are strikingly consistent with the centers of urban construction in the different periods. Appropriately, in this chapter three construction booms of cultural facilities are reviewed, as Shenzhen was transformed from a border town to a modern metropolis. The integration into public policy and the development plans of cultural resources such as performance spaces in the context of the specific historical moment are also analyzed, and the additional urban and social functions they provide are examined. In this way, the relationship between cultural buildings and political rights, urban structural readjustment, civic life, economic development, and the value of cultural space are explored, and the trajectory of urban development is revealed as well.

4.1   The Initial Stage—The First Construction Boom of Cultural Facilities (1979–1989)

From the late 1970s to the early 1980s, the cultural system of mainland China was transformed from the planned economy to reform and opening-up. During the planned economy period, the free-supply cultural system was not designed to produce economic returns, as the main function of culture was to educate and publicize. In essence it could be simply concluded as government-establishment culture. In the preliminary stage of SEZ, the cultural facility construction in Shenzhen was basically few. A People's Cinema was set up in 1949, the Shenzhen Theater opened in 1958, and the exhibition hall in 1975, and together these had cost 600,000 yuan and they served an area of 2751 km^2.[3] The positioning of SEZ, however, resulted in a major flow of capital into the economic area.

However, the extremely slow pace of cultural construction and the worry of "economic oasis, cultural desert" prompted the leaders at that time to accelerate as much as possible the pace of cultural construction.[4] The mayor at that time, Liang Xiang, had a famous saying: "We would rather go hungry but build eight cultural facilities." The first wave of cultural facility construction began in 1983, when the Shenzhen Municipal Party Committee and Government verified the cultural construction planning of the city, and confirmed that eight cultural facilities would be established: a new library, a grand theater, a television station, a stadium, Shenzhen University, a news center, and a science museum, which cost an investment of nearly 700 million yuan (Fig. 4.2). Li Weiyan, the Minister of Propaganda Department of Shenzhen at that time, noted that, "from 1981 to 1983, the total investment for the cultural construction accounted for 33% of the local financial infrastructure investment." Four of the eight projects were designed by architects of the so called "Lingnan School". In the 1950s and 1970s, the "Lingnan School of modern architecture", centered on Guangzhou, played an active role in the construction of Shenzhen at the beginning of reform and opening-up.[5]

On February 27, 1984, Shenzhen Grand Theater broke the ground. In 1983, the tax revenue of Shenzhen was only 96.77 million yuan, but the planned investment of 18 million yuan for the Shenzhen Grand Theater accounted for 18.6% of this revenue. After a five-year construction period, the theater was officially opened in 1989, and the final cost had reached 89 million yuan. According to the Memorabilia of Shenzhen Grand Theater (Infrastructure), on December 23, 1982, the Shenzhen Cultural Bureau described in their written report *Suggestions on Changing the*

---

[3]For details on the backward situation of Shenzhen culture at that time, see Wang (2007, 4), and Shenzhen Museum (1999, 626).

[4]For details on the reason why the leaders wanted to speed up the cultural construction at that time, see Cultural and Historical Records Committee of Shenzhen CPPCC (2001, 156–160).

[5]Lingnan School is represented by a group of architects in southern China in the 1970s and 1980s. See Xiao and Yin (2016, 84–90), Xue (2006, Chap. 7), and Xue and Ding (2018, Chap. 4). These books have detailed analysis of the ideas of this southern China architectural school.

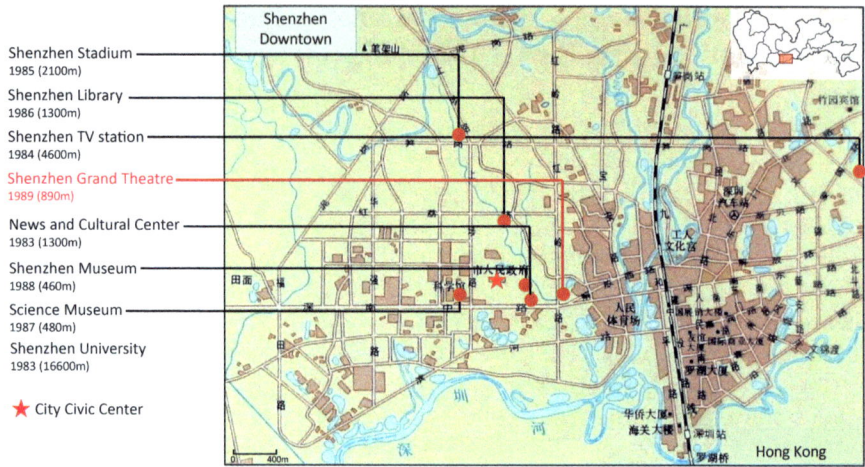

Fig. 4.2 1983—first upsurge of cultural facilities construction. Map of Shenzhen in the early 90s. Drawn by the author. (Figures in brackets above indicate the distance from each facility to the city hall)

Construction Plan of the Grand Theater to Shenzhen Municipal Party Committee and Government: as a pilot Special Economic Zone that was opening up to the whole country and the world, and which required at least one typical cultural center that could compete at a high international level; its mode of construction would make the city proud through its eye-catching architecture.[6] This is not difficult to explain why the government made such an extraordinarily large investment into constructing the Grand Theater in the early days of the special zone, even though the population was only 740,000 (both registered and non-registered) in 1984.

The theater was described as "One L-shaped building (that) occupies an area of 43,000 m², costs 18 million yuan, possesses 1600 seats and can be used for various kinds of performance" by the *Shenzhen Special Zone Daily* on February 27, 1984 (Fig. 4.3). However, due to cuts in infrastructure investment, the Shenzhen Grand Theater project was suspended from the second half of 1986 to the first half of 1988, so the original plan of completing construction by October 1986 was not achieved. In 1988, the Theater was selected as the main venue for the opening ceremony of the Shenzhen and Zhuhai International Art Festival, and with the allocation of 17 million yuan by the government, the remaining construction of the main theater and lobby was able to be completed.

The former vice chairman of the Chinese People's Political Consultative Conference (CPPCC), Gu Mu, inspected Shenzhen during the art festival. The art festival last ten days, which included 500 artists from 12 countries giving 25 performances. Although the concert hall and other affiliated projects were still

---

[6]Sourced from Memorabilia of Shenzhen Grand Theater (Infrastructure). Courtesy of Shenzhen Grand Theater.

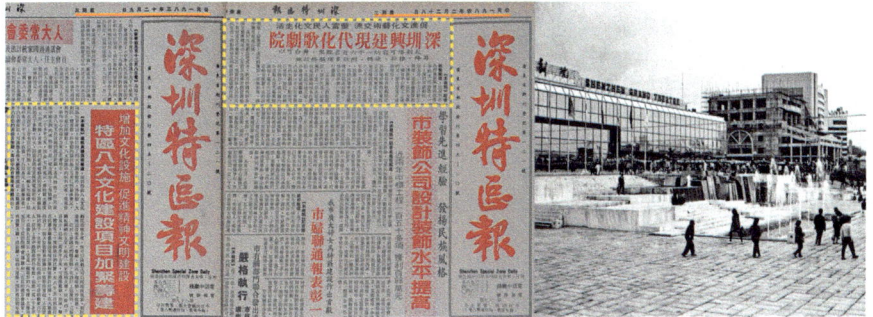

Fig. 4.3 1983 and 1984—news of the Shenzhen Grand Theater in the *Shenzhen Special Zone Daily*

incomplete, the shows attracted an audience of nearly 45,000.[7] In 2004, the financial district was reconstructed and two new roads were laid next to the Grand Theater. The government wanted to use this opportunity to re-organize the equipment room, eliminate fire hazards, renew aging facilities, and upgrade the external image of the theater. Landscape and façade renovation were planned by Shenzhen Aube Architectural Engineering Design Co., Ltd., and the interior was designed by the Beijing Institute of Architectural Design (Shenzhen branch), with an investment of 130 million yuan. The renovation was completed and business resumed in March 2006.[8] The Shenzhen Grand Theater hosted a total audience of nearly 100,000 at 171 performances throughout the year 2015, but compared with the average annual level of around 200 performances a year in other locations, there are nearly 15% room for improvement.

The completion of the Grand Theater was an ideological precursor to Shenzhen in the late 1980s, and symbolized the development direction of more advanced theaters in that era. Shenzhen Grand Theater is located at the intersection of Middle Shennan Road (the only main road at that time) and Hongling Road. To the south is the bustling financial center and to the west the beautiful Litchi Park. The theater covered an area of 43,760 m^2 and was decorated with golden glass curtain wall. It was called "the Golden Fairy" and "Pride of Shenzhen" for its magnificent appearance. It was also the first theater in China to have a stage with a "品" form, which can be rotated, pushed, and pulled up and down. In addition to a 1600-seat main hall, a 500-seat concert hall and a complete set of entertainment facilities. There is also a sunken plaza outside that diverts people and vehicles, and the traffic flow is organized through it. Audiences at the time were impressed and amazed when they entered the theater (Fig. 4.4). Thus, the Grand Theater, as an essential cultural facility of Shenzhen, has been a major provider of cultural and festival performances organized by the government. This reflects the fact that in China, theaters can play an important political role (Fig. 4.5).

---

[7]See Office of Local Chronicles Compilation of Shenzhen (2012, 212).

[8]For details on the renovation of Shenzhen Grand Theater, see Cai and Chou (2005, 46–51).

Fig. 4.4 **a** Under construction, 1985; **b** perspective from South Square, 1990; **c** lobby. Courtesy of Shenzhen Grand Theater

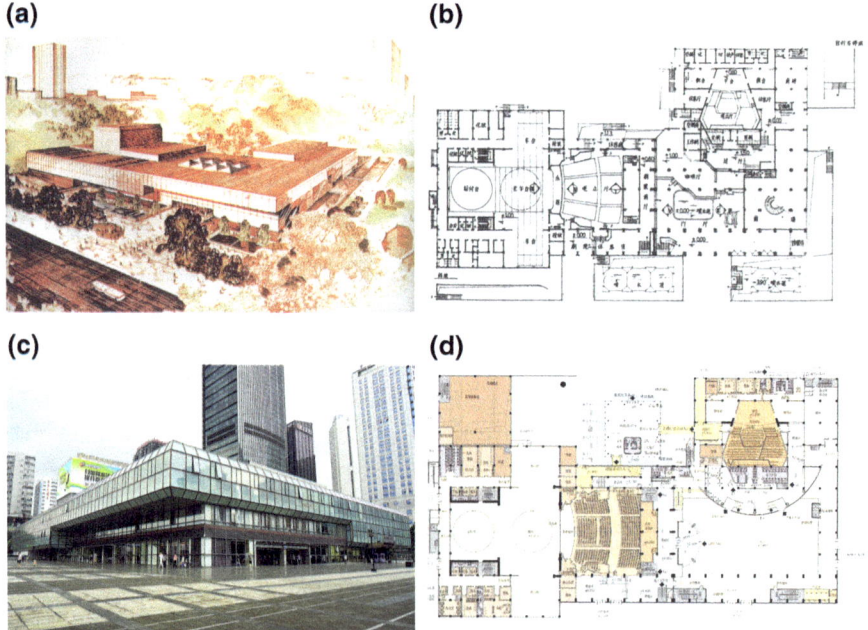

Fig. 4.5 Shenzhen Grand Theater, 1989. **a** Aerial perspective, sketch by Lin Zhaozhang, 1983; **b** plan in 1983–2004; **c** perspective after renovation, 2012; **d** plan after 2004. Photos (**a**) and (**b**) from Shi (2010); photo (**c**) by the author; photo (**d**) courtesy of the theater manager

From the urban planning perspective, the Grand Theater and the Television Station are located in Luohu District, and Shenzhen University stands in Nanshan District, while the remaining five major cultural facilities all reside in Futian District, which is the same district where the Municipal Government dwells in. The Grand Theater is located at the north side of Shennan Road, the only main road in the 1980s. The Municipal Party Committee and the Municipal Government were on the same side of the road. In fact, Grand Theater was 890 m away from the Municipal Government, which was about the distance between two bus stops or about 15 min walk. The distances of the other major cultural facilities from the Municipal Government are: Shenzhen Museum at 460 m away; the Science Museum at 480 m; the Library at 1.3 km; and the Stadium at 2.1 km. The Grand Theater is thus not the nearest cultural facility to the political center. In the 1980s, cultural facilities were planned in a dispersed way and did not form any axis order, so its political feature was not clearly reflected at the planning level. At the functional level, the Grand Theater not only holds performances by domestic and foreign troupes but also the government's major cultural festivals, including national leaders' visits, receptions, and celebration activities of the party and government. From this aspect, the Grand Theater has showed its close relation with political activities. Additionally, the theater has a full range of supporting facilities including galleries, cafes, cultural boutiques, Chinese and Western restaurants, dance halls, and semi-outdoor underground commercial streets. Shenzhen Grand Theater was the first trial to combine cultural facilities with commercial design after 1949. The functional combination of the Grand Theater at that time represented a trend in the development of new grand theaters: a strong political atmosphere with few commercial features (Fig. 4.6). It is worth noting that the public had no right to know and participation in the design and implementation of public buildings at that time.

Fig. 4.6 Shenzhen Grand Theater in 1995 and 2012. Basemaps from Ma (2013)

4.2 The Growth/Expansion Stage—The Second Construction Boom of Cultural Facilities (1989–1996)

In 1992, China's patriarch Deng Xiaoping delivered the renowned "South Tour Speeches" when inspecting coastal areas in Guangdong province. Under the slogan of "Development is the top priority," a new round of construction started, and the deadlock of Reform and Opening Up was broken. Shenzhen's development in this stage embodied the further realization of the new groups' construction and urban expansion.[9] In the 1990s, Shenzhen emphasized culture as an important part of cultural and ethical progress and established eight new cultural facilities: the Huaxia Art Center, Shenzhen Book City, Guanshanyue Art Museum, He Xiangning Art Museum, the Special Zone Daily Building, the Shenzhen Economic Daily Building, the Painting Institute, and the Stadium, all of which required a huge investment. The public cultural service system of Shenzhen took shape basically at that time.[10] This was the second construction boom of cultural facilities in Shenzhen, with the spatial distribution of cultural facilities continuing to spread westward in a decentralized approach. However, most of them were close to the new planned city center in Futian District. Only Huaxia Art Center and He Xiangning Art Museum were located in Overseas Chinese Town (OCT) in Nanshan District, which was 14 km away from downtown at that time, and the Shenzhen Painting Institute was located in Silver Lake in Luohu District (Fig. 4.7).

The construction of Huaxia Art Center started earlier and originated from the planning of Overseas Chinese Town. In August 1985, as the nationwide economic macro-control intensified, Shenzhen's radical development faction represented by the Mayor was curbed by the central government and the development scale was reduced. In November 1985, Shennan Road continued to be developed westward. According to the notice from the Overseas Chinese Affairs Office and the Office of Special Economic Zones under the State Council, 4.8 km^2 of wilderness was marked out from Shahe Overseas Chinese Industrial Park for the purpose of building an export-oriented development zone—the Overseas Chinese Town of Shenzhen Special Economic Zone (OCT). Mr. Ma Zhimin, the then director of the construction headquarters of the OCT, spent 110,000 US dollars, which was a huge amount at that time, and invited Mr. Meng Ta Cheang, a master of planning in Singapore, to design and plan this land.

Meng's planning idea was to design a relatively independent city within Shenzhen that included industry, a residential area, and an administrative, cultural, and commercial center. The principles were to respect and use the original land-form; control building height and density and let multi-story building predominate;

---

[9]For more about the key points of Shenzhen's development in different stages, see Meng (2006).

[10]The idea that the public cultural service system has basically taken shape comes from Wen (2008, 43).

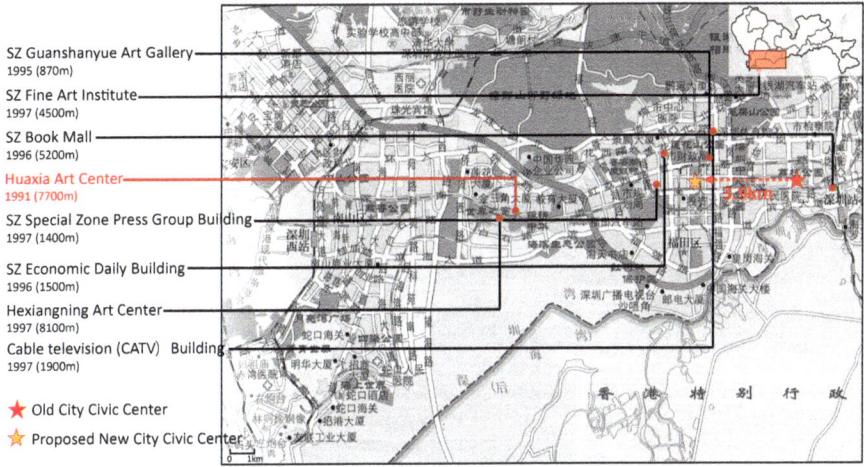

SZ Guanshanyue Art Gallery
1995 (870m)

SZ Fine Art Institute
1997 (4500m)

SZ Book Mall
1996 (5200m)

Huaxia Art Center
1991 (7700m)

SZ Special Zone Press Group Building
1997 (1400m)

SZ Economic Daily Building
1996 (1500m)

Hexiangning Art Center
1997 (8100m)

Cable television (CATV) Building
1997 (1900m)

★ Old City Civic Center

☆ Proposed New City Civic Center

Fig. 4.7 1990s—the second upsurge of cultural facilities construction. Map of Shenzhen in mid-90s. Drawn by the author. (Figures in brackets above indicate the distance from each facility to the city hall)

form a T-shaped layout for internal roads to avoid wide roads and intersections; prohibit the construction of any north-south thoroughfare that intersected with Shennan Road; set a regional center with a pedestrian street.[11] However, an unprecedented crisis struck Shenzhen when the OCT progressed from the design to the overall construction. In 1986, Shenzhen removed over 1500 infrastructure projects in the whole city, reducing the construction scale by more than half.[12] In January 1987, construction headquarters of OCT held a cornerstone laying ceremony for a miniature landscape of Splendid China in Shenzhen Bay. In November 1989, Splendid China opened for business with only an area of 31 ha, and recouped the investment cost of 100 million HK dollars in less than a year. Its success not only created a new style of Chinese theme park but also brought huge benefits to the OCT Group, thus promoting the development of other projects in the OCT, and two large construction projects—Huaxia Art Center and the Folk Culture Village were launched simultaneously (Fig. 4.8).

The Huaxia (China in a literary meaning) Art Center, located on the opposite of Splendid China, started its construction on September 5, 1990 and was put into service on October 1, 1991. It was designed by Huasen Architectural and Engineering Designing Consultants Ltd. (HSArchitects) (a company established in 1980 as China's first Sino-foreign joint venture, founded by the Architecture Design Institute of the Ministry of Construction and Hong Kong Senyang

---

[11]Planning concept extracted from CAUPD (2014).

[12]For more about the situation of the early development of OCT, see Author unknown (2010).

Fig. 4.8 **a** The planning of OCT in 1986; **b** detailed planning drawings for the first phase of OCT (1986). Courtesy of OCT

Fig. 4.9 Huaxia Art Center. Photo by Charlie Xue

International Co., Ltd.). HSArchitects gained a huge reputation by designing Nan Hai Hotel and Shenzhen Gymnasium (Fig. 4.9).

The Art Center covers an area of 4500 m² and the gross floor area is about 13,000 m². It has four floors with a height of 27.2 m. Its function allocation reflected the requirements of the times, as the ballroom industry enjoyed great success at that time. The dance hall at the eastern side of the first floor with an area of more than 800 m^2 was at the time the largest dance hall with international standards in Shenzhen. And there are 300 seats surrounding the corridor on the second floor. The main hall is located at the western side of the second floor with an area of 685 m^2 (814 seats). There is a studio with an area of 600 m^2 at the eastern side of the fourth floor and 10 activity rooms on the western side. The Center has other auxiliary facilities such as dressing rooms, a fitness room, a coffee shop and a lounge. The plan of this building is presented as an isosceles triangle. The design of the entrance is open and distinct, getting rid of the usual closeness of theaters. On the one hand, its planning complies with the extension of the commercial pedestrian street. On the other hand, it responds to subtropical climatic features well. The roof's space truss structure has the roles of both sunshade and rain cover. The opening with a width of eight meters and three-stories height in the northeast is identical to the prevailing wind direction in the summer of Shenzhen, contributing to good natural ventilation.[13]

In the initial stage of modernization practice in the Reform and Opening Up from the 1980s to the 1990s, an eclecticism appeared in architectural design, namely, the combination and coexistence of traditional Chinese culture and Western form.[14] Huaxia Art Center was a typical example. The architect combined traditional cultural elements with the function and techniques of modern architecture. First, in terms of the materials selected, traditional pink concave-convex bricks were used, with gray bricks in the interlayer forming a horizontal line segmentation. Second, for the façade detail design, red sandstone relief was used in the stairs at the western side and external wall above the water pool at the southeast side, which represented ancient China's traditional philosophy. Third, for the landscape design, a Chinese-style garden was set up at both sides of the main entrance along the street in front, and a copper-made sculpture of "Flying Apsaras" in the Chinese style with a height of nine meters was added to the water pool at the eastern side (Fig. 4.10).

In 1993, Huaxia Art Center won the Gold Award of the National Excellent Design Selecting Committee and First Prize of the Quality Engineering of Ministry of Construction. HSArchitects continued to create a group of architectural designs in the OCT, including almost 30 high-rise residential buildings, the He Xiangning Art Museum, and other noteworthy public buildings, which virtually cornered the market. After many years of construction, the OCT, as a relatively independent city group, is undoubtedly successful in its development. It has gradually developed into an urban leisure center with residence, travel, and high-end industrial functions by combining urban resources and ecological environment.

---

[13]About the architectural design of Huaxia Art Center, see Gong et al. (1993).

[14]Wang's thesis discussed that an eclecticism appeared in architectural design from the 1980s to the 1990s. See Wang (2000).

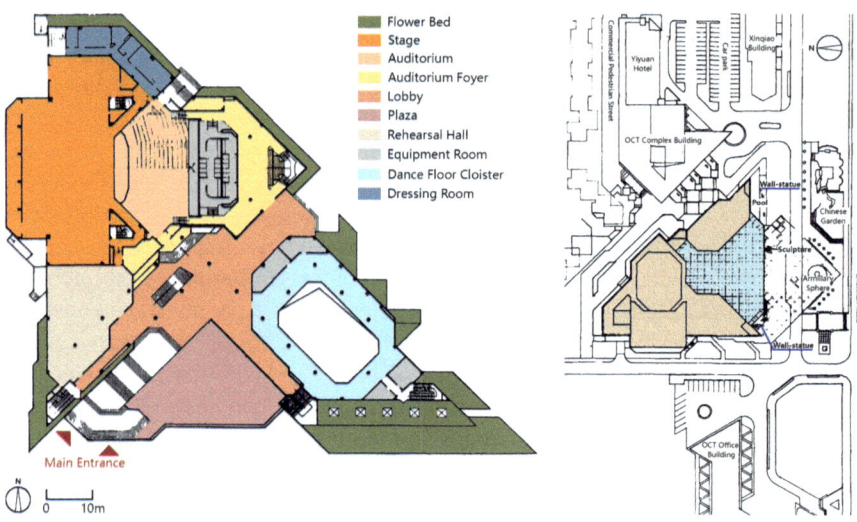

Fig. 4.10 First floor plan and master plan of Huaxia Art Center. Drawn by the author

4.3 The Development Stage—The Third Construction Boom of Cultural Facilities (1997–2010)

The planning of Futian Central District was first initiated as early as 1987. The British Llewelyn-Davies Planning Co. and Shenzhen Planning Bureau put forward the first version of the planning: on both sides of the central axis (north-south direction) was the urban public facilities land; in the north along the central axis was the municipal hall and in the south was landscaping; the land on the north side of Shennan Road (i.e., at the midpoint of the central axis) was intended for the Central Plaza; on the west side of the Plaza was the exhibition hall of science and technology, the art center, and the theater; and on the east side of the Plaza was the youth hostel, exhibition center, and library. This version of urban design laid a foundation for the design idea of arranging public buildings along both sides of the north-south central axis. *Futian District Planning*, completed in 1988, was based on the design drawings from the previous version and it basically established the planning layout of Futian Central District. In this planning, the cultural center and the information exchange center were placed on the north side of Shennan Road and along both sides of the central axis, and the financial, trade and commercial center was planned on the south of Shennan Road. The planning adopted a gridiron road structure and the design of traffic diversion (for motor and non-motor vehicles). In addition, it clearly stated that the cultural square was to be arranged in the north of the greenbelt and, in combination with the social and cultural center and the Grand Theater, provide a place for social activities.[15]

---

[15]For detail about the first version of the planning of Futian Central District, see Chen (2015a, 100–106).

In 1991, the government initiated a study on the planning of Futian Central District again. This time, Tongji Architectural Design Co., Ltd. (TJAD) and Urban Planning and Design Institute of Shenzhen (UPDIS) collaborated. While valuing the central-axis design and the principle of traffic diversion, they put forward a new master plan based on four solicited plans in the previous international consultation in 1989. In this approach, three rings were formed around the intersection of the south-north central axis and the east-west Shennan Road. In the inner ring was the leisure square. In the middle ring were large-scale public facilities for commerce, culture, etc. In the outer ring was a mixed area of commerce and residence. In November of the same year, the government began conducting site selection for large-scale cultural facilities and issued the *Report on Site Selection for Shenzhen Exhibition Center* in December, stating that the proposed Exhibition Center would be arranged on the north side of Futian Central District, the west of Jintian Road, and the south of Hongli Road.[16]

In 1992, the Shenzhen Branch of the China Academy of Urban Planning and Design (CAUPD) prepared the Detailed Plan and the Traffic Plan for Futian Central District, defining again that an oval square would be arranged at the intersection of the south-north central axis and east-west Shennan Road, and the land on the north side of the square was planned for administrations (the municipal hall) and cultural facilities (the museum, exhibition center, grand theater, etc.), and the central district would act as a showcase for the economic and cultural rejuvenation of the Chinese nation in the future. From 1995 to 1996, the government asked for an international consultation on the planning of core areas of the district (i.e., planning of an area of 1.93 km^2 along both sides of the south-north central axis and the single building of civic hall). The scheme by John M. Y. Lee/Michael Timchula Architects was recommended for its three-dimensional design of the center axis and the wavy image of the civic hall.[17] The planning ideas and the single building image of the civic hall in this plan were further developed later (Fig. 4.11).

Shenzhen entered the second pioneering stage in 1996. The government took Futian Central District as a key construction base. From 1997 to 1998 the Shenzhen Municipal Party Committee and Shenzhen Government initiated the bidding for designs of the six main infrastructures in Futian Central District and conceived a detailed planning scheme for the city's central axis. The six main constituents of the infrastructure are the Civic Hall (renamed as the Citizen Center later), the Central Library, the Concert Hall, the Children's Palace, Television Center (now known as the Media Group Building), and Crystal Island subway station (now known as Citizen Center station). Four of these are cultural facilities. This was the third boom of cultural facility construction in Shenzhen (Fig. 4.12).

The location of the library and concert hall was also determined at this time. It was relocated from the north side of Shennan Road and the west side of Yitian Road (the southwest side of the Citizen Center) to the block of the original

---

[16]The information on the planning in 1991 is quoted from Chan's book, see Chen (2015b, 71–73).

[17]The details for the international consultation on the planning of core areas of Futian Central District are from Shenzhen Planning and Land Resource Bureau (2002, 15–25).

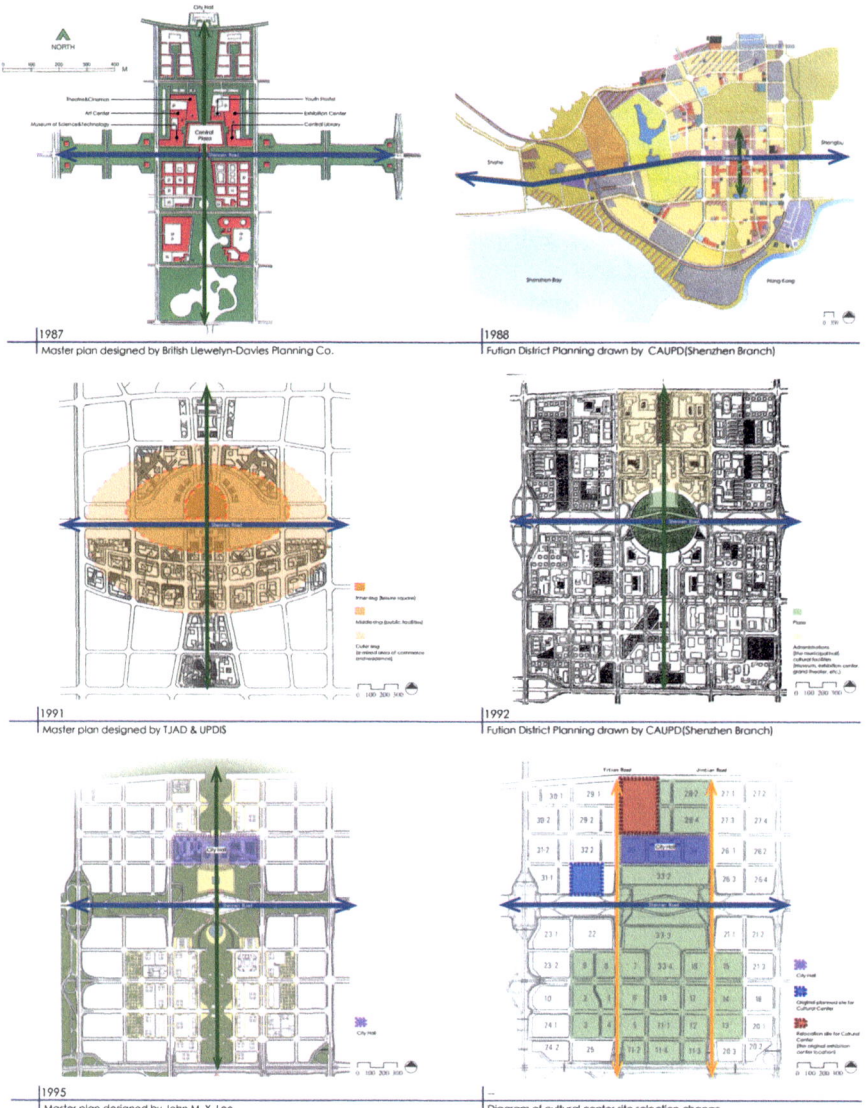

Fig. 4.11 Urban planning and design for the central district. Master plans from Shenzhen Planning and Land Resource Bureau (2002). Illustrations drawn by the author

exhibition center (the northwest side of the Citizen Center). Futian Central District was the area where the Municipal Government invested the most resources into public cultural facilities in its third pioneering stage. The Government invested 1.7

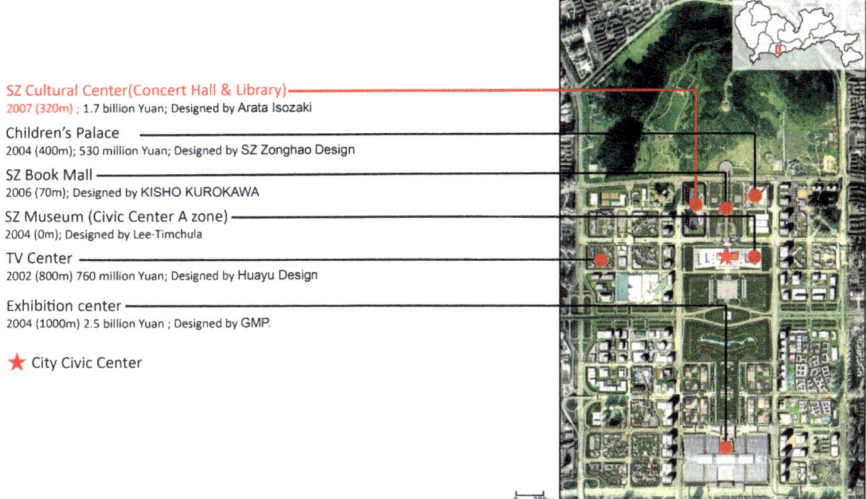

SZ Cultural Center(Concert Hall & Library)
2007 (320m) ; 1.7 billion Yuan; Designed by Arata Isozaki

Children's Palace
2004 (400m); 530 million Yuan; Designed by SZ Zonghao Design

SZ Book Mall
2006 (70m); Designed by KISHO KUROKAWA

SZ Museum (Civic Center A zone)
2004 (0m); Designed by Lee-Timchula

TV Center
2002 (800m) 760 million Yuan; Designed by Huayu Design

Exhibition center
2004 (1000m) 2.5 billion Yuan ; Designed by GMP.

★ City Civic Center

Fig. 4.12 The beginning of the 21st century—third upsurge of cultural facilities construction. Map of Shenzhen in 2008. Drawn by the author. (Figures in brackets above indicate the distance from each facility to the city hall)

billion yuan (US$2.2 billion) in the library and concert hall, 530 million yuan (US $69.7 million) in the Children's Palace, 760 million yuan (US$100 million) in the Television Center, and 2.5 billion yuan (US$0.3 billion) in the Exhibition Center.[18] By 2010, Shenzhen had completed the construction of the new administrative center, the cultural buildings, the densest rail lines and their stations.

The Futian Central District competition was the starting point of international competition among CBDs, and influenced other cities in China, which reflects the general planning model of Chinese new towns. In this planning model, the cultural buildings cluster should be built near the administration center and the layout should be designed with orderly aesthetics. Besides, the planners attempt to create a political and cultural center under the axis control, so the design of cultural buildings should first meet political tastes. The planning of Shenzhen Futian Central District adopted the Chinese traditional layout of a central axis, which stretched 2 km from the Lianhua Mountain in the north, crossing the Citizen Square to the Exhibition Center in the south. The public cultural facilities are mainly located along both sides of the north central axis. It is worth mentioning that the central axis system was designed and deepened in 1997 by Kurokawa Kisho, a Japanese modernist master. The north central axis stretches from the southern foot of Lianhua Mountain and the rooftop platform of Shenzhen's Central Book City to the platform of the Citizen Center. This is a typical "space on the drawing" pattern. The axis is

[18]The data on the investment are taken from Urban Planning, Land & Resources Commission of Shenzhen Municipality, Time+ Architecture Journal (2017, 92–117).

not visible from eye-level and pedestrians on the road are unable to see the continuing route that was carefully designed by the planners.

Shenzhen Cultural Center includes the Shenzhen Concert Hall and the Shenzhen Library. It covers an area of 55,846 m^2 and is located in the northwest of the Citizen Center. In 1998, the Government organized an open international competition for designing the Cultural Center, and a limited number of designers were invited (Table 4.1). This was six months before the International Design Competition of the National Center for the Performing Arts, which was launched in April 1998. The Shenzhen Cultural Bureau, as the client, hoped that the cultural center would "become a public cultural leisure place with landmark, time and cultural characteristics, beautiful environment, and popular with citizens and visitors in Shenzhen." According to the design requirements, the budget of the Concert Hall was about 400 million yuan (US$48.2 million) and the Library about 300 million yuan (US$36.1 million). On January 9, 1998, the preliminary design judges were composed of 12 experts from planning, architecture, structure, acoustics, music, and library science. After a week, the Planning Bureau of Land and Resources and the Cultural Bureau co-chaired and invited seven local and overseas construction experts to vote for the first and second prizes. These included Wu Liangyong and Zhou Ganci (Fellows of Chinese Academy of Sciences and Chinese Academy of Engineering), Guan Zhaoye (Fellow of the Chinese Academy of Engineering), Hong Kong architect Pan Zuyao, and acoustic expert Wang Binglin.[19]

Finally, the design plan proposed by Japanese architect Arata Isozaki stood out from the competition and got the supports from seven judges of the Committee. While the second prize went to Safdie Architects. As both schemes were submitted by globally renowned architects, the Municipal Bureau of Culture invited 15 experts from Beijing and Guangzhou once again to a symposium on February 10, 1998, to confirm the final decision. Arata Isozaki's design was approved by most of the experts. Two days later, the Communist Party Group of Shenzhen cultural bureau officially recommended to the Leading Group of Municipal Main Cultural Infrastructure Construction that Arata Isozaki's design should be implemented. However, Huang Weiwen, the planner from the Development and Construction Office of Futian Central District at that time, recalled that the leaders of the municipal government preferred Safdie's scheme.

In order to persuade the leaders to respect the choice of the judges, the leading group organized a questionnaire survey to the public after 10 days.[20] The questionnaire had a relatively small sample size with 200 questionnaires distributed, and 127 respondents of which visited the model and submitted their suggestions. At last, the outcome was that 55.9% of the respondents approved of Arata Isozaki's design. In late March, the municipal party committee held a symposium on the

---

[19]For detail about the process of the competition, see Urban Planning, Land & Resources Commission of Shenzhen Municipality, Time+ Architecture Journal (2017, 121).
[20]For detail about the process of the competition, see Urban Planning, Land & Resources Commission of Shenzhen Municipality, Time+ Architecture Journal (2017, 25).

Table 4.1 1998—the seven designers invited to the competition

1	Japan	Arata Isozaki and Associates
2	Canada	Safdie Architects
3	USA	Kling Lindquist Partnership
4	USA	L.S.H.
5	USA	Urban Construction Group
6	China	BIAD
7	Hong Kong	Rocco Design

selection of the implementation scheme. The relevant personnel of the Planning Bureau, the Construction Bureau, and the Cultural Bureau, along with architectural experts and scholars, assessed the advantages and disadvantages of the two schemes and voted anonymously. As a result, Arata Isozaki's design scored 20 compared to 15 for Safdie's.[21] Arata Isozaki has more experience in performance space design than the other architects bidding in the competition. His projects include the Kyoto Concert Hall completed in 1995, and the Nara Centennial Hall, which was almost completed at that time, and so the old Japanese master may have been quite confident in winning the bid for the cultural center. This was the first project that he won through fair competition in China, and thus opened up Chinese design market for him. And then he designed the Shanghai Symphony Orchestra Concert Hall (2008–2014), the Harbin Concert Hall (2009–2015), Datong Grand Theater (2009–2018) and other large-scale performance buildings (Fig. 4.13).

The most striking ideas in Arata Isozaki's design for the Shenzhen Cultural Center are the "Golden Glass Tree" and the gorgeous harp-type curtain wall, which was intended to display a gesture of openness in the city. The library and concert hall are connected into a unified whole through a two-story platform facing the central axis. The concert hall consists of an 1800-seat vineyard typology hall and a small 400-seat theater studio. The entrance hall is a brilliant space containing five golden pillars that support the polyhedral glass roof. In addition, the architect is very bold in the use of color, and the five colors selected—yellow, red, blue, white, and black—correspond to the traditional Chinese "five elements." Yellow is present in the north side of the concert hall in the auxiliary back hall; the red tube is vertical elevators; the blue is at the top of the black wall and there is a blue fluorescent strip at night; the large outdoor platform and the frames dividing the curtain wall are white; and the west wall is black, which the judges found controversial.

The review minutes provided an explanation of the Committee judges' decision. Compared with the other plans, the design concept of the plan was unique. It was aimed at being a local landmark after completion. Its overall design style was coordinated with the style of the CBD. In terms of functionality, the Concert Hall was designed in a "Vineyard Terrace" style, which provides the audiences with better acoustic effects. Both the curtain walls on the main (east) facade and the

---

[21]Finally, Arata Isozaki's design was 20:15 scores, and won the Safdie's. Information excerpted and modified from Shenzhen Planning and Land Resource Bureau (2002, 66–73).

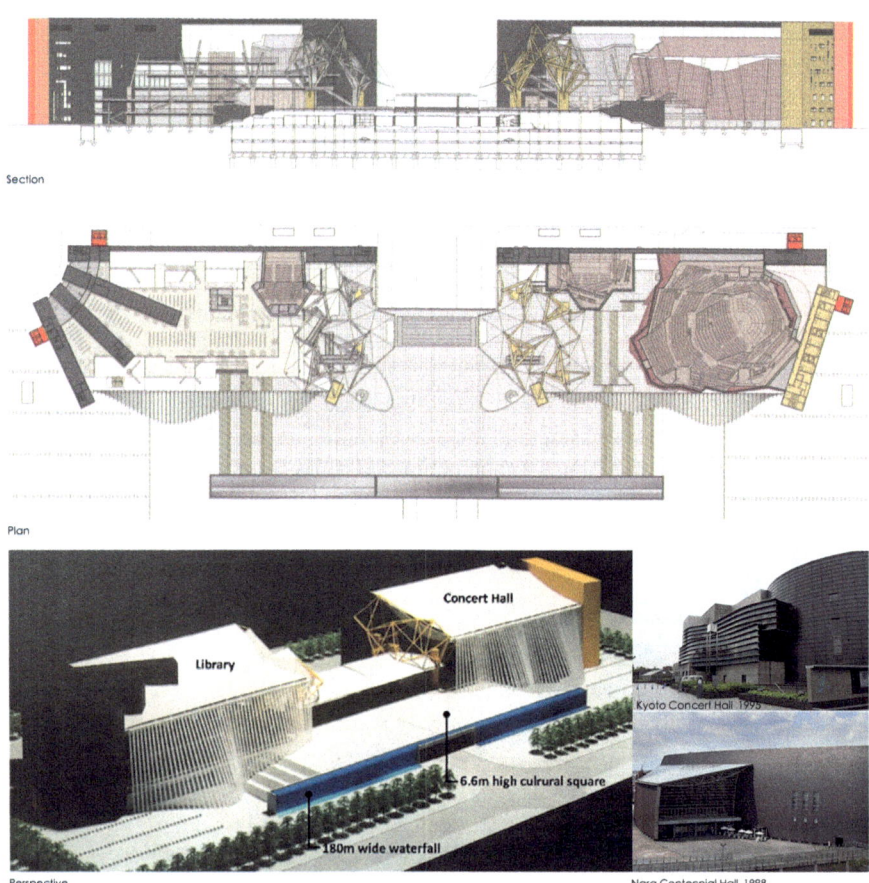

Fig. 4.13 Arata Isozaki's scheme for the Shenzhen Cultural Center competition. Sections and plan from Urban Planning, Land and Resources Commission of Shenzhen Municipality

welding technology for the cast steel joints of the Golden Tree were distinctive. Most importantly, it complemented the public space on the main axis.[22]

The judges praised the runner-up scheme designed by Safdie, saying that "it has a strong sense of sculpture and is also in harmony with the overall environment and is an excellent creation." It consisted of two independent spirals that are opposite each other. The curved surface shape provided rich changes in light and shadow. Combined with the waterscape arrangement, a level of cooperation with the urban park on the east side was noted. However, when considering the factors of originality and planning coordination, the design was deemed too similar to the

---

[22]The review minutes was published in Urban Planning, Land & Resources Commission of Shenzhen Municipality (2017, 25).

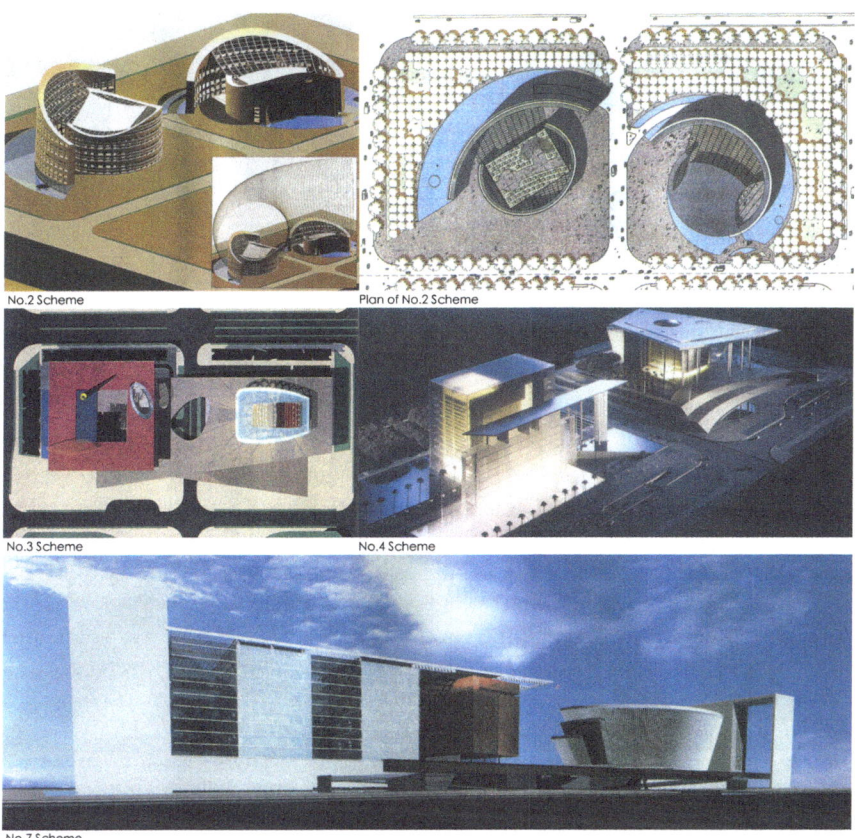

Fig. 4.14 Other schemes in the Shenzhen Cultural Center competition. Photos from Shenzhen Planning and Land Resource Bureau (2002)

Vancouver Library Square in Canada that Safdie designed in 1995, and the form of two curved walls would affect the lateral reflection of sounds, which is contrary to the form of successful modern concert halls. In summary, Isozaki's design was thus deemed superior. For the remaining schemes, the judges said that they all had more or less significant shortcomings in use or forming. Apart from No. 5 scheme (the California Urban Construction Group) and No. 7 scheme (Hong Kong Rocco Design), the designs of the other schemes are piled up too much, and the forms were viewed as being rather contrived (Fig. 4.14).[23]

[23]Information excerpted and modified from Shenzhen Planning and Land Resource Bureau (2002, 66).

Fig. 4.15 The groundbreaking ceremony of the six main infrastructures of Shenzhen Central District. Photos from Ma (2013)

On December 28, 1998, the groundbreaking ceremony of the six main infras-tructures in Shenzhen Central District was held simultaneously (Fig. 4.15). Current and previous leaders of the Shenzhen Municipal Party Committee attended the event. The public construction of Central District thus officially began. After a decade of construction, Shenzhen Cultural Center was opened to citizens and tourists in 2008. Compared with the budget cost in the requirement, however, the Cultural Center overspent 1 billion yuan. Since the application of steel structures was at a very preliminary stage in China 20 years ago, the steel structure for the golden tree was still an experimental construction. The construction team cooper-ated with Japanese structural engineers to make models, and then confirmed every joint on site, so it took a long time to construct (Fig. 4.16).

Shenzhen Concert Hall is the symbolized modern cultural facility, fully invested by Shenzhen Municipal Government after the Shenzhen Grand Theater. Its estab-lishment has provided a professional artistic space that meets international stan-dards for those activities such as performances by leading international symphony orchestras and international music competitions. In 2017, 187 performances were held throughout the year, serving nearly 160,000 visitors. However, according to the observation on the spot, we identified some problems, such as: the 180-m waterfall in front of the cultural square blocks the large staircase behind it, so that most people do not take the route originally designed, proceeding from the ground to the 6.6-m high square and then entering the concert hall, but enter the concert hall directly from the ground. Thus, the inefficient use of main entrance, including the sharing platform and external staircase, just pays for the "good appearance on drawings" (Fig. 4.17).

In addition, we interviewed the concert hall management staff, who claimed that they had purchased outdoor equipment and organized an event on the cultural square, which is the platform shared with the library. However, the management of the library took great exception to this, because the noise would be intolerable for the library users. Therefore, the manager said if the designer could consider sep-arating the outdoor platform between the library and the concert hall, there would be no mutual interference problems. Previously, street artists were invited to put on

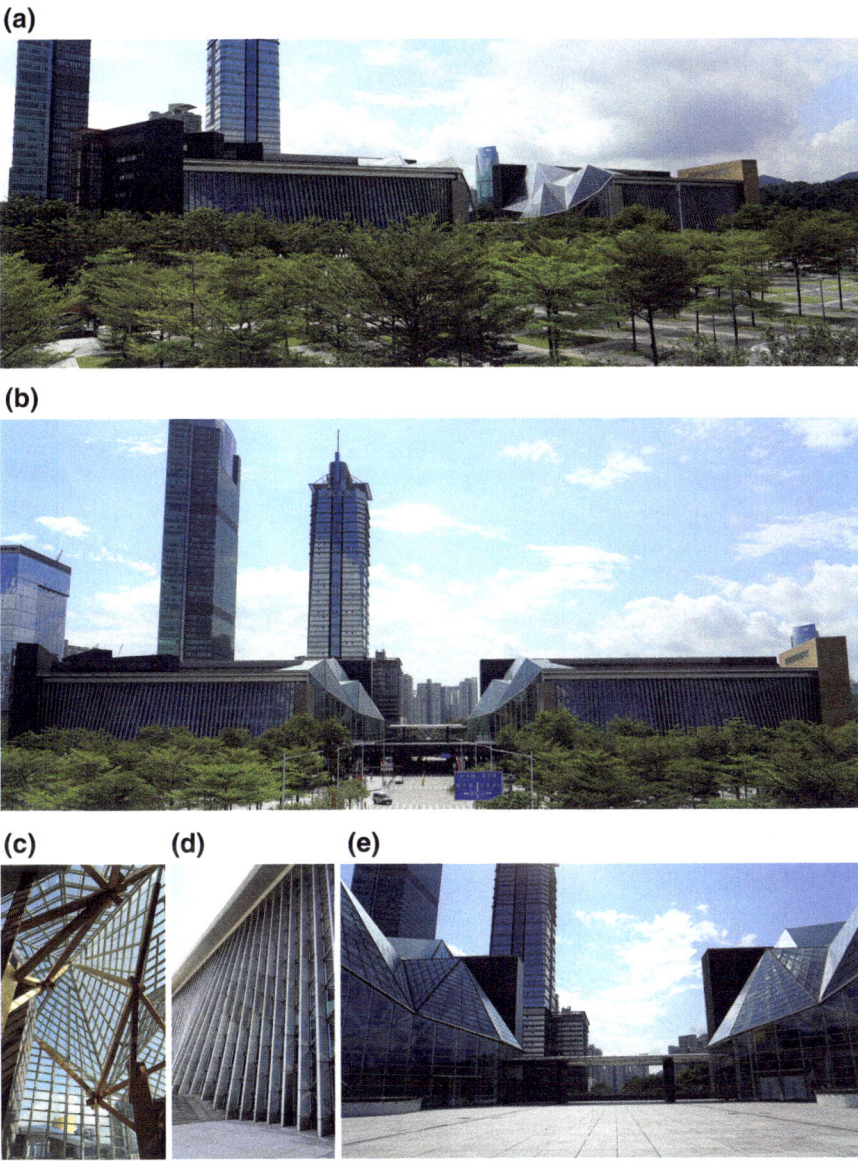

Fig. 4.16 **a**, **b** Photos of Shenzhen Cultural Center from the main façade view. **c** Photo of the polyhedral glass roof and golden pillars. **d** The gorgeous harp-type curtain wall. **e** Cultural square

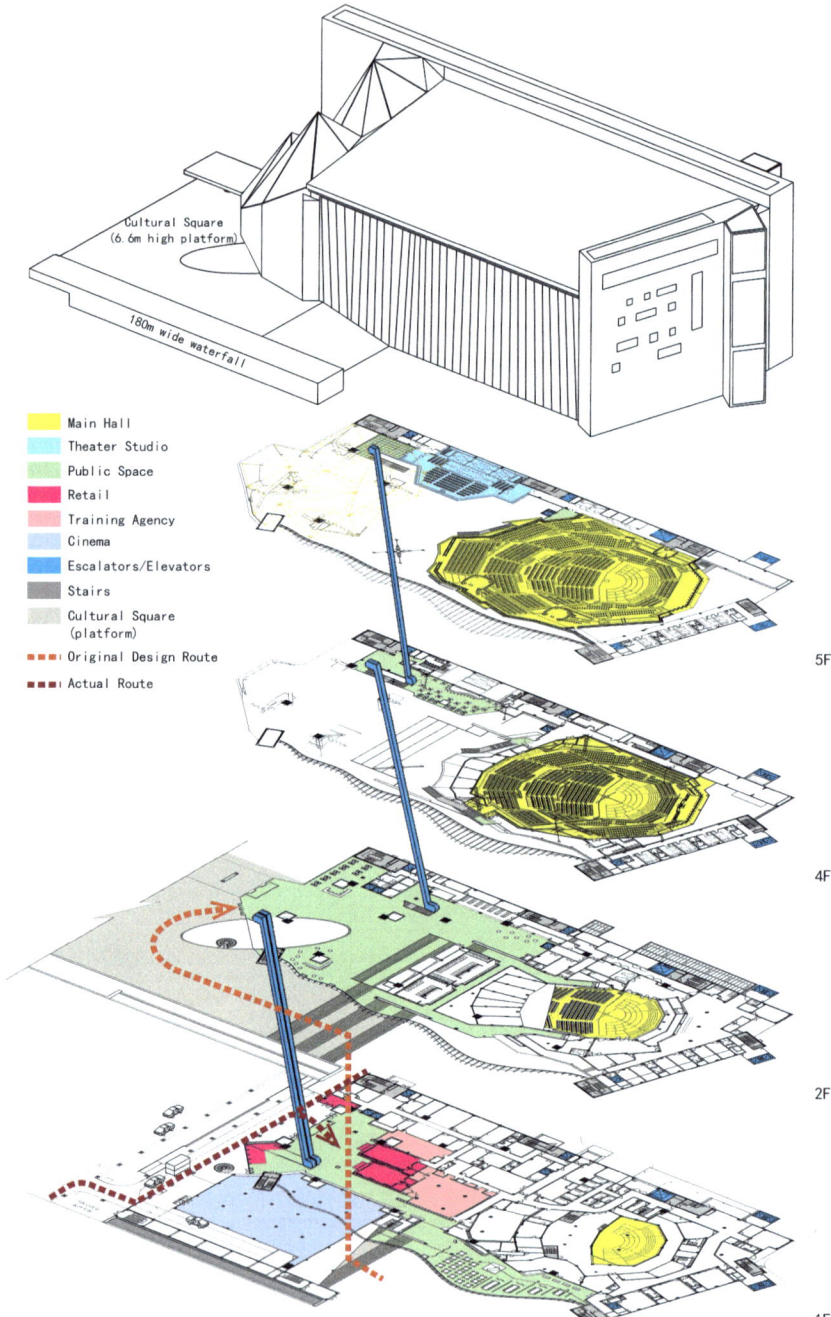

Fig. 4.17 Axonometric analysis of concert hall. Drawn by the author

a show on the cultural square, but that caused the urban management department to have concerns about safety in the open staircase due to the large crowds. After that, any organized public activity must obtain a permit in advance so street artists are not allowed to play inside the domain of the concert hall, to maintain the elegance and order of the concert hall. Thus, the original design of the outdoor theater could not be used as intended, and the architect's desire could not be respected in the real operation. The level of management and investment is critical to the quality of public facilities.[24]

4.4 The Development Stage—The Third Construction Boom of Cultural Facilities (1997–2010)

As China promotes the strategy of the "Guangdong-Hong Kong-Macao Greater Bay Area" and interconnects the infrastructure within the Pearl River Delta, the time has come to build an international megalopolis in the Greater Bay Area. In addition to technological innovation and industrial upgrading, this development also relies on the integration of cultural exchanges. Shenzhen, as a world-class city in terms of scale and economy, has been positioned as the engine for developing the Bay Area and has been tasked with a new mission. The Shenzhen Cultural Industry Development Plan (2007–2020) stated to invest more on the cultural and entertainment industry. This statement reflects people's cultural consumption keep growing. Besides, with the joining of consumer groups of the surrounding cities, the demand for cultural facilities in Shenzhen will be on the rise and witnesses a tendency of diversity.

The *13th Five-Year Plan for Cultural Development of Shenzhen* issued at the end of 2016 clearly indicated the following:

> The 13th Five-Year Plan period is a decisive stage of building a moderately prosperous society in all respects, and is also a key period for speeding up the construction of a culturally-rich city for Shenzhen. The progress of Shenzhen's cultural reform and development, as of now, still falls within an important and strategically opportune period. … Need to accelerate the construction of cultural facilities, thoroughly implement beneficial projects related to culture and sports, and plan to build a number of international-level cultural facilities that match the Shenzhen's status as a cultural giant. Various cultural spaces will be effectively integrated and improved to gradually realize the establishment of two or three international core areas of urban culture. The construction of New Cultural Center, Natural History Museum will be planned, and the preliminary demonstration for the construction of the Shenzhen Opera House will be carried out.

On February 2, 2018, the Shenzhen Culture, Sports, and Tourism Bureau held a conference to discuss tasks for 2018, and stated the main objectives of their work in

---

[24]Interview of Shenzhen Concert Hall was conducted on November 30, 2016. The interviewees include Li Shunchao of administration department, Yang Qingxi and Manager Gu from technical department.

culture, sports, and tourism until 2022, which include the establishment of a number of major cultural and sports facilities, such as the Shenzhen Reform and Opening Exhibition Hall, and the New Art Gallery. Improvements in public culture, sports, and tourism service supply were also identified, to enhance the quality of life of citizens and visitors. In addition, Zhang Heyun, the director of the Bureau, commented, "Shenzhen has experienced two booms of cultural and sports facilities construction, but it is still lacking the landmark ones and sports venues that can host top events. Actually, Shenzhen hosted Universiade in 2011 and built a large-scale sport park, stadium, indoor hall and swimming hall by using up its reservation. Therefore, they will focus on promoting the transformation and upgrading project of the sports center, and actively strengthening the planning of cultural facilities in Shenzhen Bay in the following stages." The Bureau of Public Works of Shenzhen's Nanshan District also announced in April 2018 that "Shenzhen Houhai Central Area, as an important node for the Guangdong-Hong Kong-Macao Greater Bay Area, will assume important central area functions and portal display functions of the Nanshan District, and become an international high-standard urban central area." At present, the planning of a commercial and cultural belt and the design of the major project in this area is being undertaken.

Moreover, Shenzhen International Exhibition Center is also the core project in Airport New City. The construction of the steel framework has begun, and is expected to be completed in 2019 as the largest exhibition center in the world. Recently, the Notice on the Renovation and Upgrading of the Shenzhen Sports Center has redirected citizens' attention to this old stadium. Before this, the maintenance and renovation of Shenzhen museum, which was also one of the older eight cultural facilities, had started earlier.

A new round of construction boom for cultural facilities is obviously emerging, mainly in the Qianhai and Houhai areas, while groups and public buildings in the Shangbu and Luohu areas that were developed earlier are faced with urban renewal and upgrading. This chapter reveals how urban administrators merge cultural resources into planning and public policy for urban construction, by analyzing three construction booms of cultural facilities in Shenzhen and the history of the times. The new planning trends are interpreted and the transfer path of the city center and the change of urban spatial structure are investigated. Furthermore, taking Shenzhen as an example, China's public cultural facilities are mainly funded by local governments. Political feature and the meanings of cultural symbols are added to the original basic functions of individual buildings. As competition between cities intensifies under globalization, urban design oriented by cultural strategy has become a dominant force in the urban renewal of developed countries. Obviously, decision-makers of Shenzhen make it clear that construction of cultural buildings can not only improve the city's image but also boost economic and social development. Last but not the least, perhaps because of the success of Futian Central District, the planning idea of driving the development of new districts through the construction of cultural flagship projects has been vigorously promoted.

4.5 Conclusion and Discussion

Shenzhen is the starting point for the largest city-construction movement in contemporary China. Nationwide urban construction is about 10–15 years behind that of Shenzhen. So, the planning and construction system and the phenomenal expansion of the city have served as a template for rapid urbanization. In the context of rapid urbanization in Shenzhen, excessive input of cultural facilities over the past 30 years is the most striking architectural phenomenon in its massive upsurge of urban construction.

Shenzhen Grand Theater marked the beginning of modern theater design, and ushered in the "Grand Theater era."[25] Its mechanical stage system was designed by a British company, which led the trend of looking for overseas architects to design theaters. In the 1980s, cultural facilities were planned to be distributed in disperse way, and did not form any axis order, so their political feature was not clearly reflected at the planning level. Although Huaxia Art Center is classified as one of the new eight cultural facilities, its construction is a relatively independent event, and is inseparable from the urban expansion and new group construction it emerged from. It represented an exploration of some advanced enterprises and institutions in that era, which promoted cultural exchanges and enriched leisure time. The architectural design style also has a distinctive combination of Chinese and Western characteristics.

In terms of spatial distribution in the second construction boom of cultural facilities in Shenzhen, development spread westward in a decentralized approach. However, most cultural facilities were close to the new planned city center. Shenzhen concert hall represents the now common planning model of new towns in China. In this model, cultural buildings are built adjacent to the administration centers, in an attempt to shape a political and cultural center under the control of the axis. The design of cultural buildings thus addresses political aesthetic needs first, rather than starting from the needs of the public. This type of planning reflects the close integration of political symbols and spatial elements, and also illustrates the close association of urban development and politics in China. In addition, architects have tried to figure out what decision-makers want and attempted to stand out through unique design and attractive implications. The cultural organizations, as users or managers of the theater, will only give opinions at the expert meeting, but it is difficult to measure how many of these can be actually applied. The citizens are the main users of cultural buildings, but their rights and participation are ignored or absent. What's more, local government has consciously increased investment in cultural facilities but administrators in some cities put these facilities under protection without thinking about the public's participation in a non-consumption

---

[25]See Lu (2009). Lu's book has compiled the progress of the Chinese theater since the end of the 19th century. The book has unique information and elaborates on the transformation and development of performing buildings in China. For more about the development of performing buildings in China, see Xue and Xiao (2017).

Fig. 4.18 Comparison of the elevation scales of the major theaters of different periods in Shenzhen. Drawn by the author

manner, thus replacing the public's demand with a hierarchical grade sequence. This results in distance and isolation being put between the public and these grand cultural facilities.

Shenzhen Theater was born in the 1950s, a confused era of the planned economy, as a three-story box in a conservative style that only met the basic functional needs. In the late 1980s, Shenzhen Grand Theater presented the image of a new theater and surprised the Chinese people. The "Lingnan School of modern architecture" gradually waned as globalization evolved, so the design style of the Shenzhen Grand Theater could not be followed. Shenzhen Huaxia Art Center, as the last large-scale performance venue built in the 20th century, is obviously retrogressive. Although the scale is not small, it is not eye-catching or ostentatious. The Shenzhen Concert Hall, which cost 1.7 billion yuan (US$2.2 billion), represents the theater style after the millennium: that is, a costly city landmark, which is in fact a standard auditorium cover with an expensive, shiny "coat." Although the Cultural Square (the platform shared with the library) was designed to be more open, it no longer welcomes street artists (Fig. 4.18).

According to incomplete statistics, 364 theaters have been newly built, rebuilt, or expanded since 1998 in China, with a total investment of above 100 billion yuan. More construction is being planned. However, this construction boom does not seem to be a response to the demand for performances, but only fuels competition between municipalities.[26] It is disappointing that the government does not care about whether these huge investment venues have good financial returns and whether they have fulfilled the mission of being public buildings in view of the low usage rate, the lack of openness to the public, and the poor management level.

Acknowledgements This paper is part of a study supported by the Research Grant Council, Hong Kong Government, under Grant Project No. CityU 11658816. To begin with, my greatest gratitude goes to my respected supervisor, Professor Charlie Q. L. Xue, both for his ongoing support, helpful advice and warm encouragements during the process of writing the manuscript. I also want to thank many people who had the generosity to help me undertake the field work and conduct my research: Dr. Chen Yixin from Urban Planning, Land and Resources Commission of Shenzhen Municipality; Zhu Ya, Duan Xinren, Kang Rui from Shenzhen Grand Theater; and Li Shunchao, Ms. Pan, Yang Qingxi from Shenzhen Concert Hall. Besides, I am also grateful to my colleague, Zhang Lujia and Xiao Yingbo. I benefited from every discussion with them. Finally, I would like to thank my family for always being there for me. Their love was a strong inspiration.

---

[26]See Lu (2011) & Wilkinson (2018)

I was born in Shenzhen, but my parents are not from Shenzhen. I was tagged with the 'second-generation immigrant' (Shen Er Dai) label, and Shenzhen city is only eight years older than I am. When I was a child, I lived in a Danwei housing less than one kilometre from the Grand Theater. Although the Grand Theater and the financial district behind it were the most prosperous downtown area in the eyes of others, as to me, it was a paradise for walking after dinner! The Grand Theater was open to the public then, except for the inner performance hall. Every night, my parents took me through Litchi Park to the lively commercial pedestrian street under the theater, and we took a ride on the square ... Eventually, when I was four years old, I walked into the theater which was the best art palace in Shenzhen in the 1980s and even 1990s, to watch a drama with a gift ticket provided by my father's company. After more than 20 years, I have forgotten the name and content of the show, but I remember that the next day I showed off the ticket stub to my classmates and boasted about my experience of watching the show.

In addition to holding various large-scale cultural performances, in the 1990s, the Grand Theater was the site of various high-class conferences and festivals of government agencies and institutions. High prices and outstanding political functions made it difficult for the public to enter the theater. In 2005, the underground commercial street and the up-and-down outdoor squares were turned into an underground car park after the renovation of the whole theater. The Grand Theater and the nearby Dajiale Stage, which carried the collective memory of the first two generations of Shenzhen immigrants have become cold and closed "ground-hitting" boxes.

As we all know, Shenzhen is an immigrant city in which diverse cultures collide and merge. It also seems to be more inclusive and eager to innovate than other cities. In 1987, the government took the lead in conducting an international consultation on the planning of the future central area of the special economic zone. In 1997, the government launched intensive international design competitions for the six major public buildings in the central area, all of which demonstrated the vision of Shenzhen to be open, inclusive and innovative. In 2007, a cultural centre designed by a famous Japanese architect was completed here. I, as a sophomore majoring in architecture, was delighted at the opportunity to behold the master up close. This low-key but sparkling cultural palace amidst the blocks resembling 'the City of Tomorrow' imagined by Le Corbusier, with groups of office buildings in a modern American style during the 1980s and 1990s, made me realise that library and concert hall can be open and transparent. However, for various reasons, the use of the building is not as open as the design makes it appear. This kind of high-end cultural space remains somewhat isolated from civic life.

The trend is changing and new construction is in the works. I hope that Shenzhen will create another legend and that in the next round of construction of cultural facilities it will not only transform its closed buildings into more open sharing platforms, but also bring this kind of 'high-up' cultural space closer to daily life and integrate it more positively into urban space.

References

Author unknown. (2010). OCT: Original geomorphologic heritage of Shenzhen. *Jinxiu* (12), 74–83. 佚名 (2010). 华侨城: 深圳原生地貌遗产. 锦绣 (12), 74–83.

Cai, K., & Chou, Y. (2005). Renovation design for Shenzhen Grand Theater. *Architectural Creation* (11), 46–51. 蔡克, 仇岔国 (2005). 深圳大剧院改造设计. 建筑创作 (11), 46–51.

CAUPD. (2014). *Liujue Xiecui*. Shenzhen: Shenzhen International Color Printing. 中规院深圳分院 (2014). 六觉撷萃. 深圳: 深圳国际彩印有限公司.

Chen, Y. (2015a). *Shenzhen Futian CBD: A thirty-year history of urban planning and construction (1980–2010)* (pp. 100–106). Nanjing: Southeast University Press. 陈一新 (2015a). 深圳福田中心区(CBD): 城市规划建设三十年历史研究 (pp. 100–106). 南京: 东南大学出版社.

Chen, Y. (2015b). *Exploration of urban planning: Progress report of urban planning and implementation for Central Shenzhen (1980–2010)* (pp. 71–73). Shenzhen: Haitian Publishing House. 陈一新 (2015b). 规划探索: 深圳市中心区城市规划实施历程 (pp. 71–73). 深圳: 海天出版社.

Chung, C., Inaba, J., Koolhaas, R., & Leong, S. (2001). *Great leap forward*. Cambridge: Harvard Design School.

Cultural and Historical Records Committee of Shenzhen CPPCC. (2001). *The third episode of Shenzhen Cultural and Historical Records* (pp. 156–160). Shenzhen: Haitian Publishing House. 深圳市政协文史资料委员会编 (2001). 深圳文史第三辑 (pp. 156–160). 深圳: 海天出版社.

Gong, D. S., Zhang, P. F., & Zhou, P. (1993). Shenzhen Huaxia Art Center. *Architectural Journal* (2), 41–47. 龚德顺, 张孚佩, 周平 (1993). 深圳华夏艺术中心. 建筑学报 (2), 40–46.

International New Town Institute. (2016). *Shenzhen: From factory of the world to world city*. Rotterdam: nai010 publishers.

Lu, X. (2009). *On the evolution of modern theaters in China*. Beijing: China Architecture and Building Press. 卢向东 (2009). 中国现代剧场的演进. 北京: 中国建筑工业出版社.

Lu, X. D. (2011). On China's Grand Theatre Era. *World Architecture*, (1), pp.111-115. 卢向东 (2011).中国剧场的大剧院时代.世界建筑, (1), pp. 11–115.

Ma, S. (2013). *Shenzhen glorious history: Ma Shuhua's photo album*. Shenzhen: Shenzhen Press Group Publishing House. 马树华 (2013). 深圳辉煌历程: 马树华纪实摄影集. 深圳: 深圳报业集团出版社.

Meng, J. (2006). Shenzhen architecture for 25 years. In Y. L. Zhang (Ed.), *Shenzhen survey and design for 25 years: Architectural design*. Beijing: China Architecture & Building Press. 孟建民 (2006). 深圳建筑25年. 张一莉编, 深圳勘察设计25年: 建筑设计篇. 北京: 中国建筑工业出版社.

O'Donnell, M., Wang, W., & Bach, J. (2017). *Learning from Shenzhen: China's post-Mao experiment from special zone to model city*. Chicago: University of Chicago Press.

Office of Local Chronicles Compilation of Shenzhen. (2012). *CPC: Shenzhen historical memorabilia* (p. 212). Shenzhen: Shenzhen Press Group Publishing House. 深圳市史志办公室编 (2012). 中国共产党: 深圳历史大事记. 深圳: 深圳报业集团出版社.

Shenzhen Museum. (1999). *History of Shenzhen special economic zone*. Beijing: People's Publishing House. 深圳博物馆编 (1999). 深圳特区史. 北京: 人民出版社.

Shenzhen Planning and Land Resource Bureau. (2002). *Urban planning and architectural design for Shenzhen Central District 1996–2002: The international urban design consultation for core areas of Shenzhen Central District*. Beijing: China Architecture & Building Press. 深圳市规划与国土资源局 (2002). 深圳市中心区城市设计与建筑设计 1996–2002: 深圳市中心区核心地段城市设计国际咨询. 北京: 中国建筑工业出版社.

Shi, A. (2010). *The excellent buildings in contemporary Lingnan (1949–1990)*. Beijing: China Architecture & Building Press. 石安海 (2010). 岭南近现代优秀建筑 *(1949–1990)*. 北京: 中国建筑工业出版社.

Urban Planning, Land & Resources Commission of Shenzhen Municipality, Time + Architecture Journal. (2017). *Shenzhen competition: International urban/architectural competitions in Shenzhen 1994–2014*. Shanghai: Tongji Press. 深圳市规划和国土资源委员会(市海洋局)编 (2017). 深圳竞赛: 深圳城市/建筑设计国际竞赛 1994–2014. 上海: 同济大学出版社.

Wang, S. (2000). *Explode the characteristics of Chinese architecture between 1990 to 2000* (Master degree dissertation). Southeast University, Nanjing. 王韶宁 (2000). 20世纪九十年代中国建筑发展特征初探. 南京: 东南大学. 硕士学位论文.

Wang, W. (2007). *From the edge to the center: Research on the development of cultural industry in Shenzhen*. Beijing: People's Publishing House. 王为理 (2007). 从边缘走向中心: 深圳文化产业发展研究. 北京: 人民出版社.

Wen, S. (2008). *Shenzhen cultural revolution event*. Shenzhen: Shenzhen Publishing Group & Haitian Publishing House. 温诗步 (2008). 深圳文化变革大事. 深圳: 深圳出版发行集团 & 海天出版社.

Wilkinson, T. (2018). Typology: Opera houses. *The Architectural Review*. https://www.architectural-review.com/rethink/typology/typology-quarterly-opera-houses/8653735.article. Accessed September 7.

Xiao, Y., & Yin, S. (2016). A review of the development of contemporary architecture in Shenzhen between 1980s and 1990s. In Urban Planning, Land & Resources Commission of Shenzhen Municipality, Time + Architecture Journal, *Shenzhen contemporary architecture* (pp. 84–90). Shanghai: Tongji Press. 肖毅强, 殷实 (2016). 深圳20世纪八九十年代建筑创作发展评述. 深圳市规划和国土资源委员会, 《时代建筑》 杂志 编著, 深圳当代建筑, 84–90. 上海: 同济大学出版社.

Xue, C. Q. L. (2006). *Building a revolution: Chinese architecture since 1980*. Hong Kong: Hong Kong University Press.

Xue, C. Q. L., & Ding, G. (2018). *A history of design institutes in China: From Mao to market*. London and New York: Routledge.

Xue, C. Q. L., & Xiao, Y. (2017). The jewel in the crown—The heat of Grand Theaters. In L. Li & C. Xue (Eds.), *Chinese urbanism in the 21st century* (pp. 33–51). Beijing: China Building Industry Press. 薛求理, 肖映博 (2018). 皇冠上的明珠: "大剧院"热. 李磷, 薛求理 编, *21世纪中国城市主义*, 33–51. 北京: 中国建筑工业出版社.

Zou, B. (2016). The value and significance of Shenzhen's urban planning practice. In Urban Planning, Land & Resources Commission of Shenzhen Municipality, Time + Architecture Journal, *Shenzhen contemporary architecture* (pp. 112–115). Shanghai: Tongji Press. 邹兵 (2016). 深圳城市规划时间的价值和意义. 深圳市规划和国土资源委员会, 《时代建筑》 杂志 编著, 深圳当代建筑, 112–115. 上海: 同济大学出版社.

Chapter 5
Growth with the City: Theatrical Buildings in Chongqing

Dongzhu Chu and Kai Xue

5.1 Introduction: Development of Theatrical Buildings in Chongqing

In the twentieth century, the development of Chongqing was closely related to the development of China as a whole. Local theatrical buildings and even modern public cultural facilities date from the special historical period in which the city functioned as a provisional capital (Zhang 2012).

In 1937, Japanese troops launched an all-out war of aggression against China, and Nanjing, then the capital of China, found itself in a critical situation. On November 20 of the same year, Lin Sen (1868–1943), chairman of the National Government of the Republic of China, delivered the *Declaration on the Relocation of the National Government to Chongqing* in Hankou. On September 6, 1940, the national government officially confirmed Chongqing as its "provisional capital." On December 1, 1937, the national government officially designated Chongqing as its capital, and the city became the venue of the national government and the South Bureau of the Communist Party of China. It also hosted the Central Committee and served as the command center of the World Anti-Fascist Alliance in the Far East. With this change, Chongqing, a former riverside industrial city in the southwest region, became the political, military, economic, and cultural center of China. People from all walks of life rapidly moved to Chongqing, and numerous cultural institutions, cultural groups, and outstanding talents came to Chongqing for development. For example, the Central Film Studio and China Art Troupe relocated to Chongqing and staged such famous plays as *Qu Yuan* and *The Peacock's Gallbladder*. All of this swiftly boosted the prosperity of culture in Chongqing. The theatrical buildings represented by the Guotai Grand Theater began to emerge in this mountainous city with two rivers flowing through it (Fig. 5.1).

D. Chu (✉) · K. Xue
School of Architecture and Urban Planning, Chongqing University, Chongqing, China
e-mail: c.dz@vip.163.com

© Springer Nature Singapore Pte Ltd. 2019
C. Q. Xue (ed.), *Grand Theater Urbanism*,
https://doi.org/10.1007/978-981-13-7868-3_5

序号	建筑类别	建筑名称	地址
1		国泰	邹容路
2		民众	中正路（今邹华路）
3	电影	新川	中正路（今邹华路）
4		昇平	保安路（今八一路）
5		一园	中正路（今邹华路）
6		第二书场	保安路（今八一路）
7		第一剧场	民国路（今五一路）
8	戏剧	得胜大舞台	大同路
9		实验剧场	中山一路
10		第一川剧院	金汤街
11		第二川剧院	邹容路
12		抗建堂	中山一路
13	话剧	银社	道门口
14		青年馆	中华路

Fig. 5.1 Chongqing cultural map from the "provisional capital" era (Xie 2011)

With the founding of New China in 1949, Chongqing became the most important industrial base in southwest China and gave top priority to industrial development. At the same time, the construction of cultural buildings in Chongqing was nearly stagnant until the 1980s. It is worth mentioning, however, that the "Shancheng Wide-Screen Cinema" ("Shancheng" here literally means "mountainous city") was designed and constructed in the Lianglukou area, an important nodal place of Yuzhong Peninsula, in central Chongqing in 1958. Although it was demolished in 1996, it was an outstanding representative of the theatrical buildings in Chongqing after the founding of New China. The product of a design process directed by faculty members from the Chongqing Institute of Architecture and Engineering (today's Chongqing University), such as Prof. Huang Zhongshu and Wu Deji, the building achieved a high level of design in aspects such as the treatment of a 14 m level difference on the site and the acoustic design of the auditorium. With a cylindrical roof made up of triple continuous thin shells, the cinema measured 46 m in main body width (span) and 67 m in length. Its gross floor area was 3600 m^2, allowing it to accommodate 1500 people. It was the first special-grade cinema equipped to show 70 mm stereophonic films in western China and one of the most important theatrical buildings in Chongqing of the past half-century (Fig. 5.2) (Cai 2005, NBS 2018, Sina.cn 2013).[1]

---

[1]In 1960, the architectural model of Shancheng Cinema was sent to the Leipzig International Exposition for an exhibition. In 1990, it was rated as one of the "Top 10 Buildings in Chongqing in the First Forty Years after the Founding of the People's Republic of China." In January 1996, the Shancheng Wide-Screen Cinema was demolished due to a renovation of the old urban area.

Fig. 5.2 Rendering of the Shancheng Wide-Screen Cinema

In 1997, Chongqing resumed its status as a municipality under the direct control of the central government. After having been dormant for years, this important city in southwest China began a new round of rapid development. In May 1998, the government of Chongqing Municipality took international bids for the regulatory plan of Jiangbei town, covering an area of 2.69 km^2, and the urban design for an area of 1 km^2. This space was later promoted, in the name of the Jiangbei town CBD, as a "national financial district." The Chongqing Grand Theater was designated to stand on the southeast river bank of the district and began to develop by leaps and bounds. In July 2002, the solicitation for proposals for the "Urban Image Design of Yuzhong Peninsula" formally began, and Yuzhong Peninsula, Chongqing's "mother town," ushered in plans for a large-scale urban-space renovation. In April 2009, the municipal government proposed the *Master Plan of Liangjiang New Area of Chongqing* and in the following year officially set up the Liangjiang New Area. This area was the third state-level opening-up development, after the Pudong New Area in Shanghai and the Binhai New Area in Tianjin, and it was set up with the direct approval of the State Council (Fig. 5.3).

Meanwhile, Chongqing made great efforts to upgrade its previously feeble cultural infrastructure with the aim of blossoming into a "cultural center in the upper reach of the Yangtze River." At a key project meeting held in June 2003, Huang Zhendong, then the Communist Party Secretary of Chongqing, proposed the

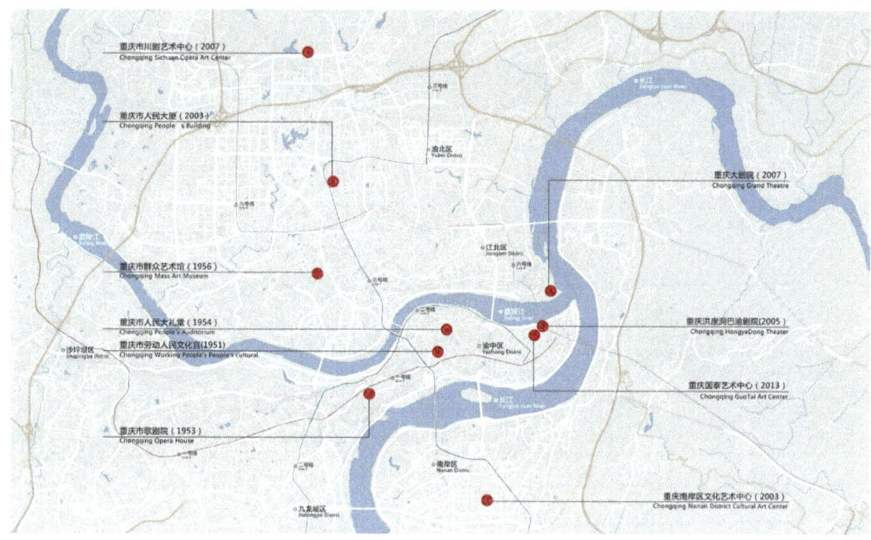

Fig. 5.3 Map of main performance buildings in Chongqing

"Ten Major Cultural Facilities Construction Project."[2] The theatrical building projects included the Chongqing Grand Theater, Chongqing Guotai Arts Center, Chongqing Sichuan Opera Theater, and People's Mansion, and their construction pace accelerated, fully compensating for the chronic lack of cultural activity centers in Chongqing. Large-scale theatrical buildings gradually became a focus in the renewal of the old urban area and the construction of the new urban area and acted as new drivers of the city's economic growth. Since 2003, Chongqing's GDP has maintained a growth rate of more than 11% annually (Table 5.1), making Chongqing the fifth city in China in 2017, although it was only eighth in total GDP in 2003 (NBS 2017).[3]

---

[2]In Chongqing's "10th five-year plan" formulated in 2001, Chongqing proposed to promote the construction of major cultural facilities, i.e., Chongqing Library, Shancheng Cinema, the Chongqing Grand Theater, the Chongqing Art Museum, the Guotai Grand Theater, and the Chongqing Children's Library. In June 2003, Huang Zhendong, then the Communist Party Secretary of Chongqing, proposed to complete the construction of ten major cultural facilities before 2008, i.e., Chongqing Library, the Shancheng Cinema, the Chongqing Grand Theater, the Chongqing Art Museum, the Guotai Grand Theater, the Chongqing Science and Technology Museum, the International Convention and Exhibition Center, the Children's Palace, the City Planning Exhibition Hall, and the Nanshan Botanical Garden. See Chongqing Daily, *Compose a New Chapter of Social Development,* August 19, 2004.

[3]In 2017, the top four Chinese cities ranked by GDP were Shanghai (RMB 3013.3 billion), Beijing (RMB 2800 Billion), Shenzhen (RMB 2228.6 billion), and Guangzhou (RMB 2150 billion). The data are from National Bureau of Statistics website, http://data.stats.gov.cn/easyquery.htm?cn=E0105. Accessed December 1, 2018.

Table 5.1 Changes in Chongqing's GDP since 1997, when Chongqing became a municipality directly under the central government (Li et al. 2014)

Year	Total GDP (RMB 100 million)	Growth rate (%)	Ranking among cities nationally
1997	1510	11.20	5
1998	1602	8.60	5
1999	1663	7.80	6
2000	1791	8.50	6
2001	1977	9.00	6
2002	2233	10.20	6
2003	2556	11.50	8
2004	3035	12.20	8
2005	3468	11.50	8
2006	3907	12.20	8
2007	4676	15.90	8
2008	5794	14.50	8
2009	6530	14.90	8
2010	7926	17.10	8
2011	10,011	16.40	8
2012	11,410	13.60	7
2013	12,783	12.30	7
2014	14,263	10.90	6
2015	15,717	11.00	6
2016	17,741	10.70	6
2017	19,500	9.30	5

5.2 The Chongqing Grand Theater in the CBD

Before the construction of the Chongqing Grand Theater, the main performance venue in Chongqing, in addition to the aforementioned Shancheng Wide-Screen Cinema, was Chongqing Auditorium (Fig. 5.4). Chongqing Auditorium, built in the 1950s, consists of four parts—the assembly hall and the east, south, and north towers. The assembly hall has a gross floor area of 18,500 m^2 and can accommodate over 3400 people. It hosts Chongqing's important political conventions and international conferences and some domestic and foreign performing arts activities. It is the most important cultural venue for the citizens of Chongqing. With the reform and opening-up of the 1980s, the level of cultural exchanges at home and abroad steadily increased, and the layout of Chongqing Auditorium came to seem inadequate to accommodate modern large-scale performances. After Chongqing became a municipality directly under the central government in 1997, the demand for a new theater became more urgent. In 2003, the planning scheme of

Fig. 5.4 Chongqing Auditorium

Fig. 5.5 Jiangbeizui CBD planning aerial view

Chongqing's CBD area was formally adopted. The site for a new grand theater was chosen at the tip of Jiangbeizui, where the Yangtze River and the Jialing River intersect (Fig. 5.5) (Gerkan et al. 2012).

In the same year, the government of Chongqing Municipality launched a global call for architectural design proposals for the Chongqing Grand Theater. As an "elegant and mass public cultural facility" (in the words of the design solicitation document), the grand theater project consisted of a grand theater with 1800 seats, a medium-scale theater with 800 seats, and a multi-functional rehearsal hall that could accommodate 300 audience members with corresponding ancillary and supporting facilities. It would satisfy the performance requirements for large-scale operas, ballets, variety shows, dramas, symphonies, and chamber music. The project had an overall footprint of 7000 m^2 and a projected total construction cost of up to RMB 800 million (USD 123 million).

The strikingly situated design project attracted extensive attention at home and abroad. Five companies—China Southwest Architectural Design and Research Institute Corp. Ltd, gmp from Germany + East China Architectural Design and Research Institute Co., Ltd., Hassell from Australia, the China Architecture Design and Research Group, and Arup Corporation from the UK—took part in the design competition. In February 2004, seven experts[4] from China, Spain, and the USA selected two of the five competing proposals and submitted them to the municipal government for its finalization and public announcement.

Proposal No. 2 (submitted by gmp from Germany + East China Architectural Design and Research Institute Co., Ltd.), called "a cruise on the river," highlighted the strong identity of the architecture by molding the building into the distinctive shape of a cruise ship. It called Chongqing "a giant ship heading for modernity and the future." The most eye-catching part of the design was the large glass façade: the roof and envelope of the building were made of organic glass similar to Chinese jade. The building thus made an intensely differentiated visual impact. Proposal No. 4 (designed by the China Architecture Design and Research Group) made separate arrangements for the three functions: a large-scale theater, a medium-scale theater, and a multi-functional rehearsal hall. The spaces were connected via corridors to reduce the total volume of the building. The image of "cobblestones" embodied the alignment between the characteristics of the building and the riverside environment. The most important feature of this proposal was its handling of and adaptability to the local terrain. In addition, the outstretched building lay on the site's slopes, integrating the circular plane of vision with the surroundings and the land form (Fig. 5.6).

Among the proposals that were not selected, No. 5, titled "Phoenix" and submitted by Arup Corporation from the UK, attracted widespread attention. By including an irregular curved façade, this proposal broke with the form of traditional theaters and was full of imagination and visual impact. Because of its complicated structure and high cost, however, it was not selected (Fig. 5.7) (Feng 2004).

In March 2004, the Chongqing Grand Theater Design Competition concluded. The municipal government decided after careful study to award the contract to the submitter of Proposal No. 2. It is unsurprising that the proposal designed by gmp and led by the German master architect Von Gerkan won the competition, because it had certain advantages in the control of the integral shape and construction costs. Although some online commenters called the shape a "tank" in the wake of the

---

[4]The Expert Evaluation Committee was composed of seven members, including professor and academician Zhong Xunzheng from Southeast University and the Spanish architect Ricardo Bofin.

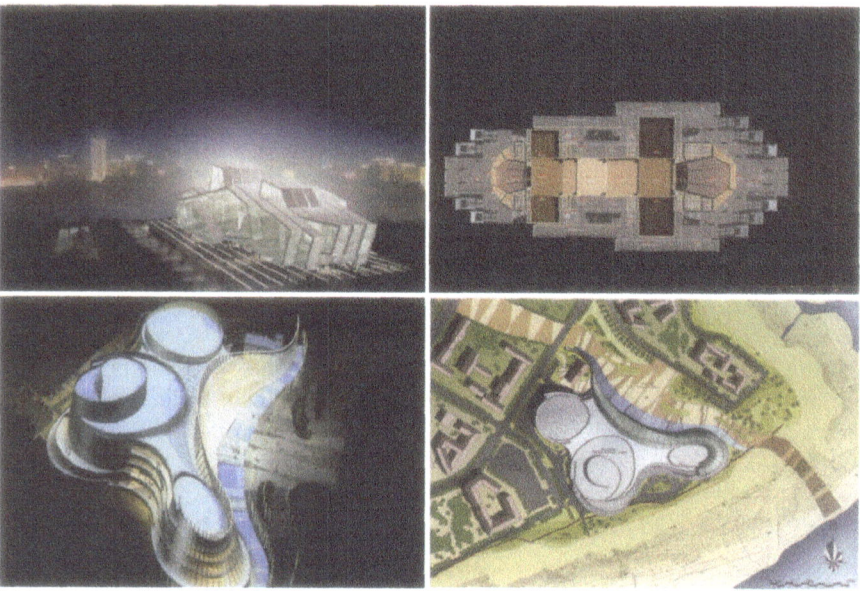

Fig. 5.6 Renderings of proposals No. 2 and No. 4

Fig. 5.7 Rendering of proposal No. 5

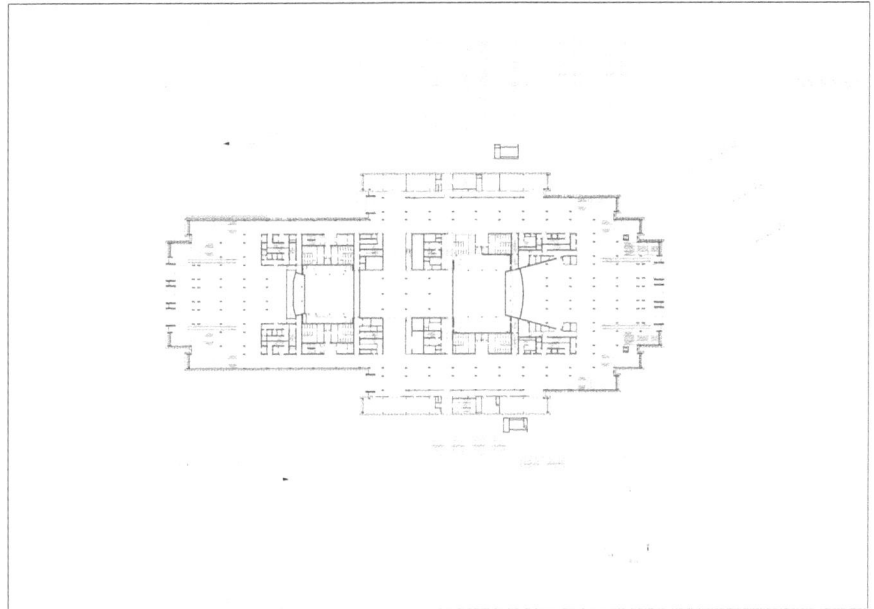

Fig. 5.8 First floor plan of the Chongqing Grand Theater

public announcement, Proposal No. 2's compact modeling and suggestion of "setting sail" appealed to the municipal leaders facing excellent development opportunities.

The Chongqing Grand Theater was completed in December 2009. Judging from the result, the proposal was implemented smoothly. The theater is about 220 m long from east to west and 110 m wide from north to south. The maximum height of the building is approximately 64.06 m. The internal structure of the theater is divided into seven floors above the ground and two underground floors with a 1826-seat large-scale theater and a 930-seat medium-scale theater. Like the National Center for the Performing Arts (Beijing, see Chap. 1) completed in 2007, the theater space of the Chongqing Grand Theater is enclosed in two glass envelopes, producing unity in its "imagery presentation" and "functional requirements" (Fig. 5.8). The main body of the theater stands on a stone base, hiding auxiliary rooms for electromechanical equipment and stage facilities. The dining facilities are widely distributed. A large-scale platform facing the boulevard of the city can also be used as an outdoor catering area. Since its completion, the Chongqing Grand Theater has become a top-grade theater with complete functions. It was ranked second in size in 2009, after only the National Center for the Performing Arts. It hosts numerous high-level domestic and foreign performances, with more than 160 shows on stage every year. It has become one of the most important centers for civil and cultural activities in Chongqing (Figs. 5.9 and 5.10) (Jiangbei 2006, Liang et al. 2005, Qi 2015).

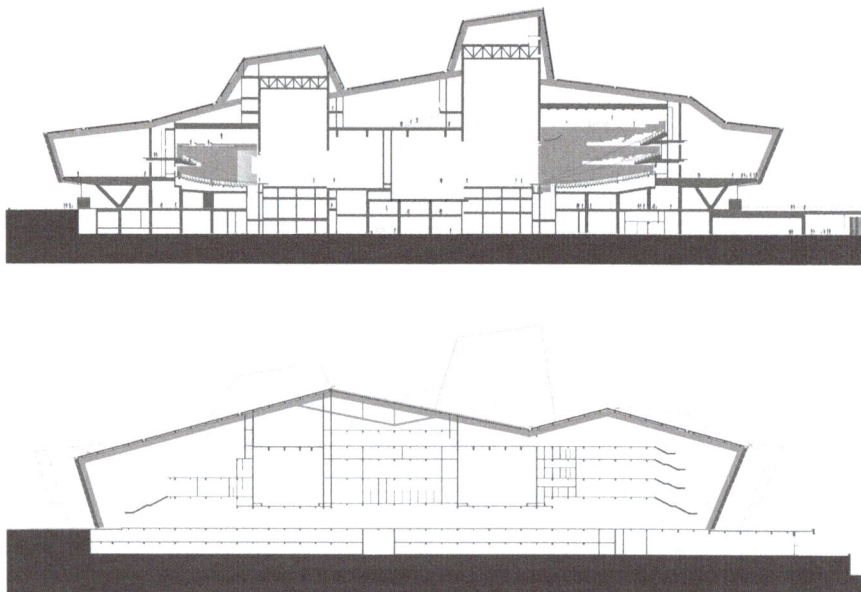

Fig. 5.9 Section plane of the Chongqing Grand Theater

Fig. 5.10 Chongqing Grand Theater—building, lobby and hall. Photo by Charlie Xue and Sun Cong

Nearly 10 years have now passed since the Chongqing Grand Theater was completed, and the Jiangbeizui CBD has also taken shape. If we take a closer look at this landmark building, it is not difficult to make the following objective appraisals (Li 2003).

(1) Although there was concern about certain obvious similarities that connect this design with the image presented in the proposal for the Oslo National Theater in Norway (not implemented) previously designed by gmp, it is undeniable that with its unique undulating body, the Chongqing Grand Theater has its own clear identity, standing in contrast to the multitude of cubic office buildings in Jiangbeizui. Its image is unforgettable from the first glance. Although the glittering and translucent façade presented in the design proposal did not completely materialize, the colorful and changing patterns and videos displayed on the huge wall at night improve the building's media presentation function, attracting people across the banks of the Jialing River and the Yangtze River.

(2) Although the Chongqing Grand Theater has a prominent image, it is unfortunately not perfectly integrated with the surrounding environment. As far as image is concerned, the highly complete modeling and rigid outdoor base make it a big city showpiece at the confluence of the two rivers, humorously called "a green tank without a barrel" by locals. Its colossal dimensions deprive it of intimacy. Because of its sharp boundaries, the building lacks spatial permeation between the interior and exterior and lacks a semi-outdoor entertainment space that would shelter people from sunlight and rain. In addition, these boundaries result in insufficient support for commercial space. Occasional shops have to be "hidden" in the theater with quiet business. The shortage of daily public facilities means that the large square is seldom visited by citizens.

(3) The main entrances and exits of the theater lie on both ends of the building, leading to an insufficient connection between its lateral sides and the environment. In addition, because the volume of the building is enormous, people have to walk long distances to watch performances. This feature is especially troublesome in bad weather.

(4) On the level of urban design, the Chongqing Grand Theater lacks a comprehensive connection to the peripheral traffic, and the planned underground walking system to connect with monorail stations has not yet been built. In addition, the parking lot is insufficient and occupies a large outdoor space, which makes the theater even less welcoming (Fig. 5.11).

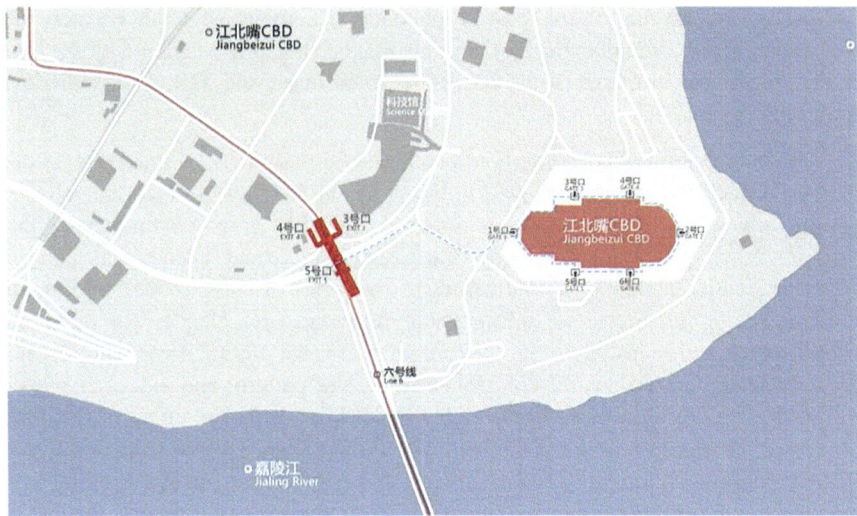

Fig. 5.11 Context of the Chongqing Grand Theater

5.3   The Rebirth of Guotai: History of the Guotai Arts Center

The predecessor of the Guotai Arts Center is the Guotai Grand Theater, which was the first modern large-scale theatrical building designed and constructed by Oriental Architects in 1937. Shortly after the completion of this building, the following comment was made: "In terms of magnificence, it occupies a leading position even in cinemas of Shanghai, and as far as exquisiteness and comfort are concerned, it epitomizes the achievements of modern science." In 1952, it was dismantled and rebuilt according to the design directed by Professor Ye Zhongji, Dean of Chongqing University's Department of Architecture, and renamed "Heping (peace) Cinema." During the period of the Cultural Revolution (1966–1976), it was renamed "Dongfanghong (the east is red) Cinema" (Table 5.2). As time went on, this once glorious center for the performing arts in Chongqing gradually declined and became a "wasteland" in the bustling downtown (Cui et. al 2013).

Table 5.2 History of the Guotai Grand Theater's name changes

Time	Event
1943	Drama performance was stopped; only films were shown
1951	Taken over by the department of culture and education in Southwest China
1953	Renamed "Heping (peace) Cinema"
1966	Renamed "Dongfanghong ('the east is red') Cinema"
1979	Resumed its previous name, "Heping (peace) Cinema"
1993	Renamed "Guotai Cinema"

In 2003, while the global bidding for the Chongqing Grand Theater Project was in full swing, the international tendering for the *Urban Image Design of Yuzhong Peninsula of Chongqing* (hereafter referred to as the *Image Design*) was completed, and its planning was eventually implemented through legislative protection.[5] Six famous design organizations at home and abroad competed for this urban renewal project: Pesch and Partner Architekten Stadtplaner from Germany; Architecture-Studio from France; Skidmore, Owings and Merrill LLP from the USA; Gensler from the USA; Shanghai Xian Dai Architectural Design (Group) Co., Ltd.; and Chongqing Planning and Design Research Institute. The evaluation experts set out to "fully tap the six design proposals, particularly the pros and creativities of the three winning proposals, based on the proposal by Pesch and Partner Architekten Stadtplaner from Germany to absorb the pros of all proposals." Finally, ten major image elements, including an "urban cap," an "urban balcony," and a "green corridor," were proposed, reinforcing the framing of Yuzhong District as Chongqing's "mother town."

In the nine key plots mentioned by the *Image Design*, the Guotai Arts Center (Fig. 5.12) was shifted from the plot where the former Guotai Cinema was located to a new plot for a cultural performance center. The project was defined as "an arts center integrating a grand theater and an art museum." Furthermore, the connection between the riverside plot and the non-riverside plot was taken into consideration to allow for elements such as "an urban balcony, a recreational waterfront, a mountainous city footpath, and a green corridor (Chongqing Planning and Natural Resources Bureau 2006)."

In October 2005, the "Solicitation for Architectural Proposals for the Chongqing Art Museum of the Guotai Grand Theater" was officially launched. This was the second theater project among the "ten major cultural facility projects" in Chongqing. It was conducted by domestic competition. The art museum was composed of a medium-scale hall with 800 seats, 2 small-scale halls intended for traditional dramas with 350 seats each, and a medium-scale art gallery. The total planned area was 9670 m². The government's proposal solicitation document defined it as "a palace of art embodying the elegant culture and the landmark building in Chongqing" and stated that the intention was to adopt "the architectural form in the traditional Chinese national style."[6]

At the beginning of the planning process, the project was filled with challenges: unlike the Chongqing Grand Theater, the Guotai Grand Theater project was located

---

[5]On November 24, 2003, the 6th Session of the 2nd Standing Committee of the People's Congress of Chongqing deliberated and passed the document titled *Regulations on Urban Image Design of Yuzhong Peninsula of Chongqing*, which offered legislative protection for the contents of the urban image designed through international bidding, such as "ten major creativities" and "nine major plots.", webpage of the Sina.cn., http://finance.sina.com.cn/g/20040115/0758603810.shtml.

[6]The text was excerpted from the circular titled *On the Solicitation for Architectural Proposals for Chongqing Art Museum of the Guotai Grand Theater issued by Chongqing Urban Planning Bureau*. See webpage of the Chongqing Planning and Natural Resources Bureau, http://www. cqupb.gov.cn/content.aspx?id=2487&iscehui=false. Accessed February 14, 2006.

Fig. 5.12 The design and
research range of the Guotai
Arts Center

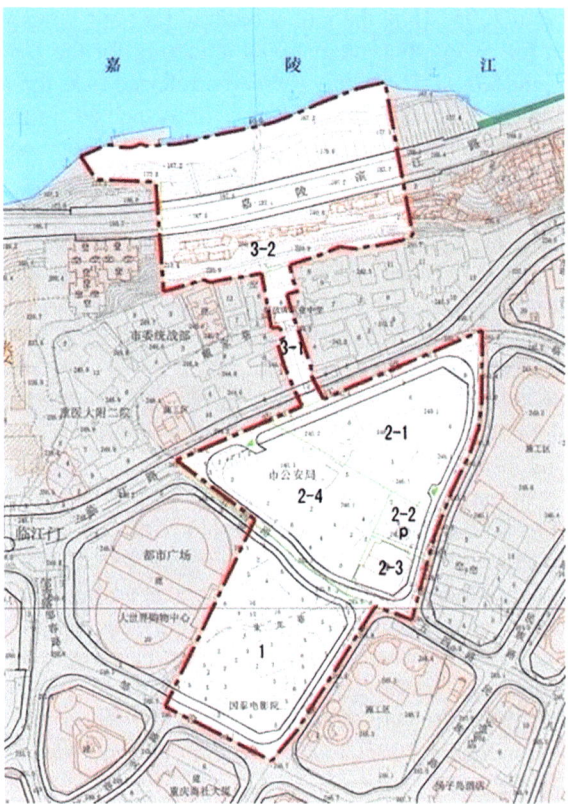

in the heart of Jiefangbei CBD in Yuzhong District, in a complicated surrounding environment containing both dense CBD high-rise buildings and time-honored residential buildings; with a height difference of 14 m, the site was connected to several main urban roads and central pedestrian streets; although neither the planned gross floor area nor the site area was large, a theater, an art gallery, and an auxiliary art classroom required a complicated functional mixture.

Two months later, 14 famous domestic architectural design units, including the China Architecture Design and Research Group, Chongqing University, the Central-South Architectural Design Institute, the China Southwest Architectural Design and Research Institute, and Tanghua Architect and Associates, submitted their proposals. According to the experts' voting results and a study by the leaders of Chongqing Municipality, four units, including the Central-South Architectural Design Institute, the China Southwest Architectural Design and Research Institute,

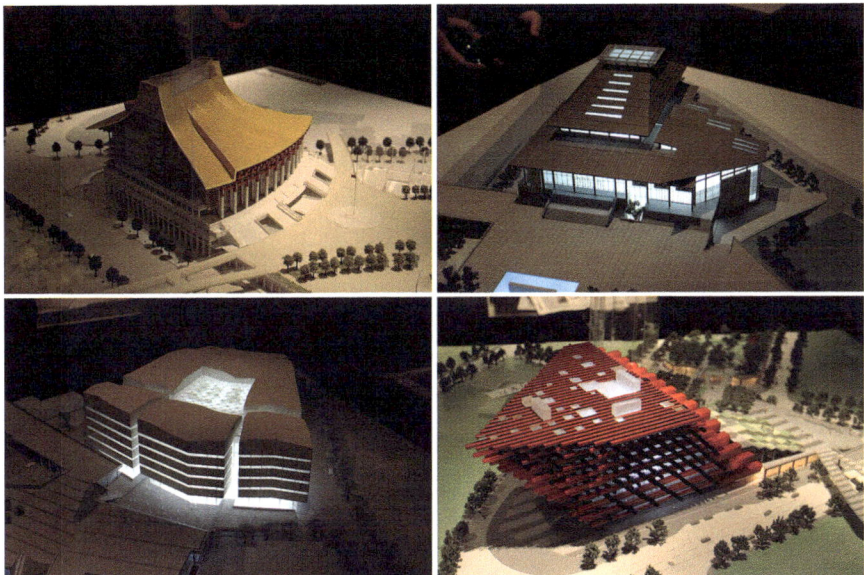

Fig. 5.13 Models of four proposals in the second round

and the China Architecture Design and Research Group,[7] entered the second round and made the corresponding modifications. Finally, the proposal by Chief Architect Cui Kai from the China Architecture Design and Research Group won the bidding process and began construction (Fig. 5.13) (Zhang et al. 2014).

In 2013, the Chongqing Guotai Arts Center[8] was officially completed after an eight-year effort. Composed of the Guotai Grand Theater and the Chongqing Art Museum, the Guotai Arts Center is divided into 10 floors, with 7 floors above ground and the others underground. It has one medium-scale theater with 800 seats,

---

[7]Among the four proposals that entered the second round and made the corresponding modifications, the proposals submitted by both the China Southwest Architectural Design and Research Institute and the Central-South Architectural Design Institute were biased toward pseudo-classical architecture and made use of traditional Chinese architectural elements to create a modern theater space, which conformed to the related requirements for architectural form as prescribed in the bidding document. The China Architecture Design and Research Group, which adopted modern design technique in its proposal, ranked only fourth in the first round and should not have entered the second round. However, the Communist Party Secretary and Mayor of Chongqing deemed that its proposal "would be really favored by civilians" after seeing the model at the bid evaluation scene, and recommended that the proposal enter the second round as a supplement with modifications made, so that the red building using the ancient Chinese wooden structure could win the voting in the second round.

[8]In September 2006, the Chongqing Guotai Grand Theater Project was officially named the Guotai Arts Center in its scheme. See the webpage of Sina.cn., http://cq.sina.com.cn/city/cqfb/2013-01-16/49640_2.html. Accessed January 16, 2013.

Fig. 5.14 The Chongqing Guotai Arts Center after completion

2 small-scale theaters with 350 seats each, 1 art museum exhibition hall, and 1 underground garage. With building coverage of 6500 m² and a gross floor area of 30,200 m², it has become an important public cultural space in Jiefangbei CBD (Fig. 5.14). By abstracting the collective memories of Chongqing, such as tenon-through dwellings, ancient Chines design vocabulary and skills to transform architectural forms, space, structures, colors, etc. In addition, through the connection with urban roads in different directions and at different elevations, the urban square, "urban forest," "urban balcony," urban art center, and other spaces have been created with an emphasis on the openness and connectivity of the building. E wooden structures, urban tree shades, and hot pot, Guotai Arts Center makes use of modern (Shi 1995).

Despite various setbacks encountered in the process of bidding and construction, the Guotai Arts Center shows favorable architectural qualities after completion.

(1) In consideration of the base elevation difference and the need to streamline the organization, the Guotai Arts Center was constructed in such a manner that the art museum and the Guotai Grand Theater are vertically arranged. Theaters and other large spaces are set up in the lower part, while the art museum and other relatively small spaces are in the upper part. Contrary to common practice and

Fig. 5.15 Main structure construction

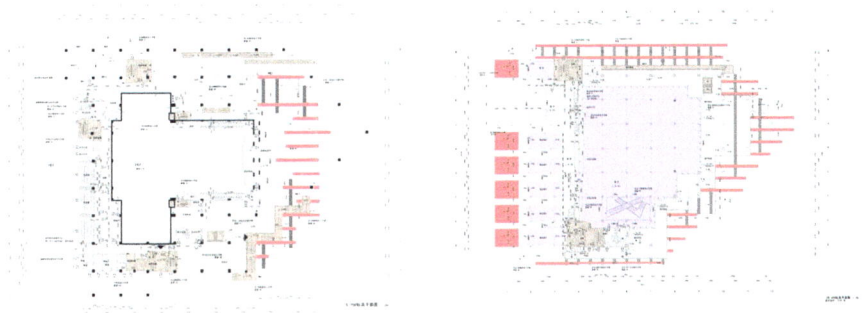

Fig. 5.16 The theater plane (left) and the art gallery plane (right)

despite structural challenges, the design offers an extensive spatial experience (Zhang et al. 2014).[9] (Figs. 5.15 and 5.16)

(2) In the treatment of the elevation difference, the Guotai Arts Center provides two outdoor platforms at different elevations, which form a rich spatial hierarchy and create many steps, platforms, and exhibition spaces that interact with the city. This means that the building is not an isolated body, but invites multi-layered exchanges with the city.

[9]The original structural scheme for the Guotai Arts Center was an all-steel framework system that could facilitate connections among various parts of the structure and realize a good integral ductility. However, to minimize costs, a system composed of a reinforced concrete framework shear wall and partial steel structures was eventually selected. See Zhang et al. (2014).

Fig. 5.17 Research model with BIM technology

(3) The architectural themed element called *ticou* (an ancient Chinese wooden
    structural element) was implemented in such a way that *ticou* is not only an
    important hallmark of the building, but also has functional importance: about
    40% of the *ticou* serve as equipment pipes, about 30% serve as load-bearing
    components, and about 30% serve as decoration components (Fig. 5.17). The
    ticou are integrated with the structures and equipment of the building through
    3D BIM technology. Although the application of hundreds of *ticou*[10] in the
    all-steel truss structure was somewhat controversial, the functional complexity
    is realized to some extent, achieving coherence between the building's skin and
    its generative logic.

On July 4, 2013, at the Seminar on the Chongqing Guotai Arts Center jointly
sponsored by the China Architecture Design and Research Group and *Urban
Environment Design* (UED), design experts from the design teams and all walks of
life in Chongqing shared their understandings of the scheme. Terms such as "fu-
sion," "urban space and built environment," and "order" were repeatedly mentioned, reflecting the design field's recognition and appreciation of this project.

The relationship between architecture and the city is never simple, however, and
the birth of an outstanding building depends not only on the designer's ability, but
also on the decision maker's vision. In the treatment of the relationship with the
city, the Guotai Arts Center presents distinctiveness in addition to controversy.

(1) In terms of publicity, Guotai Arts Center takes advantage of the two elevation
    differences to realize a connection with the periphery and takes into consid-
    eration the connection between underground business and metro stations
    (Fig. 5.18). These connections are commendable for such a new public struc-
    ture with complicated functions, built in the old urban area center. The public
    footpath connecting to Binjiang Road in the original proposal was canceled,
    however (Fig. 5.19), and the planned escalator connecting different elevations
    and many public activity spaces such as platforms and ramps are closed
    because of safety issues. Despite all this, it is obvious that the lack of openness
    caused by "management issues" goes beyond the scope of a discussion on
    architecture.

---

[10]To increase the richness of the architectural space and control costs, the more than 1300 pieces of
ticou in the original design were reduced to more than 680.

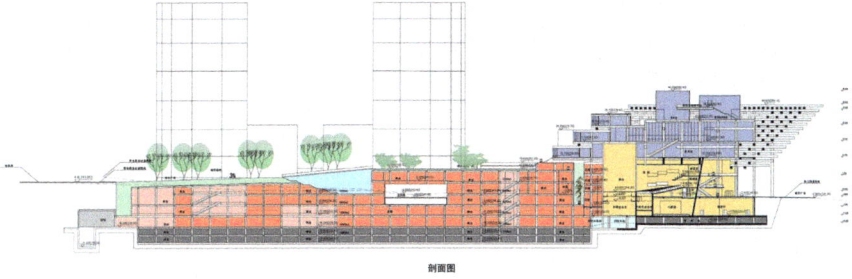

Fig. 5.18 Section plane of the Chongqing Guotai Arts Center with its surroundings

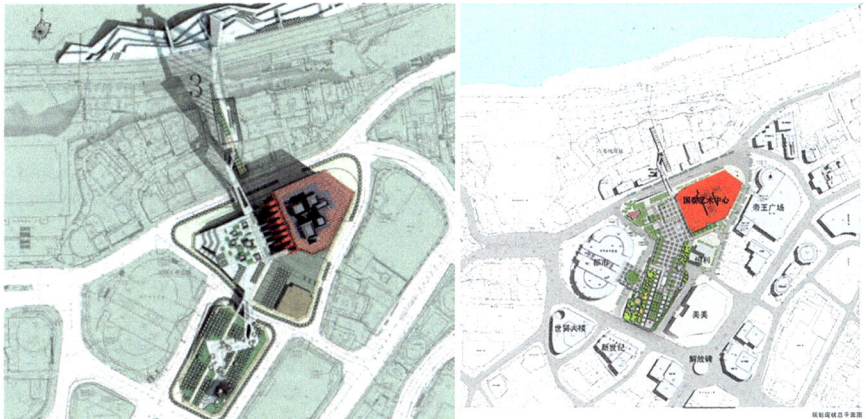

Fig. 5.19 Comparison of the master planes adjustment (left: design, right: implementation plan)

(2) In terms of architectural image, the torch-shaped architectural modeling is still flamboyant, and the "historical memory" and "genius loci" proposed in the design philosophy are not sufficiently presented. Nonetheless, the positive thinking on open space in a complicated urban environment, as reflected in the construction of the Guotai Arts Center, deserves appreciation and emulation.

5.4   Conclusion

Theatrical buildings are important embodiments of the cultural facility development level of a city, although there are usually few per city. Since opening to the world in the late nineteenth century, Chongqing has witnessed ups and downs—after the "opening" (1891), it became a "Yuan-controlled municipality" (1929), a "wartime capital" (1937), and the victim of the "Chongqing bombing" (1938–1943). It then became New China's "municipality directly under the central government" (1949), a "provincial city" (1954), a "municipality with independent planning status" (1983), a "municipality directly under the central government" for the second time (1997), a "national urban-rural coordinated and synthetically reformed testing district" (2009), and "one of the first batch of national central cities" (2010). Today, Chongqing has definitively developed into a center for economy, finance, scientific innovation, shipping, and business logistics in the upper reach of the Yangtze River, the important strategic pivot of West China Development and the important junction point between the "Belt and Road Initiative" and the Yangtze River Economic Zone. It is not hard to grasp that whenever the fate of a city undergoes a change, theatrical buildings are affected as well. The changes in culture, economy, and even political status are inevitably mapped onto the development and use of theatrical buildings.

During the War of Resistance against Japanese invasion (1937–1945), cultural and political resources from throughout China were gathered in Chongqing, owing to its status as the wartime capital. This development gave rise to the birth of important theatrical buildings such as the Guotai Grand Theater. Moreover, because performing arts activities could intuitively and vividly reflect current affairs, eulogize culture, and enhance morale, a large number of patriotic performing arts workers used the stage as a smokeless battlefield and made important and distinctive contributions to the war. After the founding of New China, Chongqing, shouldering a different historical mission, stood at a new starting line. A rich and novel cultural life was still its people's common desire. With cutting-edge technology and an audacious design, the Shancheng Wide-Screen Cinema brought to the citizens of Chongqing a brand-new experience of watching films and a strong sense of civic pride. The cinema was the earliest new-type cinema especially designed and built for showing wide-screen films in China and the first special-grade cinema that was capable of showing 70 mm stereophonic films. The Shancheng Wide-Screen Cinema left numerous citizens in the mountainous city with wonderful memories. Regrettably, the neglect of culture in the subsequent decades led to Chongqing's lackluster efforts in the construction of theatrical buildings.

It was not until 1997, when Chongqing once again became a municipality directly under the central government, that the theatrical buildings were developed in a real sense. Without leaving Chongqing, local citizens could now enjoy abundant high-level performances. Today, attending plays, operas, concerts, children's plays, *quyi* (Chinese folk art forms), etc. has become a leisure activity for citizens wishing to upgrade their cultural attainment. In this mega-city with a population of over 10 million, further improvements in the number and types of theatrical buildings are needed. In addition to the large-scale iconic buildings, more medium- and small-scale theatrical buildings with a wider distribution need to be developed. In the future, the features and advantages of this mountainous city with its complicated terrain will be enhanced by these buildings, which are more flexible and amenable to everyday use. We are looking forward to the emergence of theatrical buildings with more Chongqing characteristics.

My personal experience in Chongqing began in 1997, when it was directly administered by the central government. In the 1990s, the GDP of the city hovered between third and fifth for all of China. However, the funds used for urban cultural infrastructure were meagre.

The provincial city of Chengdu, around 300 km from Chongqing, built a comprehensive artistic 'Jincheng' palace with a GFA of 20,000 m^2 in the 1980s that could accommodate various performances, conferences and exhibitions. There was no such cultural facility in Chongqing even in the 1990s, and people there have waited a long for high-class cultural buildings.

I clearly remember the process of several important design competitions, such as those for the Chongqing Grand Theatre and Guotai Arts Centre. The model and perspective drawings were showcased to citizens in exhibitions and online when China's internet was in its infancy. We viewed those pictures in our student dormitory, enduring slow Internet speeds. We enthusiastically participated in the construction of this old industrial city with high hopes. This change was tremendous and unforgettable. After my overseas study, I decided to return to Chongqing because this once rough and derelict industrial base was rapidly becoming a modern city. It called to a young man doing architectural study.

After the construction of several landmark buildings, the cultural genes should penetrate to micro urban spaces and bring culture to the city and people. I expect to see a rich and diversified performing art space established in Chongqing. The hilly topography complements the architecture of this city. In the years ahead, the performing art buildings in Chongqing will present more varied characteristics and colours.

References

Cai, Z. (2005). Good foundation and pragmatic planning—Introduction to the controlled detailed planning experience of Chongqing Jiangbeicheng (CBD). *Beijing Planning and Construction, 2005*(01), 98–105. 蔡震(2005). 良好的基础与务实的规划—重庆江北城(CBD)控制性详细规划经验介绍. 北京规划建设, *2005*(01), 98–105.

Cui, W., Qin, Y., Jing, Q., Zhang, G. Y., & Xia, Z. (2013). Character from tradition to modernity—Chongqing Guotai Art Center Construction Ji. *Urban Environment Design, 2013*(12), 38–77. 崔愷,秦莹,景泉,张广源,夏至(2013). 品格,从传统到现代—重庆国泰艺术中心建造纪. 城市环境设计, *2013*(12), 38–77.

Chongqing Planning and Natural Resources Bureau. (2006). About the collection of the architecture plan of Chongqing Art Museum of Guotai Grand Theatre. 关于国泰大戏院重庆美术馆建筑方案征集. 重庆市规划和自然资源局. http://www.cqupb.gov.cn/content.aspx?id=2487&iscehui=false. Accessed February 14, 2006.

Feng, N. (2004, Feb 10). Two programs compete for the Chongqing Grand Theatre. *China Construction News*. 冯宁(2004年2月10日). 两方案角逐重庆大剧院. 中华建筑报.

Gerkan, M., Wrentz, K., Esch, H., & Heiner, L. (2012). Chongqing Grand Theatre. *Urban Environment Design, 2012*(07), 74–83. 曼哈德·冯·格康, 克劳斯·楼茨, Hans-Georg Esch, Heiner Leiska (2012). 重庆大剧院. 城市环境设计, *2012*(07), 74–83.

Jiangbei Today. (2006). Chongqing Jiangbei City. *Chongqing and the world, 2006*(02), 44–47. 今日江北(2006). 重庆江北城. 重庆与世界, *2006*(02), 44–47.

Liang, D. S., Lei, Z. Y., & Shi, M. (2005). Analysis of the collection plan of Chongqing Grand Theatre. *Architectural Journal, 2005*(01), 59–61. 梁鼎森, 雷尊宇, 石玫(2005). 重庆大剧院征集方案评析. 建筑学报, *2005*(01), 59–61.

Li, G. (2003). For the Chongqing Grand Theatre before the construction. *Art Science and Technology, 2003*(02), 18–19. 李国棋 (2003). 为建设前的重庆大剧院. 艺术科技, *2003*(02), 18–19.

Li, X. R., Fan, J. F., & Xiao, Z. Y. (2014). Environmental achievement landmark building— Taking Chongqing Grand Theatre and Sydney Opera House as examples. *Huazhong Architecture, 32*(09), 33–38. 李小蓉,缪剑峰,肖紫怡(2014). 环境成就地标建筑—以重庆大剧院与悉尼歌剧院为例. 华中建筑, *32*(09), 33–38.

NBS. (2018). National Bureau of Statistics of China. *Data.stats.gov.cn.* http://data.stats.gov.cn/easyquery.htm?cn=E0105. Accessed December 1, 2018.

Qi, X. M. (2015). *The urban form and evolution of the Yuzhong Peninsula in Chongqing.* Chongqing University. 綦晓萌(2015). 重庆渝中半岛城市形态及其演变. 重庆大学.

Shi, M. (1995). Chongqing Guotai Grand Theatre replays the glory. *New Cultural Historical Materials, 1995*(02), 10. 石曼(1995). 重庆国泰大戏院重放光辉. 新文化史料, *1995*(02), 10.

Sina.cn. (2013). Guotai Grand Theatre turned gorgeously to a new identity. 国泰大戏院华丽转身. 新浪网. http://cq.sina.com.cn/city/cqfb/2013-01-16/49640_2.html. Accessed January 16, 2013.

Xie, X. (2011). Research on urban construction and planning in Chongqing from 1937 to 1949. South China University of Technology. 谢璇 (2011). 1937–1949年重庆城市建设与规划研究. 华南理工大学.

Zhang, J., Jing, Q., & Shi, W. (2014). Searching for the spirit of the place in the historical memory of the city—Interview with Guotai Art Center. *Architectural Skills, 2014*(08), 64–75. 张洁,景泉,施泓 (2014). 在城市的历史记忆中寻找场所精神—国泰艺术中心访谈. 建筑技艺, *2014*(08), 64–75.

Zhang, T. (2012). Research on the development of Chongqing and Changchun cities during the Anti-Japanese war. Zhejiang University. 张涛(2012). 抗战时期重庆与长春城市发展研究. 浙江大学.

Chapter 6
The Henan Art Center: From Dilemma to Ambition

Lujia Zhang

In China, the Yellow River is called the "mother river." It flows through the central part of China and has been a center of agriculture for thousands of years, with the Central Plain Civilization spreading out from its fertile edge. Cities extend across the river plains, forming Henan Province, which has a large population that still mainly depends on agriculture. Zhengzhou, the capital city, has historically been strategically and culturally important.

Since the People's Republic of China was established, the increasing demand for railway lines and logistics has made Zhengzhou an important transportation hub, with the largest railway marshalling yard in China. However, due to weak industrial base, Henan's provincial cities have fallen behind other Chinese cities in development, with general economic policies and slow economic growth. Compared to other provinces, Henan's economic strength is ranked in the middle or below.

The Reform and Opening policy began a period of rapid urbanization in China, which brought an acceleration in the rate of economic growth in the 1990s. Cities made ambitious plans for urban expansion and thousands of development zones and new urban districts were planned and constructed, creating a large "Urbanization Wave." At that time, the old city area of Zhengzhou was more than 120 km^2 with a population of almost 2 million, while the level of urban expansion was ranked at the bottom for Henan province, and 10% lower than the national average (Fig. 6.1). All of these backward indicators created a dilemma for the government. To address this embarrassing situation, the Henan government set a new goal in their 10th Five-Year Plan and further confirm it in the 11th Five-Year Plan[1]

---

[1] The 10th Five-Year Plan and the 11th Five-Year Plan both explicitly mention the development and meaning of Zhengdong New District, as well as other development zones, to reach the goals of urbanization construction. See People's Government of Henan Province (2001a, b, 2006).

L. Zhang (✉)
Department of Architecture and Civil Engineering, City University of Hong Kong, Kowloon, Hong Kong
e-mail: luj.zhang1989@foxmail.com

© Springer Nature Singapore Pte Ltd. 2019
C. Q. Xue (ed.), *Grand Theater Urbanism*,
https://doi.org/10.1007/978-981-13-7868-3_6

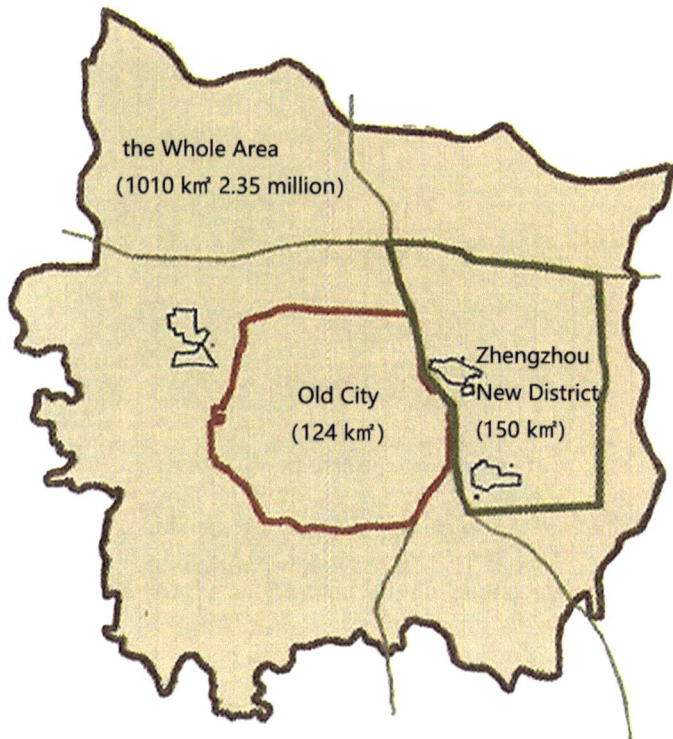

the Whole Area
(1010 km² 2.35 million)

Old City
(124 km²)

Zhengzhou
New District
(150 km²)

Fig. 6.1 Old city and the planned Zhengdong New District (1990s)

(People's Government of Henan Province 2001a, 2006): to establish large-scale development zones and buildings. The aim was to achieve the same speed of development as other cities, and even gain a top ranking in the future.

6.1 City Development—The Zhengdong New District

As the urban expansion experiences in other districts worldwide, the attempt at the first stage is not always successful as expected. Same situations happened in Zhengzhou. Early in 1988, when large cities with advanced economic conditions in China started to accelerate their urbanization speed, a major urban expansion project also began in the northwest area of the old city in Zhengzhou: the Zhengzhou High-Tech Industrial Development Zone. In the first few years, groups of high-tech industries moved in and the zone grew rapidly. In a short period, the city achieved an efficient and fruitful outcome in the form of many factories being built and put into use. The number of half completed city blocks seemed to indicate future expansion.

However, after the initial infrastructure was constructed, the dangers of blindly following a trend were revealed. Large factories made the blocks unsuitable for walking and the low number of residential communities and shops made it hard to attract people to live in the area. The commercial street at the zone entrance, which imitated other famous cases, had received thousands of negative comments even before its real opening. The tertiary industry declined quickly. Even worse, several suburban villages became urban villages due to urban expansion, and it was difficult to manage this diverse area in a unified way. All these poorly planned elements resulted in an embarrassing situation—a 70 km² high-tech development zone with a population of only 200,000. There were hardly any people to be seen on the streets, and transportation was inconvenient from the city center to the development zone (Xia and Yin 2006).

This high-tech development zone soon became a negative example of blindly imitating successful cases of urban planning. As a result, the government appeared to be very cautious and hesitant about extending construction to the eastern district of the city. Furthermore, their original plan for the eastern district still expressed short-sighted ambitions and few creative ideas. At the beginning of 2001, the Eastern District Plan initiated by Zhengzhou Municipal Government proposed a new district of less than 20 km² on the site of the former Air Force Airport. Unsurprisingly, the plan was rejected by Li Keqiang, the governor of Henan Province at that time. He suggested that Zhengzhou should abandon the "big cake" style of urban expansion and seek higher vision and goals to formulate more successful long-term plans and layouts (The People's Government of Henan Province 2001a, b).[2] In response, in July 2001, the Urban Planning Compilation and Research Center was set up by the government, which launched an international competition for an overall master plan for the Zhengdong New District.

At the beginning of the competition, 16 famous national and international design companies were invited to join the competition. After the first round of selection and negotiation, six companies entered the second round: the Arte Charpentier Architects from France, the PWD Corporation from Singapore, the COX Architects from Australia, the Chinese Institute of Urban Planning and Design, SASAKI Associates from the USA, and Kisho Kurokawa Architect & Associates from Japan.

Zhengzhou is an old city on the North China Plain. The old city area has a typical latitude and longitude square road grid with hardly any slopes, as is common in China's central plains. Zhengzhou has been called the "Green City" for a long time, and big plane trees can still be seen everywhere shading the city roads. Two important railways—the Longhai Line and the Beijing-Guangzhou Line—pass through the city center and join at the old railway station. Balancing the characteristics of new districts with the old city is a difficult challenge for urban planners.

In the end, Kurokawa's plan seemed to have an absolute advantage over the other five entries. He interpreted the two main railway lines as two "V" axes joined at the cusp. The layout clearly distinguished the new district from the old city, and

---

[2]Li Keqiang was the vital person who made the decision of the Zhengdong New District. In 2015, Li Keqiang visited Zhengdong New District as Prime Minister. He affirmed the achievements and directions that the government had chosen. See Qiao (2015).

boldly used a circular road grid that formed two circular central business districts (CBDs). Impressed by these surprising designs, the government favored Kurokawa in an obvious way (Fig. 6.2). During the 1990s, Kurokawa had participated in big planning projects for several new districts in China, including the Futian Central District of Shenzhen, Changfeng Culture and Business District of Taiyuan, and so on and his accumulated experience may have given him a better idea of what the governments like and how Chinese culture is expressed in a city (Xue 2006, 2010). In contrast, the designs of the other five companies had relatively obvious drawbacks. The plans of PWD Corporation, the Arte Charpentier Architects, and the Chinese Institute of Urban Planning and Design seemed too generic with few creative elements, whereas the plans of the SASAKI Associates and COX Architects were not suitable for the real situation of Zhengzhou. Unsurprisingly, Kurokawa's plan impressed the judges, and his years of work in China were capped with success (Fig. 6.3) (Zhengzhou Zhengdong New District Administration Committee and Zhengzhou Urban Planning Bureau 2010a, b).

The CBD of Zhengdong New District has a ring-shaped road grid. Kurokawa explained that this type of road grid reduces vehicle congestion during peak hours. Kurokawa was expressing his ideal city as metabolism concept through this form. This also met the needs of the government, which was eager for a unique urban design that would break up the existing rectangular road grid. Similar choices were made throughout China during that period. Urban layouts in China were being transformed from central administrative buildings within a grid with straight axes to cultural architecture centered in grids with gentle and changeable forms. Older planning embodied a strong orientation, whereas a circular shape without a single directional trend was the preferred choice of the new governments (Fig. 6.4).

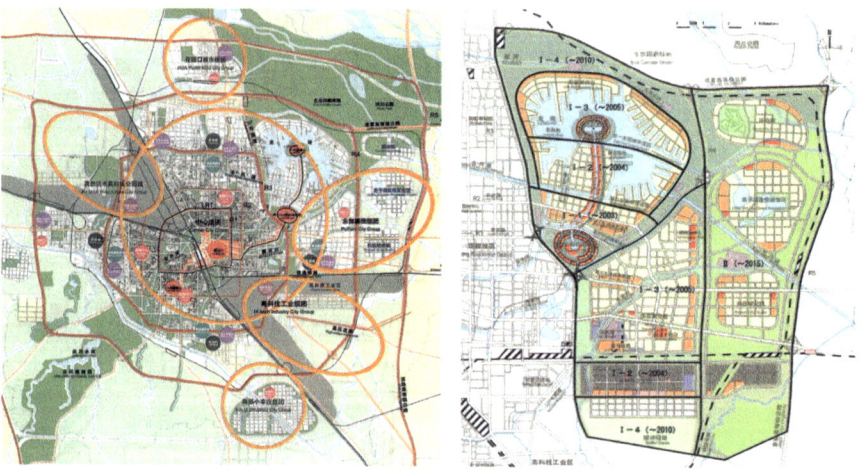

(a) Two important railways pass across the city center. Kurokawa made them the main axis with "V" shape in his master plan.

(b) Kurokawa's Plan for the Zhengdong New District

Fig. 6.2 Design proposal of Kurokawa Kisho

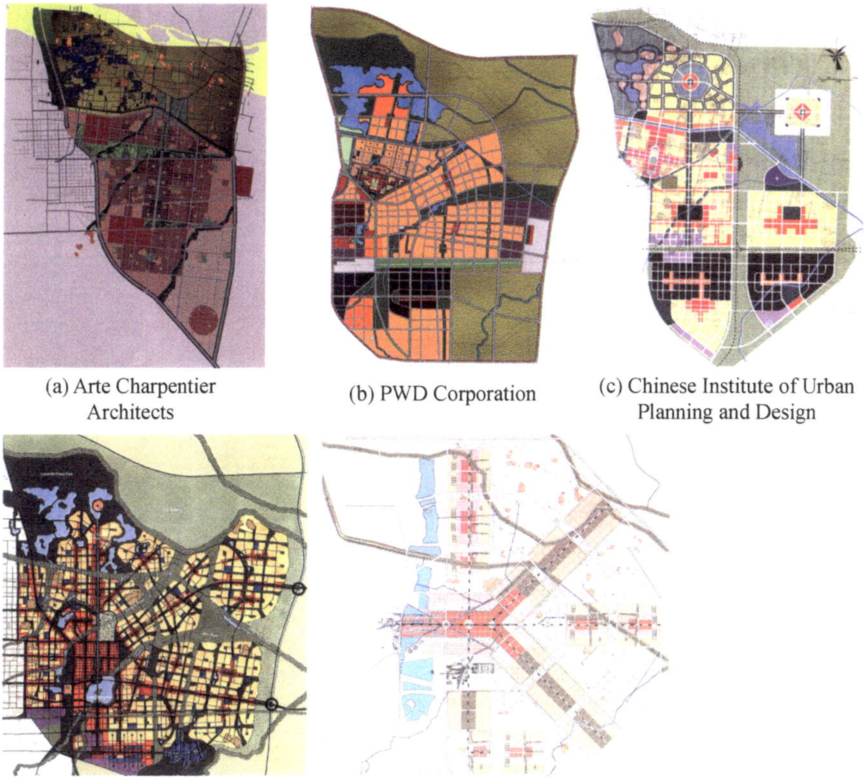

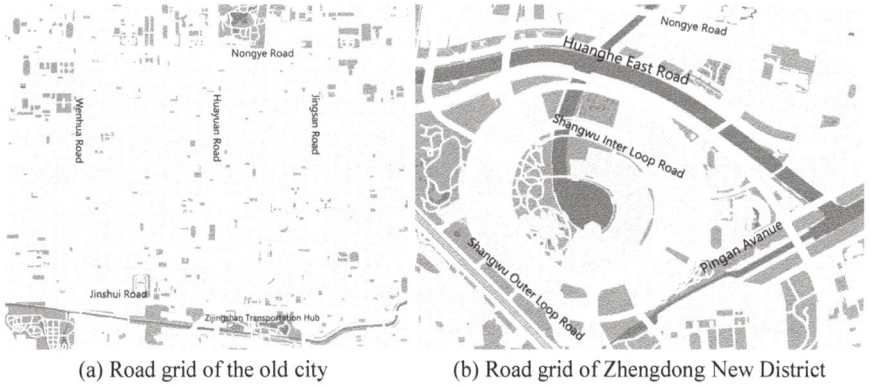

(a) Arte Charpentier Architects

(b) PWD Corporation

(c) Chinese Institute of Urban Planning and Design

(d) SASAKI Associates

(e) COX Architects

Fig. 6.3 Competition plans of the five other design companies

(a) Road grid of the old city

(b) Road grid of Zhengdong New District

Fig. 6.4 Comparison of the old and new road grids

6.2   CBD Construction and Group Building Development Strategy

The planned construction area for Zhengdong New District was 150 km^2, which was almost the same scale as the original old city. To avoid a blind "big pie" expansion, the plan set out a comprehensive strategy of developing groups of buildings. Kurokawa's scheme divided the new district into several groups, including the CBD, Longhu Business District, Commercial and Residential Logistics Zone, Longzihu University Zone, High-Tech Zone, and Economic and Technological Development Zone. Mixed functions were planned and built sequentially.

The first buildings in the CBD were three iconic public buildings in the center of the district: the Zhengzhou International Convention and Exhibition Center, the Zhengzhou Greenland Plaza (the Convention Hotel), and the Henan Art Center. They are the most eye-catching structures in the plan. Around an artificial lake in the center, there are two circles of commercial buildings. The height of the buildings in the inner circle is a bit lower than that of the buildings in the outer circle. The construction also extended outward to other building groups, particularly residential buildings and basic infrastructure facilities. As Zhengzhou's importance as a logistics center and transportation hub grows, the exhibition center will meet the urgent demand for a large-scale and high-quality exhibition space. Reflecting the government's emphasis on cultural development, the Henan Art Center was designed as not only a theater building, but also a unique artistic symbol in its own right. On January 20, 2003, the Zhengzhou International Convention and Exhibition Center held a groundbreaking ceremony, to officially begin the construction of Zhengdong New District.

The government slogan was "Image establishment in three years; scale forming in five years." In the first few years of construction, the three iconic buildings and circle of office buildings described above were quickly completed and put into use. Even so, Zhengdong New District was once criticized in the media as one of the biggest "ghost towns" in China. The residential areas had incomplete supporting facilities, keeping the occupancy rate low, and leading to empty streets and an unwelcoming atmosphere. The controversial large-scale ring-shaped road grid made it difficult for people to find their way. Some taxies even refused to take guests there (Yu et al. 2010).

The "Rise of Central China" policy greatly increased investment in cites in central China, but the amount was still not satisfactory. After the rapid large-scale construction projects in the first decade, the growth slowed to less than the planned rate. Luckily, with the increasing number of residential quarters and ancillary facilities, the area has gradually got rid of the "ghost city" title. Now the CBD area has bustling businesses and crowds of people.

6.3   Site Selection of Henan Art Center

The construction of the Henan Art Center had already been proposed by the government in the 1990s, during the period of the "Ninth Five-Year Plan." Due to complications in the site selection process, it was not implemented during this period. After 2000, the government once again pursued the construction of the Henan Art Center, and organized experts to propose new sites. Three locations were originally proposed: the experimental field of the Henan Academy of Agriculture Science, a site to the west of the Henan Museum, and the former Air Force Airport. The first two were located on the Nongye (agriculture) Road, which is the main road of the old city, very close to the Henan Museum. The third site was located at the Air Force Airport, which is now the CBD of Zhengdong New District. The Henan Museum designed by Academician Qi Kang is one of the landmark buildings in the old city. With its large number of archaeological artifacts, it is a symbol of the city's deep history and culture. In the site selection process, the government noted that in the first two options an influential building group could be formed by juxtaposing the Henan Museum with the new cultural building. The third option would create a building group in the CBD with the exhibition center and the high-rise hotel, producing an iconic skyline (Fig. 6.5).

After several rounds of discussion, the government chose the site in Zhengdong New District for a number of reasons: a wide geographical area for construction, a large potential audience, convenient transportation, enough space for evacuation, and suitable for creating a grand impression. On January 23, 2002, at the No. 135 executive meeting, the government officially confirmed the selection of the Zhengdong New District site (former Air Force Airport). The project proposal was approved on July 1, 2002.

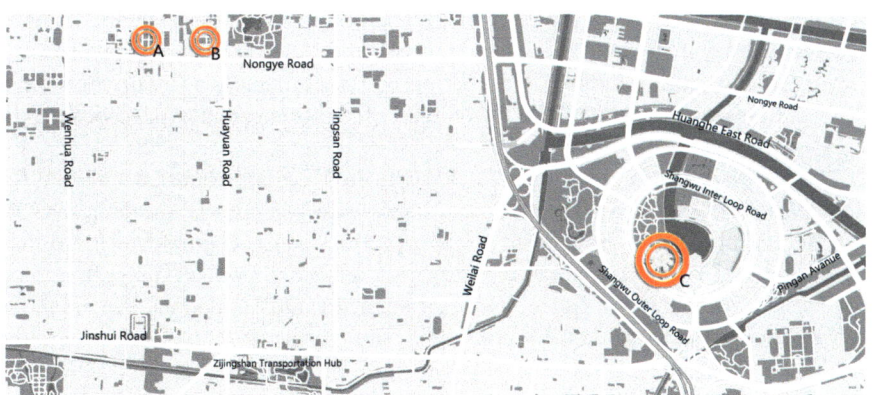

Site A: East side of the Henan Museum.

Site B: South of Henan Academy of Agricultural Science, in the experimental field.

Site C: Center of the CBD.

Fig. 6.5 Potential sites

The final confirmation and implementation of the Henan Art Center project has greatly improved the city's cultural architecture and the standard of performing venues in Zhengzhou, which was lower than other provincial capital cities. The best existing performance venue at the time was the Henan People's Hall. The others were small-scale venues that usually included a cinema.

6.4 Previously Existing Performance Venues in Zhengzhou

The city of Zhengzhou used to be a county. In 1954, the government made it the capital of Henan Province. Since then, the Henan People's Theater, Dongfanghong ("The East is Red") Theater, Zhongzhou Theater (now renovated as the Zhongyuan Grand Stage), and the Henan People's Hall were successively built.[3] They have all played important roles in the daily culture and entertainment of the city. The Henan People's Theater and the Henan People's Hall have been the main performing arts spaces, with traditional stages, conference rooms, and other ancillary functions, whereas the Dongfanghong Theater and the Zhongzhou Theater are smaller venues with successful operations.

Traditional theaters do not require high standards of physical environments. Most of the daily cultural activities are local operas and similar performances. Western operas and dramas are rare. Local dramas, such as the Yu Opera, Peking Opera, and Huangmei Opera are the most common performances. The Henan Yu Opera Troupe, which is one of the eight major opera groups in China, and the Henan Peking Opera Troupe are well-known local opera groups.

The Dongfanghong Theater, built in 1949, was originally a cultural station (club) of the Youth League of the Fourth Field Army. It has had a series of names, including the Zhongyuan (central China) Theater, People's Theater, and Baihua (hundred flowers) Theater. In 1969, it was named the Dongfanghong Theater. Playing movies during the day and offering live performances at night, the theater gradually took on a crucial role in the cultural life of Zhengzhou over its decades of successful operation.

The Zhongzhou Theater was built in 1979. It is a comprehensive building for stage performances, film projection, and conference receptions. The largest of its four auditoriums is equipped with a big stage that can accommodate more than 1600 people. In the twenty first century, the technical level of the Zhongzhou Theater had without doubt fallen below the standards of commercial theaters in the fiercely competitive market. Accordingly, the government has renovated the

---

[3]At that time, Chinese theaters usually had names with political meanings.

theater, changing the name to the Zhongyuan Grand Stage and made it a relatively high standard performing venue without a cinema.

The Henan People's Theater was built in 1953. It had the best facilities in Zhengzhou for years and was the first choice for welcoming political leaders. When the Erqi District was renovated in 2005, the demolition of the Henan People's Theater triggered wide-ranging discussions in the city. A new high-rise shopping mall and a hotel representing an investment of over 2 billion RMB (around $US290 million) was built on the original site. On the sixth floor, there is a small theater with 239 seats that is a pale shadow of the Henan People's Theater.

Founded in 1978, the Henan People's Hall was completed in 1979 with a performing hall of 2450 seats. Larger than the Henan People's Theater, it was able to host large-scale cultural performances. Before the opening of the Henan Art Center, the Henan People's Hall was the only locale for various large-scale performances. Halls are mainly used for gatherings, cultural performances, and conferences and have average basic requirements. The standards for sight lines and reverberation times are much lower than in professional modern theaters.

As this discussion shows, since the 1990s, medium-sized Chinese cities like Zhengzhou have been planning modern theater buildings to meet the urgent demand for professional performing venues (Fig. 6.6).

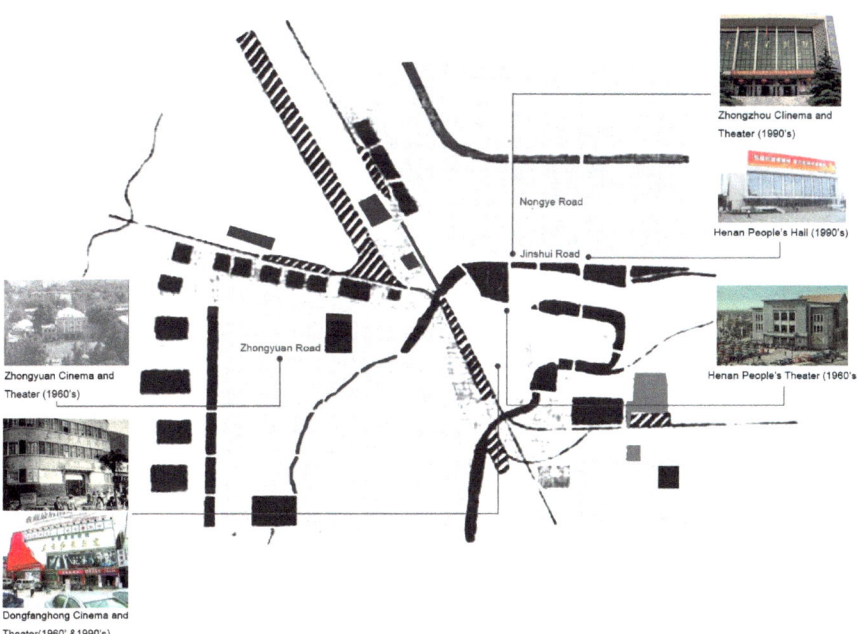

Fig. 6.6 Main theater buildings in Zhengzhou

6.5   Competition and Construction of the Henan Art Center

Since 2000, the demand for larger and more frequent cultural activities has greatly increased. Existing theater buildings limited this development and some influential international cultural exchange activities could not be held. According to government statistics, in 2003 there were approximately 90 international cultural exchange programs organized in Henan Province. Building a high-standard multi-functional art center became an extremely urgent issue.

The city had great expectations of the Henan Art Center. Establishing a dedicated group of experts and officials for the project, the government authorized the Cultural Department of Henan Province to take the lead. On January 6, 2003, the Henan Art Center Construction Engineering Office published an announcement in *China Daily, China Construction News*, and *China Procurement and Tendering Network* that international bids would be sought for planning the Zhengdong New District. Nearly 20 national and international design companies signed up to participate.

After a round of screening, seven design companies entered the second round: OTT/PPA Architects; Beijing Institute of Architectural Design; Central South Architectural Design Institute; China Aviation Planning and Design Institute (Group) Co., Ltd; LMK Architects; Shanghai Xian Dai Architectural Design (Group) Co., Ltd Group; and the Architectural Design and Research Institute of Henan Province Co., Ltd.

On March 26, 2003, a ceremony showcasing the bids was held in Zhengzhou Huanghe Hotel. The judges reviewed the seven plans and finally recommended three companies for the shortlist: the OTT/PPA Architects, Beijing Institute of Architectural Design, and Shanghai Xian Dai Architectural Design (Group) Co., Ltd. On April 4, 2003, provincial leaders including Li Chengyu and Li Ke and relevant units such as the Department of Culture heard presentations for the architectural design plans after which they decided to publicize the plans of the OTT/PPA Architects and the Beijing Institute of Architectural Design. Program photos and brief design descriptions were published on the Internet and in the largest circulation newspaper in the province, the *Dahe Daily*. Finally, the OTT/PPA Architects won. Canadian architect Carlos Ott, originally from South America, was appointed the chief architect to further improve the plan.

The government invited Carlos Ott to visit locations and famous spots related to the history and culture of Henan Province, such as the Henan Museum and the Zhengzhou Museum, hoping that the cultural elements would inspire further design improvements. This process reflects the value of tradition in Henan. As in northern China, people emphasize local culture and its meaning in their daily lives in both abstract and concrete ways. Reflecting its rich collection of archaeological artifacts, one slogan used by the government is the province of powerful culture and profound history. Therefore, the government intended the Henan Art Center to be not only a theater, but also a symbol of local culture to encourage self-identification (Wang and Lv 2012a, b).

The final plan consisted of five gold metal ellipsoidal objects connected by two huge glass panels, forming an outdoor platform above the ground. Two open squares in the front and back are for open air activities. The front area faces the main entrance and the back area is an open stage facing the artificial lake at the center of the CBD. The five ellipsoids are placed on two sides, with three performing halls on one side and two exhibition halls on the other. These buildings are the abstract representations of three historical relics unearthed in Henan Province—Tao Xun, Shi Pai Xiao, and the Bone Flute[4]—dating back to the ancient cultures of the central China area from thousands of years ago. The government hoped to highlight the depth of local history and culture through this symbolic building, to enhance the public's interest in the performing arts and architecture, and to inspire more cultural consumption (Fig. 6.7).

On June 10, 2008, after four years of construction and much effort, the Henan Art Center was completed. In the first few years, the fate of the Henan Art Center was very similar to that of the Zhengdong New District. The shape and form that the government leaders had been so proud of were criticized by the netizens and other independent media, and was called one of the "Top Ten Ugly/Strange Buildings" in China. Local media have also heatedly discussed the impact of this theater on the city, affirming its iconicity and scale, but criticizing its strange shape and unsatisfactory operation.

6.6   Grand Theater Modernism in China

The Henan Art Center was not unique at that time in China. Round shapes and curved lines were the biggest design trend after the construction of the National Center for the Performing Arts. Following the high standards of the capital city, other cities adopted similar styles in creative ways.

The first decade of the twenty first century can be classified as a period of explosive growth in cultural buildings. An increasing number of cultural buildings showed people that culture can be visualized (Table 6.1). Governments took advantage of this trend to pursue political aims at the city level and the residents were thrilled to see strange and new buildings (Sudjic 2006). At that time, the majority of the people in society appreciated things that were totally different than in the past. Therefore, in some cities, the new grand theaters had modernist styles (Lu 2009).

Very few new theaters were designed with square shapes, because blocks were seen as old-fashioned and traditional. Influenced by the National Center for the Performing Arts, round-shaped small buildings forming a larger group became a popular choice (Andreu 2009). The Henan Art Center is part of this trend; it has a mixed and immature modernist style that represents the desires of the residents and the government (Fig. 6.8).

---

[4]These are three ancient musical instruments, used more than 3000 years ago.

(a) Design competition    (b) Competition picture

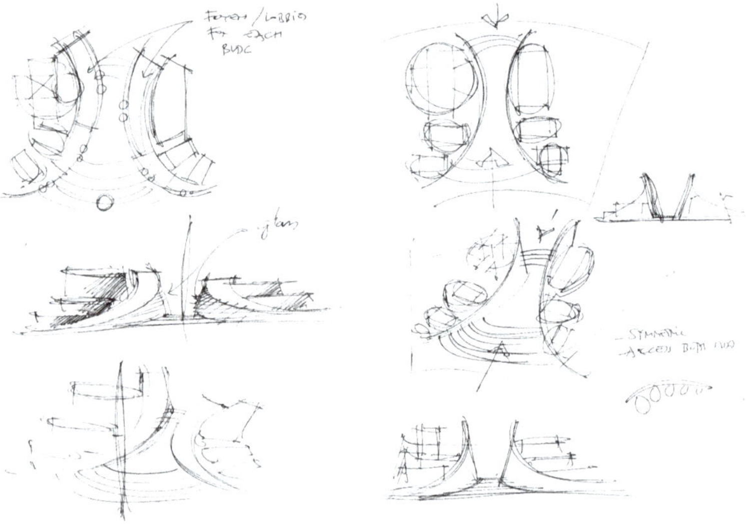

(c) Some sketches

Fig. 6.7 Process before the construction

Fig. 6.8 Grand theater buildings with round shapes since 2000

Table 6.1 Increasing number of grand theaters built in the first decade of the twenty first century

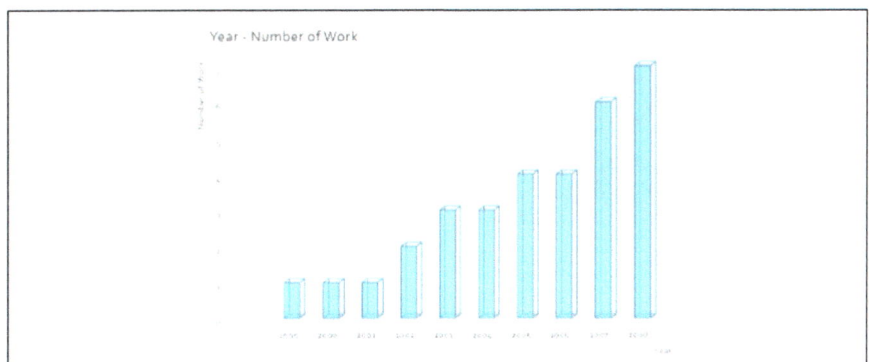

The architect Carlos Ott made his international debut when he built the Bastille Opera of Paris in 1983. His style can be partly classified as "post-modernist." He participated in several grand theater building projects in China from the late 1990s to the early 2000s including the Henan Art Center. He was first invited to China in 1997 to join the competition for the Jiangsu Grand Theater. Although his plan won the first prize, the project was canceled for political reasons. In 1998, he was invited to the international competition for the National Center for The Performing Arts. He entered the second round but did not win the bid. He then achieved first prizes in competitions to design the Hangzhou Grand Theater, Hangzhou International Convention Center, Wenzhou Grand Theater, Dongguan Yulan Grand Theater, Henan Art Center, and some other important iconic buildings. Judging from his company's portfolio, Carlos Ott is not an expert in designing cultural buildings; his main focus is commercial buildings, residential buildings, hotels, and apartments. Among his portfolio, cultural buildings are in the minority and, strangely enough, all are located in China except for one in Paris (Fig. 6.9).

Carlos Ott is an architect from South America. For grand theater projects that require huge investments, he prefers golden materials, using golden facades with greenish or bluish glass curtain walls to create a relationship between illusion and essence. In terms of shape, Carlos prefers round and curvilinear lines. Since his design of the Bastille Opera House, he has not built any theater buildings with square shapes. Even the Wenzhou Grand Theater, which has some square corners, has a curved gradient. Perhaps this golden arc style was the mainstream government aesthetic around 2000. Carlos was popular during that period and build many such buildings in cities at the middle economic level.

These buildings have sometimes been criticized by the media and the public, but are mostly welcomed in daily life. The shape means something but not everything, especially for the people who live near the buildings. Governments prefer shapes that are totally different from traditional ones, whereas residents are curious about

(a) Hangzhou Grand Theater (2000)   (b) Wenzhou Grand Theater (2001)

(c) Dongguan Grand Theater (2002)   (d) Henan Art Center (2003)

Fig. 6.9 Theater buildings of Carlos Ott

how modern architecture can create new and stimulating living environments. These buildings are indeed practical. In daily life, the shape and color may not be relevant, but big squares and up-to-date facilities are really attractive to most users.

6.7   Ten Years of Ambitious Operation

The Henan Art Center is conveniently located in the central CBD, 6 km from the Erqi Tower, the city's iconic historic building, 7 km from the Central Railway Station, and 10 km from the National G30 Expressway. At the beginning, when the infrastructure and rail transportation were still under construction, no public transportation was available after evening performances, which was an operational problem. To solve this problem, the manager of the Henan Art Center established a free commuter bus service from the art center to an important city transportation hub—the Zi Jing Shan Transportation Hub—to serve the audiences and to operate as soft publicity. In 2013, Zhengzhou Rail Transit Line 1 was established and the transportation situation improved. Over time, there were more subway stations and multiple bus lines near the theater. In addition, the number of private cars in the city increased rapidly from 20 vehicles per 100 people (2008) to nearly 57 vehicles per

100 people (2017).[5] Even so, the manager chose to continue the free bus services to attract more people. According to statistics, the cumulative number of bus shifts in the first decade of operation is more than 1000.[6]

The completion of the Henan Art Center has greatly improved the standard of performing venues in Zhengzhou. Unlimited and simultaneous high-profile performances and cultural exchange programs can be held in the city. The large performing hall, which has more than 1800 seats, and the concert hall are the settings for most of the daily performances. The small performing hall is usually used for meetings and small indoor activities, and occasionally for experimental drama. The three performing halls fulfil various other functions, as needed. The plan is beautiful, but the reality is cold. Furthermore, the performing operations faced great difficulty. With only 191 performances in 2009, the manager had to find realistic solutions for the shortfall.

The Dongguan Yulan Theater, opened in 2005, is also the work of Carlos Ott and is roughly the same size as the Henan Art Center. Although Dongguan is an ordinary city in Guangdong Province with a relatively high economic level, it was not as urbanized as Zhengzhou at that time; however, the consumption level is not insignificant. According to the former manager, the operation of Dongguan Theater (Fig. 6.10) was more immediately successful than that of the Henan Art Center in Zhengzhou. In 2008, the management of the Henan Art Center hired an experienced general manager from the Dongguan Yulan Theater, Mr. Chen, to expand the market. (In 2008, Mr. Chen, the experienced general manager of the Dongguan Yulan Theater, was deployed to the Henan Art Center to expand the market.) In an interview, Manager Chen was bitter when describing the early years of operation of the Henan Art Center.[7] The problems were almost the same for all capital cities with large populations and average economic levels in China. The governments of these cities undertook ambitious plans to build large theater buildings. They cited examples such as the Sydney Opera House, the Bastille Opera House, and the Bilbao Effect as successful cases to follow, inventing powerful slogans and choosing fantastic styles. They hoped to replicate the brilliance that these cultural buildings brought to those cities. However, in most cases, a few years after opening, they had to face the bleak reality that the operational status was not satisfactory. Then, negative reports and media comments flooded in.

Theaters and theater buildings became a trend in China in the twentieth century. They have been increasingly popular in the last 30 years, and this situation is not unreasonable. In China, traditional culture is deeply rooted. In the first decade of the twenty first century, living standards have changed dramatically, and people's material lives have been gradually enriched. For people who live in mid-level cities

---

[5]The data are from the government's website. See Henan government.

[6]The data are from the Ten-Year Anniversary of Henan Art Centre Report and videos provided by Mrs. Li, a staff member at Henan Poly Art Center Management Co., Ltd.

[7]A conversation with Mr. Chen, the manager of Henan Poly Art Center Management Co., Ltd, at the Henan Art Center in March 2018.

Fig. 6.10 Dongguan Yulan grand theater. Photo by Charlie Xue

such as Zhengzhou, cultural life is still in its infancy. In the Chinese cultural market, foreign art has a higher value than local cultural performances of the same level. Even though some people are curious and interested in local performances, the high price makes them hesitate to attend them. Lower prices and free activities, the usual measures taken by theaters to attract audience around the world, are needed to increase cultural consumption, which takes time to cultivate. This is the job of the management team of Henan Art Center. In the first ten years' operation, they have provided 222 public performances (free) and 228 popular art lectures, which are the performances attended by the most people.

In recent years, with the rapid economic growth, there has been an increasing number of exchange programs, demonstrating the acceptance of multiculturalism. The awareness and amount of cultural consumption is also rising year by year. In 2017, there were 452 performances, and there have been 2875 in the first ten years, including 1089 self-operated performances. The average attendance rate has gradually increased from 37% in 2009 to more than 75% in 2017. The number of visitors has grown from nearly 150,000 in 2009 to 364,000 in 2017, bringing the total number of visitors to more than 4.1 million.[8]

The Henan Art Center has relatively more open space than other theater buildings of the same scale. Although the shape is controversial, the exterior space of the theater is smoothly connected to the interior space. The two big glass curtain walls produce a strong visual guide from the square to the entrance and toward the open stage. The entrance square is gradually becoming livelier as more pedestrians pass through it. The completion of more residential neighborhoods has increased the space's popularity and usage rate. Afternoon and evening are the peak times in the square. Throughout the year, except in winter, nearby residents and pedestrians like to stop and rest on the square. Many spontaneous activities take place here. It is a positive addition to the Henan Art Center and the new district, although it also brings some management tasks, such as the use of the pool, the maintenance of the landscape, and so on (Fig. 6.11).

The use of open stage is more regular. A variety of popular free outdoor performances are conducted on weekends from May to October every year, usually for brand promotion and charity events. The public's habit of evening walks promotes these activities. In the past ten years, there have been more than 300 performances on this open stage, for more than 2 million audience members (Hu 2018). This program also provided opportunities for some traditional performances that were on the verge of closing. Saving traditional culture and providing diversified performances has earned the Centre a "Stars Award" at the 10th China Arts Festival. The Henan Art Center seems to have achieved a win-win result (Wen 2018).[9]

Although the operation status has improved with increasing rankings year by year compared to other provincial capital cities, audiences still need to be continuously cultivated. Grand theaters in China cannot be fully commercialized. The only one that does not require financial subsidies to maintain normal operations is the Shanghai Oriental Art Center. The Henan Art Center has accepted six million yuan in sponsorship from the government every year continuously since opening. Compared to other first- and second-tier cities with better economic levels, Henan Art Center has room for improvement (Table 6.2).

6.8 Concluding Remarks

During China's rapid urbanization wave, grand theater buildings were the most eye-catching additions to CBDs. For most mid- and upper-level Chinese cities, the construction of grand theaters was beyond individual cities' own means, especially as the public and government expected iconic and symbolic architecture. That was

---

[8]The data are from the 10th year celebration ceremony. See Henan Poly Art Center (2018).

[9]The information comes from a conversation with Ms. Yuan, member of the Henan Art Center management team in February 2017.

(a) Front square

(b) Outdoor stage

(c) The Henan Art Center (From the front square to the lake)

Fig. 6.11 Square of the Henan Art Center

Table 6.2 Statistic of performance number in total of 2010, 2017 and 2018

Item	2010	2017	2018
Total	197	424	454
Self-operated performance	106	132	159
Rental performance	50	195	190
Cooperative performance	0	14	13
Charitable performance and lecture	41	53	52
Art training	0	40	40

Source Management office of Henan Art Center

the case for the Henan Art Center. In five-year plans such as the "Ninth Five-Year Plan" and "Tenth Five-Year Plan" in Henan Province, the construction and operation of such buildings were key projects. The process has been dominated by local governments, with little public participation.

A government's perception of an appropriate architectural style embodies the characteristics of the times. These particular shapes not only represent the mainstream aesthetic preferences of the government, but also the attitude of the times. It is not surprising that they all participate in the current trends. After all, no one can resist the wave of the times.

The history of the Henan Art Center represents the general situation of grand theater projects during this period. Fortunately, with government subsidies, most of them have evolved into a new stage of operation. Looking back at this period helps us to critically understand modernism as more than a typology or style, but as an ideology.

The past three decades have been a period of rapid urbanization in China. Urban expansion has been accompanied by the construction of cultural buildings. These large-scale public projects usually require a large amount of funds and policies to support normal operations in their early stages of operation, which are relatively long. Over time, more people take advantage of cultural services. The growth of urban cultural consumption drives the development of the city, and many medium and upper level Chinese cities have constructed and operated buildings similar to the Henan Art Center.

In the past three decades, grand theaters have been built and put into operation in many cities. With economic growth, the art market is becoming more active and includes diverse performances and larger audiences. Many cities like Zhengzhou are no longer satisfied with one grand theater building. Urban expansion can create new problems such as accessibility issues. In 2014, just as the operation of the Henan Art Center appeared to improve, the Zhengzhou Grand Theater was proposed for the western part of the city. It will be located in the northwest part of the city, and will be one of a group of cultural buildings in the future civic center. The project completed the bidding, selection, and final design competition in February 2017. Many well-known national and international design companies participated in the competition. The domestic design company Architectural Design and Research Institute of Harbin Institute of Technology won the competition. The project began construction in March 2017 and it is expected to be opened at the end of 2019. The total costs are expected to be 2.08 billion RMB (around $US302 million) with a gross floor area of 124,000 m². The scale and investment are far beyond that of the Henan Art Center (Fig. 6.12).

In December 2015, the SCO (Shanghai Cooperation Organization) was held in Zhengzhou.[10] The city has proved its economic strength by hosting high quality

---

[10]Shanghai Cooperation Organization was launched in June 2001, including such six countries as China, Kazakhstan, Kyrgyzstan, Russia, Tajikistan and Uzbekistan. India and Pakistan joined in 2017. Summit was held every year in different cities.

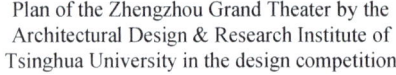

Plan of the Zhengzhou Grand Theater by the Architectural Design & Research Institute of Tsinghua University in the design competition	Final construction plan for the Zhengzhou Grand Theater by the Architectural Design and Research Institute of HIT

Fig. 6.12 The Zhengzhou grand theater

international conferences. In 2017, Zhengzhou was designated one of the 12 National Central Cities in China. This designation is both a reward and a catalyst. This city in the Central Plain, which is speeding-up, is constantly exploring new directions and its path to the future.

Acknowledgements This chapter is part of a study supported by the Research Grant Council, Hong Kong government, project No. CityU 11658816. I am grateful to Dr. Charlie Q. L. Xue who gave me valuable advice and supported my writing in all stages of this chapter's development. I would like to thank Manager Chen Zeli, Yuan Dian, Li Ya, Ding Zhimin and Wang Suli for generously offering great help and valuable one-hand materials to me. Special thanks to Sun Cong and Xiao Yingbo for the discussions and suggestions on the improvement during the writing.

I grew up in Zhengzhou. I grow up with the city. When I was a child, my family lived in the southeast region of the old town, not far from where the Zhengdong New District is now. At that time, the area was all farmland. My father took me there by bicycle on weekends to experience nature and teach me some knowledge of crops. I have precious memories of this area.

As I grew up and began to read and write more, my father started taking me to the cinema with him. Sometimes we watched films in the auditorium of his university, sometimes in the Henan People's Hall; there was no single place for cinema. I consider Henan People's Hall one of the best high-class places I have ever been. Every time I went there, I was excited, and I could see joy and delight on the faces of others as well.

About 10 years ago, my cousin's family moved to a new home in the eastern part of the old town, close to the Zhengdong New District. When we go to visit them, we usually have a big dinner in the shopping centre along the CBD area. After the meal, we walk along Ruyi Lake, just as many residents do. Almost every time we pass the Henan Art Centre and the landmark Greenland Plaza, we hear comments from others about the shape and meaning of the theatre and about its performances and exhibitions. Unlike the public media's reports and judgements, most of what can be heard is praise rather than criticism . Some of my other relatives who live not far from the CBD say that they enjoy the lake and the squares of these public buildings provide. Many of my friends are registered members of Henan Art Centre and go to the theatre more than once a month. To some extent, they represent the voice of the new generation. They can buy tickets to high-level performances, and they benefit from them a lot, whether in daily life or in their careers. The new generation may be critical about the shape and style of the building, but they cannot deny the effects that it has on them and the living environment.

Last year, my best friend held his wedding ceremony on the lake platform of the Green Plaza, with the landmark and the Henan Art Centre as the background. Their ceremony was not a traditional one as most new couple would choose; they had a buffet and their favourite German beers. They said that the place and the background environment meant a kind of new city life and a different future. This is also what I hope that the new district and buildings can bring to this conservative inland city.

References

Andreu, P. (2009). *National center for the performing arts.* Beijing: China Architecture and Building Press.

Henan Poly Art Center. (2018). *Henan Poly Art Center 10th Anniversary Video.* Retrieved from https://v.qq.com/x/page/e05432lwklu.html. Accessed January 12, 2019. 河南艺术中心 (2018). 河南之约——河南艺术中心十周年发布会视频.

Hu, L. D. (2018). *To meet Henan at this 10th anniversary.* Henan Art Center will launch a series of grand performances this year. gov.hawh.cn. Retrieved from http://gov.hawh.cn/content/201802/02/content_411335.html. Accessed January 12, 2019. 胡玲娣."河南之约·相聚此10"河南艺术中心今年将推系列盛大演出. 河南文化和旅游厅.

Lu, X. D. (2009). *On the evolution of modern theaters in China—A history from grand stage to grand theater.* Beijing: China Architecture & Building Press. 卢向东. (2009).中国现代剧场的演进–从大舞台到大剧院. 北京:中国建筑工业出版社.

Qiao, W. H. (2015, September 26). Prime Minister Li Keqiang got on the 58th floor of the "Big Corn" (the Greenland Plaza) for overlooking Zhengzhou, A04. *Dahe Daily.* http://newpaper.dahe.cn/dhb/html/2015-09/26/node_70.htm. Accessed January 12, 2019. 乔伟辉 (2015年9月26日). 总理登"大玉米"58层俯瞰郑州. 郑州:大河报. A04.

Sudjic, D. (2006). *The edifice complex: How the rich and powerful—And their architects—Shape the world.* London: Penguin.

The People's Government of Henan Province. (2001a). *The 10th five-year plan of Henan Province.* gov.hawh.cn. Accessed 21 December 2006, from https://doc.docsou.com/bdea68f7299454b82ffeec30c-4.html. 河南省政府办公厅. (2001). 河南省"十五"规划. 郑州:河南省人民政府.

The People's Government of Henan Province. (2001b). Henan Provincial Government Work Report of 2001—The Fourth Session of the Ninth People's Congress of Henan Province. henan.gov.cn. https://www.henan.gov.cn/2006/08-11/226996.htm. Accessed 11 August 2006. 李克强. 2001年河南省政府工作报告——河南省第九届人民代表大会第四次会议. 郑州:河南省人民政府.

The People's Government of Henan Province. (2006). *The 11th five-year plan for urbanization in Henan Province.* Accessed 21 December 2006, from http://www.henan.gov.cn/ztzl/system/2006/10/27/010011294.shtml. 河南省政府办公厅. (2006). 河南省城镇化"十一五"规划. 郑州:河南省人民政府.

Wang, S., & Lv X. (2012a). *Mei De Lichen—Henansheng Yishu Zhongxin Jianshe Huimou. (The Process of Beauty—Reviewing Henan Art Center Construction Process).* Beijing: Guang Ming Daily Press. 王仕俊,吕寻珠(2012). 美的历程——河南省艺术中心建设回眸. 北京:光明日报出版社.

Wang, S., & Lv, X. (2012b). *Yishu De Xinjing (Artistic Mood).* Beijing: Guang Ming Daily Press. 王仕俊,吕寻珠(2012). 艺术的心境. 北京:光明日报出版社.

Wen, X. J. (2018, January 3). A new chapter to continue the glory on the reform and innovation policy—Interview with Guo Wenpeng, Deputy General Manager of Poly Culture Group Co., Ltd. and general manager of Beijing Poly Theatre Management Co., Ltd. (p. 06). *Henan Daily*. http://newpaper.dahe.cn/hnrb/html/2018-01/03/node_6.htm. Accessed January 12, 2019. 温小娟(2018年1月3日). 改革创新谱新篇,乘风破浪续辉煌—访保利文化集团股份有限公司副总经理、北京保利剧院管理有限公司总经理郭文鹏. 郑州:河南日报. p. 06.

Xia, J., & Yin, S. (2006). *Juzhu Gaibian Zhongguo (Living changes China)*. Beijing: Tsinghua University Press. 夏骏.阴山(2006). 居住改变中国. 北京:清华大学出版社.

Xue, C. Q. L. (2006). *Building a revolution: Chinese architecture since 1980*. Hong Kong: Hong Kong University Press.

Xue, C. Q. L. (2010). *World Architecture in China*. Hong Kong: Joint Publishing Ltd.

Yu, X. A., Wang, J. G., & Wan, S. W. (2010). *Zhongguo xinchengshi jianshe yanjiu—Zhengzhou xinqu jianshe de shijian yu tansuo (Research on the construction of the new urban area in China—On practice and exploration of Zhengzhou New District)*. Beijing: Social Sciences Academic Press (China). 喻新安,王建国,完世伟等(2010). 中国新城区建设研究——郑州新区建设的实践与探索. 北京:社会科学文献出版.

Zhengzhou Zhengdong New District Administration Committee, & Zhengzhou Urban Planning Bureau. (2010a). *Zhengzhoushi Zhengdong Xinqu Chengshi Guihua yu Jianzhu Sheji (2001–2009) Zhengdong Xinqu Zongti Guihuapian (Urban planning and architectural design for Zhengdong New District of Zhengzhou (2001–2009). The master plan for Zhengdong New District)*. Beijing: China Architecture & Building Press. 郑州市郑东新区管理委员会,郑州市城市规划局 (2010). 郑州市郑东新区城市规划与建筑设计(2001-2009)郑东新区总体规划篇. 北京:中国建筑工业出版社.

Zhengzhou Zhengdong New District Administration Committee, & Zhengzhou Urban Palning Bureau. (2010b). *Zhengzhoushi Zhengdong Xinqu Chengshi Guihua yu Jianzhu Sheji (2001–2009) Zhengdong Xinqu Shangwu Zhongxinqu Chenshi Guihua yu Jianzhu Shejipian (Urban planning and architectural design for Zhengdong New District of Zhengzhou (2001–2009). Urban planning and architectural designs for CBD of Zhengdong New District)*. Beijing: China Architecture & Building Press. 郑州市郑东新区管理委员会, 郑州市城市规划局 (2010). 郑州市郑东新区城市规划与建筑设计(2001–2009)郑东新区商务中心区城市规划与建筑设计篇. 北京:中国建筑工业出版社.

Chapter 7
The Shanxi Grand Theater: The "Renaissance" of Chinese Drama Land

Yingbo Xiao and Min Ni

7.1 History: Shanxi's Performance Space

Shanxi Province, one of the main cradles of Chinese performing arts, is located in the North China region. Studies on no fewer than four inscriptions prove that buildings dedicated to the performing arts (known as dance halls) appeared as early as the Northern Song Dynasty (AD 960–1127).[1] This type of construction is often located inside the temple courtyard, and its location is similar to that of Xian Hall (the hall of consecration) of the later Ming Dynasty. It can be inferred that the dance hall was adapted to the need to worship the gods with drama and dance performances. In the traditional daily life of northern China, theatrical performances are popular and auspicious elements of religious rituals (Fig. 7.1).

With the rise of the "Hua Bu" (local operas that differed from the orthodox Kunqu opera), drama activities in Shanxi flourished even more during the Ming and Qing Dynasties (1368–1912). "According to statistics, there were more than 300 opera troupes performing in Shanxi, with more than 10,000 employees, and nearly 2000 shows each year during the Ming and Qing Dynasties." (Chinese Opera Chorography Editing Committee 1990) The art form of local operas was inclusive and popular. Performances often took place in the open spaces of villages, towns, and temples where villagers gathered, and trade fairs were held. As time went on, the dance halls of the

---

[1]Stone tablet record of a newly built Houtu goddess temple(including 'Dance Building') in Wangquan county, Hezhong prefecture, 2nd year of the reign of Jinde (1005 A.D.), Song Dynasty. See Che (2011).

Y. Xiao (✉)
Department of Architecture and Civil Engineering,
City University of Hong Kong, Kowloon, Hong Kong
e-mail: yingbxiao2-c@my.cityu.edu.hk

M. Ni
Tourism Department of Normal College, Shenzhen University,
3688 Nanhai Ave, Shenzhen, Guangdong, China

© Springer Nature Singapore Pte Ltd. 2019   149
C. Q. Xue (ed.), *Grand Theater Urbanism*,
https://doi.org/10.1007/978-981-13-7868-3_7

Fig. 7.1 Stage and poetic drama figurine (1210 A.D. JIN Dynasty). Excavated from Dongming's tomb in Houma city, Shanxi province. Photo by the author; from the Shaanxi History Museum

Song Dynasty were transformed into ancient stages. No walls enclosed the open space, and people could enter it freely and easily without tickets. The rural opera performances were related to folk ritual activities[2] (Fig. 7.2). The performances" costs, instead of being covered by ticket fees, were paid by the festival organizers, who believed the popularity of their shows would bring good fortune. It is recorded that to make the shows more attractive, organizers even invited multiple opera troupes to perform similar repertoires at the same time. In a model that created incentives for troupes to perform well, the audience members, acting as judges, freely choose which rival show to watch by gathering in front of the chosen stage.

In addition to folk ritual activities, commerce was an important force driving the development of performing arts spaces. Due to its relatively restricted and independent geographical environment, Shanxi Province was less affected than other areas by the external social unrest and war of the Late Qing Dynasty and the Early Republic of China Period. With the development of the city and the prosperity of commerce and trade, interior performance places, such as tea gardens and opera gardens, appeared on bustling streets. In tea gardens, people could watch Shanxi local operas while enjoying Chinese tea or other refreshments, so driving up food and beverage sales. Clever businessmen soon discovered the commercial value of the performance market. In 1915, a tea garden was transformed into a fashionable "opera garden." From then on, spectators had to queue up for show tickets to opera gardens. These profit-oriented theatrical performance venues hosted Shanxi local operas and stage plays, and sometimes movies. After renovations, opera gardens became the era's main site of urban cultural consumption. Some even continued as famous theaters after the founding of the People's Republic of China (Fig. 7.3).

---

[2] The folk ritual activities called "Shaishe-showing," shows for gods and ancestors, these rituals were one of the main ways of performing opera. See Duan (2008) pp. 56–60.

Fig. 7.2 Mural of the theatrical scene to the east of the door on the southern wall in Mingying Wang Hall. The Water God's Temple of the Guangsheng Monastery, Hongdong County (1324 A. D. Yuan Dynasty). Photo by the author, from the Shanxi History Museum

After the war, the People's Republic of China had just been founded, and the national economic base was weak, with a general pattern of underdevelopment in all sectors. After 1953, the authorities committed to rebuilding the country. Shanxi had a solid foundation and distinct advantages in industry and rich minerals. Taiyuan, the provincial capital city of Shanxi, became one of the first of China's heavy industrial bases in the construction of priority cities. Each such city was given a complete set of cultural and recreational facilities for workers in the new factories, mines, and other corporations. At the time, Taiyuan had nearly 50 performance spaces, which enriched

Fig. 7.3 The Changfeng Theater. Formerly the guild hall of 'Eight Banners' (military-administrative organizations of the Man nationality) in the Qing Dynasty. In 1928, it was transformed into the 'Mingsheng Building,' one of the most important theatres in Taiyuan. In 1958, it was modernized as a model theatre. Photo by Mr. Xiao Ying

the cultural life of the people and promoted the development of the entertainment industry. Since the advent of modern times, Western culture and entertainment had gradually been accepted and imitated by Shanxi's people, with some changes and innovations. The traditional opera gardens soon appeared too dim, small, and crowded for modern life. Accordingly, opera troupes gradually moved their performances into Western-style theaters. The performances were adapted to fit their new spatial circumstances. As early as 1954, Yue Weifan, the mayor of Taiyuan, was determined to make the city into a modernized industrial metropolis following the "urban comprehensive plan (1954–1974)." Yingze Avenue, in the south of the old town of Taiyuan, was designated as the major thoroughfare. On both sides of Yingze Avenue, modern urban infrastructure was built, including hotels, restaurants, emporiums, office buildings, and theaters (Fig. 7.4).

The Taiyuan Worker's Cultural Palace is located on the south side of Yingze Avenue. Designed by the Shanxi Architectural Design and Research Institute, the building is the only large Soviet-style building in Taiyuan. (For more information about performing spaces in the Mao period, see Chap. 1.) As the earliest and biggest large-scale comprehensive cultural and entertainment center in Taiyuan, the palace, built in the Socialist Classicist style, represents the most sophisticated construction technology available in Taiyuan in the 1950s (Figs. 7.5, 7.6). The architectural plan is in an E shape, with a width of 130 m from east to west and 80 m from north to south. The building mass is organized high and low with rhythm along the main façade. The overall dimensions appear distributed at random, abounding in variation coupled with exquisite details and conveying a sense of stereoscopic vision. The main body and the two wings are connected by an arched corridor. By casting the Worker's Cultural Palace as both modern and traditional, the Nationalist era gave the building a new identity. The main façade is constructed in the Socialist Classicist style, with a

Fig. 7.4 Yingze Avenue. This is one of the main streets, planned in 1954 and constructed in 1956 in Taiyuan, Shanxi Province. It was designed to be 70 m wide and was second only to Chang'an Avenue in Beijing (120 m)

Fig. 7.5 The Taiyuan Worker's Cultural Palace. Photo by Xiao Ying

Fig. 7.6 Stills from the films "Platform", showed the typical scene of troupe performing in the 1960s–1970s. From Zhantai (Platform). Director Zhangke Jia. Artcam International, Bandai Entertainment Inc. and Hu Tong Communications, 2001 (Hong Kong)

symmetrical layout of five bays and three longitudinal sections and ethnic-style decoration, see Yang and Gu (1999). Its prime location made the hall the city's most important theatrical performance and conference space. The annual "Xinhua Prize" ceremony, the highest award given to local operas, was held in the Taiyuan Worker's Cultural Palace (Table 7.1).

After 1978, the next 30 years of reform and opening up constituted a process of mental emancipation. Artistic creativity in the performing arts slipped the leash of censorship. With the influx of pop music, karaoke, and video games, which have become the dominant entertainment mode of the young urban generation, the traditional performing arts have been gradually marginalized in this generation's aesthetic identity and consumer choices. As development continues, this traditional performance space has also been profoundly affected by the market. To cope with

Table 7.1 Representative performance spaces located near Yingze Avenue

Project	Design and year of completion	Architects	Construction area (m^2)	Site area (m^2)	Theater	Multifunctional hall
The Taiyuan Worker's Cultural Palace	1956–1958	Fang Kuiyuan, Yin Gu	8216	approximately 14,000	1425 seats	500 seats
The Great Hall of Lakeside	1958		8000	30,000	2100 seats	400 seats

competition, a number of theaters have had to lease their space in pieces, becoming classrooms, shopping malls, ballrooms, restaurants, and so on. The unplanned reconstruction and transformation have destroyed the original setting and the general tone of the art centers (Figs. 7.7, 7.8).

Unfortunately for opera troupes performing in urban areas, the performance market is becoming more competitive, while the survival of opera troupes performing in rural area is at greater risk than in any preceding generation. Between 2000 and 2017, Shanxi province's urbanization rate increased from 34.91 to 56.2%. With the rapid industrialization and urbanization occurring in the suburbs of the metropolis, it is inevitable that more and more opera troupes will lose their audiences and performance spaces. Because the development of modern mechanized agriculture has led directly to a substantial reduction of the rural population, fewer villagers remain to enjoy local opera in the slack season. Some villages used to be located on the outskirts of the city, but with the expansion of the city, they are now encircled by urban areas, which are associated with overcrowding and social problems. As a result, very little open space remains for stage shows. Because the impact of urbanization has been greatest on China's villages, these villages are experiencing an unprecedented rate of change in their social life. The impact has not

Fig. 7.7 Shanxi Theater. The first modernized theater in Taiyuan. From the billboard of the façade, we can see that the space was split and rented out as an Internet bar, a karaoke space, and now a cinema. Photo by Xiao Ying

Fig. 7.8 The Bingzhou Theater. Completed in 1955, the theater is being converted into a hot pot restaurant. Photo by Xiao Ying

only undermined their socioeconomic structure and everyday life, but also affected the transmission of the traditional performing arts culture.

7.2 Strategy: Taiyuan City, the Culture Industry, and the Grand Theater

The theater, whether referring to stage shows or to motion pictures, has long been a keyword for Chinese urban modernization (People's Government of Shanxi Province 2017). After 2000, city administrators became concerned with the relations between cultural infrastructure and urban and regional economic development (Xue and Xiao 2018). Yu Youjun, who governed Shanxi province from 2005 to 2007, was a key figure in this relationship. Mr. Yu was viewed as a reformer who was determined to steer Shanxi toward prosperity. Rather than following bureaucratic tradition, he preferred to get expert advice.[3]

While he was mayor of Shenzhen, Yu accumulated rich experience in urban construction and the improvement of people's welfare in one of the most developed coastal cities. As a typical central city, however, Taiyuan has lagged far behind Shenzhen and lies in the downstream level of the middle China area. Yu's major

---

[3]Although every government official in Shanxi emphasized "reproducing the green mountains and rivers of Shanxi" as an official routine, Yu abandoned the inefficient and propagandistic measure of planting trees for the barren mountains every spring and left the task of upgrading the urban environment to professional specialists and companies.

policy focus was opening up Shanxi and invigorating its domestic economy. The first Investment and Trade Symposium was held in Taiyuan at the beginning of the Yu administration; many businessmen were invited as Governor Yu's friends (Yu 2005). Unfortunately, the infrastructure and investment conditions of Taiyuan failed to impress them. Furthermore, the over-exploiting energy industry has always been the pillar industry of Shanxi Province since 1949. Yu was one of the few who recognized the hidden risks of this industry early on and planned an economic transition to control the consequences (People's Government of Shanxi Province 2016). In cases of the economic transformation of cities and regions that are dependent on natural resources, like the Ruhr of Germany, Lorraine of France, and Pittsburgh of the US, success is generally ascribed to the development of the service industry. In Shanxi Province, both the unfavorable investment conditions and the need to develop the service industry called for a massive infrastructure upgrade. The Changfeng Quarter, which occupies a 2.56 km^2 site, was the center of upgrading construction in the southern part of Taiyuan during the 11th Five-Year Plan period (2006–2010). According to meeting minutes, the Changfeng New Quarter was to be designed and built according to the "modern concept." It would host political, economic, cultural, and exhibition activities that epitomized the character and landscape of Taiyuan for citizens and investors.

On January 27, 2007, Governor Yu chaired an executive meeting that resulted in a decision to begin a new round of urban infrastructure upgrades. Shanxi province raised RMB 0.5 billion yuan (US$65.8 million in 2007) as an investment in public welfare and public infrastructure, including the International Exhibition Center, Shanxi Grand Theater, Science and Technology Museum, Provincial Library, Sports Center, and Geological Museum. The authority believed the lack of those buildings had created a bottleneck that restricted urban development. The "historical outstanding debt" of public infrastructure was to be repaid as soon as possible.

> The meeting analyzed the situation of the lag in the construction of social welfare infrastructure in Shanxi Province. Most of the existing social welfare infrastructure in Shanxi Province was built in the 1950s and 1960s. It is in disrepair; the equipment is aging; it is functionally outdated. Some facilities are basically nonexistent. These buildings are unable to support and promote the rapid and healthy development of cities. At present, there is no grand theater, concert hall, or convention and exhibition center capable of hosting large-scale conferences and exhibitions in Shanxi Province.[4]

Taiyuan lies between two long mountains chains to its east and west. The current major districts of Taiyuan are distributed mainly along the east bank of the Fen River. According to the general development plan, the city would expand to the

---

[4]The meeting analyzed the situation of the lag in the construction of social welfare infrastructure in Shanxi Province. Most of the existing social welfare infrastructure in Shanxi Province was built in the 1950s and 1960s. It is in disrepair; the equipment is aging; it is functionally outdated. Some facilities are basically nonexistent. These buildings are unable to support and promote the rapid and healthy development of cities. At present, there is no grand theater, concert hall, or convention and exhibition center capable of hosting large-scale conferences and exhibitions in Shanxi Province. See the People's Government of Shanxi Province (2007).

southwest. Much of the "public infrastructure" mentioned above would be located in the Changfeng Quarter (Fig. 7.9). In May 2006, an international competition organized by the Municipal City Planning Bureau of Taiyuan invited five architectural firms to submit detailed outlines of their design and planning work. One bidder in the competition, Kisho Kurokawa, is famous for the Zhengdong New Area of Zhengzhou (see Chap. 6), which is not far from Taiyuan, and Futian CBD of Shenzhen (see Chap. 4). This double magnum opus is widely considered to be one of the most significant examples of his symbiotic thought. Kurokawa's plan placed a municipal administrative center in the south and a convention and

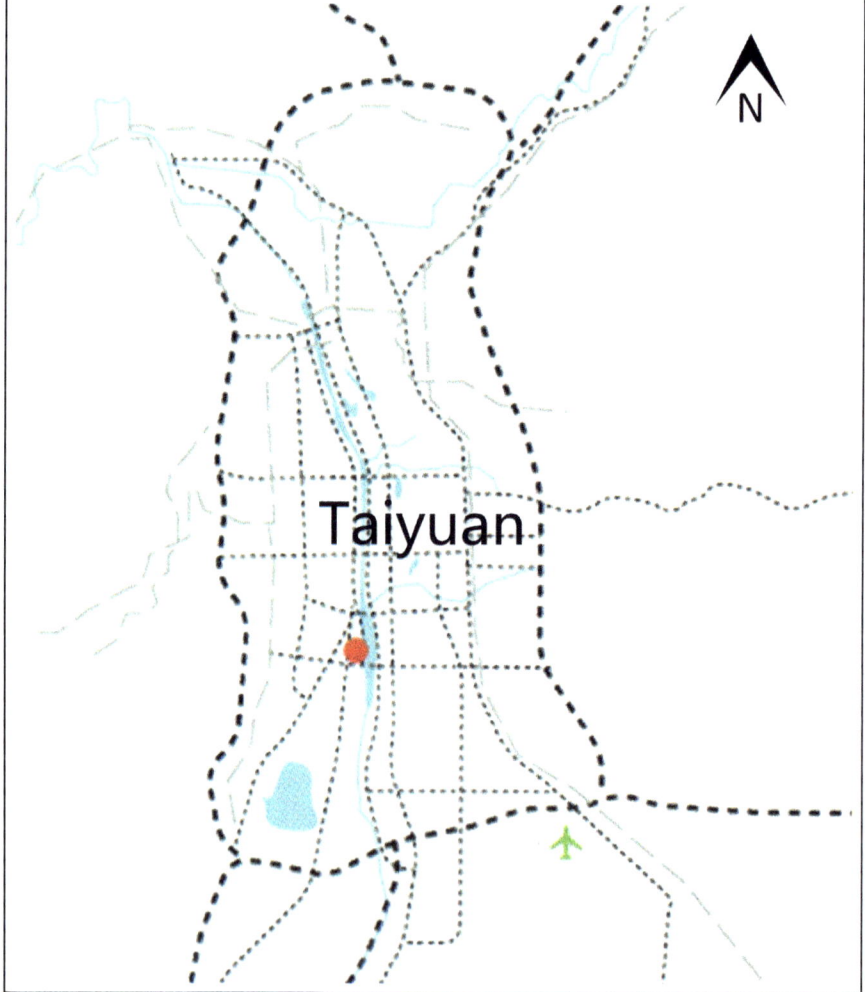

Fig. 7.9 The city of Taiyuan, showing the location of the Changfeng Quarter. Copyright © Arte Charpentier Architectes

exhibition center in the north. These centers were envisioned as the poles of a magnet, intended to function as sources of vitality for the quarter. All of the other functions of planning would be integrated into the field generated between the poles (Figs. 7.10 and 7.12). In the case of Futian CBD, Shenzhen, a similar prototype can be seen in the multi-layered central axis of "Lotus mountain (central park)–Civic Center (municipal administrative center)–Convention and Exhibition Center." As the former mayor of Shenzhen, Yu was familiar with the Futian CBD plan (Fig. 7.11), but Arte Charpentier was the eventual winner of the competition.

In contrast to the north-south axis of Kurokawa's scheme, which is parallel to the bank of Fen River, the first distinct strategy of the scheme from Arte Charpentier was the concept of making the axis cross the river perpendicularly. Arte Charpentier saw the project as both a transitional and an extended area connecting the current urban areas to new areas. Referring to the historical relationship between the Seine River and Paris's urban expansion, large public buildings and green square were organized through the axis perpendicular to the river bank, so that the urban texture was extended on both sides of the river bank and a complete urban space system was formed (Fig. 7.13).

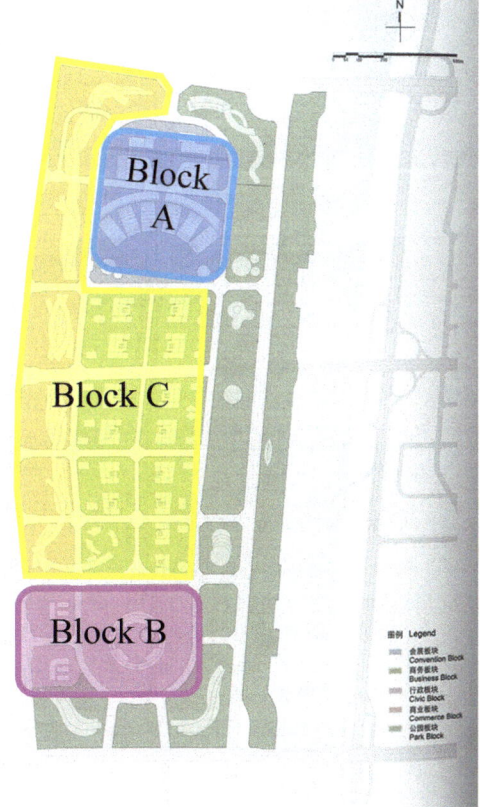

Fig. 7.10 The zoning plan of the Changfeng Quarter designed by Kisho Kurokawa. From Book: Urban Planning Commission of Taiyuan, The Book Series of Taiyuan Urban Planning Projects (Beijing, China Building Industry Press, 2008), pp. 220, illustrations drawn by the authors. Block A: Convention Block. Block B: Administrative Block. Block C: Business Block

Fig. 7.11 The zoning plan of
Futian CBD in Shenzhen.
Copyright © Chen Yixin,
illustrations drawn by the
authors. Block A: Convention
Block. Block B:
Administrative Block. Block
C: Business Block

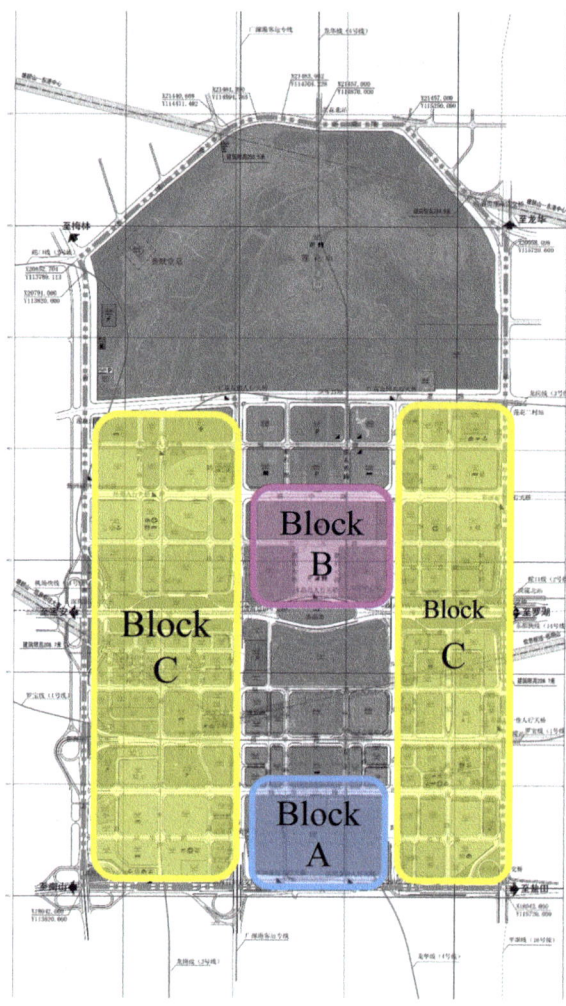

In Paris, several urban axes were drawn perpendicular to the Seine to locate major
infrastructure among them. To create public spaces converging on the water in Taiyuan, we
decided to bring the Fen River into our site to create a green island from which three axes
would radiate. (Zhou and Chambron 2012)

These axes and avenues provided both a link to the city and extensions along
which future growth would be located. Because of the city's geographical distribution, this link could cause the axis to be oblique. In the traditional thought of
northern China, the positioning of urban fabric along a north-south axis symbolized
legally constituted authority, and it was believed that the articulation of the
administration center dominating north–south axis organized the city in a

Fig. 7.12 Structure map of
the development plan of the
Changfeng Quarter designed
by Kisho Kurokawa. The
administrative and exhibition
centers are like the poles of a
magnet. The poles become
sources of vitality for the
quarter. See Urban Planning
Commission of Taiyuan
(2008), pp. 220

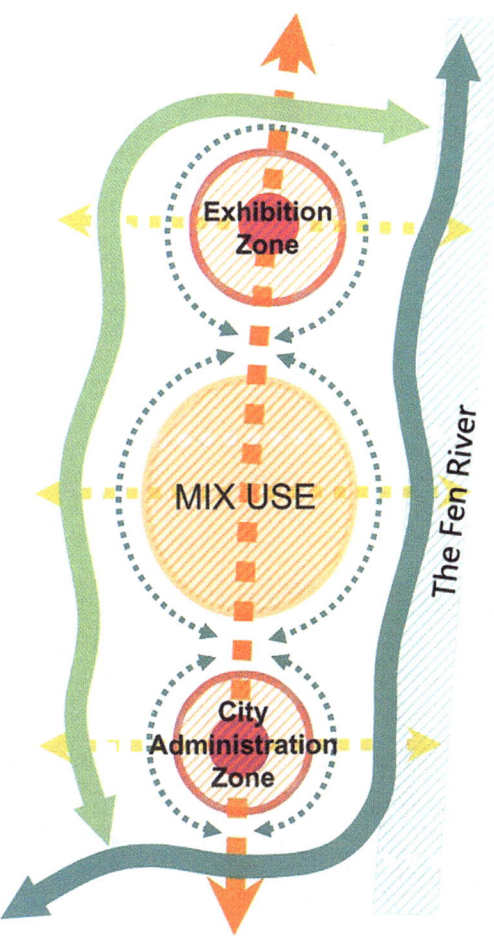

symmetrical layout, and it is well-known as central uprightness.[5] Luckily, however,
the authority accepted Arte Charpentier's thoughtful but challenging concept
(Fig. 7.14).

The second strategy of Arte Charpentier's plan was to regard the cultural
complex as the core area of the new city (Fig. 7.15). Three axes radiated through
the cultural complex, composed of the Shanxi Grand Theater, a library, a museum,
an art gallery, and a science center. To further strengthen the position of the cultural

---

[5]The squareness, the three gates on the southern front of the Capital City and the symmetrical
positioning of the gates and courtyards in this frontal area, the assertive orthogonal structure in
relation to the four cardinal points, the use of axes, the domination of the north-south axis, the
articulation of the center, and the elaboration of the southern front of the center, were eminent in
Beijing. See Zhu (2004), p. 99.

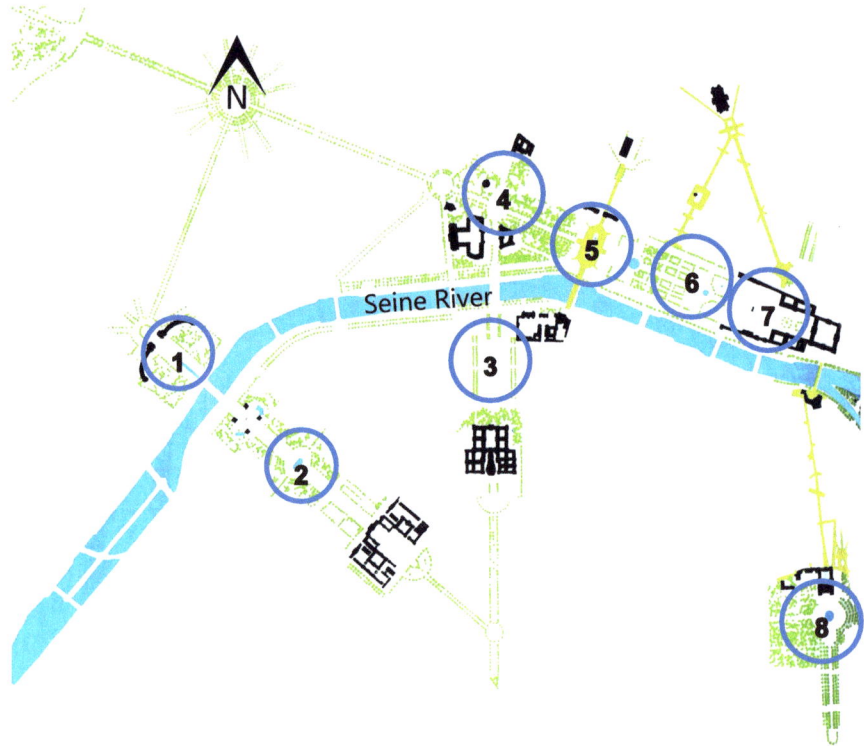

Fig. 7.13 The urban axes and open space perpendicular to the Seine River. Arte Charpentier captured the imaginations of the judges with the idea of turning the Fen River into the Seine River. Legend: (1) Gardens of the Trocadero; (2) The Champ de Mars Park (Eiffel Tower); (3) Esplanade des Invlides (Les Invalides); (4) Jardins des Champs Elysees Gardens; (5) The Place de la Concorde; (6) Tuileries Garden; (7) Louvre Museum; (8) Luxembourg Gardens; Copyright © Arte Charpentier Architectes

complex, the architect dug a water channel in the site to form a cultural green island. Shaped like a port, the cultural green island clustered five public cultural facilities. Because the 6-m embankment could have interrupted the experience of the waterfront space, buildings were set on the podium with embankments of the same height. As a result, the platform with its immense volume seems to float on the river, which is of special significance in the cultural context of East Asia.[6] In the practice of an urban designer with a French background, the cultural facilities are highly respected in the architectural hierarchy of the Changfeng Quartier.

[6]For example, the Japanese prints that were popular among Westerners in the nineteenth century are known in Japanese as ukiyo-e, literally "Pictures of the Floating World', which is a common reference to "the life one lives." Contemporary Asian architects often revisit the concept of floating space:' By seeing a garden as a metaphor for the process of time interminable, a life of some sort, there might be a chance that I can express a living architecture, an architecture floating amidst time'. See Tang (2018), 17 and Andō et al. (1997), 512.

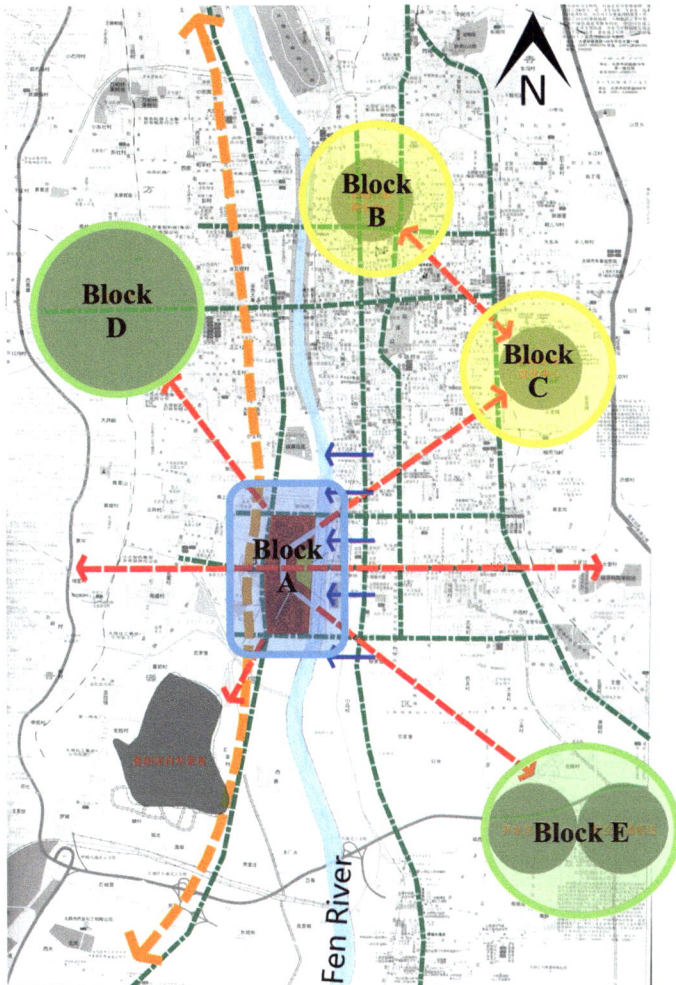

Fig. 7.14 Structure map of the development plan of the Changfeng Quarter designed by Arte Charpentier. These axes and avenues provide both a link to the city and extensions along which future growth will be located. Copyright © Arte Charpentier Architectes, illustrations drawn by the authors. Block A: The Changfeng Quarter. Block B: The administrative and commercial center of the old city. Block C: The historical and cultural center of the old city. Block D: The industrial development zone of the new city. Block E: The commercial development zone of the new city

Neither Kisho Kurokawa's nor Arte Charpentier's plan is a home-grown solution to the grass-roots problems of Shanxi. We wish to emphasize two aspects of this Western-style adaptation in the midst of China's urban transformation. First, the theoretical means were borrowed from and influenced by the Western mode, which creates conflict with Chinese cultural and social conventions; second, the adaptation made a collective use of architecture that is frequently transformed by

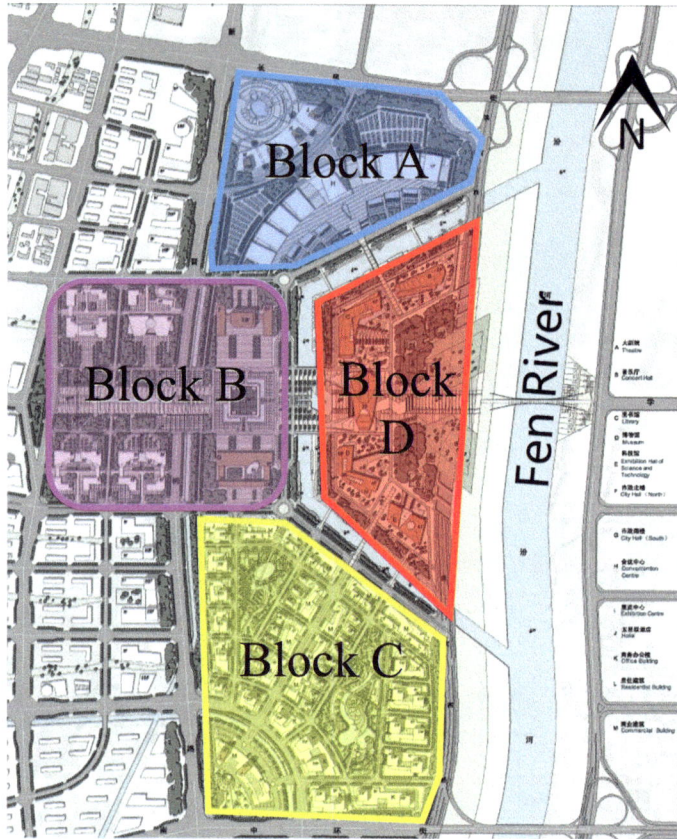

Fig. 7.15 The zoning plan of the Changfeng Quarter designed by Arte Charpentier. Copyright © Arte Charpentier Architectes, illustrations drawn by the authors. Block A: Convention Block. Block B: Administrative Block. Block C: Business Block. Block D: Cultural Block

changing modes of cultural consumption and that presents a new vision that is diversified and open (Tang 2018). As a result, the architectural and urban design is regarded more as a common motif of collective practice than as a matter of the wishful thinking of individual architects. Looking at the beginning of the decision-making process, we can trace several changes in the decision makers" mindset regarding which building types should dominate the construction and development of the new city. The Changfeng Commercial District was assigned four main functions: it was to be a provincial-level cultural and art exhibition area, a provincial-level exhibition area, a municipal-level administrative center, and a business district. Because office space accounts for a large area, it often becomes the background pattern of urban design. Most of this debate, however, focused on whether the convention center or the cultural area would dominate the Changfeng Quarter. From the changes in the name of the quarter, we can see that the urban decision makers gradually changed the concept of this area. It was originally named the "Changfeng New District," serving as the main venue of the "Expo Central China" held in Taiyuan in 2011. The name was later changed to the "Changfeng Business District." The final official name was the "Changfeng Cultural and Business District." In conclusion, we can discern a change in mindset from regional development led by the exhibition economy, which pursues short-term benefits, to regional development guided by a culture that pursues long-term benefits.

In fact, the preparation for the Shanxi grand theater significantly predates the Changfeng Cultural and Business District. Since the beginning of Chinese economic reform, the programming of the Shanxi grand theater has been on the agenda. In 1982, the planning commission of Shanxi Province officially approved the project and purchased the seating area at the same time. The project was to be transferred to the Provincial Department of Culture after the early-stage work was finished. Influenced by Shanxi's ambition, many neighboring provinces joined the surge in the construction of cultural facilities. In 1989, however, the provincial government decided to postpone construction because of financial problems. In 1996, the original site of the grand theater was sold to a foreign investor by the government to "expand the investment." During that time, there was not a single room for the preparatory office, let alone a site for the grand theater.[7] Ironically, the Shanxi grand theater project received unprecedented attention, which led the theater to become the core building of the new commercial district. In "The Outline of the Cultural Development Plan for the 11th Five-year Plan Period of Shanxi Province," the authorities asserted,

> We should improve the network of public cultural services and implement the cultural infrastructure construction project. The project will focus on large-scale public cultural facilities (including the Shanxi grand theater) and strengthen the network of public cultural infrastructure based on the cultural facilities in communities at the grassroots level. These key construction projects should be designed as one of the most recognizable symbols of Shanxi.

To return to governor Yu: he left his position as governor of Shanxi Province in the middle of 2007 and has since devoted himself to academic research. His most important political achievement in Shanxi has been his efforts to reform and reorganize the coal industry. For example, one housing improvement project was the transformation of a shantytown for 300,000 mineworkers in Datong. In October 2013, he donated a community cultural center for this project with a total contribution of RMB 1.6 million yuan from his publication royalties. One local resident said gratefully, "Now the miners have their own modernized life." (State Council Information Office of China 2013) The Shanxi grand theater and community cultural center in Datong can be regarded as part of the two-pole practice of Mr. Yu Youjun in the public cultural service network.

---

[7]In March 1982, to change the backward situation of the provincial capital's cultural infrastructure, the provincial department of culture applied to the provincial planning commission for a report, hoping to build a new theater in Taiyuan with modern features, complete functions, and advanced equipment. See Sang (2002), B04.

7.3 Importation and Adaptation: Arte Charpentier's Urban Practice in Shanxi

The architectural revolution triggered by China's economic reform since 1978 drew a large number of international architecture firms into China. Their practices in China inevitably influenced contemporary Chinese architecture (Xue 2010). While most of the performing arts centers in the Western world are financially strapped and slow to develop, Chinese grand theaters and other cultural facilities are springing up like mushrooms, making the Chinese market an ideal arena for cultural architecture design. Western architects, who have been immersed in mature markets for years, have perceived the opportunity brought by this development, and they have joined the gold rush in the East without hesitation. Compared with local Chinese architects, who started to build up the grand theaters only at the beginning of the 1990s, Western architects have relatively rich experiences. Western architects therefore dominated the round of "grand theater construction booms" that have taken place since 2000.

Meanwhile, the construction booms are also influenced by external experiences. The last round of massive city revitalization was the Grands Projets of François Mitterrand. The Grands Projets, which included the Opéra Bastille, were described as "eight monumental building projects that in two decades transformed the city skyline." (Muscat and Peel 2002) The architectural program of the project aimed to provide modern monuments for Paris that would symbolize France's position in politics, culture, and the economy. The relationship between the cultural monuments and the city's revitalization traces one continuous line. In Haussmann's renovation of Paris, the Palais Garnier was in the dominant position. The Center Georges-Pompidou, regarded as the most remarkable achievement in former president Pompidou's career, was said by the Pritzker jury to have "revolutionized museums, transforming what had once been elite monuments into popular places of social and cultural exchange, woven into the heart of the city." (Pogrebin 2019). These cases were widely reported and discussed in China's architecture circle in the 1980s.[8] In 1998, then French president Jacques René Chirac (who had been mayor of Paris during the Grands Projets, 1977–1995), proposed a cultural exchange program of "150 Chinese architects in France." This activity gathered a group of talented young architects in China and cultivated their friendship and affinity for French architecture (Architectural Times 2005).

Admittedly, it is important to avoid the 'post hoc ergo propter hoc' fallacy when examining the reasons for the Chinese preference for French architects. There is no doubt, however, that the cultural exchange between China and France inclined Chinese architects and urban policymakers to approve the "French prototype". As a

---

[8]For example, the review of the Grands Projets written by Guan Zhaoye, Academician of the China Engineering Academy. See Guan (1989) pp. 10–19.

result, the "French style" designers became more competitive in the construction boom of China's cultural facilities in the twenty-first century. There is an essential difference between the form of "self-colonization" and architecture importation. As Ledderose notes, classical Chinese belief that 'by artificially making a replica of something one wields power over the real object' (Ledderose 1983) according to Bosker book, the movement might be intended as a projection of China's power: its ability to control and rearrange the cosmos by metaphorically transplanting Europe and the United States into China's domain (Bosker 2013). On the Chinese perspective side, there is wide acknowledgment of the almost miraculous power of cultural facilities in Western cities, especially the grand theatre. Chinese leaders want to follow the example of successful cases by "importing" authentic modern monuments from the Western world for celebrating country's progress and accumulated wealth after the Chinese economic reform.

As a representative of French architects who have achieved success in China's market, Arte Charpentier tries to bridge importation and adaptation by understanding cultural differences and identity. The first contact traces back to 1984, when Mr. Charpentier began to participate in the cooperative cultural and technical exchanges that occurred as the Shanghai municipal government conducted architectural seminars to improve the quality of its housing. In May 1994, Arte Charpentier won the international competition to design the Shanghai Grand Theater (see Chap. 2). The first signature-built project garnered nation-wide appreciation for the firm and for French architects (Zhou and Chambron 2012). Later, the firm gained opportunities to contribute to cities all over China. So far, the Arte Charpentier has completed three performance spaces. The Chinese cities in which the performance spaces are located range from first-tier to third-tier (Table 7.2).

7.3.1 A Synchronized Fashion

As the achievements of urban design were recognized and rewarded, Arte Charpentier was invited to the International Design Competition of the Shanxi Grand Theater. Located in the heart of the Changfeng Quarter, the theater had been sketched out during the urban design competition. The architectural centerpiece is in some senses a prolongation of the urban design concept. Architects from Arte Charpentier are adept at working on urban design, architecture, and landscaping in a synchronized fashion. Ms. Zhou Wenyi, the project manager of the team, had received a thorough French education in architecture and urban design. Arte Charpentier holds the view that

> A plaza, visual axes, or the landscape have to be worked out in conjunction with the architecture to create a strong sense of place. At the same time, we did an analysis of the site and the relationship between the city and the topography so that the architecture, the city, and the landscape form an integral ensemble as if the architecture had grown out of the site. (ICI, p. 25)

Table 7.2 The performance space projects designed by Arte Charpentier in China

Project	Competition winner	Completion	Construction area (m^2)	Theater	Concert hall	Multifunctional theater	Remarks
Shanghai Grand Theater	1994	1998	64,000	1800 seats	600 seats	300 seats	The Architectural Creation Award of the Architectural Society of China(1949–2009)
Shanxi Grand Theater	2008	2012	77,000	1628 seats	1170 seats	458 seats	Awarded a special prize from UIA–Interarch, 2009
Xinzhou arts center and opera	2012	2015	73,000	1200 seats	None	600 seats	Workshops for painting, music, and literature

Data summarized by the author, accordance with the latest information form official website of the Arte Charpentier, see Arte Charpentier Architects (2018)

The composition and succession made "the Changfeng Quarter and the Shanxi Grand Theater" an ideal project package with which Arte Charpentier could practice its philosophy (Fig. 7.16).

7.3.2   Entrance-Face (Façade)

The architectural work benefited from the synchronized style of the urban design. Because the building is set upon the main axis leading from the City Hall Plaza to the bank of the Fen River, its axial orientation alone assigns it unmistakable importance, just as Haussmann's boulevards created the ideal site for the Opéra Garnier (Chaslin 1989). A large opening in the Shanxi grand theater was regarded as the passage for the axis (Fig. 7.17). All of the axes of the Changfeng Quarter converge on the grand portico under the opening. The grand portico stands on a terrace of steps, which form a continuum. In the center of the design composition, the terrace enjoys the greatest view: from the city hall plaza in the west to the hydrophilic landscape opposite. As an analogy, the Grande Arche in Paris uses the symbolic Roman triumphal arch not only to identify the city's northwestern extension but also to welcome new business interests to La Défense (Fig. 7.18). Edelman's discussion of the hierarchy of some public spaces is applicable to La Grande Arche and the Shanxi Grand Theater, a building embodying public investment but accentuating governmental control (Fig. 7.19).

> The scale of the structure reminds the mass of political spectators that they enter the precincts of power as clients or as supplicants, susceptible to arbitrary rebuffs and favors, and that they are subject to remote authorities that they only dimly know or understand. (Gartman and Edelman 1996)

 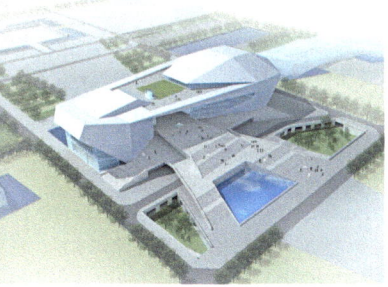

(a) The key building design in the former urban design competition.   (b) The final design of Shanxi Grand Theater.

Fig. 7.16 The design of Shanxi Grand Theater. Copyright © Arte Charpentier Architectes, illustrations drawn by the authors

Fig. 7.17 The Shanxi Grand Theater and the axis. Photo by the author, illustrations drawn by the authors

In traditional architectural thought, the term "entrance-face (façade)" (门面) often associates the entrance of the building with the human face. Literally, "mian" suggests a mask, a painted or sculptured face that is worn by a person to enhance, hide, or alter his or her physical appearance. A face is therefore simultaneously a representation and a means of performance and disguise (Cody 2004). Analogously, at the entrance of the Changfeng Quarter, the Shanxi Grand Theater would invite guests, repel strangers, and indicate various relationships between inside and outside. Furthermore, in the traditional Chinese context, people often place more emphasis on the "depth" of such an architectural "entrance-face" than on the vividness of its "facial expression." (Tang 2018).

In conclusion, the homoplastic buildings of the Grande Arche and the Shanxi Grand Theater have taken on different meanings in different social contexts. In premodern Chinese society, such positioning or contextualizing was often associated with the art of governance (Wu 2013). Following the construction of the Changfeng Quarter, a newly designed shopping mall occupied the former plaza that links the administrative center and the terrace of theater steps. The immense volume of the five-story building unreasonably obstructs the original axis between the administrative center and the cultural center. The axis was disregarded by the consumption capital, presenting the cultural empathy between France and China as evidence (Figs. 7.20, 7.21).

Fig. 7.18   The Grande Arche and the axis. Photo by the author, illustrations drawn by the authors

7.3.3   *Axes that Reach/Paths that Wander*

In fact, the grand steps" continuum has been acknowledged since the period of the Changfeng Quarter's urban design. All of the participants in the design competition applied the steps motif. In contrast to its competitors (Fig. 7.22), Arte Charpentier showed its proficiency in the language of modern architecture without the imitating a cultural symbol. The theater building contains an opera hall, a concert hall upon the terrace, and a small theater under the belvedere platform. On the opposite side of the portico, the opera hall and the concert hall shape the solid appearance of the building. The carefully folded roof allows sunlight to shape the more dynamic form of free plasticity, which reminds visitors of the Casa da Musica designed by Rem Koolhaas. The plaza, the steps, the esplanade, and the halls are treated as a continuous visual sequence. By using stone of the same shade, the sequence achieves an immersive experience of purity and serenity. Near the performance halls, the red color in the interior space emphasizes the heart of the structure and activates spectators" emotion (Fig. 7.23).

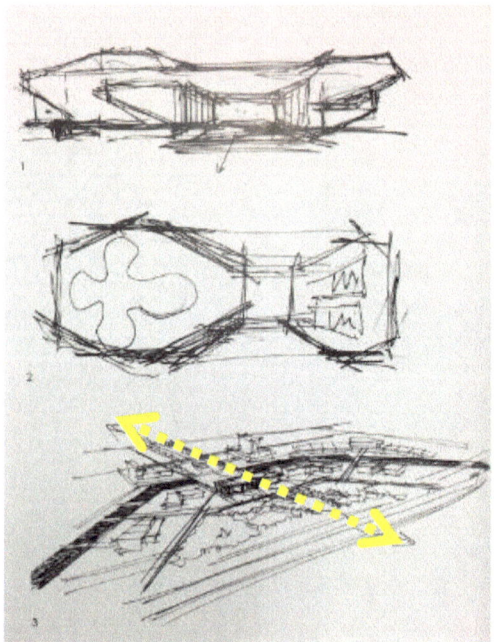 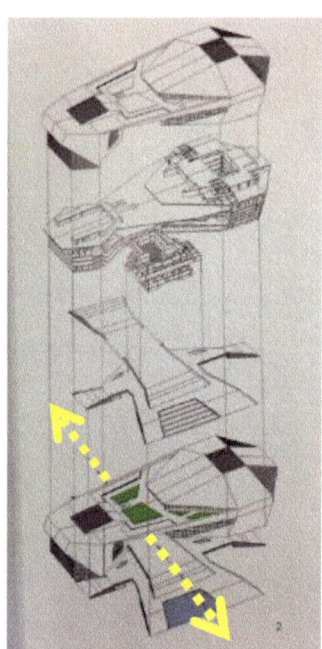

(a) Sketches of the urban design and architectural form   (b) Volumetric exploded view of the
of the Changfeng Quarter.   Shanxi Grand Theater.

Fig. 7.19 The axis within the design of the Changfeng Quarter and the Shanxi Grand Theater.
Copyright © Arte Charpentier Architectes

7.4 Conclusion

This chapter focuses on Taiyuan city, a second-tier city with a brilliant history that
had been gradually reduced to mediocrity. When an ambitious governor took office,
he planned to carry out an urban revitalization process in which cultural facilities
would become symbols of power and represent the city's identity or define its
character. The leaders of this process found, however, that the majority of cultural
spaces nourished by local traditions had been eliminated by the tide of market
forces. The importation of Western-style architecture and urban design for the
performing arts seemed to offer a way out. We examine the Shanxi Grand Theater
in terms of designs, layouts and uses, expectations, and disappointments in spatial
terms both within and in relation to urban spaces.

From an optimistic perspective, the extensive discussion of the construction of
the grand theater could be the beginning of public participation in the architectural
criticism of public buildings. Before this change, unique representations of buildings were propagandized to the public: glorious palaces, splendid great halls, and
soaring skyscrapers. Unlike administration buildings, which are linked to national

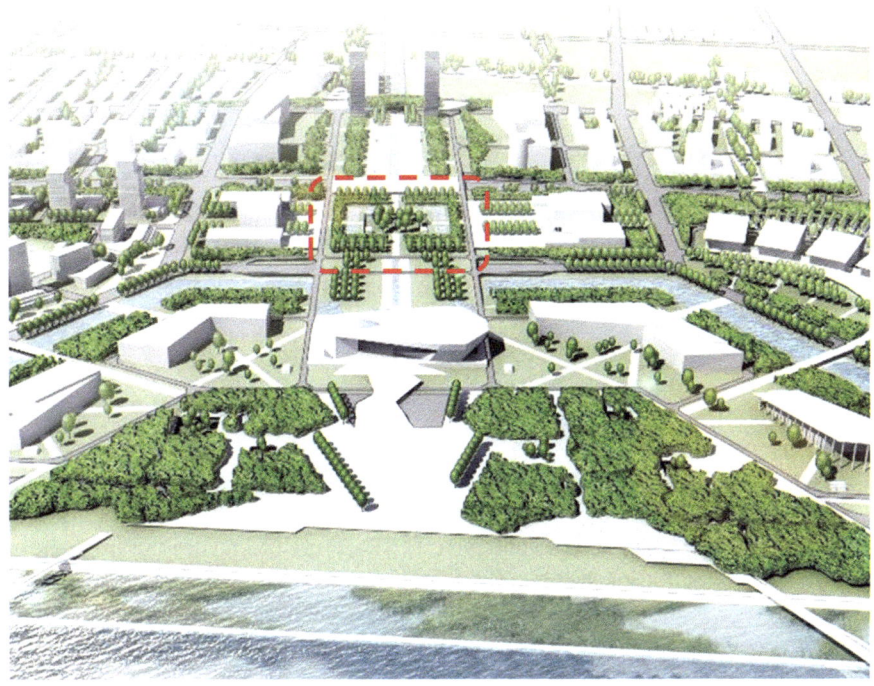

Fig. 7.20 The plaza link to the administrative center and the terrace of steps. Copyright © Arte Charpentier Architectes

Fig. 7.21 Rendering shows a newly designed shopping mall occupying the former plaza. Copyright © Arte Charpentier Architectes

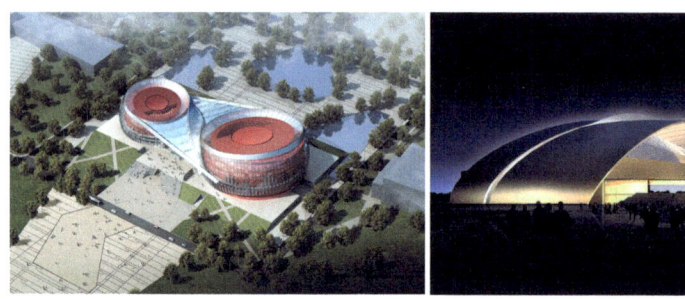

"Pair of Drums."   "Winds of Shanxi."
                                            See Mi et al. (2009), pp. 158-159.

Fig. 7.22 Competitors' design of the Shanxi Grand Theater. Copyright © Urban Planning Commission of Taiyuan

dignity, cultural facilities vary widely and are rarely politically sensitive. Although market economic entities in early stages like to display skyscrapers symbolizing the wealth and glamour of the metropolis, cultural facilities display more creative freedom in their architectural modeling because their architects face fewer structural constraints. The grand theater is an appropriate example of public discussion and vision. During the building boom, the public gradually participated in comprehensive and thorough architectural criticism, and eventually formed its own aesthetic criteria.

From the authority's perspective, the construction of large-scale architectural projects served as a gesture: when an outstanding building appears in a traditional area, it must have a significant meaning. After several years of large-scale construction, the authorities have already learned to release special information through the construction of a grand theater. The opening-up policy, that is, allows the government to present cultural wonders to the Chinese people through the integration of global intelligence. In this way, people "silently" enhance their sense of national identity and pride. Talented architects, moreover, are attracted from a wide field to develop the city to its utmost architectural potential.

In view of the overall situation of China's urban modernization, large public cultural buildings have been placed in a dominant position in this urban revitalization movement. All levels of government have carried out this consensus: influenced by the grand theater boom in the capital and in first-tier cities in China, the provincial capitals started a new round of competitions for such urban spectacles, and third-tier cities have made less pragmatic urban planning decisions because of the weight of this criterion for "modern cities." When the mass media focuses on the construction of large public buildings like grand theaters and exhibition centers, buildings devoted to minority groups" welfare are inevitably neglected. Because Paris can no longer afford to carry out "Grands Projets" like those of the 1980s, massive urban construction represents a precious "historic

Fig. 7.23 Photographic view of the Shanxi Grand Theater. **a** The façade. **b** The side foyer. **c** The interior of the theater. Copyright © Arte Charpentier Architectes

opportunity" for contemporary China. China must, however, select a course for its urban development with limited time and complex options.

Acknowledgements This paper is part of a study supported by the Research Grant Council, Hong Kong Government, Project No. CityU 11658816. The authors thank the constructive comments and suggestions from Dr. Zhang Liang, Mr. Cai Wenyue, Ms. Zhou wenyi, Mr. Pierre Chambron, Ms. Liang Jia, Dr. Tang Keyang, Dr. Xiao Ping and Mr. Xiao Ying.

My father was trained as a surgeon in Beijing. His professor habitually listened to J. S. Bach's works during preoperative preparation. Since graduating, my father has applied this musical philosophy in our family, and he took us to performing arts shows as much as possible.

I spent my childhood in Taiyuan, where there was little chance for a young boy to attend high-grade performances. My only visit to the Grand Theatre in Beijing will always remain in my memory, although then, I lost myself in the comfortable seats and dazzling lights rather than the performance. If readers can empathise with me as a young boy, they may understand what motivates the Shanxi people's ambitious behaviour regarding grand theatre.

In addition to the modern grand theatre, many Soviet-style performing spaces were built in the 1950s–1960s that were still functional at the end of the 20th century. I lived in a unit compound ("danwei dayuan", unit yard community) with an auditorium for conferences, drama shows and movies. The small square in front of the auditorium became the center of the community. I would do my homework with my friends on the wide railing after school. When children played football or basketball on the square, their parents sat on the entrance steps, watching over them. My grandfather always had numerous tickets to every performance in the auditorium.

The building made a favourable impression on me. As an adult, I have experienced many performing spaces in Asian and European countries, but the way I think about performing spaces has been and continues to be influenced by nostalgia for my happy childhood.

References

Andō, T., Dal Co, F., & Gregotti, V. (1997). *Tadao Ando* (p. 512). London: Phaidon.

Architectural Times. (2005). Long-term and win-win cooperation-interview with the French director of '150 Chinese architects in France' project. *ABBS*. Retrieved August 7, 2018, from http://www.abbs.com.cn/jzsb/read.php?cate=5&recid=13240. 建筑时报. (2005). 放眼长远 合作共赢—就"150名中国建筑师在法国"项目采访法方负责人. *ABBS*.

Arte Charpentier Architects. (2018). The official website of the Arte Charpentier. *Home | Arte Charpentier*. Retrieved December 4, 2018, from http://www.arte-charpentier.com/en/.

Bosker, B. (2013). *Original copies: Architectural mimicry in contemporary China* (p. 90). Hong Kong: Hong Kong University Press.

Chaslin, F. (1989). A monument in persepective. In F. Chaslin, V. Picon-Lefebvre, & R. Theuil (Eds.), *La grande Arche de la Défense* (pp. 19–25). Paris: Electa Moniteur.

Che, W. (2011). A new discovery of the 'dance building' inscription in the northern Song Dynasty. *Literary Heritage, 5*, 144–147. 车文明. (2011). 北宋"舞楼"碑刻的新发现. 文学遗产, 5, 144–147.

Chinese Opera Chorography Editing Committee. (1990). *The chorography of China opera, volume on Shanxi* (p. 17). Beijing: Culture and Art Press. 中国戏曲志编辑委员会. (1990). 中国戏曲志·山西卷. 北京:文化艺术出版社. p. 17.

Cody, J. (2004). Making history in Shanghai: Architectural dialogues about space, place, and face. In P. Rowe & S. Kuan (Eds.), *Shanghai: Architecture and urbanism for modern China* (pp. 128–141). New York: Prestel.

Duan, J. (2008). *Stages and society: Study on Stages of Shanxi Province in Ming and Qing Dynasties* (Ph.D. Dissertation). Central China Normal University. 段建宏. (2008). 戏台与社会:明清山西戏台研究(博士学位论文). 武汉: 华中师范大学.

Gartman, D., & Edelman, M. (1996). From art to politics: How artistic creations shape political conceptions. *Contemporary Sociology, 25*(1), 44. https://doi.org/10.2307/2076951.

Guan. Z. (1989). Review of the grands projets. *World Architecture, 5*, 10–19. 关肇邺. (1989). 巴黎国庆工程述评. 世界建筑, *5*, 10–19.

Ledderose, L. (1983). The earthly paradise: Religious elements in Chinese landscape art. In B. Murck, *Theories of the arts in China* (p. 166). Princeton: Princeton University Press.

Muscat, C., & Peel, C. (2002). *Museums and galleries of Paris.* Singapore: APA.

Mi, J., Li, D., & Qiu, J. (2009). Schematic design of Shanxi Grand Theatre. *Architectural Creation, 7*, 158–159. 米俊仁, 李大鹏, 邱健伟. (2009). 山西大剧院方案. 建筑创作, *7*, 158–159.

Nelson, R., & Shiff, R. (2003). *Critical terms for art history.* Chicago: University of Chicago Press.

Pogrebin, R. (2019). British Architect Wins 2007 Pritzker Prize. *Nytimes.com.* Retrieved October 13, 2018, from https://www.nytimes.com/2007/03/28/arts/design/28cnd-pritzker.html?hp.

Sang, J. (2002). To Shanxi grand theater: Where are you. *Shanxi Daily*, p. B04. 尚晋生. (2002). 山西大剧院:你在哪里? 山西日报 (2月4日), p. B04.

State Council Information Office of China. (2013). Yu Youjun donated 1.6 million yuan from his publication royalties to build a cultural center for the Datong miner community. *Public Welfare of China.* Retrieved August 28, 2018, from http://gongyi.china.com.cn/2013-10/16/content_6375918.htm. 中国互联网新闻中心, 公益中国爱心联盟. (2013). 于幼军捐160万稿费 为大同矿工社区建文化中心. 公益中国.

Tang, K. (2018). Forming and performing: Conditioning the concept of Chinese space in the case of National Theatre of China. *Space and Culture, 13*(5). https://doi.org/10.1177/1206331218774486.

The People's Government of Shanxi Province. (2007). The provincial government raised five billion yuan to build six buildings for the public welfare. *Shanxi.gov.cn.* Retrieved August 7, 2018, from http://www.shanxi.gov.cn/yw/zwlb/gsdt/200701/t20070129_48758.shtml 山西省人民政府办公厅. (2007). 省政府筹资五十亿元兴建社会公益六大建筑. *Shanxi.gov.cn.*

The People's Government of Shanxi Province. (2016). *Thoughts on the development of new urbanization in Shanxi Province* (p. 7). Taiyuan: The People's Government of Shanxi Province. 山西省人民政府. (2016). 山西省"十三五"综合能源发展规划 (p. 7). 太原: 山西省人民政府.

The People's Government of Shanxi Province. (2017). Thoughts on the development of new urbanization in Shanxi Province. *Stats-sx.gov.cn.* Retrieved August 5, 2018, from http://www.stats-sx.gov.cn/sjjd/sjxx/201706/t20170605_82101.shtml. Accessed 14 Aug 2018. 山西省人民政府人口处(2017)山西省新型城镇化发展的思考.山西统计信息网.

Urban Planning Commission of Taiyuan. (2008). *The book series of Taiyuan urban planning projects* (1st ed., p. 220). Beijing: China Building Industry Press.

Wu, H. (2013). *Remaking Beijing: Tianmen Square and the creation of political space.* London: Reaktion Books.

Xue, C. (2010). *World architecture in China.* Hong Kong: Joint Publishing.

Xue, C., & Xiao, Y. (2018). The jewel in the crown-The heat of grand theatres. In L. Li & C. Xue, *Chinese urbanism in the 21st century.* Beijing: China Building Industry Press. 薛求理, 肖映博. (2018). 皇冠上的明珠: "大剧院"热. 李磷, 薛求理 主编, *21*世纪中国城市主义 (pp. 33–51). 北京: 中国建筑工业出版社.

Yang, Y., & Gu, M. (1999). *Chinese architecture in the 20th century* (p. 235). Tianjin: Tianjin Science and Technology Press. 杨永生, 顾孟潮. (1999). *20*世纪中国建筑. 天津: 天津科学技术出版社.

Yu, Y. (2005). Speech at the press conference of the 2005 Shanxi Investment and Trade Fair. *Scio.gov.cn.* Retrieved August 7, 2019, from http://www.scio.gov.cn/xwfbh/gssxwfbh/xwfbh/

shanxi/Document/321029/321029.htm. 于幼军. (2005). 在2005山西投资贸易洽谈会新闻发布会上的讲话. *Scio.gov.cn.*

Zhu, J. (2004). *Chinese spatial strategies* (p. 99). New York: Routledge.

Zhou, W., & Chambron, P. (2012). *From architecture to the city.* Paris: ICI Consultants. 周雯怡, 皮埃尔. (2012). 从建筑到城市:法国*ARTE*-夏邦杰建筑设计事务所在中国. 沈阳: 辽宁科学技术出版社.

Chapter 8
A Butterfly by the Lake—Wuxi Grand Theater

Lin Li

8.1 Background of Wuxi

Wuxi, a city in Jiangsu Province, is located about 40 km from its eastern neighbor Suzhou and about 128 km west of the metropolis Shanghai (Fig. 8.1). Despite its population of 6.55 million (2017), Wuxi still seems small when compared with its larger neighbor Suzhou (10.26 million in 2017) and the megacity Shanghai (24.18 million in 2016). Although its proximity to Suzhou and Shanghai is a geographical limitation that reduces Wuxi's potential to become a regional center, it has never lacked for confidence and ambition in catching up with the trends of other large cities. For example, the construction of Wuxi Grand Theater is a milestone project in the city's history of cultural development in terms of providing a high-class facility for the performing arts.

The historical water city of Wuxi was founded during the Yuan Dynasty (1335) as an unusual diamond-shaped county town surrounded by a city wall and an outer moat. According to historical records (i.e., the county gazetteer of Wuxi), the perimeter of the city wall during the Ming Dynasty was about 17,836 Chinese feet (approximately 6 km). Two crossing rivers were used as main traffic arteries or thoroughfares: the Beijing-Hangzhou Grand Canal originally ran through Wuxi as its north-south semi-major axis (now Zhongshan Road; about 2.13 km), and an east-west river acted as a semi-minor axis (now Xongning Road and Houxixi Street; about 1.5 km). Because Wuxi had access to a large water transportation network, it gradually evolved into a logistical center and a famous dock for the rice and cloth trades along the Grand Canal (Figs. 8.2 and 8.3). It was also prosperous in commerce and handicraft production.

With Huishan Mountain to the west of the city and Lake Tai (Taihu) just less than 6 km. to the southwest, many people consider Wuxi a landscape city. Erquan

L. Li (✉)
Chinese Civilization Center, City University of Hong Kong, Kowloon, Hong Kong
e-mail: cililin@cityu.edu.hk

© Springer Nature Singapore Pte Ltd. 2019   179
C. Q. Xue (ed.), *Grand Theater Urbanism*,
https://doi.org/10.1007/978-981-13-7868-3_8

Fig. 8.1 Geographic location of Wuxi

Fig. 8.2 Wuxi old town was a canal city. The Beijing-Hangzhou grand canal once ran from S to N. 1 —Wuxi County Government Office, 2—Jingui County Government Office, 3—Temple of Literature, 4—College, 5—Temple of Military, 6—Temple of the City God, 7—Temple of Shanhuang, 8—Chongan Buddhist Temple, 9—Dongxu Daoist Temple. N—North city gate and canal pass, S—South city gate and canal pass, E—East city gate, W—West city gate, Wp—West canal pass

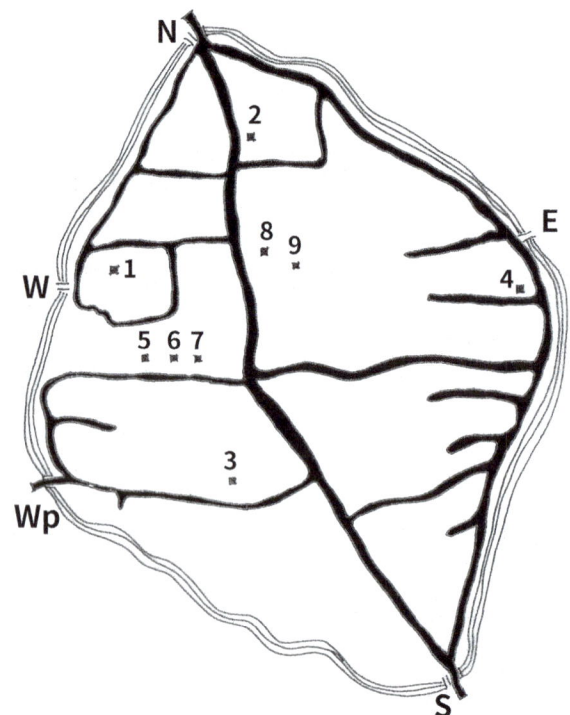

Fig. 8.3 A model of Wuxi old town shows the city wall and canals of the southern portion

Spring, Jichangyuan Garden in Huishan Mountain, and Yuantouzhu Park in Lake Tai are three beautiful attractions that are well-known nationwide (Fig. 8.4).

8.2 Urban Development

The urban area of Wuxi was about 10.5 km^2 in 1949, but by 2005 it had grown to 193 km^2, nearly 20-fold growth. The urban development of Wuxi occurred in three phases: (1) 1950–1979; (2) 1980–1999; and (3) 2000 to the present.

The first phase was characterized by the demolition of the city walls, the rerouting of the Grand Canal from the city center to the western and southern suburbs, and the transition from water transportation to land transportation. The city extended along the axis of the Shanghai-Nanjing railway and motorway, stretching in the northwestern and southeastern directions like a spindle. The key projects during this phase included many new vehicular bridges constructed for land transportation over canals and rivers (Fig. 8.5). According to government plans from 1953 and 1959, Wuxi was developed to be a city of light industry with textile and electromechanical production, with scenic health resorts as a secondary function.

In the second phase, Wuxi was planned to develop from 640,000 people and 52 km^2 (1982) to 1 million people and 130 km^2 (1986) as an "important city of economic center and scenic tourism of Jiangsu Province." The city grew in a ring pattern outward from the old town, and Huishan Mountain was embraced by new districts (Fig. 8.6). The key projects of this phase included high-rise hotel towers such as Wuxi International Hotel (1997), Wuxi Jinjiang Grand Hotel (1998), and

Fig. 8.4 Wuxi regional map. W—Wuxi old town, H—Huishan mountain, L—Lake Li, T—Lake Tai

the 100-ha Wuxi Movie and Television City, built since 1987 as a filming location for CCTV.

In the third phase (the current phase), Wuxi development has been planned within six zones: The Central Urban Core (old/center), Huishan Xincheng[1] (new/ north), Xidong Xincheng (new/east), Keji[2] Xincheng or Wuxi Xinqu (new/ southeast), Taihu Xincheng (new/south), and Lixi Xincheng (new/west) (Fig. 8.7). Each zone is provided with a new center, such as Taihu Square Park in the Central Urban Core, Central Park in Huishan Xincheng, Yingbin Square in Xidong Xincheng, Xinzhou Eco-park in Wuxi Xinqu, Jingui Park in Taihu Xincheng, and Wuxi Sport Center in Lixi Xincheng. The numerous key projects of this phase fall into various categories such as infrastructure, public open spaces, cultural facilities,

---

[1]Xincheng means new zone or new city.

[2]Keji means science and technology.

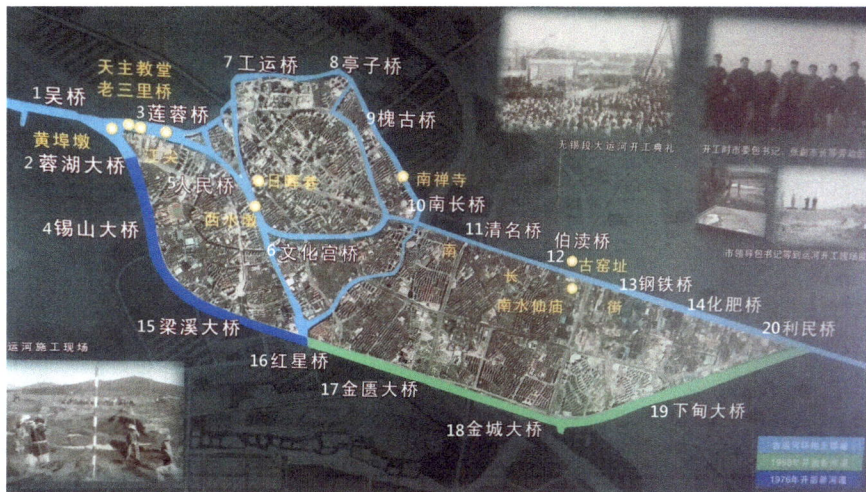

Fig. 8.5 Twenty vehicular bridges were built during the first phase. 1—Wu Bridge, 2—Ronghu Bridge, 3—Lianrong Bridge, 4—Xishan Bridge, 5—Renmin Bridge, 6—Wenhuagong Bridge, 7 —Gongyun Bridge, 8—Tingzi Bridge, 9—Huaigu Bridge, 10—Nanchang Bridge, 11—Qingming Bridge, 12—Bodu Bridge, 13—Gangtie Bridge, 14—Huafei Bridge, 15—Liangxi Bridge, 16— Hongxing Bridge, 17—Jinkui Bridge, 18—Jincheng Bridge, 19—Xiadian Bridge, 20—Limin Bridge

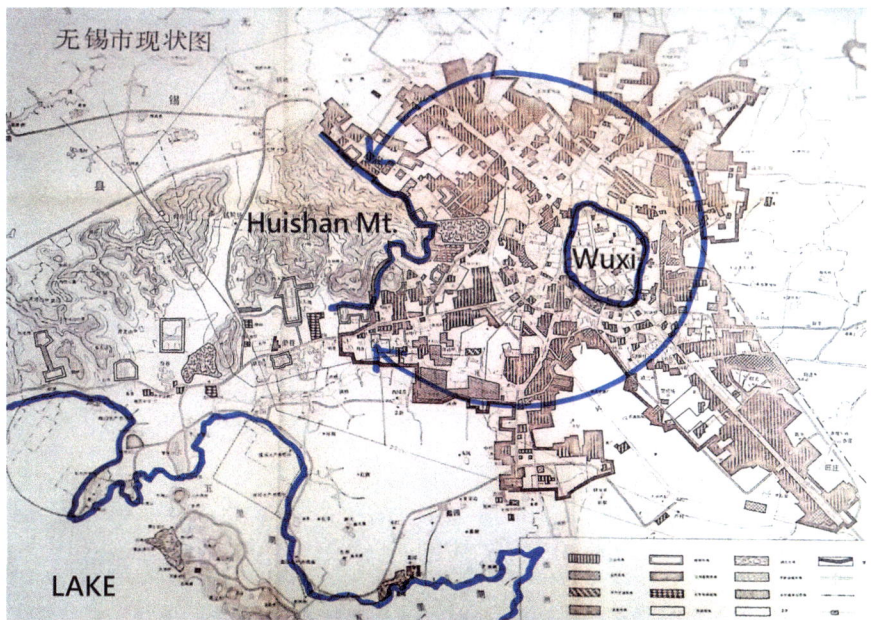

Fig. 8.6 Map of Wuxi in 1982 shows urban development in a ring-pattern

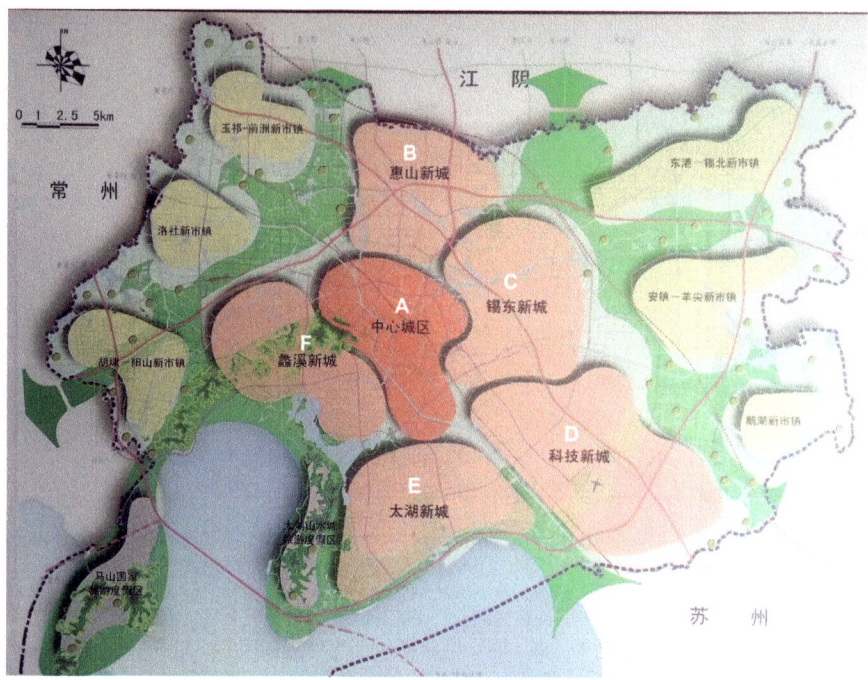

Fig. 8.7 Recent master plan of Wuxi. A—Central Urban Core, B—Huishan Xincheng, C—Xidong Xincheng, D—Keji Xincheng, E—Taihu Xincheng, F—Lixi Xincheng

and commercial buildings. Large projects in addition to the parks mentioned above include Shuofang International Airport, Wuxi High-Speed Rail Terminal, Wuxidong[3] High-Speed Rail Terminal, Wuxi Civic Center (a government building), Wuxi Museum and Wuxi Grand Theater, Center 66 or Hang Lung Plaza (a 270-m office tower/shopping mall), Maoye Center (a 304-m office/hotel), and Wuxi International Financial Square (a 339-m office tower) to outline a new image of the city.

By keeping pace with China's rapid urbanization over the past 10 years (Xue 2006), a multicentered Wuxi is emerging. Sanyang-guangchang, or Sanyang Square, the traditional heart at the intersection of Renmin Road and Zhongshan Road in the historical town, has been transformed into a central business district (CBD) with dense skyscrapers that see much hustle and bustle in shopping and entertainment in the city (Fig. 8.8).

Taihu Square Park, south of the diamond-shaped old town, is a new center of the Central Urban Core. The park is about 450 m wide and 800 m long and is surrounded by Wuxi Great Hall of People, Wuxi Museum, Library, Urban Construction Archive, Revolutionary Museum, Science and Technology Museum,

---

[3]Wuxidong means Wuxi East.

Fig. 8.8 Skyline at Sanyang Plaza, from middle to left: Hodo International Plaza (pyramidal top/248 m), Center 66, Yunfu Building (flat top/264 m), Suning Plaza (angled top/328 m)

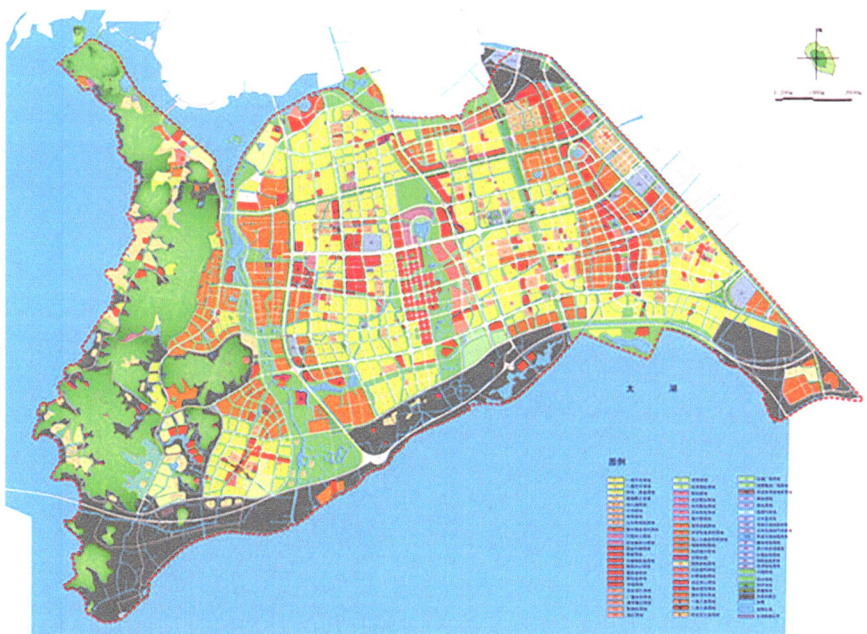

Fig. 8.9 Master plan of Taihu Xincheng (new town)

Youth and Children Activity Center, International Financial Square tower, Maoye
Center tower, World Trade Center tower, Intercontinental Hotel tower, Kempinski
Hotel tower, and a high-end shopping mall (Xue 2010).

South of the Central Urban Core is the Taihu Xingcheng new zone. According to
the master plan, the land uses of this 150-km^2 new zone are for leading business
firms, financial institutions, corporate headquarters, professional services, administration, science and education, cultural and creative industries, and housing
communities of a resort lifestyle (Fig. 8.9). The centerpiece of the Taihu new zone
is the 6.5-ha Jingui Wetland Park (Li and Xue 2017), which includes Wuxi Civic
Center as the new home of the city government (Figs. 8.10 and 8.11).

Fig. 8.10 Jingui Wetland
Park

Fig. 8.11 Wuxi Civic Center, designed by gmp

The Civic Center, designed by German architectural firm gmp and completed in 2010, is a curved building, 740 m long and 105 m high, that follows the configuration of the circular lake to its south. In addition to offices, this 335,000-m^2 administrative complex also houses a conference center and an exhibition center.

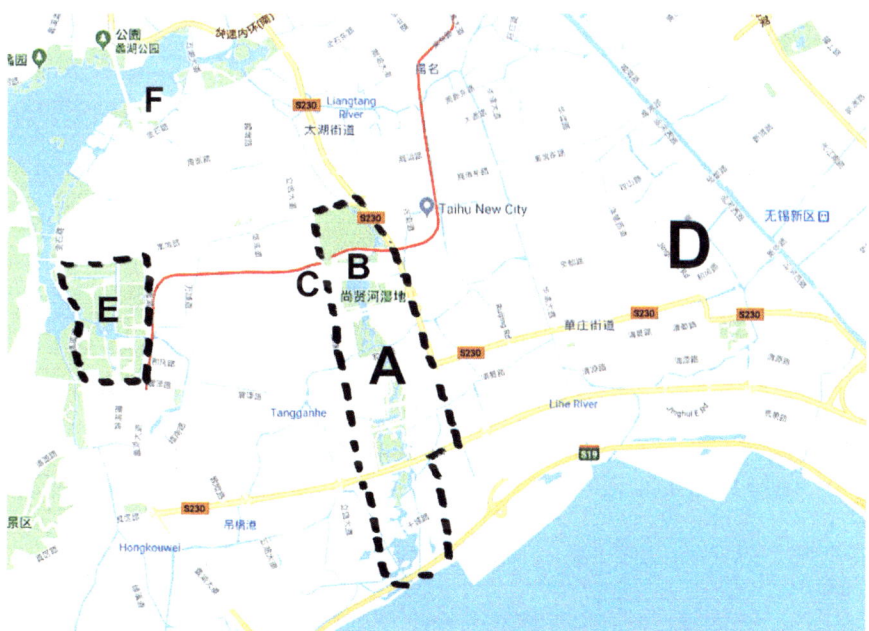

Fig. 8.12 Key projects of the Taihu Xincheng. A—Jingui Wetland Park, B—Civic Center, C—Financial Center, D—Science Park, E—Jiangnan University, F—Wuxi Grand Theater

Across the street to the west is a 270 × 850-m block dedicated to finance, with the Wuxi Financial Center facing the main boulevard, Guanshan Road. Near the eastern edge of Taihu Xingcheng (new town) is the 23-km^2 Wuxi International Science Park (2009), near the western edge is Jiangnan University's new 215-ha campus (2005), and at the northern edge (i.e., the south bank of Lake Li[4]) is Wuxi Grand Theater (Fig. 8.12).

Wuxi Grand Theater is located on the south bank of Lake Li and on the east side of Liwu Dadao Avenue. It was designed by the Finnish architectural firm PES; construction began in 2009 and was completed in 2012. The total investment in the theater, which takes the form of a butterfly with eight wings, exceeded RMB1 billion.

8.3   Historical Review of Musical Arts and Performing Venues in Wuxi

Xiju is a local Xiqu (or Chinese folk opera) of Wuxi. Its origin can be dated to the early Qing Dynasty (1644–1911). According to historical records, a retired imperial official Zhao Yi described a folk performance on a temporary stage built by wooden benches during a Buddhist Festival of Xiaomaoshan Miaohui in the countryside of Wuxi. As a folk art, Xiju used to be performed in rural areas such as the market-places of villages and small towns, but occasionally it was performed inside the city. In 1919 and 1920, two Xiju companies introduced commercial performances in Shanghai and saw immediately success. However, Xiju in Wuxi was rather frustrated, because it contained obscenity and was banned by the local government. In 1930, some Xiju artists formed a company in Suzhou and their performances were successful too. In 1955, the Wuxi Xiju Company was officially established by the city government. Xiju performances were suspended during the Cultural Revolution (1966–1976). In the 1980s, Xiju recovered and again achieved popularity for a short time. It began to decline after 1990 because of competition from other forms of popular entertainment. Like other local Xiqus in China, performances of Xiju in the past often took the form of tours to villages, small towns, or large factories. It was seldom performed in a fixed theater.

Wuxi is associated with one of the most famous pieces of erhu music, *Erquan Yingyue* ("Reflection of the Moon in Erquan Spring"). This solo erhu piece had no name when first played by the blind street musician Ar-Bing (Hua Yanjun). He often played this music at the open piazza of the Erquan Spring (the Second Spring) in Huishan Mountain and asked for donations to make a living. In 1950, a professor from the Central Academy of Music recorded Ar-Bing's playing and named it after Erquan.

---

[4]Lake Li is a bay defined by the Lake Tai coast and the Yuantouzhu Peninsula to the southwest of Wuxi.

Before 1949, Zhongyang Theater was one of the large movie theaters in Wuxi (Fig. 8.13). In 1954, the Wuxi Worker's Cultural Palace (1 Qingyang Road) was completed, and its theater served as a major place for the performing arts for 60 years. In 2014, a New Worker's Cultural Palace was built in Taihu Xingcheng (299 Guanshan Road), and the old one was demolished (Figs. 8.15 and 8.16). The

Fig. 8.13 Zhongyang Theater is one of the oldest movie theaters in Wuxi

Fig. 8.14 Performing Arts Center

Fig. 8.15 The new worker's cultural palace

Fig. 8.16 The theater of the new worker's cultural palace

new complex also includes a modern theater. The Performing Arts Center in the old town of Wuxi was converted from the old Auditorium of the CPPCC (Chinese People's Political Consultative Conference) for children's theater (Fig. 8.14). Opened in 1999, the Wuxi Great Hall of People (gross floor area [GFA], 28,362 m^2) is also a venue for the performing arts, with a 1248-seat grand theater (Figs. 8.17 and 8.18).

Fig. 8.17 Master plan of
Taihu square park. Red dot
shows the great hall of people

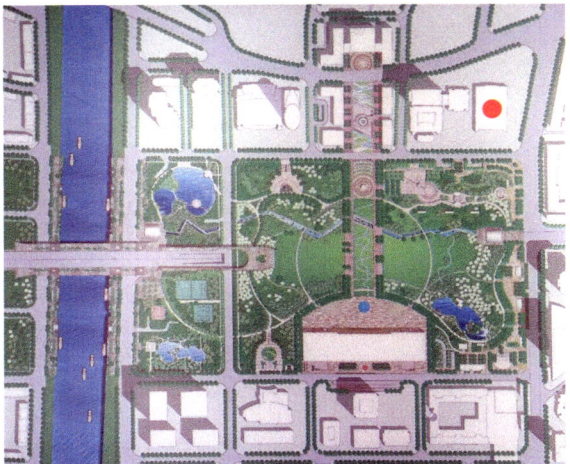

Fig. 8.18 Great hall of people, Wuxi

8.4   Wuxi Grand Theater

8.4.1   Site

The theater project, originally called the Art Center, was planned in Lot No. 1 Taihu
Xingcheng, south of the Lake Li (Lihu), southeast of the Lihu Bridge, east of the
Lihu Dadao Avenue, and north of Jinshi Road. It is a waterfront site 6 km from the
old town center, and the planned site area was about 55,000 m^2.

Fig. 8.19 Lihu (Lake Li) Scenic zone

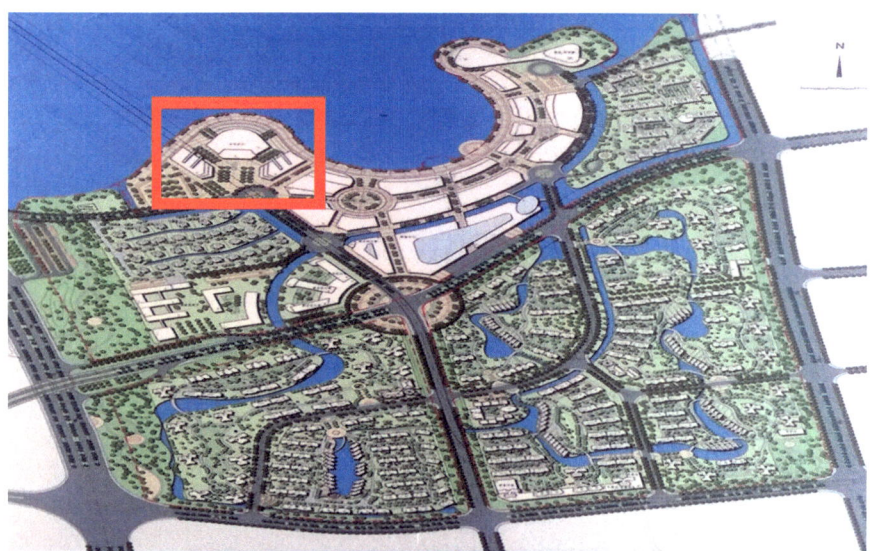

Fig. 8.20 Taihu international community

Lake Li is a bay of Lake Tai formed by the Yuantouzhu peninsula and the coast to the southwest of Wuxi old town, with a water surface of about 8.6 km². Wuxi once had a plan to develop Lake Li, called Lihu Scenic Zone, in 1995. The objective of the plan was to develop the lake and its surrounding coastlines into a huge landscape garden and a wetland park with elements of tourism, aquatic activities, culture, and entertainment, including resorts, conference services, and public facilities (Fig. 8.19).

The theater lies on the southern shore of Lake Li and the northern edge of Taihu International Community (Fig. 8.20), which is a joint-venture real-estate development by two Hong Kong developers: China Resources Land Limited and Sun Hung Kai Properties. The total area of the Community is about 111 ha, and the total GFA is about 1,450,000 m^2, of which residential buildings comprise 1,100,000 m^2 and commercial buildings comprise 360,000 m^2. The northern edge of the Community features a U-shaped commercial zone whose central portion is occupied by a large shopping mall, Mixc. The theater is built at the upper-left end of the U, projecting into the lake (Figs. 8.21 and 8.22).

Fig. 8.21 Site map of the grand theater

Fig. 8.22 The theater was built on a manmade peninsula

8.4.2 Objective

For Wuxi, the construction of a Grand Theater is the creation of an iconic and functional project to complete the city's urban functions and to raise the standard of performing art facilities, and to improve its cultural status. The city believed that it would promote the development of art and cultural industry and regional or international exchanges of culture. Local mass media also expected that, as a flagship project of cultural industry, the construction of Wuxi Grand Theater should be a new milestone and increase Wuxi's international influence.

8.4.3 Architect

PES Architects of Finland won first prize in an invited international architectural competition in 2008. Pekka Salminen was the design team leader. The idea of the theater came from its site along a lake and a man-made peninsula with a bridge nearby. The waterfront environment led to an easy association with the image of the Opera House in Sydney Harbor.

Founded in 1968 by Pekka Salminen, the Helsinki-based PES Architects is a leading architectural design firm in Finland. PES has designed complex public buildings such as theaters, airports, railway terminals, university buildings, schools, sporting facilities, retail developments, office buildings, and housing developments. Since 1986, the firm has consistently worked on design commissions for Helsinki Vantaa Airport, with the main projects being the International Terminal T2 completed in 1999 and the non-Schengen Terminal Phase 1 completed in 2004. Sustainable design, in terms of ecological, economical, and architectural quality, is an essential and self-evident part of PES' design solutions.

Before establishing PES, Pekka Salminen worked for the notable Finnish architect Timo Penttilä on the design of the Helsinki City Theater (completed in 1967), which was Penttilä's most important project. Salminen has won many professional awards, including the Finnish Concrete Prize, the Finnish Steel Prize, the European Union Prize for Contemporary Architecture—Mies van der Rohe Award, the German Concrete Architecture Prize, and the German Architecture Prize. His other representative works include Lahti Sports Centre and Ski Museum, Lahti City Theater, the Police College of Finland, Helsinki-Vantaa Airport, and the Concert Hall at St. Mary's Church in Neubrandenburg, Germany. Another major project in China that will be completed after the Wuxi Grand Theater is the Strait Culture and Art Center in Fuzhou (October 2018).

PES has operated in China since 2003. When he was asked about appreciation for Finnish architecture in China during an interview with EARs, Salminen expressed that smart and user-friendly solutions in building were typical characteristics of Finnish architecture. He also smoothly criticized Chinese clients who ask ed(?) first about a building's looks, then the price, and finally the functionality.[5]

8.4.4 Form

Like Sydney Opera House, whose roof structures ("Shells") are built atop a podium, according to the architect, Wuxi Grand Theater "consists of eight leaves, or wings, which, together with the terraced stone plinth give the impression of a butterfly descending onto the shore of the Wu-Li Lake".[6] "PES-Architects wanted to give such a form to this new art institute so that the building itself becomes a work of art —a big sculpture. In addition to this the wings are an important part of the ecological concept as they protect the building mass from the direct heat of the sun."[7] The theater's footprint is 67,600 m^2, and the GFA is about 78,000 m^2. The plinth is 6 m high, and the building's height exceeds 50 m. The architectural form of the theater beautifully interprets its scenic context (Figs. 8.23 and 8.24).

---

[5]Interview with Pekka Salminen, EARs, retrieved: http://ears.asia/2015/07/30/interview-with-pekka-salminen/.

[6]Wu-Li Lake is another name of Lake Li.

[7]From PES Architects official website, retrieved: http://www.pesark.com/wuxigrandtheater.html.

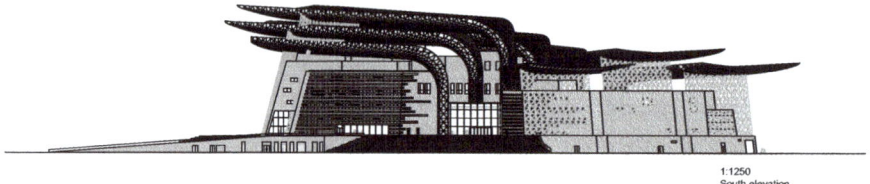

Fig. 8.23 South elevation. Courtesy of PES architects

Fig. 8.24 The theater and the lake

8.4.5 Function

The theater is accessed from the south plaza, where a grand stair rises to the top of the plinth leading to the main entrance. The lobby is a see-through design with an open view to the northeastern water scenery of Lake Li. The central lobby also subdivides the complex into two parts: a 1680-seat Grand Theater with a five-leaf roof on the northwestern side for opera, music, and ballet and a 690-seat Comprehensive Performance Hall with a three-leaf roof on the southeastern side. Outside the theater, terraces, paths, and landscapes surround the complex and integrate well with the lakeshore, providing a pleasant walking experience at the edge of the peninsula (Figs. 8.25, 8.26 and 8.27).

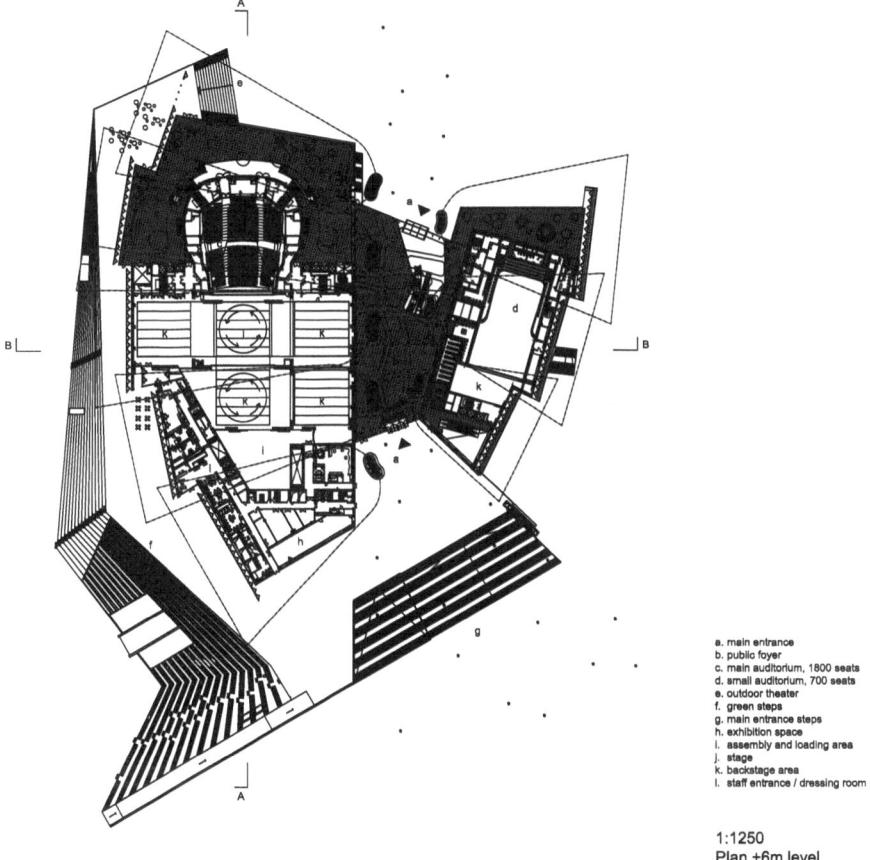

a. main entrance
b. public foyer
c. main auditorium, 1800 seats
d. small auditorium, 700 seats
e. outdoor theater
f. green steps
g. main entrance steps
h. exhibition space
i. assembly and loading area
j. stage
k. backstage area
l. staff entrance / dressing room

1:1250
Plan +6m level

Fig. 8.25 Floor plan +6 m level. Courtesy of PES architects

8.4.6 Structure

The eight-leaf metal roof is an independent structure that completely detaches from the two auditoriums, which are concrete enclosures cladded with stones on the exterior walls. The main entrance, the central lobby, and two foyers that face the lake have glass curtain walls and glass roofs (Figs. 8.28, 8.29, 8.30 and 8.31).

8.4.7 Interior

The most special feature of the theater is the extensive use of bamboo as a finish material for the auditorium's interior walls. According to Dezeen, "new methods for

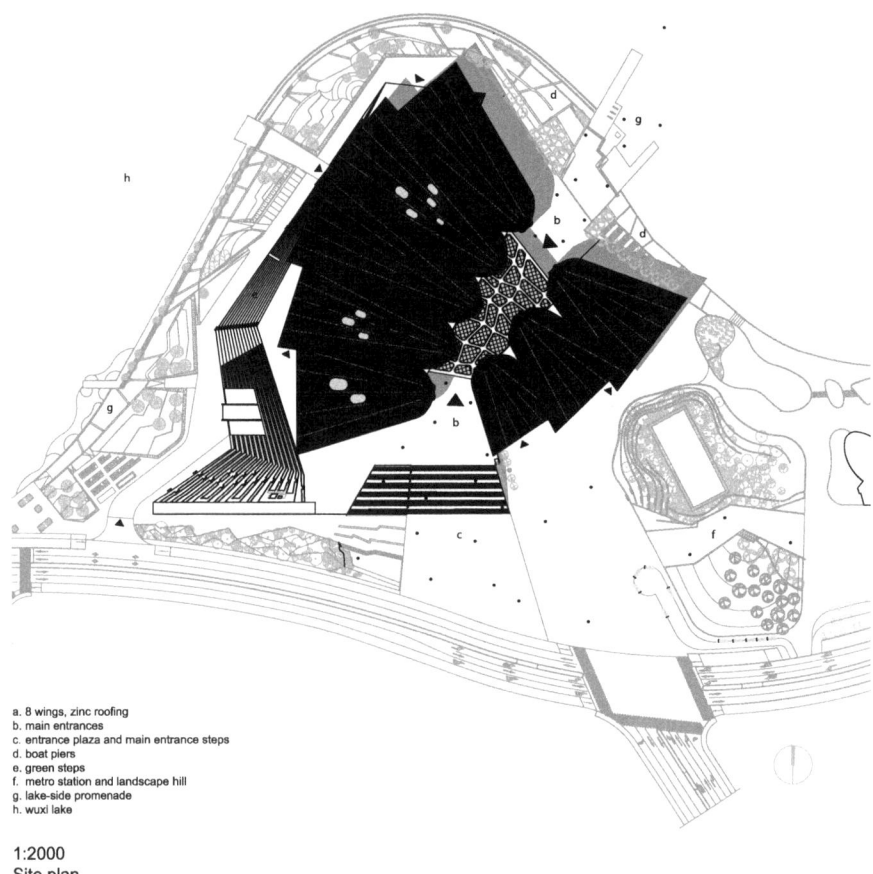

a. 8 wings, zinc roofing
b. main entrances
c. entrance plaza and main entrance steps
d. boat piers
e. green steps
f. metro station and landscape hill
g. lake-side promenade
h. wuxi lake

1:2000
Site plan

Fig. 8.26 Site plan. Courtesy of PES architects

the production and use of bamboo have made it possible to cover the Main Opera Auditorium with over 15,000 solid bamboo blocks, all individually shaped according to acoustic needs and architectural image."[8] (Figs. 8.32, 8.33, 8.34 and 8.35).

---

[8]Wuxi Grand Theater by PES-Architects, Dezeen. Retrieved: https://www.dezeen.com/2012/09/09/wuxi-grand-theater-by-pes-architects/.

Fig. 8.27 Top level of the plinth

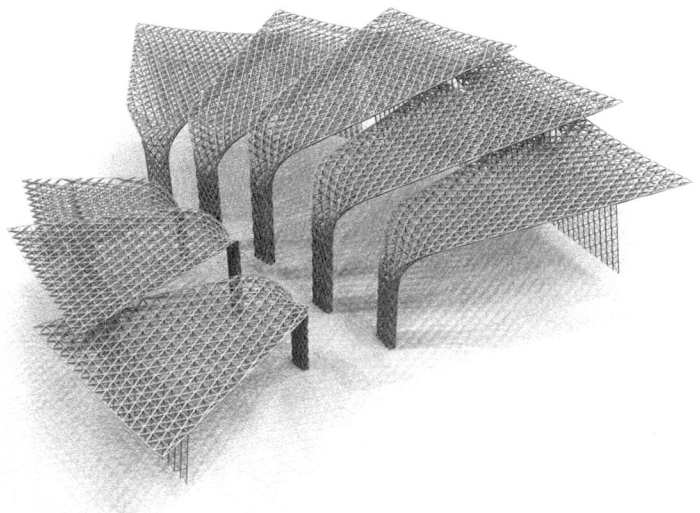

Fig. 8.28 Steel structure wings as the roof. Courtesy of PES architects

Fig. 8.29 Wings viewed at night. Kari Palsila/courtesy of PES architects

8.5 Reflections

As a small city that concentrated on the development of light industries until the late 1990s, Wuxi had never been a prime venue in terms of high-profile performing arts. To the east, not far away, is the cultural center of Shanghai. To the west lies the provincial capital Nanjing (the capital of the Republic of China from 1927 to 1949). The construction of a large-scale, high-standard performance space was only realized in 1999 when the Wuxi Great Hall of People was completed.

With reference to Fig. 8.36, it is interesting to see that the locations of new theaters are moving farther from the Wuxi old town: the old Worker's Cultural Palace (1954), the Great Hall of People (1999), the Grand Theater (2012), and the new Worker's Cultural Palace (2014) (Fig. 8.36). It seems that Wuxi does not want to build new cultural facilities in its historical city center, in which only an old auditorium of the CPPCC is being converted into a children's theater. The planning concept of new theaters is apparently associated with the development of new

Fig. 8.30 Main entrance. Jussi Tiainen/courtesy of PES architects

Fig. 8.31 Lakeside view. Kari Palsila/courtesy of PES architects

Fig. 8.32 Central lobby.
Jussi Tiainen/courtesy of PES
architects

Fig. 8.33 Foyer of the Opera
house. Jussi Tiainen/courtesy
of PES architects

Fig. 8.34 Interior of the Opera hall. Jussi Tiainen/courtesy of PES architects

Fig. 8.35 Bamboo finish

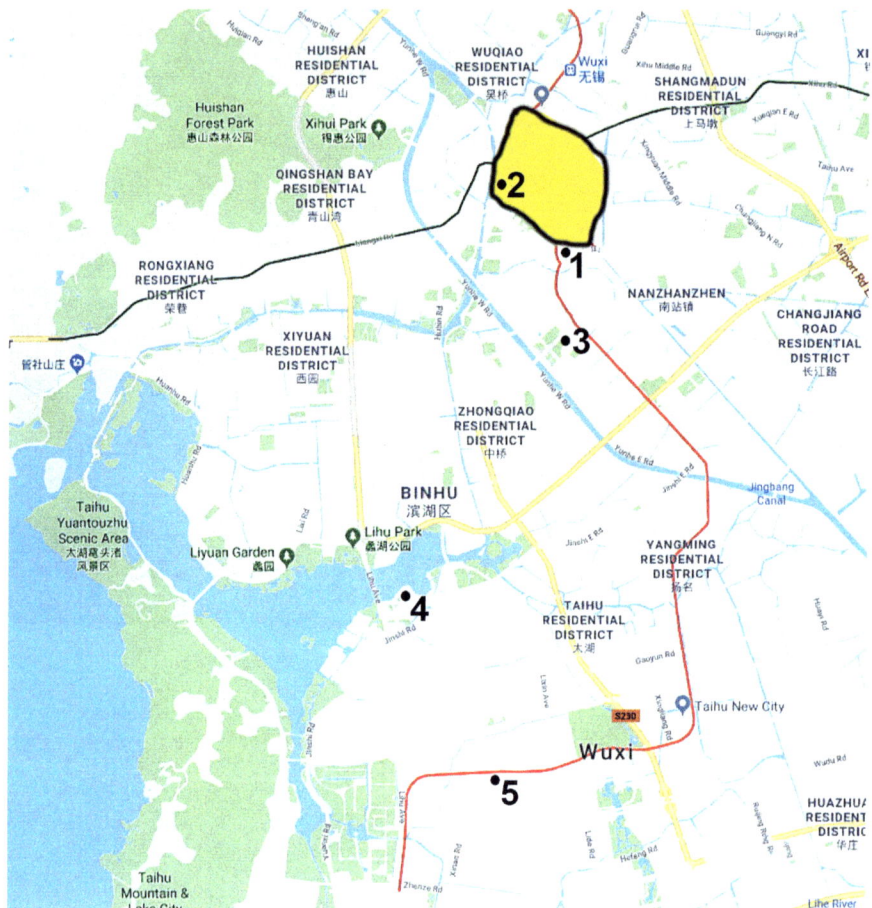

Fig. 8.36 1—Old worker's cultural palace (1954), 2—Auditorium of the CPPCC (unknown), 3—Great hall of people (1999), 4—Wuxi grand theater (2012), 5—New worker's cultural palace (2014)

districts or new zones. For example, the Wuxi Great Hall of People, located in Taihu Square, is a new city center outside Wuxi old town, and Wuxi Grand Theater and the new Worker's Cultural Palace are located in the new zone Taihu Xincheng (Taihu New Town).

Although it has an elegant, state-of-the-art design against a beautiful and stunning landscape surrounded on three sides by Lake Li, the impressive Wuxi Grand Theater is currently somehow detached from the urban center, other cultural facilities, and the public realm. The masterplan of Taihu Xincheng shows the new city center around the manmade lake inside Jingui Wetland Park (Figs. 8.10 and 8.12), with many public, administrative, cultural, and entertainment buildings and the CBD. The selection of a lakeshore site for the existing Grand Theater could have been influenced by Sydney Opera House and the Suzhou Culture and Art Center (2007), which was also built on a lakeside manmade peninsula. Although these three theaters are all near water, the Wuxi one is currently quite remote, unlike the Sydney one, which is near downtown, and the Suzhou one, which is adjacent to the CBD of Suzhou Industry Park. Even with its proximity to a large shopping mall complex, Wuxi Grand Theater is still isolated by vast residential districts from the rich public and commercial lives in the central area of Taihu Xincheng. It is now quite clear that the site selection for the Grand Theater was more inclined to the natural environment of Lake Li than to the urban context of Taihu Xincheng. Indeed, it is true, as the architect said, Wuxi Grand Theater is "a work of art—a big sculpture" against the beautiful backdrop of Lake Li. Perhaps Wuxi prefers the Grand Theater to promote the image of the Lihu Scenic Zone rather than Taihu Xincheng, or Lihu Scenic Zone is the central park of Greater Wuxi in its city planning. Based on a government document, the location of the current site at the "golden bay" of Lake Li, with its waterfront scenery, is also a convenient point of transportation with Lihu Avenue as an expressway to the old town and Wuhu Avenue as a main traffic artery nearby. The city plans to construct a subway line with a designated stop at the Grand Theater.[9]

Today, Wuxi has more than 6 million residents, and the Taihu Xincheng is a new zone with a planned population of 1 million. A majestic theater may be common for a city of such scale in Western society, where classical music, opera, and ballet are traditional parts of urban culture. However, Western performing arts are new to Wuxi, which has no local symphony orchestra, ballet company, or opera company. According to an official report,[10] Wuxi had four performing arts companies in 2016. Three were Xiqu companies, and the other featured acrobatics, puppets, and shadow play. Their staffs totaled 120 people. No art education organizations existed in 2016. The Grand Theater's unique design was conceived as an architectural landmark to promote Wuxi to the outside world by local officials, who intended to learn from Beijing and Shanghai by organizing international art festivals to support the traditional Xiju, musical shows, and local creative industry.[11]

Wuxi Grand Theater is the most expensive and largest cultural facility ever built in Wuxi. Its design and construction have been aimed at "first class standards, the new urban landmark and a graceful art temple" since its inception.[12] The opening ceremony and premiere performances were held April 30, 2012.[13] An inscription on a tablet in front of the theater's entrance says: "Here is the cultural icon of Wuxi, a

---

[9]From the exhibition script at Wuxi Urban Planning Exhibition Gallery.

[10]Publicity Department of Wuxi Municipal Committee, Wuxi Bureau of Statistics, Wuxi Bureau of Culture, Broadcasting, Television, Press and Publication (2017).

[11]From ChinaNews.com. Retrieved: http://www.chinanews.com/cul/2012/04-26/3849670.shtml.

[12]Jiangnan Evening Post. 江南晚报. Retrieved: http://www.wxrb.com/news/cjgh/201202/t20120222_971740.shtml.

[13]Wuxi Daily News. 无锡日报. Retrieved: http://www.wxrb.com/node/news_wuxi/2012-4-28/73c8fafk1294135.html.

Table 8.1 Program list of Wuxi grand theater, 1st quarter 2018

Date	Event	Artist
January 2	Dance	River Dance (Ireland)
January 9–10	Chinese Comedy Dialogue	Deyun (Beijing)
January 19	Snow kid (musical show)	Zhao Yu, Zhang Xiaoke, Zhang Wei
January 23	Man of La Mancha (Chinese Version)	SEVENAGES
January 26	The Nutcracker	Russian National Ballet Theater
January 27	OCTONAUTS (Chinese Version)	Tianjin Bo Yi Media
January 30	Citizen Concert	Wu Na (Guqin/local)
February 2–3	Chinese Comedy	Kai Xin Ma Hua
February 8	Swan Lake	Children's Ballet of Kiev, Ukraine
February 21	Thomas & Friends (Chinese Version)	Tianjin Bo Yi Media
February 24–25	The Three Sisters Waiting for Godot	Beijing Fengshuo Guoshi Media
March 1	Citizen Concert	CLARI-TET (Quintet/local)
March 13	Chinese Comedy Dialogue	Xingye Xiangsheng (Beijing)
March 17	Piano Trio	Russian musicians
March 21	The Sky Kingdom Show	N/A
March 22	Taipei Li-Yuan Peking Opera Theater	Wang Zhao Xin
March 30	Modern Dance	Shanghai Jin Xing Dance Theater
March 31	Jin Xing Talk Show	Jin Xing

new fulcrum of thriving and developing cultural industry. It will change the cultural ecology of Wuxi critically."

The Grand Theater is commissioned to Poly Theater Management Co., Ltd., which is the largest theater management and performance marketing company in China. Table 8.1 presents a calendar of the Spring Performance Season[14] from January 2 to March 31, 2018.

Table 8.1 shows that 21 performances/shows were scheduled within a 3-month calendar, or about 7 performances in an average month. The official website[15] of Wuxi Grand Theater lists approximately 14 performances for June 2018. Compared to the 44 performances at Hong Kong Cultural Center[16] during June 2018, Wuxi Grand Theater is apparently underutilized. In terms of architectural design, Wuxi Grand Theater is definitely a world-class venue of performance; however, some

[14]From the booklet '2018 Wuxi Grand Theater Spring Performance Season'. 2018无锡大剧院新春演出季.

[15]Wuxi Grand Theater website. Retrieved: https://wxdjy.polyt.cn/ (June 5, 2018).

[16]Hong Kong Cultural Center website. Retrieved: http://www.lcsd.gov.hk/en/hkcc/programmes/currentmonth.html (June 5, 2018).

events might not suit or live up to the same artistic class of the theater. The demand for appreciation of "pure art" in Wuxi has also been questioned.

Now the young "butterfly" is quiet, a public sculpture standing alone by the lakeshore, away from the dense and crowded downtown. We wish that she will soon become an active cultural engine with open wings and take off into the infinite sky of performing events. The value of a Grand Theater is not simply to present a visually impressive architectural landmark to the general public and visitors, but also to substantially enrich and promote the cultural lives of the local community.

Acknowledgements   This chapter is part of a study supported by the Research Grant Council, Hong Kong Government, Project No. CityU 11658816. The author heartily thanks Professor Pekka Salminen for his kind provision of valuable pictures of Wuxi and Fuzhou projects.

I have been to Wuxi four or five times. Each time, I was in a rush, or only there for a short time. My longest visit to Wuxi was about three days. I enjoyed the beautiful landscape of Yuan-tou-zhu Peninsula in Lake Tai and explored the delicate and intricate Ji-chang-yuan Garden in Huishan Hill. Wuxi once was a canal town. Although the in-town canals and typical waterfront houses with white walls and dark roofs disappeared long ago, I still like the old town very much because it is small and convenient, and I can go anywhere by foot. The sense of it being small mostly comes from the ancient moat that encircles Wuxi old town. Walking along the moat in the morning is one of the most pleasant things I do there, and it reminds me that Wuxi is a historical city. In the old days, rural areas and small villages could be found beyond the moat.

Today, Wuxi is rapidly developing new towns, and its urban area has increased continuously. During my last visit in spring 2018, it took me more than an hour to reach the Grand Theater from the old town by subway and taxi. It was a quiet afternoon; there was no performance event scheduled that day, and I saw no more than 10 visitors. I was very surprised to see that the theater was situated in a tranquil environment, with a wide open plaza and an expansive green lawn in front, and a calm lake at the left and rear. The bridge is 300 m away, and no vehicular noise comes from there. Through a grand stairway, I stepped up to the top of the plinth six metres above ground level, where I was able to look over the wide expanse of misty water. I walked around the theater, along the terrace of the plinth and the lakeside promenade, and was amazed by how well the building had been designed to harmonise with the natural landscape, especially the transparent glass curtain walls in the public foyers facing the lake, which allowed the scenery to be viewed inside the theater. Indeed, I had not just an appreciation of the architecture of Wuxi Grand Theater, but also an appointment with Lake Tai.

References

Li, L., & Xue, Q. L. (2017). *Chinese urbanism in the 21st century*. Beijing: China Architecture and Building Press. 李璘、薛求理. (2017). *21世纪中国城市主义*. 北京:中国建筑工业出版社.

Publicity Department of Wuxi Municipal Committee, Wuxi Bureau of Statistics, Wuxi Bureau of Culture, Broadcasting, Television, Press and Publication. (2017). Statistics of Wuxi culture 2016. Wuxi: Government Printer. 无锡市宣传部、无锡市统计局、无锡市文化广电新闻出版局. (2017).无锡文化及相关产业统计概览2016.无锡:无锡市政府.

Xue, C. Q. L. (2006). *Building a revolution: Chinese architecture since 1980*. Hong Kong: Hong Kong University Press.

Xue, C. Q. L. (2010). *World architecture in China*. Hong Kong: Joint Publishing (H.K.) Ltd.

Chapter 9
The National Taichung Theater: Experimenting Publicity of Metropolitan Urbanism

Jing Xiao

9.1 Urban Regularization and Re-planning of Taichung in History

That Taichung becomes one of the leading cities in Taiwan is part of a story that is less than one century old. Historically, the plateau in the central basin of the island of Taiwan where the city is located was cultivated under the supervision of Tainan, Chiayi, and many other traditional cultural centers. Changhua, today a comparably minor city close to Taichung, was established in 1722 and dominated the region for a long time because of its good seaside location and available transportation. There was a brief bureaucratic reformation that transferred the power from Tainan to Taichung in 1887, and later further north to Taipei. This transfer led to the reconstruction of Taichung in 1889, and the new city had eight main-gate buildings with single pitched roofs that were surrounded by newly established walls.[1] After the Sino-Japanese War in 1895, Taiwan was ceded to the Japanese and became a colony. During the first decade of the twentieth century, the Japanese government planned to build a new railway system called the West Coast Line. Several emerging colonised cities along the line proceeded with a new round of modern development under a series of experiments called the Urban Regularization

---

[1]See Lee (1980, 2005) for the history of Taiwan architecture and the unfinished project of building Taichung city before the Japanese occupation.

J. Xiao (✉)
School of Architecture and Urban Planning, Shenzhen University,
3688 Nanhai Rd., Shenzhen, China
e-mail: xiaojing.arch@szu.edu.cn

© Springer Nature Singapore Pte Ltd. 2019
C. Q. Xue (ed.), *Grand Theater Urbanism*,
https://doi.org/10.1007/978-981-13-7868-3_9

Schemes (URS).[2] What distinguished the URS from ordinary land rezoning and land readjustment in Imperial Japan was that the orthogonal grid system of the modern city was of top priority. New streets were supposed to penetrate the old district in the name of providing modern sanitation and gentrification. However, the urban context was disregarded, and land interests were deprived of by force, without compensation.[3]

As a central metropolis, Taichung received special attention from the colonial government and thus became the first city in Taiwan to suffer the destructive power of the URS in 1900, even one year before Taipei. However, the original purpose of rebuilding Taichung was to accelerate the progress of local industries by accommodating more immigrants. In doing so, both the first draft of the URS and later the Expanded Regularization Scheme issued in 1911 managed to regulate the urban patterns of Taichung with a monotonous gridded order. It was said that all of the residential houses along the streets presented a strong Japanese Meiji style.

Sanitary functions predominated in the scheme for Taichung. Under the guidance of William K. Burton, no underground drainage was allowed in the new plan; water channels and drains had to be exposed to sunlight for sterilisation purposes.[4] Therefore, the majority of the new streets were intentionally shifted to an angle of 55° from the meridian line. Taichung applied this method with the aim of developing cleaner urbanisation, while the citizens endured sub-tropical sunlight in the morning and afternoon to such a degree that even the Japanese admitted the failure in the 1940s (Shirakura 1943). Today, visitors find the streets to be confusing, specifically those around the city center of Taichung and the National Taichung Theater, extending from southeast to northwest and from southwest to northeast. This confusing layout was part of the colonial legacy and not due to topological urban growth like those of medieval towns.

The third round of urban re-planning occurred after WWII. In December 1964, Dr. Donald Monson from the United Nations came to Taiwan and reviewed the metropolitan planning for Taipei and Keelung. He wrote reports and urged the government to ask for help from the Special Fund for Assistance in Metropolitan

---

[2]See Huang (1997) and Chang (1993). The Urban Regularization Scheme was officially announced by the Japanese government for the first time in the 1930s. However, its large-scale experiments in colonized countries, such as Korea and Taiwan, literally started in the early part of the twentieth century. The implementation of urban planning system was part of institutional control over the colonies. By the end of the World War II, there were up to 72 cities in Taiwan that completed the urban regularization scheme.

[3]See Aoi (2013). In comparing the colonial urban growth of Changhua with that of other cities in Taiwan, Aoi examined in detail how the Urban Regularization changed the trajectory of cities in Taiwan. For him, the scheme only meant to construct new cities and had a very limited focus on the subjects of urban street and drainage system.

[4]See Otsuji (1943). William K. Burton (1856–1899) was a British engineer who lived in Meiji Japan since 1887. From 1896 to 1899, he worked in Taiwan as the Adviser in Sanitary Engineering. He helped to improve the sanitation systems with the support from the Governor-General of Taiwan. His exemplary projects include the water-works at Tamsui and Kelung, and the drainage system of Taihoku. See Davidson (1903).

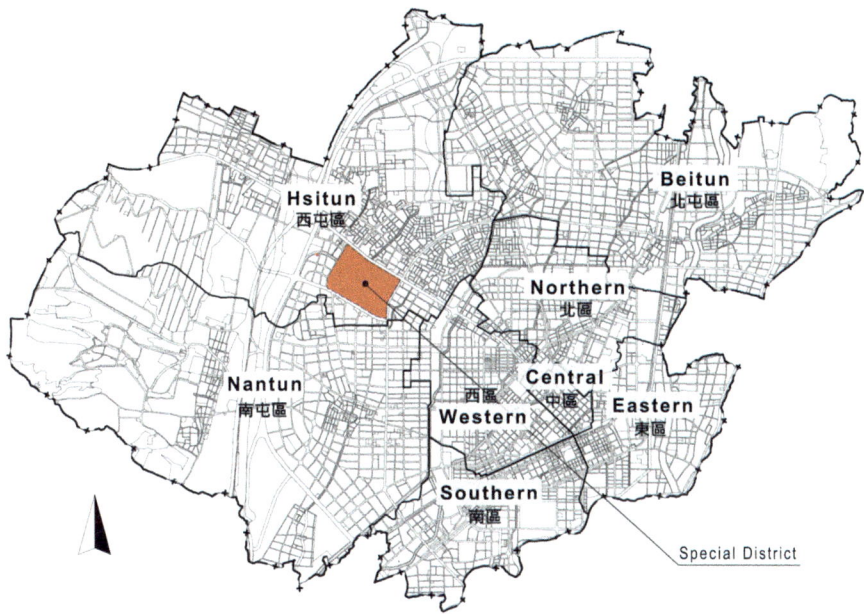

Fig. 9.1 Metropolitan area of Taichung city, showing the location of the SDSC. The orientation of the streets reflects the urban pattern of the old city center. Drawn by the author

and Urban Planning of the UN. In 1966 the UN passed the proposal, and a special Urban and Housing Development Committee (UHDC) was founded to make new plans for all of the metropolitan cities in Taiwan.[5] Accordingly, the first regional plan for Taichung was issued in 1971 and confirmed that the city would be one of the three future first-tier metropolises. The other two regions were Northern Taiwan and Kaohsiung/Tainan.

There was a first-round official review of the original regional plan in 1986. The proposal for the then Taichung Concert Art Center accompanied the original regional plan. It envisaged a public facility within the special district in the northwestern suburban area for the new metropolitan center (Special District for Sub-civic Center, SDSC), dedicating the No. 7 Rezoning Area to a series of municipal facilities and public space (Fig. 9.1). The district was basically an

---

[5]See Chen (2011). The consulting team members of UHDC specialized in urban design and planning included Donald Monson, Karl J. Belser, Lweis R. Coyle, and Edmund T. Ames, etc. They examined approximately 132 items, covering the subjects of urban planning, housing, land development, transportation, administration, urban environment, industry and economy. For Taichung region, they completed at least several major preliminary reports and drafts for urban planning, including the Regional Plan for the Metropolitan Taichung, Docking District Plan, Urban Outline Plan, Public Water Resource Survey, Statistical Analysis of Population Density and Growth, Assessment for the Future Thirty Years' Industry Development, and Statistics for Land Use and Rice Production.

extension of the urban fabric of the old city center, and therefore still reflected the legacy of colonisation and maintained its road grid of 55°. Proposals for the detailed plan were drafted in September 1989. In 1992, a proposal for the National Concert Hall replaced the former proposal for the Taichung Concert Art Center, which was then named the National Taichung Theater in 1999 by the Cultural Development Board of the central government. After the horrifying earthquake on September 21st that year, the district soon recovered and boomed with many new commercial high-rises and condominium towers.

9.2 International Competition(s): Changing Ideals in the Posthumous Guggenheim Garden

Taichung claimed to have a collection of first-class cultural institutions for art, sports, and education. The National Museum of Natural Science was inaugurated in 1980 and was chaired by Professor Pao-Teh Han, a leading architect and educator in postwar Taiwan. The National Taiwan Museum of Fine Arts opened in 1988 and remains the only national museum for the exhibition of Taiwanese modern and contemporary works of art. After the new millennium, there was a series of international competitions held around the topics of the No. 7 Rezoning District of the special metropolitan area. The international competition for the new Taichung City Civic Center in 1995 was said to be the first large-scale competition of this type in Taiwan's public sector. The winning design was made by the Zurich-based architects Weber Hofer Partner AG and was completed in 2010. In recent years, the city has accumulated many new installations, including the Taichung Condominium Tower by Richard Meier, the Gateway Eco Park Competition in 2011, the City Cultural Center in 2016 designed by SANAA, and the Asia Museum of Modern Art by Tadao Ando in 2012. The latter two were both Japanese laureates of the Pritzker Architecture Prize.

In 2002, the then-city mayor Jason Hu persuaded the Guggenheim Museum Foundation to establish a new branch in Taichung. This museum was planned to be located at the northeast corner of the new No. 7 Rezoning District, mirroring the national theater along the central axis of a green park. The City Council was supposed to be situated between the buildings. The City Municipal Building was to be at the far west end of the parkland. The Guggenheim Foundation claimed that the entire district, then called—the Guggenheim Garden—would incorporate different land plots and inaugurate a new cultural park with a unique urban landscape for art, culture, exhibition and political events (Fig. 9.2).[6] An international commission for

---

[6]Online resource via: http://www.99ch.com.tw/info-detail.asp?lang=1&doc_id=1389 (Access date: 2018/05/12). The Urban Design for the Guggenheim Garden invited three international leading architects, including Frank Gehry (for the Municipal Building), Zaha Hadid (for the Museum), and Jean Nouvel (for the National Theater). The proposed museum would have a gross floor area of up to 88,000 m^2, compared with 38,000 sq. for the National Theater, 35,500 m^2. for

Fig. 9.2 Map of the No. 7 Rezoning district showing the changes in the locations for different civic institutions. The green-coloured areas represent the proposed Guggenheim Garden. The original location for the National Theater was in the southeast corner of the garden. The map was modified according to the modification to the detailed plan for the Taichung metropolitan planning —SDSC 变更台中市都市计划(新市政中心专用区)细部计划, issued by the Taichung municipality in August 2008. Re-drawn by the author

the projects in the Garden proceeded one year later, and it was announced that the British-Iraqi architect Zaha Hadid would provide the design for the Guggenheim Museum Taichung. She upheld her iconic design philosophy by offering a kinetic urban spectacle (Fig. 9.3). Her design gained publicity by configuring access to open spaces and accommodating daily activities. The gallery space underwent a

the Municipal Building and 31,000 m². for the Parliament Building. The final contract for the feasibility study and evaluation agreement was co-signed by Mayor Jason Hu, CEO for the Guggenheim Foundation Thomas Krens, and the then Director of the Guggenheim Museum Bilbao Sr. D. Juan Ignacio Vidarte in Bilbao.

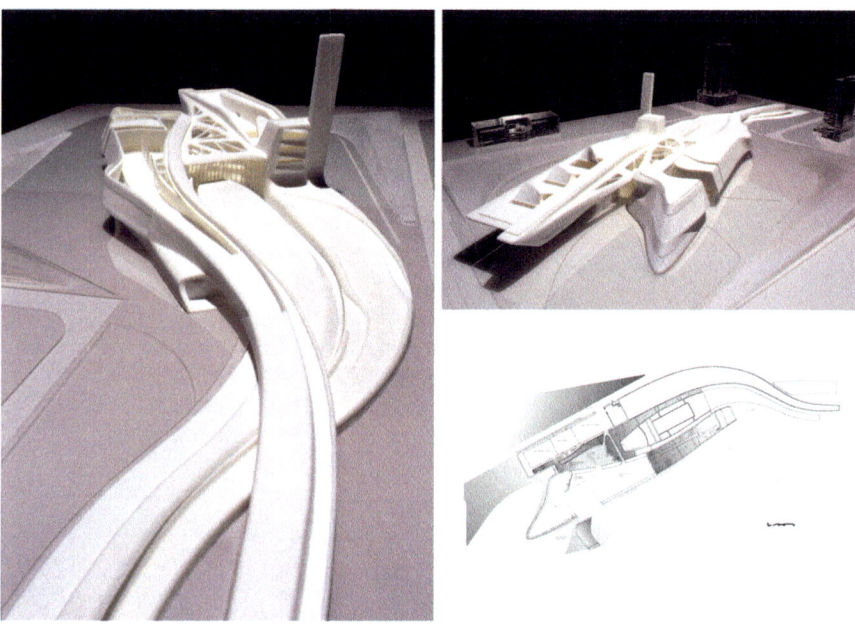

Fig. 9.3 Design proposal for the unbuilt Guggenheim museum by Zaha Hadid. Website: http://www.zaha-hadid.com/archive (latest access date: 2018/06/25). Courtesy by Zaha Hadid architects

radical transformation of space and became visible from the outside. Visual expression and perception intertwined along the interior ramps, movable exhibition walls, and platforms. Similar ideas witnessed her successive designs of the same period, including the Guangzhou Opera House in 2003 (see Chap. 3 of this book). Zaha Hadid was the winner of the Pritzker Architecture Prize in 2004. Unfortunately, the central government gave up on her museum design due to its limited annual budget and eventually cancelled the whole project later that year.

The competition for the National Taichung Theater was also blemished by the interruption, although not to the degree of cancellation.[7] Due to a similar unsatisfactory budget, it was downgraded to—the Metropolitan Opera House of Taichung —expecting only a regional influence and service coverage. Luckily, under the auspices and insistence of the Taichung Municipality, an international competition for the project was announced later in December 2005 (Table 9.1). Due to the promotion of the cultural industry in Taiwan, which required new representatives in each of the metropolitan areas, there was a series of negotiations between the Taichung municipality and central government regarding the ownership of and administrative authority over the theater. In 2014, the central government promised

---

[7]The administrative office of the central government granted 1.2 billion NTD (40 million USD) for the project. See Administrative Office of the Central Government (2003).

Table 9.1 Time schedule for the National Taichung theater design competition (Information excerpted and modified from Cheng 2006)

Date	Content	Details
2005/09/01	Announcement of competition	
2005/09/01– 2005/10/03	Release of design specification	Background and specification of planning, including the geographical and cultural environment of Taichung, and local transportation. Principles of the spatial design. Tender notice including the requirement of the floor area
2005/09/12	Deadline of inquiries	Collection of thirty-two questions about the competition and tender
2005/09/19	Feedback to inquiries	–
2005/10/03	Deadline for the first-round submission	Submission of the files for qualification, tenders of the concept design, and achievements of potential collaborators before 12:00 am
2005/10/03	Qualification check	Starting from 14:00 pm. Thirty-two design companies from twelve countries passed the qualification check
2005/10/04– 2005/10/05	First-round peer review by the jury panel	Based on the tenders of the concept design, five nominees entered the second round
2005/10/05	Exhibition of results	At the meeting hall of the Evergreen Laurel hotel, Taichung
2005/10/14	On-site survey	–
2005/12/15– 2005/12/16	Final design presentations	Five nominees presented tenders of the final designs to six international jurists
2005/12/16	Announcement of the winner	Closed-door discussion in the morning
2005/12/16– 2006/01/01	Exhibition of final designs	Two-week exhibition at the Taichung cultural center

to promote the project once again as the National Taichung Theater. The construction of the entire project started in 2009 and was completed in 2016.

The jury panel included several world-class scholars and critics at the beginning of the competition: Mohsen Mostafavi from Harvard, USA; Francesco Dal Co from IUAV, Italy; Hiroshi Hara from Japan; as well as Kuo Chao-li from Tunghai University and Chen Mai as the representatives of local architectural practices. One special jury member was Stanley Lai, a renowned theater director of artistic performance in Taiwan. For the first time, he became involved in an international architectural competition in theater design. In the design specification, Francesco Dal Co noted that the binary composition of life and drama had a long history and therefore spiritualized that function of performance in the varieties of civic architecture (Tseng 2006). In reflecting on Dal Co's postulation, leading international architects, such as Thom Mayne of Morphosis, Itsuko Hasegawa, Hans Hollein, Antoine Predock, Christian de Portzamparc, and Richard Rogers explored the idiosyncratic interplay between architecture and performance. By contrast, Studio

Sputnick from Holland, Mehrdad Yazdani from the USA, Robert Ofero (former student of Rem Koolhaas), Yasuyuki Ito from Japan, the Kay Ngee Tan Architects from Singapore, and several local designers including J. J. Pan, Kris Yao, and Jou Min Lin chose to integrate everyday life with landscape and tectonics. In the first round of peer reviews, five nominees qualified and passed into the second phase of the competition. Among them, Claus en Kaan was an emerging architectural firm based in Amsterdam. Shuhei Endo had practised the idea of "para-modern architecture" for 15 years and, at that time, had just received the 9th International Architecture Exhibition Special Award in La Biennale di Venezia 2004. The third nominee, Hsueh-Yi Chien, had completed several key museum projects including the Yingko Ceramics Museum in the then Taipei County (2002) and the Ilan 228 Memorial (2004). However, the public spotlighted the designs by two leading figures, Toyo Ito and Zaha Hadid.

Kinetic architecture had always been the signature of Zaha Hadid (Fig. 9.4). As it was the second time she participated in the district, Hadid was determined to win the competition for the National Taichung Theater with exactly the same design philosophy. Her proposal recalled the phantom of the posthumous Guggenheim Gallery and introduced the external dynamics of land formation. The building's architectural circulation originated across the street and flowed into the main lobby. The entire body of the building seemed to consist of a submerged armature extending from the central axis. Accompanying this was the lifted corridor assigned to the artists' studios, workshops, and boutique shops, which had unlimited access. The cultural plaza, outdoor performance space, and grand steps were to the north in the expectation that potential visitors might arrive via the closest subway station where the Shin Kong Mitsukoshi Department Store oversaw the passage. To a

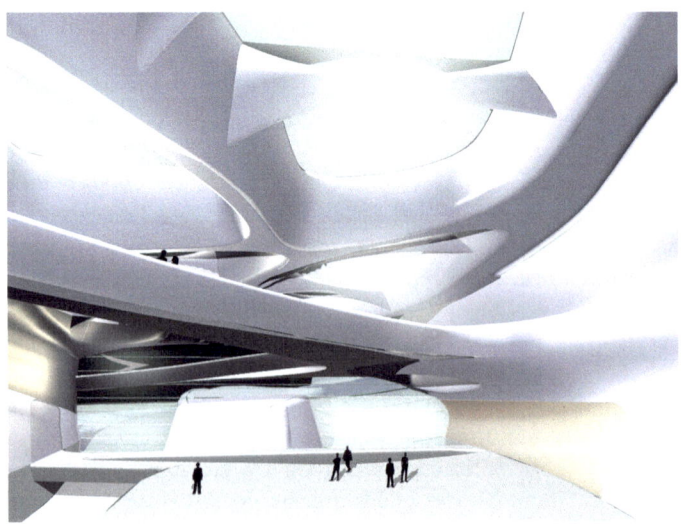

Fig. 9.4 Kinetic architecture of the Guggenheim Museum. Courtesy by Zaha Hadid Architects

Fig. 9.5 Southeast façade of the National Taichung theater (upper) and the interior design of the music gathering space (lower). Designed by Toyo Ito. Photo collage by the author

certain extent, Hadid envisaged an even better urban strategy in this proposal than that of the former Guggenheim project, in that she re-configured the theater with the cultural and administrative axes, commerce, and public access. Ultimately, the open ground was to be interiorized as part of the everyday civic performance. By contrast, what Toyo Ito conceived of was, as he preferred to call it, "a potted life". It was this powerful idea and imagery of design that led him to his final victory. As Ito himself explained, the proposed geometrical structure, which the critics later renamed the "Sound Cave", should be able to breathe, demarcate and interchange with the new era of social progress (Fig. 9.5).

9.3 Theater Design: Emerging Grid, Sound Cave and Geometrical Truss System

Toyo Ito claims to have completed more projects than other foreign architects in Taiwan (Hsieh 2014). He finished the main stadium for the Kaohsiung World Games in 2009, the Plaza of the World Trade Center in 2011, and the Taipei Center for Creative Culture and the Academy for Social Sciences at National Taiwan University, both in 2013 (Fig. 9.6). His experiments on civic housing after the "311 Earthquake" in Japan—みんなの家, Home for all—in 2011 won him the First Prize in La Biennale di Venezia in 2012, due to his humanistic thinking on architectural adaptation. His laureate for the Pritzker Architectural Prize in 2013 confirmed his contribution to the frontier of architecture.

The design for the National Taichung Theater reflects Toyo Ito's willing to return to nature. The project triumphs the cross-shaped central garden and has a gross floor area of up to 51,166 sq., covering a designated public space of 57,020

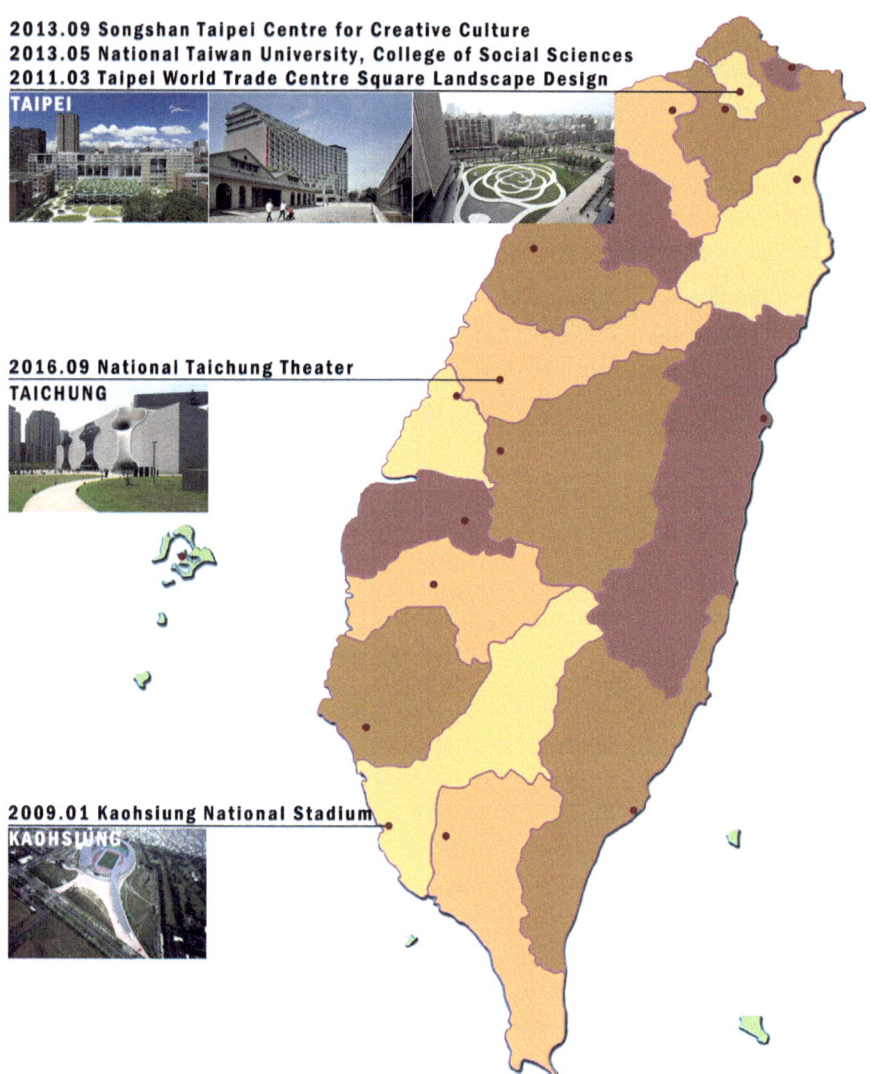

Fig. 9.6 Toyo Ito's complete projects in Taiwan. Map revised by the author

sq. The main building has two underground levels and another six levels above, with a total height of 32 m. It comprises three performance spaces—a grand theater, playhouse, and creative performance hall called the "Black Box", with 2014, 800, and 200 seats respectively. There is also the Art Plaza, Arts & Creative Workshop, restaurant, café and many other public facilities on the first, fifth and sixth levels. The budget for the construction was 3.6 billion NTD (USD 121 million).

Fig. 9.7 Design sketches by Toyo Ito, showing the functional spaces in the cave system (upper). Photos of the entrance hall (lower left) and the lobby to the grand theater (lower right)

In Toyo Ito's design concept, the building represents the idea of an "emerging grid" that circulates a spatial system of horizontal and vertical tubes. The tube system lends itself to daily facility maintenance and provides an excellent acoustic effect for both performance and public visits (Fig. 9.7). The emerging grid, on the other hand, explores the surrounding landscape by incorporating water, greenery, and human activity. To generate a platform of communication for multiple cultures, the design goes beyond the boundary of traditional performance architecture and seeks the possibility of an open structure, which can define a new dialogue between visitors and officers, and spectators and performers, inside and outside. Acoustic space is the key focus. A series of "caves" are the tunnels for both sound and people who move freely in the public space, following the curved boundaries into the entrance halls of the grand theater and the playhouse on the second floor. There were several major revisions in design, including that the Black Box for creative performance moved to the underground level, where people found it easier to reach. The platform and seating area were completely changed in a direction for the convenience of costume operation.

It is challenging to dissolve the rigid pattern of both the architecture and streets. Meanwhile, how to stimulate the on-site activity by improvising participatory performance is of critical importance for architectural publicity. A curved wall system makes use of tube structures to lift the theater space onto the upper levels, sparing the permeability of the ground floor. Openings of different sizes and directions manipulate the circulation toward the exhibition and cafeteria space on the fifth floor and the vertical two-story-high lobby of the grand theater. The maximisation of publicity and greenery is achieved by the openness of the building's outer rim as well as by the unlimited access to the roof garden. Therefore, the structural design became so challenging that the first several rounds of construction tendering turned out to be fruitless.

The executive architects, in cooperation with Toyo Ito, were Yang Yi-yong and Yang Li-hwa, who were both graduates of the National Cheng Kung University and founding partners of the Da-ju Architects & Associates. They worked closely with structural engineers and consultants, including those of Arup London and Evergreen Consulting Engineering, Inc. (Taiwan). During the competition, the engineering research team of ARUP came up with the building method, which consisted of a steel structure with concrete layers. However, this method of construction appeared to be too expensive and time-consuming, and it is needless to mention that no specific building regulations for this structure were available except for certain cases of tunnels or revetment construction. The traditional system of shaping forms does not help to build curved panels with different shapes. Environmental issues were also prohibitive to the design. The Asahi Glass Build, Kankyo Engineering Inc. Takenaka Corporation provided an alternative to make use of reinforced steel bar trusses. This internal truss consists of multiple fixing anchors and three layers of wire mesh that gently hold concrete in its curvilinear shape. The entire 'truss cage' was prefabricated and moved to the building site later. Therefore, the entire structure was designed to comprise two levels with 29 continuous curved-wall units. Each unit was to be controlled by four geometrical points and merged into a fluent surface. However, the three-dimensional structure was not ready for the two-dimensional drawing system. It was quite difficult to represent the curves with the coordinates of each controlling point. The architects categorised thousands of construction details into a group of building types, according to their

Fig. 9.8 (Left) Construction detail of the curved wall system, with steel mesh finishes holding concrete. Photo by the author. (Right) Scaled model for sound testing at the National Taiwan University of Science and Technology. Courtesy by Prof. Chiang Wei-Hwa, NTUST

principles of connection and formation. Lacking the Building Information Modeling system, they had to check the details one by one manually. For the sections of the curved wall system and steel structure alone, this involved reviewing more than 10,000 construction drawings (Fig. 9.8).

In the early simulations by Arup, the proposed walls of reinforced concrete of up to 80 cm thick were too heavy to support themselves. Additional layers of infilling materials foresaw considerable deficiencies and problems of finishes. Fortunately, the automobile design department of Arup had a different view upon seeing this proposal. According to their automobile protocols, a sheer wall that was only 40 cm thick, if compatible with careful simulation, would be enough.

In its custom acoustic design, the building structure considers little of the interior acoustic effect and decoration, both of which require a secondary interior design consisting of a reflection installation. However, in the case of the Taichung Metropolitan Theater, the world-class acoustic design by Nagata Acoustic Inc. promised to come to fruition with the help of the building's own shape. The reinforced concrete shell of the sculptural vacuums is sound-proof to external noises and is available for the diverse sounding environment regarding shape casting. Both the testing on the 1:10 scaled model made by the National Taiwan University of Science and Technology and the on-site mock-up trial show that the Arup system of curved walls of less than 40 cm in thickness is an excellent option to maintain both structural and acoustic requirements.

9.4 Primitive Openness Versus Publicity: An Infrastructural Retrospection

There are progress and transition in Toyo Ito's mind about the relation between openness, publicity[8] and architecture. Sendai Mediatheque, as one of his first projects that were acknowledged internationally, is a multi-use space consisting of a civic gallery, library, and information center. With new media and advanced technologies, architecture can be a transmitting platform to keep the urban function evolving and to reflect what citizens create and share every day. In the book *Generative Order*, Toyo Ito explains that Sendai Mediatheque is a new version of

---

[8]There are different definitions of public space. To explain the publicity in Taiwan, the author would like to borrow the concept of public typologies made by the architectural critic Hsia Chu-Joe: (1) the tectonics of a critical public forum, which works as a mediating institution to regulate the citizenship between the nation power and private interests; (2) the national administrative system; (3) the community defined by self-authorization; (4) an urban symbolic representation that holds indispensible political principles. In this chapter, 'publicity' refers to the first and fourth categories—citizenship regulation and urban symbolic representation. Publicity should not be identified according to the property and user alone, but by a *bourgeoise* operation of space that qualifies the citizenry and control over the daily access to particular space of symbolism. See Hsia (1994).

the Domino system that blurs the hierarchical order of space through the homogeneity of different floors. Meanwhile, the deliberate dichotomy between inside and outside is meaningless because the servicing and serviced parts merge to provide a seamless mutual communication (Ito 2008). In his early project of the White U House, we see a special consideration of materiality upon fluidity, the membrane and the site. The circulation of air, light, and space promotes a rhythmic connection between architecture and the environment. Ito struggles to reflect what modern urban cities could offer and receive, even reflecting on how cities challenge everyday life. In this new context, the dynamism of force would be free from the built environment, and architecture appears to represent a primitive placeness emerging from the modern-minimalist slogan *Less is More* (Ito 2008).

In the "Blurring Architecture" Shows exhibited in Tokyo and Aachen, Germany, Toyo Ito, for the first time, addressed the instability of thingness in architecture in a metaphorical way whereby both the exterior and interior should interact like an ambiguous reflection on water, intermediate but always subject to change. When people move around the building, it should be quite difficult to define whether they are within a physical body or walking along an urban street. An interplay of the building and surroundings is intended to blur the boundary between them (Ito 2000). Cecil Balmond, the chief structural engineer and Deputy Chairman of Arup, was vital to Toyo Ito's updated version of this morphology. He began to cooperate with the Japanese architect in the project of the Serpentine Gallery Pavilion in 2002. In Kensington Gardens, a central park in London, they studied a system of flat steel bars (Balmond 2002). The camouflage of hollow triangles, in fact, underlined a specific algorithm of cubes. Computation programmed the degrees of how the cubes rotated and constantly inscribed with one another. Unlike an ordinary structural system, space was wrapped up by a flowing geometrical surface that defied the gravity of the load-bearing elements, such as pillars, walls, and window frames.

Another case that reflects a closer genealogy with the National Taichung Theater is the Brugge 2002 Pavilion in Ghent, Belgium. This summertime installation is devised of a system of a honeycomb core made by an aluminium alloy. The thin layer of this perforated board could not sustain itself. Architects had to attach additional oval panels to either side of the box, providing a discontinuous 'door frame'. It composed of a weird folding structure of translucent surfaces—a semi-tube—that receives air, light, sound and cityscape from outside. It was from here that Toyo Ito began to think about an architecture of receptive tubes. Its functionality is not only born from its formal nature but also decided by the algorithmic control of permeability.

What Toyo Ito refers to is a sort of tectonic permeability. The primitiveness reflects the appropriate materiality in structure, and the openness results from the calculation of the very appropriateness based on algorithm. This ontological thinking on architecture and its ambient power is comparably self-sufficient. Thus in many circumstances, Toyo Ito repeated his reluctance to return to the urban context and history for design inspiration, for which it seemed to him a rigid yet passive manipulation of architecture to the physical environs. The design of the

National   Taichung   Theater,   in   fact,   indicates   Ito's   reluctance   and counter-contextualization.

On the one hand, the architecture claims to be open to the public in terms of its many features. For example, the main square facing the central axis is free from any viewing obstacles and is very convenient for visitors to take photos. The small amphitheater at the south corner steps down from the surrounding landscape and invites people to sit down and take part in sunset shows. On the other hand, the accessibility of the space is compromised by the factor that many urban connections are not yet available or in full operation.

In the design proposal, Toyo Ito also foresaw an underground public plaza that would link to the central park. This plaza would have been a perfect connection between the theater and central green axis, providing easy access and indispensable shade for people coming from the planned G9 subway station. Upon reflection, it seemed that both Toyo Ito and Zaha Hadid noticed this potential benefit (for Hadid, it highlights the iconic second-floor sinuating corridors). However, after the fourth-round inspection on the SDSC planning, the system of underground passes along the axis was largely cancelled, which further reduced publicity of the open space around the green park (Fig. 9.9 left).

Since its opening in 2016, the National Taichung Theater has welcomed visitors and audiences from all over the world. Performances are staged almost every day, from indigenous shows to those of international masters. Tickets are available at affordable prices even for students. People without tickets can freely stroll in the lobby of various levels and roof garden to sit, chat and look out across the park and city. Visitors who do not pay for a ticket may outnumber the regular audience. They can enjoy the ethereal environment created by designers and constructors. This scenario sharply contrasts with those in Chinese mainland cities, where 'grand theaters' are heavily guarded like a vase both day and night and are only for viewing, not entering. The government and city council in Taiwan are elected by the people, and therefore each penny of public funding should be accounted for.

Returning to Taichung, the revised urban scheme issued in 2008 resulted in serious problems and jeopardised the publicity of the theater. After the Second Detailed Planning Revision of the New Civic Center Special District, higher-density real estate development in the area became an option. The plan was for the central green axis to have more underground parking lots and leisure, but that proposal was confronted with a financial shortage. To solve this problem, the government applied the scheme called the *Plot Ratio Transfer* or *Transfer of Developmental Rights* (TDR).[9] If the developers and industries assisted public interest, an additional plot ratio and beneficiary rights would accordingly be

---

[9]*Plot Ratio Transfer* 容积移转 is also called the transfer of development rights in Western scholarship. It aims to deal with the conflict between the protection of spatial right and the marketing development. It is useful especially wen ordinary statutory plans cannot offer a flexible solution to the different actual requirements of plot ratio control. See for example Levinson (1997).

Fig. 9.9 The upper-left map shows the change of the underground passes extending from the proposed G9 subway station to the National Grand Theater. The first draft of the plan meant to introduce visitors to the main green axis and then further to the main plaza of the theater (as shown in red). However, the revision made in May 2016 shows that people would have to turn around to the corner of the Shin Kong Mitsukoshi department store and the mega city, and then access the theater through the northeast street corner (as shown in thin black). This new plan would provide more commercial convenience but leave the central green axis not fully used by the public in the future. Information modified according to Second Review to SDSC of the Urban Planning of Taichung (2005), also see Mass Transit Railway (2009). The upper-right map shows the plan for building setbacks and corridors along the streets

rewarded in other plots nearby (called the receiving area),[10] which occurred for the cases of public spaces of more than 500 m^2 and other public facilities, such as schools, fire stations, and cultural institutions. For the case of the National Taichung Theater, the entire scheme allowed the stakeholders to build more floor areas than was regularly permitted, which demonstrated some disorder in the urban development quotas and the absence of governmental management in addressing market incentives and compensation mechanisms (Hsieh and Juang 2009). The consequence was that the central axis of the green land was isolated from the larger urban context and surrounded by higher residential buildings. Visitors would be surprised to find the theater hidden in the skyline of luxury serviced apartments of various

---

[10]See Jin and Dai (2010). The first experimental application of the plot ratio transfer in Taiwan came along with the Cultural Heritage Preservation Law in 1982. During that time, there was an emerging social consciousness in protecting cultural heritage. The subsequent issues of the specific protection law, however, violated the property rights of the owners within the protection district. Plot Ratio Transfer was thus one of the potential schemes that promoted economic compensation to the stakeholders. According to the guideline for transfer (2004), a new amount of plot ratio would be rewarded by a careful calculation, and the receiving area for that could be a different plot in the same or any other special district.

decorative styles. The acclaimed publicity was thus challenged, largely by private property holders.

What the Taichung Municipality wanted from the plot ratio transfer was to create a system of public corridors beneath the private apartments. The corridors and covered pedestrian ways imitated the typical shophouse in Taiwan and were important to connect the public space with the transportation system of the Green Line and the Blue Line (Fig. 9.9 right). Unfortunately, little specification about the corridor design was mentioned in the urban plan, except for several minor requirements of width and height.[11] Actually, apartment developers sought to maximise spatial occupation by keeping an intermediary zone downstairs along with the entrance pass-ways. There is a lack of spatial perception of public ownership due to the varieties of building styles and installations. With security guards patrolling, people may wonder if they were entering a forbidden domain rather than passing through a public corridor of the park. The architectural critic Hsia Chu-joe already warned in 2006 that the plot ratio transfer might compromise the publicity of local communities in the receiving areas (Hsia and Peng 2006). In fact, when Taichung applied the scheme for the first time in 2005, there was no specification to control the receiving areas. The situation deteriorated even further with the *laisser-faire* strategy of the local housing market, under which TDR applications in Taichung skyrocketed, much more so than in Taipei and Kaohsiung.[12] The final result was that the theater showed a high degree of tension with, and contrast to, the adjacent residential towers in all directions except in the direction of the main square (Fig. 9.10).

Another factor that we should address to is the ongoing mass transit system planning and construction for the Taichung metropolitan area. The blueprint of subways, which costs 48.6 billion NTD (1.63 billion USD), was first drafted in 1990, and a detailed plan for the prior route—the Green Line—from Wurih, Wenhsin to Beitun was issued in 2004. It will provide two stations for the Wenhsin district (G9, G10) where numerous old residential buildings would give way to the future conglomerate of the theater and other civic buildings. Another Blue Line to the north was changed to a BRT route and was thus highly dependent on the availability of public corridors to access the theater. As there were rounds of political turnovers in the city's administration, the completion of both the BRT and subway system had long been postponed, further depriving the urban area of public access. Today, most visitors walk here via the Shin Kong Mitsukoshi Department Store and the Mega City, as they are the most convenient places to eat, shop and rest. The central park axis turned into a lonely island as it is largely abandoned and

---

[11]See for example, *Third Review to SDSC of the Urban Planning of Taichung* (2012).

[12]The City of Taichung issued the guideline for plot ratio transfer in urban planning in June 2005. By the time of March 2008, there had already been around 144 TDR cases in relation to public space development, which means 11,224,500 sq. of floor area subject to the scheme. According to the overall planning, Taichung had more than 54,283 ha of public space to be reclaimed from private owners. This means more than 13.8% of the future residential and commercial areas was about to be transferred accordingly.

Fig. 9.10 (Upper-left) Overview of the residential buildings from the central parking lots; (upper-right) the central green axis; (lower-left) the new city council designed by Weber Hofer Partner, also surrounded by residential buildings; (lower-right) the 'public corridor' of 4 m wide along the central garden, covered by the arches and pillars of Japanese imperial style

isolated by the public who are reluctant to be exposed to the humid climate and sunlight.

In the latest *Fourth Review to SDSC of the Urban Planning of Taichung* in December 2016,[13] the government report identified the insufficiency of publicity along the central axis to the theater. Documents show that the architectural styles of the corridors and overhangs are extremely different from each other, and in certain cases, the public passes are occupied by private properties with plants or obstructive decorations. However, the rewarding scheme for public space approved approximately 55 cases till October 2015. There are six major checkpoints that control the publicity which they promised.[14] More than 32 cases violated the restriction of exposed signage. Another two cases have illegal construction that transformed the public corridor into a private entrance lobby. Some projects reduced publicity to the

---

[13]Especially see *Chapter Seven: Open Space*, p. 94 and pp. 106–107.

[14]Ibid. p. 94. The check list includes: (1) no surrounding fences higher than 1.2 m; (2) no bushes higher than 1.2 m; (3) fully exposed public signage; (4) no illegal construction; (5) no safeguard inspection; (6) no illegal usage.

location with few entrances, and thus destroyed the entire public nature of the system.

In summary, this chapter explores the project of the National Taichung Theater in its historical context and aims to interpret the design's publicity according to the urban scheme of the entire rezoning district by the government in the 1970s. Both the original architectural design and posthumous urban design for the Guggenheim Garden and Museum indicate an even longer consideration about publicity in the future metropolitan center. The creation of penetrating boundaries, underground lobbies, public corridors and overhangs, which featured in a series of international design competitions, invites more publicity, openness and symbols of citizenship inside and outside of the building. However, in later constructions and infrastructural development, the theater itself showed more self-indulgence with its iconic tectonics and algorithmic materiality, losing the balance between the ontology of architecture and urban context. The total accessibility around the theater was further jeopardised by the developmental schemes issued by the government, including that of *plot ratio transfers*. In the exchange of publicity for project funds from real estates, both the central green axis and mass transit system made way for private ownership of luxury apartments and hotels over the immediate interfaces with the public space.

Despite the above unsatisfactory policies and implementations, the National Taichung Theater itself makes efforts to be open to the public and represents a friendly gesture in a democratic society. Taichung may be backward in terms of GDP compared with Shanghai or Shenzhen, but its theater offers more warmth to ordinary people. It is truly a prevailing issue, deserving of our special attention. Further research should be conducted for other developing metropolitan cities in the context of pan-Chinese diasporas.

Writing about National Taichung Theater is always difficult, not only because of the constant transitions of power since the city was built and the political agenda of the physical environment, but also because of the competing economic and administrative struggles, which have resulted in the postponement of a national project for ideological and budgetary reasons. These same reasons led the government to 'commercialise public interests', even at the expense of impairing long-conceived publicity and the very nature of modern cultural institutions.

However, we see exceptional contributions from various bodies to this marvellous building. Without persistence in design philosophy and fabrication technology, citizens of Taichung would have no opportunity to explore the magical caves of Jules Verne or dream within the musical palace of Alice's wonderland. I felt like an intruder exploring its architectural qualities on my first visit, but like a close friend on my second. This change in mind-set about belonging shows the embodiment of human experience and how modern citizens can engage in social life while being inspired and motivated by artistic intervention in the built environment. I have frequented Taichung for family reasons, and when my year-and-a-half-old son stared at the musicians playing Bach in the central lobby, I know that another round of self-enlightenment has begun.

228 J. Xiao

References

Aoi, A. (2013). *Changhua 1906: Urban renewal project runs the city* (T. F. Chang, Trans.) (pp. 35–49). New Taipei City: Common Master Press. 青井哲人 (2013). 彰化1906: 一座城市被烙伤而后自体再生的故事. 张亭菲译. 新北: 大家出版 (pp. 35–49).

Balmond, C. (2002) *Network, Serpentine gallery Pavilion 2002: Toyo Ito with Arup*, telescoweb.com, Japan.

Chang, J. S. (1993). *The urban planning of Taiwan 1895–1988*. Taipei: Chang Yung-Fa Foundation & Institute for National Policy Research & Yeqiang Publisher. 张素森 (1993). 台湾都市计划 1895–1988. 台北: 张永发基金会, 业强出版社.

Chen, X.-Q. (2011). A historical research on the 'urban planning act' presented by Urban and Housing Development Committee and U.N. Advisor Group. *Journal of Environment & Art,* (9), 47–67 (in Chinese). 陈湘芩 (2011). 都市建设与住宅计划小组和联合国顾问团研议台湾"都市计划法"之历史研究. 环境与艺术学刊, (9), 47–67.

Cheng, M.-Y. (2006). Work journal of the international competition of the Taichung metropolitan opera house. *Taiwan Architects, 32*(3), 111–112. 郑明裕 (2006), 台中大都会歌剧院竞图工作纪实, 建筑师, *32*(3), 111–112.

Davidson, J. W. (1903). *Formosa under Japanese rule* (p. 43). London: Japan Society. Online access via: https://babel.hathitrust.org/cgi/pt?id=uc1.31175035157232;view=1up;seq=29, access date: 2018/05/06.

Hsia, C.-J. (1994). *Public space* (p. 13). Taipei: Artists Press. 夏铸九 (1994). 公共空间. 台北: 艺术家出版社 (p. 13).

Hsia, C.-J., & Peng, Y. K. (2006). The plot ratio transfer should be cautious. *Chinatimes* (Taiwan), A19, September 3, 2006. 夏铸九, 彭扬楷, 容积移转不可不慎. 中国时报, A19, September 3, 2006.

Hsieh, C.-C., & Juang, H.-H. (2009). The niche characteristic of urban land use strength in Taichung city: A case study of T.D.R. *Journal of Geographical Research, 51*(11), 23–43. 谢琦强, 庄翰华 (2009). 台中市都市土地使用强度 "区位特性" 之研究: 以容积移转制度为例. 地理研究, *51*(11), 23–43.

Hsieh, T. C. (2014). Spotlight on Toyo Ito. *Cultural Taichung Quarterly,* (14), 37–39. 谢宗哲 (2014). 特写伊东丰雄. 文化台中季刊, (14), 37–39.

Huang, W. D. (1997). *Investigation and research on the history of urban planning during the Japanese occupation*. Taipei: Institute for Taiwan Urban Planning. 黄武达 (1997). 日治时代台湾都市计划历程基本资料之调查与研究. 台北: 台湾都市史研究室.

Ito, T. (2000). *Blurring architecture 1971–2005* (U. Schneider, Ed.). Milan: Edizioni Charta.

Ito, T. (2008). *Generative order* (T. C. Hsieh, Trans.) (pp. 354–357). Taipei: Garden City Publishers.

Jin, G. J., & Dai, J. (2010). Discussion on Taiwan transfer of development right institution. *International Urban Planning, 25*(4), 104–109. 金广君, 戴铜 (2010). 台湾地区容积转移制度解析. 国际城市规划, *25*(4), 104–109.

Lee, C.-L. (1980). *A history of Taiwan architecture 1600–1945* (p. 246). Taipei: Peiwu Publisher. 李乾朗 (1980). 台湾建筑史 1600–1945. 台北: 北屋出版社 (p. 246).

Lee, C.-L. (2005). *Taiwan architecture in the 19th century* (pp. 152–159). Taipei: Yushan Publisher. 李乾朗 (2005).十九世纪台湾建筑. 台北:玉山出版社 (pp. 152–159).

Levinson, A. (1997). Why oppose TDRs? Transferable development rights can increase overall development. *Regional Science and Urban Economics, 27*(3), 283–296.

Otsuji, K. (1943). Reflections on Taiwan architecture. *Architectural Journal of Taiwan,* (15), 134. 尾辻国吉 (1943). 台湾建筑界の回顾. 台湾建筑会志, (15), 134.

Shirakura, Y. (1943). The architectural transformation … in the new regime. *Architectural Journal of Taiwan,* (15), 22. 白仓好夫 (1943). 改隶以后 … 建筑的变迁. 台湾建筑会志, (15), 22.

Tseng, D. (2006). Expecting Toyo Ito effect, report on the Taichung metropolitan theater competition. *Taiwan Architects, 32*(3), 108. 曾成德 (2006). 期待伊东效应: 台中市大都会歌剧院竞图纪实. 建筑师, *32*(3), 108.

Government Documents

Administrative Office of the Central Government. (2003). Official Document No. 0921113281, 06/03. 行政院 (2003). 文壹字第*0921113281*号函. 06/03.
Fourth Review to SDSC of the Urban Planning of Taichung. (2016). December. 变更台中市都市计划 (新市政中心专用区)细部计划(第四次通盘检讨). 2016/12.
SDSC of the Urban Planning of Taichung. (2009). No. 0980221090 for Mass Transit Railway, August. 新市政中心专用区南侧(配合台中都会区大众捷运系统乌日文心北屯线建设计划), 2009/08.
Second Review to SDSC of the Urban Planning of Taichung. (2005). No. 0940148260, August. 变更台中市都市计划(新市政中心专用区)细部计划(第二次通盘检讨). 2005/08.
Third Review to SDSC of the Urban Planning of Taichung. (2012). No. 1010043533, April (pp. 35–43). 变更台中市都市计划 (新市政中心专用区)细部计划(第三次通盘检讨), 2012/04 (pp. 35–43).

Chapter 10
From Colonial to Global—Performing Art Space in Hong Kong

Charlie Qiuli Xue

Hong Kong, a Chinese territory located at the tip of the South China Sea, was the last British overseas colony. During its 150 years of colonial rule from 1841 to 1997, the colonial leadership combined with a Chinese effort from the administrative to grass-roots levels made Hong Kong unique. In addition to its values and lifestyle, this city-state has its own social, political and economic systems. Hong Kong laid down the framework for the city proper during its first hundred years of development from 1841 to 1945. The 50 years following World War II saw Hong Kong transition from a defensive outpost into an international financial hub. The urban architecture seen in the city today was formulated mainly during the 1980s and fermented to maturity. Since 1978, when China opened its doors, Hong Kong has served as an example of economic success, and its experiences have directly contributed to the success of mainland China (Akers-Jones 2004; Caroll 2007; Shelton et al. 2011).

In the 1950s and 1960s, Hong Kong was busy relocating refugees and developing local industry. From the 1970s to 1990s, the rise of the "four Asian dragons"—Hong Kong, Taiwan, South Korea and Singapore—was manifested in their remarkable construction boom. Hong Kong architecture during the half century from 1946 to 1997 was shaped by government's policies, local social and technical forces and products created by local and expatriate planners, architects and builders. The tiny island took its own path apart from the U.K. and China. Hong Kong's architecture is the result of a pragmatic economy and property speculation, and is free from political ideology (Sit 2015).

C. Q. Xue (✉)
Department of Architecture and Civil Engineering, City University of Hong Kong,
Kowloon, Hong Kong
e-mail: bscqx@cityu.edu.hk

© Springer Nature Singapore Pte Ltd. 2019
C. Q. Xue (ed.), *Grand Theater Urbanism*,
https://doi.org/10.1007/978-981-13-7868-3_10

In the 1990s, the per capita GDP of Hong Kong once surpassed that of UK, its suzerain. In 1997, Hong Kong's GDP per capital was US$27,000, while China's was 781.[1] In 2017, the GDP of Beijing, Shanghai, Shenzhen and Guangzhou steadily surpassed that of Hong Kong.[2] In the past 30 years, Hong Kong's economic development relied on the benefits of open-door policy in the Chinese mainland, while its speed could not be compared with that of many Chinese cities.

During this relatively slow growing period, Hong Kong's cultural buildings fit into two categories of question. (1) How public facilities were initiated, built and nurture people's life? (2) How cultural buildings help the city to define its future? This chapter tries to answer the questions by investigating the buildings of performing art space in several stages while Hong Kong was in transition from colonial to global. It is hoped to present a different scenario of development compared with the cities in other chapters.

Before entering the description of Hong Kong's cultural building, we may have a look of American architect Richard Dattner's suggestions for the goals of civil architecture. First, it must present a modest monumentality and not be excessive or insufficient in scale. Second, it must have the noble aspiration to preserve and enhance public life. Third, it must be sustainable, exhibit an economy of means. Public architecture must set a special example by being efficient, long lasting and energy conserving. Fourth, it must have contextuality, in that it should respect and express the natural topography. Fifth, it must offer inclusiveness and accessibility. A public building should include necessary functional parts to serve the people well, be convenient to access and offer a space in which all are included, valued and welcomed. Sixth, it must accept the contradictions raised by a multicultural society's multiple interpretations of civic structure appropriateness. Seventh, it must educate. Winston Churchill recognized the didactic dimension of architecture in his statement that "we shape our buildings, and then they shape us" (Dattner 1995).

The above seven points are around a central concern that how to make a civil architecture civic. The cultural and performing arts buildings in Hong Kong are examined with these seven principles in the following text. Cultural buildings in the twenty first century divert to a new direction.

---

[1]During 1993 to 1998, the per capita GDP of Hong Kong was higher than that of the UK. The data of per capita GDP is available from International Bank for Reconstruction and Development, 2014. The GDP figures of Hong Kong and China in 1997 are from Census and Statistics Department, Hong Kong government, 2016; and China Statistic Bureau, 2016.

[2]Shenzhen's GDP surpassed that of Hong Kong, see "hujin libao lingxian, shenshui chuangxin zhumu" (Shanghai and Beijing maintain to be pioneers, Shenzhen and Guangzhou intend to be innovative), *Ta Kung Pao*, Jan 22, 2018.

10.1   City Hall

Among the public buildings built in the post-war construction, City Hall is a most prominent case. A city hall is a type of public building commonly found in continental European and British cities since the end of the nineteenth century. It usually embodies the pride, and serves the needs, of citizens. However, during the first 100 years of colonial rule, Hong Kong did not have a decent city hall. Small scale performances were carried on cinemas, private club houses or clan houses. In his preliminary planning for Hong Kong, Sir Patrick Abercrombie (1879–1957) acutely pointed out the lack of city hall and public facilities for such a large city (Abercrombie 1948). The proposal to build one arose during the post-war reconstruction of the early 1950s. A city hall council was formed in 1950 to represent voices from 55 civic organizations. In 1954, the government completed reclamation of the sea in front of Statue Square. The land was designated for the construction of a ferry pier and a city hall, and architects were recruited from Britain.

The Hong Kong government first committed Professor Gordon Brown (1912–1962), head of architecture department of Hong Kong University, to make a design. The scheme was produced in 1955 and later passed to two architects from PWD (public work department)—Alan Fitch (1921–1986) and Ronald Phillips (1926–). These architects from Britain firmly embraced the modernist principles and the design embodied the minimal elegance. City Hall was completed in 1962, located in Central on Hong Kong Island. It was the territory's first-ever entirely local-oriented center for culture, comprising facilities such as a concert hall, a library, a theater and a marriage registry.

The low block of Hong Kong City Hall houses a 1434-capacity concert hall, a 463-capacity theater and 3 restaurants. The high block houses the marriage registry and a public library. The memorial garden and shrine located in the center were built to honor those who died in World War II. The low block of the concert hall is located on one side and the high block of the library is located on the other. The two are skillfully linked by the small theater and courtyard colonnade around the memorial garden. A crisp and simple design language was used in the construction of the building, which exhibits a well-balanced horizontal and vertical composition. Hong Kong City Hall is an example of a Bauhaus building (Fig. 10.1).

Hong Kong City Hall was built to communicate a modest monumentality for important ceremonial occasions such as governor inaugurations and the welcoming of British Royal family members. Its performance venue, library, marriage registry and garden have enhanced and enriched public life. The building was also constructed according to a minimalist philosophy. Its functional provisions did not consume more materials than needed. "Less is more" was a sustainable notion in the 1960s, when the economic situation was stringent. City Hall is located in the heart of Central. Originally aligned with the Queen's Pier and Edinburgh Place Ferry Pier, it was easily accessible to visitors from across Victoria Harbor. It is

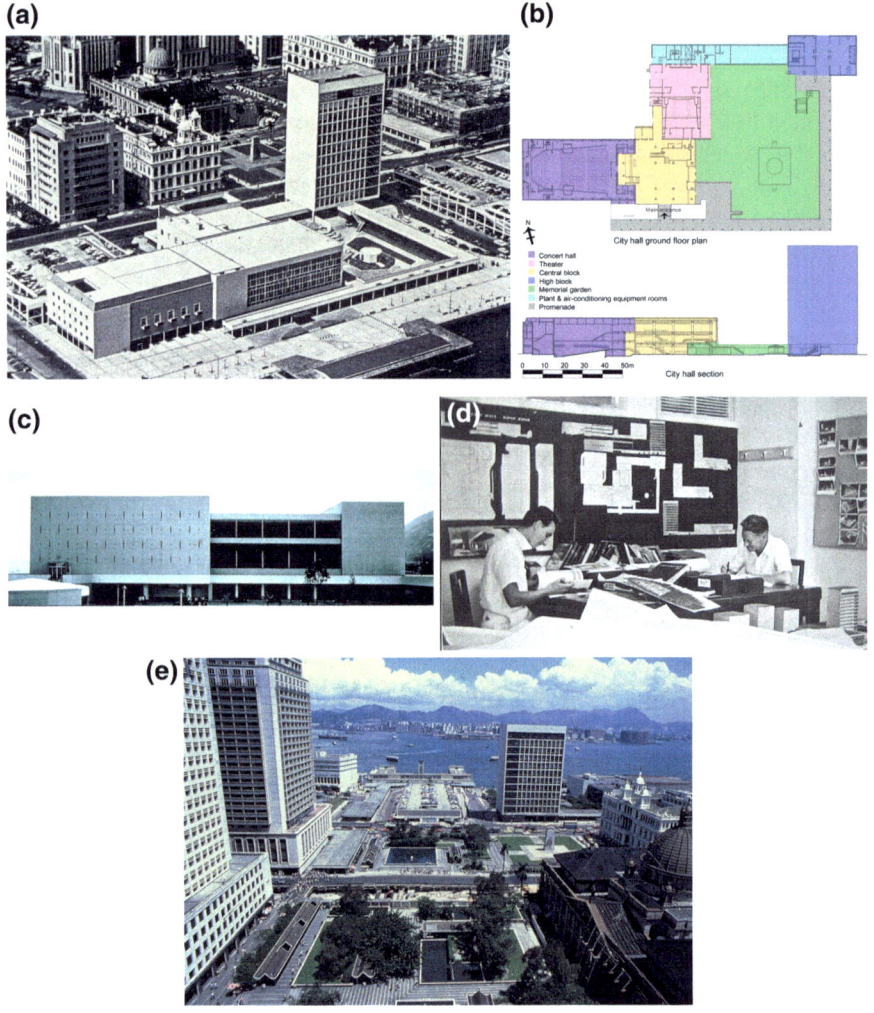

Fig. 10.1 City Hall, 1962. **a** A model of modernist architecture in Hong Kong. **b** plan, **c** elevation facing the courtyard, **d** designers Alan Fitch (right) and Ronald Philips. Courtesy of Mr. Ronald Philips. **e** City Hall seen from Hong Kong Bank. Courtesy of Mr. Chung Wah Nan

multifunctional and welcomes all age groups for any purpose. It educates the public in music, culture and literature, creating a diversified civic life for citizens inside and outside the building.

When City Hall was conceived in the mid-1950s, the surrounding buildings in Central were mainly classical (including the Supreme Court, completed in 1905; and the Hong Kong Club, completed in 1897) and Art Deco (including the Hong Kong Bank headquarters, completed in 1936, and the Bank of China, completed in 1951). The other commercial offices were designed according to an obscured and cliché language. City Hall served as a venue for royal rituals, such as inaugural ceremonies of new governors sent by Her Majesty and to welcome the Queen, princes and princesses. The design did not adopt the model of royal family buildings, but embraced an asymmetrical, open and light-hearted aesthetic. The young designers from the U.K. bravely followed new examples from their home country, such as the Team X, Brutalism and "tropical modernism" movements of the 1950s. They sought to make the building plain and intimate for its citizens.[3] City Hall provoked a modernist movement in Hong Kong.

10.2 Shatin and Other District Town Halls

When City Hall was completed in 1962, Hong Kong was in industrialization stage. More people had job, although compensation was odd. In 1967, partly influenced by the Cultural Revolution in China, riot happened in streets of Hong Kong and took the toll of decades of life. The government gradually came to the under-standing that more housing and activity places should be provided so that people would have a feeling of belonging. When Crawford Murray MacLehose (1917–2000) was installed as governor in 1971, he declared on behalf of the government to launch an ambitious "Ten-year plan of housing", which would house 1.8 million people in public housing. Where can these 400,000+ housing units be built? Government actively found the way of dispersing the population pressure in the city area. Tsuen Wan, Sha Tin and Tuen Men were developed as new towns early in the 1960s, and this process expedited in the 1970s. These new towns were planned as self-sufficient with residential, industrial, commercial and cultural facilities.[4] Town halls were built in town centers of Tsuen Wan (1980), North District (1982), Shatin (1987) and Tuen Men (1987). Town halls in other districts were later completed.

In Hong Kong, there is only one level of government without district admin-istration. Hong Kong government controls the town planning and basic provisions for citizens' daily life. Therefore, around 100 "municipal service buildings" are almost same, stacking wet market, indoor sport and library in one building. Similarly, town halls in various districts bear same contents and characteristics—a major multi-function theater of over 1200 seats, functional rooms for cultural activity rental and exhibition. Library and marriage registration are planned next to town hall. The design and standard are by and large the same in most new towns.

Take Shatin as an example. Shatin new town was planned for a population of 475,000. Shatin Town Hall was located at the town center, designed by government architects and completed in 1987. The 1400-seat theater can stage concert, opera and dancing. The exhibition hall, entertainment hall, rehearsal room, musical room

---

[3]The design intention of City Hall was reported in *Ming Pao Daily News*, 10 May 2007. For an explanation of "tropical modernism," see Uduku (2006).
[4]About new towns in Hong Kong, see Bristow (1989).

and calligraphy room are ready for rental. The gross floor area is about 15,600 m^2. Building design followed modernist principles and emphasized functionality.

Like Hong Kong City Hall, the town halls were built as local-oriented centers and offer cultural amenities and facilities such as concert halls, libraries, performance venues and marriage registries. All of the town halls are located in traffic junctions or town centers and enjoy heavy patronage on weekdays and weekends. Unlike the "grand theaters" in China in the twenty first century which mostly occupy a large street block of ten hectares with a monumental gesture, town halls in Hong Kong are modest part of the pedestrian bridge network. People can access town hall directly from subway or home, without interrupted by busy traffic. People go to see performances in the evenings and on weekends, children visit to attend various extra-mural art courses and the elderly engage in dance exercises at the podium (Xue and Manuel 2001). The building designs are plain, but meticulously serve the daily lives of the local citizens. Table 10.1 shows that town halls averagely held performance twice a day, and received 300,000 audiences each in a year.

In Shatin, the New Town Plaza, a large-scale transit-oriented development, also entered into planning as Shatin Town Hall was being prepared. The shopping mall, office buildings and high-rise residential towers around the train station were developed by the private sector, mainly Sun Hung Kai, and involve floor areas more than 200,000 m^2 in size. The public and private sectors collaborated in the construction of the town center. The elevated podium connects the shopping mall, town hall and public library. All of the high and low buildings in the town center are integrated via the same

Table 10.1 Number of performances and attendance 2013–2016

Cultural venues		2013/14	2014/15	2015/16
Hong Kong City Hall	No. of performances	573	554	628
Concert Hall and Theater	Attendance ('000)	355	336	373
Tsuen Wan Town Hall	No. of performances	720	733	756
Auditorium and Cultural Activities Hall	Attendance ('000)	282	284	297
Tuen Mun Town Hall	No. of performances	1009	1062	977
Auditorium and Cultural Activities Hall	Attendance ('000)	366	382	352
North District Town Hall	No. of performances	245	225	286
Auditorium	Attendance ('000)	58	56	66
Shatin Town Hall	No. of performances	640	608	624
Auditorium AND Cultural Activities Hall	Attendance ('000)	352	329	302

Source Leisure and Cultural services Department Statistic Report, 2017

(a)   (b)

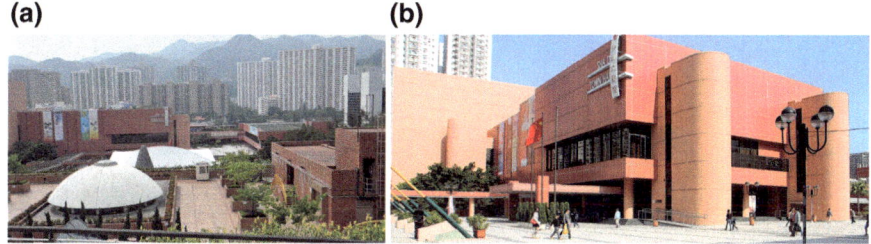

Fig. 10.2 Shatin Town Hall, 1987. **a** Seen from shopping mall, **b** Town hall standing on a platform. Its ground floor links to park and river

tile cladding. Shatin Town Hall and the town center separate pedestrians and vehicles effectively (Tan and Xue 2014). Pedestrians can walk 600 m or longer distance from the train station through the mall and town hall to the waterfront central park and their homes. They move along the upper level, while vehicles run along the street level.[5]

The government had more money in the 1980s than it did in the 1960s. However, the demand for public facilities drastically increased. When both town halls in Shatin and Tuen Men were completed in 1987, Hong Kong was in its heyday—subway starting to run and more people moving to the new towns. Shatin has gathered over 600,000 people, while town center and other cultural buildings strengthen the town center functions. The district town halls are standard physical configurations for new town construction. They were built in modest budget and offer more functions and accessibility to local residents. These buildings are more closing to the seven principles Dattner suggested (Figs. 10.2 and 10.3).

10.3   Performing Art Space in Institutions

During the colonial rule, many civil related matters were not led by government, but initiated by civil groups from bottom up. Performing art spaces in the 1970s and 1980s were good examples of this phenomenon.

At the beginning of the 1970s, aware of the lack of cultural venues, architect Tao Ho and his friends set up the Hong Kong Arts Center, which was later supported by the Governor, Sir Murray MacLehose. The government allocated a plot of land on the Wanchai seafront, but the budget was only five million Hong Kong dollars.[6] The arts center is located on a street corner. The new building closely abuts older buildings and the two sides are cut at 45° to reduce the bulkiness and follow the site

---

[5]Transit-oriented development and pedestrian convenience are characteristics of urban architecture in Hong Kong. Shatin town center is one of the typical examples. See Xue (2016), Lu et al. (2018a, b).

[6]To visualize how much was five million dollars in 1972, a university graduate could earn 700–1000 Hong Kong dollars a month at the time. See Zhang (2005). A new unit of two bedrooms, 585 ft.^{2}, in Taikoo Shing asked for HK$124,500 in 1976, according to the Archive of Swire Group.

Fig. 10.3 Town halls are usually in the pedestrian network. **a** Tusen Wan Town Hall; **b** Lobby of Tusen Wan Town Hall, changing of floor level in lobby is used in all town hall designs; **c** Interior of auditorium, Shatin town hall; **d** Tuen Men town hall shares podium with library

coverage requirement. A theater, music hall, gallery and classroom are stacked from the basement to the fifth floor. On top of the theater, the gallery makes use of the height difference by splitting the space to create half a floor. This method is workable in the high density environment. Over the past 40 years, the arts center has held numerous arts exhibitions of high and indigenous arts. The arts center school has run many visual and performing arts classes. The tower houses the offices for arts and cultural organizations. In the cultural desert of Hong Kong, a small tower in the downtown hustle sprays water droplets of Muse (Fig. 10.4).

At the time of constructing Hong Kong Arts Center, Academy for Performing Arts was in active preparation. In 1981, the government allocated a plot of land in Wanchai next to the Hong Kong Arts Center, and the Jockey Club donated a sum for the development of an Academy for Performing Arts. Architect Simon Kwan's design won first prize. Beneath the site lay sewage pipes that drained into the harbor. The buildable area consisted of only two triangles. The design placed a vehicular drop-off area between these two triangles. Entering the lobby, visitors take the escalator and arrive at the huge atrium, from where they can reach the concert hall, grand theater, chamber hall, dancing hall, recording studio and experimental theater. According to the program brief, all of these performing venues were to have their own lobby. The design gathers them together and lets them share a big atrium, which expresses the spatial order and sequence, and also provides a social and communication area. The variously sized performing spaces

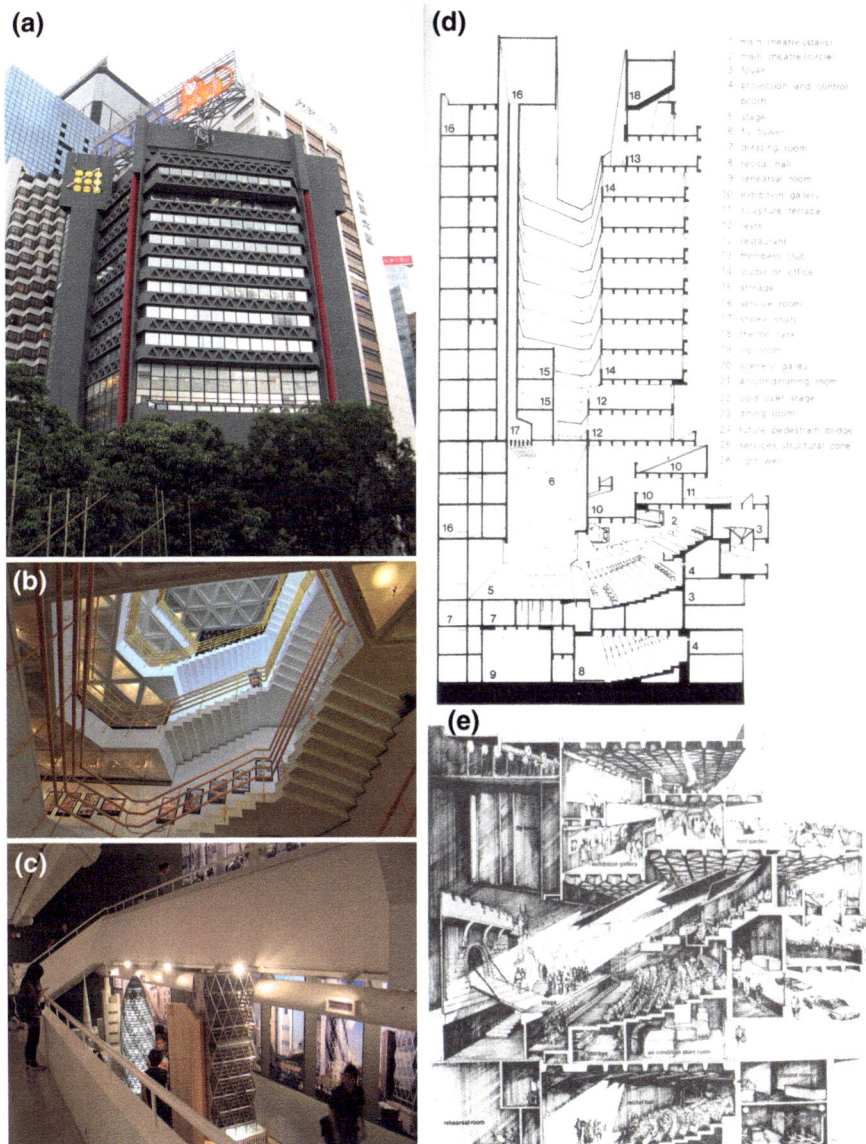

Fig. 10.4 Hong Kong Arts Center, 1977. **a** The main elevation facing the street corner. **b** Stair along the wall is the main feature of design. **c** Section showing the flexible usage of level heights. **d** Gallery. **e** Design sketch. Drawings courtesy of Dr. Tao Ho

are all woven into the modular grids of a triangle. The acute angles are used for stair shafts or storage, while the functional parts are rectangular. The building was completed in 1985 and echoed with I. M. Pei's design for the East Building of the National Gallery in Washington, 1978 (Fig. 10.5).

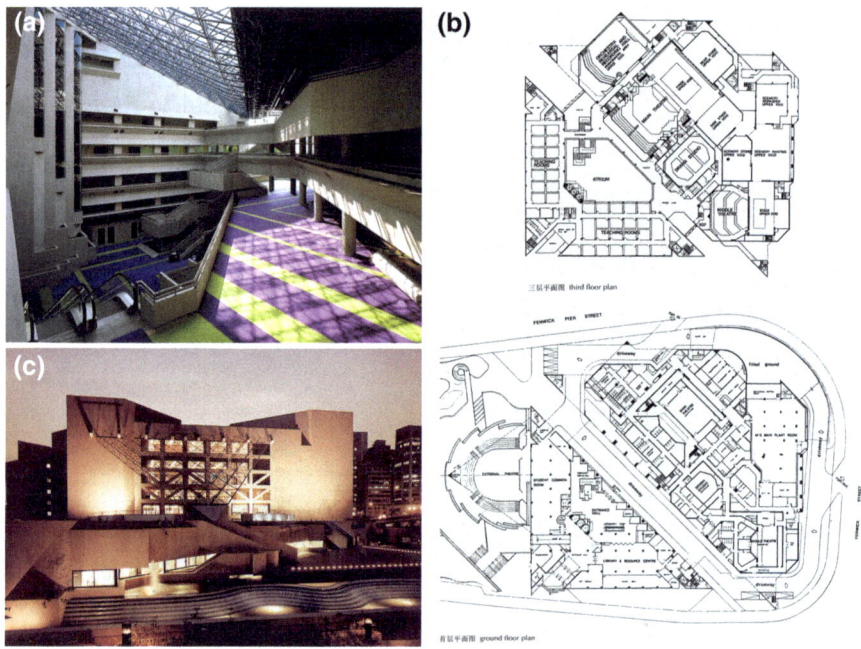

Fig. 10.5 Hong Kong Academy of Performing Arts, 1985. **a** The atrium gathers waiting and social functions for all theaters. **b** Plan drawings. **c** The outdoor space serves for open performance and social events. Courtesy of Dr. Simon Kwan

The two institutional art buildings were built for experimental and small scale performances in the same area. If town halls were built for leisure of local people, institutional performing art buildings are more for the art sake. They supplement the formal performance venues. The design language continued the method used in City Hall. The designers dug the potentials in high-density environment, and created clean building form. The buildings provide public space in busy downtown area, and they themselves merge into the street blocks of Wanchai. After 30 years' operation, the architect Simon Kwan was awarded honorary doctorate by the Academy in 2016.

10.4 Hong Kong Cultural Center

In the late 1960s, the government was planning to move the Kowloon-Canton Railway terminus to Hung Hom on reclaimed land. A cultural complex was suggested to be built on the extension of train station platform. In 1982, an indoor-stadium was built next to the train station in Hung Hom.

Located in Tsim Sha Tsui, Kowloon, the Hong Kong Cultural Center was built on the site of the old Kowloon-Canton Railway terminus station in 1989. The area of 11 ha was designated for "Cultural Complex" use for auditoria, an art museum, a planetarium, outdoor activity space, Chinese and European style restaurants in the early 1970s. In the documents of Urban Council, building Cultural Complex was "to promote local culture", and more important, "progress made on recreation and amenities has had an uplifting effect on the quality of life led by the hard-working people in Hong Kong". "Hong Kong has long joined the league of big cities first in the commercial field and then in the industrial field. But what about the cultural field? We have not much to be proud of and a lot to be ashamed of. A lot of the cultural facilities which are regarded as basic in big cities in the world simply do not exist in Hong Kong."[7] The project was first called Kowloon Civic Center to fill the gap in peninsula, but later it was loaded with more expectations for high-end performance. When the cost of HK$225 million was estimated in 1975, Hong Kong was experiencing the low economic tide after oil crisis. The Urban Council had to make up its mind and defer decades of small items to "take the Cultural Complex off the ground", as the voice in Urban Council almost unanimously supported this significant work for the public.[8]

The cultural center is located on a 5.2 ha harbor-front site and has a gross floor area of 82,231 m². There are three major performing halls in the center, the concert hall (2019 seats), grand theater (1734 seats) and studio theater (303–496 seats when used), in addition to numerous ancillary facilities like gallery, exhibition area in foyer and lecture room. The schedule of accommodation was discussed between the Urban Council and Cultural Complex sub-committee for several years in the mid-1970s, and the client finally adopted the proposal from a British consultant Theater Projects Ltd. The main concern was to build an international concert hall for unamplified music only, and a multi-purpose lyric theater. A famous pipe organ builder from Germany was employed to build and install pipe organ on one side of concert hall, costing HK$2.5 million in the 1980s.[9]

The concert hall and grand theater form the two wings of the L-shaped floor plan, with two atriums located in between. The ancillary facilities are positioned at the perimeter of the L-shape along a tight corridor. Although the L-shape appears dominating from far away, the brutal superimposition and expression of the pure form masses in the atrium and corridor provide an interesting spatial experience.

The Cultural Center was built on the Kowloon Peninsula to parallel City Hall on the island across the harbor. It was a statement of the ambition of the Hong Kong government's public architectural design during the prosperous 1980s.

---

[7]Minutes of Urban Council Annual Conventional Debate, Jan 16, 1975.

[8]Speech by Mr. Peter P. K. Ng, J. P., at the Annual Convention Debate of the Urban Council on Jan 14, 1975; Speech of Mr. Wong Shiu-Cheuck (M.B.E.) at the Urban Council Annual Conventional Debate, Jan 16, 1975. "Special lottery for Cultural Complex?" reported the possibility of raising fund, *South China Morning Post*, May 30, 1975.

[9]Memorandum for Members of the Cultural Complex and Indoor Stadia Sub-committee, Hong Kong Government, March 29, 1978; July 14, 1978.

The shoebox-shaped concert hall satisfies the performance requirements of international philharmonic orchestras and the outdoor steps accommodate open-sky shows on weekend afternoons. The clock tower retained from a demolished railway station is one of the hall's few pleasing design efforts.

A notable part is its foyer. The foyers in the City Hall and town halls were around 9000 ft.^{2} and they obviously felt crowded. The foyer in cultural center was proposed to be 20,000 ft.^{2} on ground level. Lounge and box office are arranged in this level. The design made "inner foyer" and "outer foyer". Inner foyers are from second floor, lavatories are closing to the auditorium, and outer foyer is on ground floor, exhibition area, souvenir shop, lounge and lavatories all open to the public. The center is easily accessible for visitors from the Star Ferry Pier and bus terminal. It is located in a location popular with tourists and welcomes all age groups for any purpose. It educates the public in music, culture and literature, creating a busy and diversified civic life for citizens on weekdays and weekends alike.

In the two-year period from 2014–2016, Hong Kong Cultural Center held 644 performances, with 604,299 audiences. These numbers are similar with those of town halls, but the performance was in higher class (national or international). During the same period, Hong Kong Cultural Center rented the space to 2244 groups for exhibition or social activities, 829 got rental subsidy. Four art troupes are venue partners—Hong Kong Philharmonic Orchestra, Hong Kong Chinese Orchestra, Hong Kong Ballet and Zuni Icosahedron.[10] Without such a venue, these art troupes will have no proper home to practice (Fig. 10.6).

The monumentality of Hong Kong Cultural Center is frequently challenged. Located at an eye-catching position near the harbor, its emotionless L-shape form does little to inspire the imagination of visitors. However, it has undoubtedly enhanced and enriched public life by providing a performance venue. The center was built according to a pragmatic philosophy. The lack of design character is emphasized by the building's completely concealed envelope, which never takes advantage of window openings to provide a spectacular harbor view and access to the cooling sea breeze.

In the 1980s, Hong Kong was touted as one of the "Asian Dragons." Hong Kong Bank, Bank of China and other commercial buildings stood proudly in the central business district and symbolized the arrival of global capital. The government received more revenue and reserves in the 1980s. Together with the Arts Museum in Tsim Sha Tsui, the Hong Kong Cultural Center was proposed to enforce the city's economic "dragon" status. It was built when public building construction and the newly established ASD (Architectural Services Department, originally PWD) were in full swing. Hong Kong Institute of Architects, particularly Mr. Jon A. Prescott the president of HKIA, offered to help the design competition so that the cultural center could be compared with Sydney Opera House. However, the client

---

[10]Data from *Hong Kong Cultural Centre, Bi-annual Report*, 2014–2016.

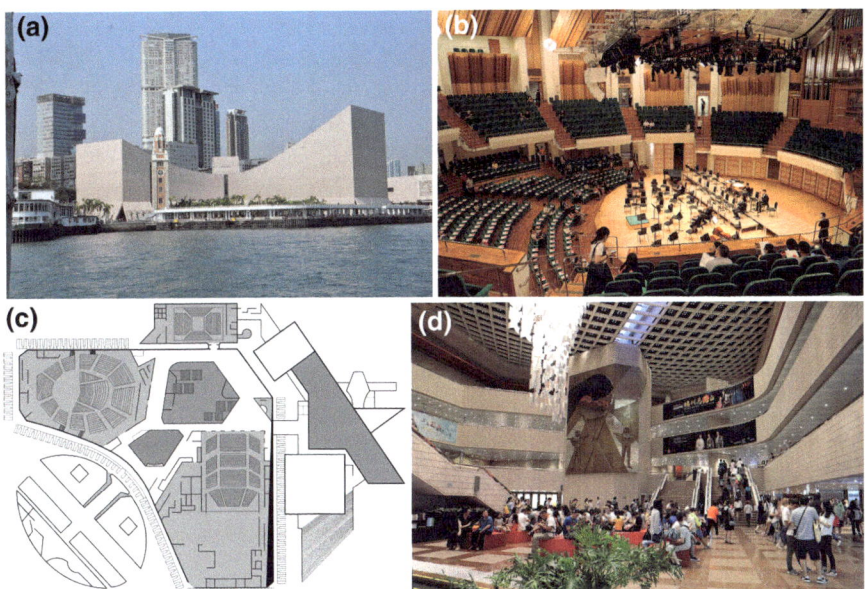

Fig. 10.6 Hong Kong Cultural Center, 1989. **a** Cultural Center from Victoria Harbor; **b** Concert hall; **c** Plan; **d** Lobby open to the public. Drawing by Zang Peng

felt that the time was too tight to hold competition.[11] A senior official at the ASD was mainly responsible for the design of the center before his retirement. The center has been severely challenged by citizen groups, architectural students and professionals since its completion.[12] In recent years, colorful laser beams have often been projected on the solid walls of the center to celebrate events. Although some people have found this use of the center to lessen its value, critical voices have generally seemed to subside (Fig. 10.7).

10.5   West Kowloon

In 1998, Beijing held an international design competition for the national theater. The three rounds of competition aroused extensive international interest and the results were fiercely debated. No matter which form of building was eventually

---

[11]Jon A. Prescott, "Kowloon Cultural Complex: Architects Institute's proposal", *South China Morning Post*, June 3, 1975; "Cultural complex design contest plea", *South China Morning Post*, June 3, 1975.

[12]The designer of the Cultural Center was an engineer, not an architect. He was in a high position in the ASD. The Cultural Center was criticized by architectural students from the University of Hong Kong, see *South China Morning Post*, Nov. 15, 1989.

Fig. 10.7 The solid wall is
good for laser show in the
evening—a rediscovered
function after 2010

selected, the process of the design competition demonstrated the opening up of China, which was long considered a country behind a curtain (Xue et al. 2010). China's bold opening up to international design firms stimulated Hong Kong to a great extent.

In 2000, the Housing Authority and HKIA first held design competitions for public housing in Shui Chuen O of Shatin, which received a warm response.[13] Around the same time, Chief Executive Tung Chee-hwa mentioned youth services in a policy address. The government suggested building a youth development center in Chai Wan with public funding of HK$900 million. In June 2000, the Home Affairs Bureau and HKIA jointly held a design competition and in December received more than 60 entries. After two rounds of competition, a scheme designed by a young team won first prize. Construction started in 2001 and stopped in 2003 due to a looming economic downturn. Construction resumed in 2005 and the building was completed and opened in 2010.

Following this warm-up period, the West Kowloon Cultural District design competition was held. West Kowloon began as a plot of 42 ha reclaimed from Victoria Harbour when the Western Harbor Tunnel, international airport and airport expressway were built. In 1996, the land was designated as a cultural district. Although the land is only one twelfth the size of the 2010 World Expo site in Shanghai, it is valuable given its location in the city center of Hong Kong. In April 2001, an international open design competition was held and five schemes were selected from 140 entries. Foster & Partners from the U.K. won first prize. The winning scheme installed a "sky canopy" above the buildings and public space, which the authority highly appreciated. After the financial crisis of 1997, Hong Kong is more concerned its image as "an Asian global city". Sky canopy has large and strong image in front of Victoria Harbor, and is written into design brief for the next stage.

---

[13]After several rounds of start and stop, Shui Chuen O Estate was completed in 2015 and accommodates 3039 households. Data is from the author's investigation.

With some concepts in mind, the government issued an invitation to develop the West Kowloon Cultural District in September 2003. The tenderer was asked to have experience developing, selling and managing large-scale comprehensive buildings and to inject HK$30 billion into the project. In April 2004, the government received five tenders. In November 2004, three entries were confirmed. An exhibition of three plans was displayed to the public for 15 weeks from December 2004 to March 2005. The tenderers comprised big property developers such as Cheung Kong, Sun Hung Kai, Henderson Land and Sino. The developers brought in international architects, engineers and various consultants. Each tenderer spent HK$10 million on models, display halls, lighting and brochures for its plan. The questionnaire sheet administered to the public was as long as a toilet tissue roll. The general public usually felt puzzled and did not know how to answer the questions. The tenderers and property developers transported their employees to "visit" and fill in the sheet (Fig. 10.8).

The people doubted the method of running the cultural district via a single consortium. The consortium invested huge amounts of money into "promoting" culture and expected the sum to be recouped through the development of commercial properties. The people questioned why this company was selected out of all of the other companies. Moreover, they questioned whether the property developers had enough experience to manage the cultural facilities. Under societal pressure, the

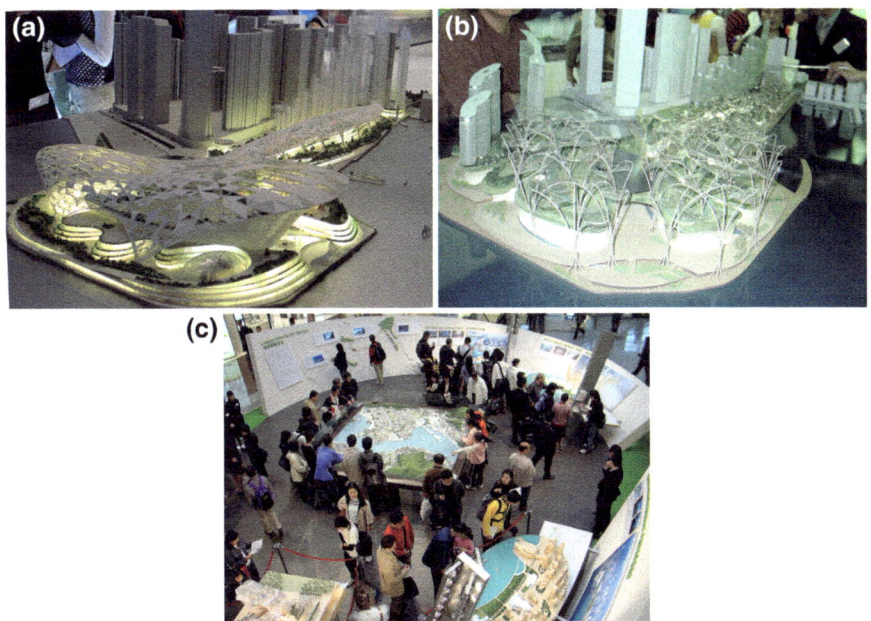

Fig. 10.8 Schemes of West Kowloon Cultural District in 2004–2005. **a, b** Shortlisted master plan. **c** Swire Properties' scheme was not shortlisted. It exhibited "Vision of the Harbor" in its own shopping mall. The design was led by Frank Gehry and Partners

Fig. 10.9 Three entries of West Kowloon Cultural District, 2010. **a** Scheme of Foster & Partners, **b** Scheme of Rocco Design, **c** Scheme of OMA, 2010

government gave up the single-operator plan, sending 10 years of government, consortium and public effort went down drain. In 2008, the government established the authority of the West Kowloon Cultural District and applied for funding of HK $21.6 billion from the Legislative Council. In 2009, an invitation for a master plan competition was sent to international designers. Master plan works from three companies, including Foster & Partners, OMA and Rocco Design, were displayed to the public for three months starting in August 2010 (Fig. 10.9).

Lord Foster first came to Hong Kong in 1979. He participated in the design of Hong Kong Bank and the Hong Kong airport, train station and cruise pier. His designs paid attention to both the environment and technology. Foster & Partners demonstrated the theme of the "park in the city," according to which a park would be featured prominently in West Kowloon with all vehicular traffic diverted underground. The dragon canopy was highlighted in the 2002 and 2004 designs. In this master plan, the canopy was replaced by large pieces of lawn and forest. The design made West Kowloon appear decent and elegant.

Rocco Design focused on pedestrian and vehicular circulation. Its plan was relegated to a compact part of United Plaza that gradually gave way to a smooth path toward the sea. Local factors such as a market and stone slab streets were integrated into the site. Artistic raft pieces were floated on the sea as metaphors of Hong Kong fishing rafts.

OMA is famous for many spectacular buildings including the CCTV head-quarters in Beijing. Its designs have centered on circulation and people movement

Fig. 10.10 Foster & Partners won the master plan of West Kowloon Cultural District, 2011

and have continuously broken through conventional concepts of "architecture." In the planning of West Kowloon, OMA designed three clusters of buildings, including the "East arts," "West performance" and "Central market" clusters. The grid layout of the "East arts" cluster was the Hong Kong version of CCTV headquarters from a visual standpoint. The "Central market" cluster was crowded. The design included a surprising stroke by adding a suspension bridge linking the Jordan and Austin Roads. There was no such requirement in the design brief and it extended the design beyond the site boundary. However, this ring bridge strengthened the celebratory atmosphere of the West Kowloon Cultural District and also connected the cultural district to the old city.

All three of the plans considered internal and external traffic and prioritized pedestrian and bicycle routes. However, the quality of the works did not meet with people's expectations. The three companies were paid HK$50 million (US$6.45 million) each in compensation. Design competitions of a similar scale in mainland China typically pay HK$200,000–500,000 at most and attract similarly famous companies.[14] Foster & Partners ultimately won the bid for the master plan of West Kowloon Cultural District. The southwest portion of the district is a large park positioned on a gentle slope. Most of the district's performance and exhibition buildings are located close to Canton Road. Vehicular traffic is hidden underground. The roads and basement parking add to the problems of pollution and ventilation (Fig. 10.10).

The cultural district will eventually be home to 14 buildings. In 2013, two buildings were confirmed. Bing Thom (1940–2016) of Vancouver and Ronald Lu of Hong Kong jointly won their bid to design the Xiqu (Chinese opera) Center. Herzog & de Meuron from Switzerland, TFP Farrells and Arup & Partners HK won

---

[14]For more information about the West Kowloon Cultural District; and the webpage of the Authority of West Kowloon Cultural District, http://www.westkowloon.hk/tc/home.

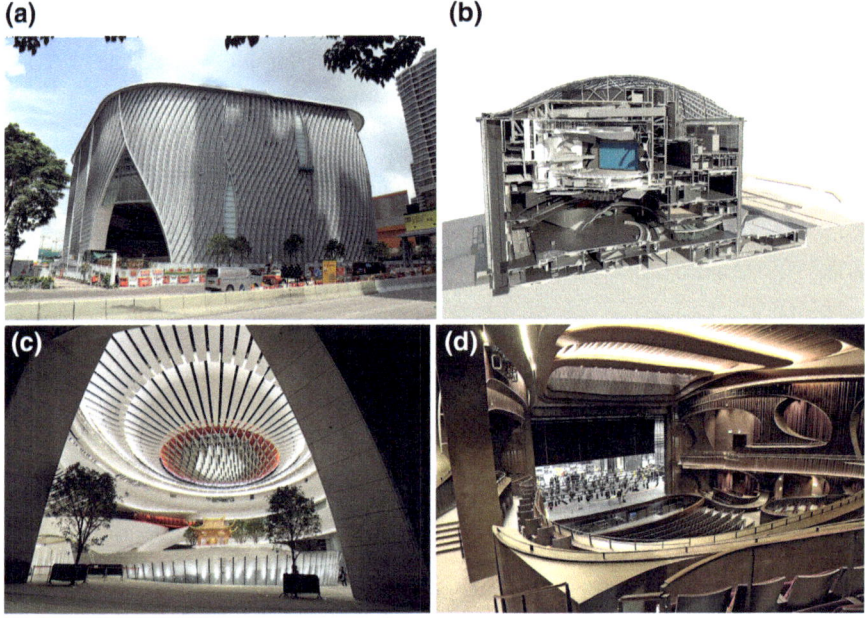

Fig. 10.11 Xiqu Center. **a** Building in 2018, **b** Model, Courtesy of Ronald Lu & Partners. **c** The concourse, **d** Theater

their bid to design the M+ Museum. Administration has been underway since 2008, with directors and many officers employed from overseas. With the "generosity" of the Hong Kong government, infrastructure construction began in 2013, and the estimated cost has already escalated to HK$47 billion, doubled the government's estimation in 2008.[15] Xiqu Center opened to public in December 2018. The building inherits the characteristics of public buildings in Hong Kong, and opens its three-floor lobby-corridors (lecture hall, "tea garden" restaurant-performance stage) to the public and fans of Chinese opera (Figs. 10.11 and 10.12).

---

[15]Chan Yuen-han, *Xijiu xin de guo?* (How can you trust the West Kowloon?) *AM730*, July 3, 2013. The escalation of construction fee is partly attributed to the shortage of construction workers. Young people are not willing to join the building industry, and the importation of labor is banned by worker's union and some politicians. In 2015, a rebar bending worker's wage is around HK $2200 (US$270) a day. The high salary heavily burdens the development and city construction. See the report from *Financial Time* (M.ftchinese.com 2015).

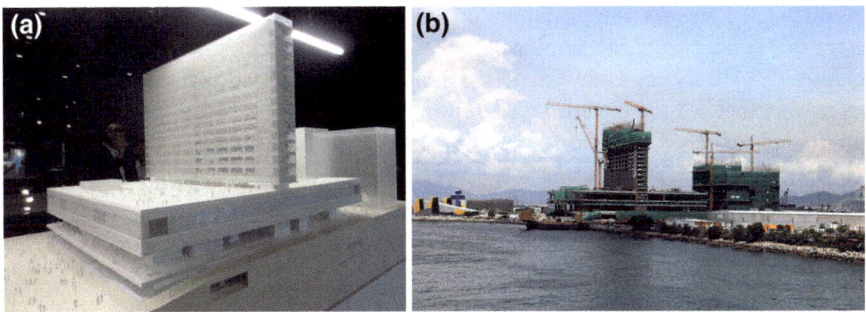

Fig. 10.12 M+ Museum, Herzog & de Meuron won the design, 2013. **a** Model, **b** construction site of M+ Museum at West Kowloon Cultural District, July 2018

10.6   Conclusion

This chapter reviews the road Hong Kong government provided performance space in the city from the 1950s to now. The milestone buildings mentioned in this chapter witnessed the transition Hong Kong evolved from a colonial outpost to an international metropolis. Unlike the intentions of Chinese cities in the 21st century for the city branding in the globalization, the provision of town hall in Hong Kong was for the betterment of residents' everyday life, and part of new town's physical configurations. The limited funding was approved from Legislative Council, which scrutinized usages and how money was spent. Modernist architectural method can well fulfill the task, with minimum input and maximum output. The buildings bring some pride for local people, but their images are never arrogant and crazy. Their easy access, plain and intimate atmospheres form a contrast with those "grand theaters" in the new millennium.

Designed mainly by government architects (some were from the UK), the buildings adopted clean design language without redundant decorations. The City Hall, facing the Queen's Pier, partly shouldered the reception of royal families and personnel from the UK. Even with this function, it resolutely got away with any colonial emblem and "Victorian" symbol. Since the 1950s, democratic ideas and modernist architecture widely dominated society and designs in the UK and Europe. Hong Kong was benefitted from the influence. Two institutional buildings in Wanchai continued the exploration of modern architecture. They skillfully fit into busy townscape in the Hong Kong Island. Both designers Ho and Kwan were educated in modern architectural spirit in the US and Hong Kong.

Entering the 21st century, Hong Kong is part of China and facing the keen competition from cities in Asia and China. If Hong Kong's public buildings including town halls before 1990 followed what Dattner suggested, the initiation of cultural buildings in the 21st century was in a different discourse. The whole country was determined to "connect with the international track", learn from and catch up with the advanced western countries. Cultural and civic buildings in China are planned rather for the city branding, cultural competitiveness and better environment for economic investment. The old type civic buildings designed by local architects in Hong Kong look shabby and outdated compared with those glamorous peers in other Chinese cities. Therefore, design market of important cultural buildings in Hong Kong had to open for international architects. Planning of West Kowloon Cultural District was the first open international competition in Hong Kong. People in Hong Kong see the amazing ideas from international architects and potential fame associated with star architects.

After sovereignty handover, Hong Kong became more democratic and debate in legislative council and society was fierce around various topics. This inevitably slows down the process of infrastructure and construction. The West Kowloon Cultural District was initiated in 1996. After 22 years, only one building has been completed. On the contrary, the World Expo site in Shanghai is more than ten times larger than the size of West Kowloon Cultural District. It was planned for four years. All buildings were completed in 3–4 years. After the expo in 2010, most land plots were auctioned and new office, residential, cultural and sport buildings constructed or in operation. After 2015, the appeal for integrating into "Guangdong-Hong Kong-Macau Great Bay Area" is loud, the construction speed in Hong Kong side demonstrated an embarrassing slow pace.[16]

So far as the design, the "newest" major performance building is Hong Kong Cultural Center, which was completed in 1989. The designers of West Kowloon Cultural Center in the 2010s include such firms as Norman Foster, OMA, Rocco Design, Herzog & De Meuron, TFP Farrells, UN Studio, Arup & Partners, Bing Thom and Ronald Lu & Partners. They can be or actually are same active in the two sides of Taiwan Straits. Some "story-telling" methods are similar with those popular in the Chinese mainland. Performance buildings in this round eventually merge into the trend of Greater China—building should (partly) serve the people, communicate with the society and bring fame, pride and profits for the city and municipal leaders.

Notwithstanding the changing trend and motivation in the twenty first century, performing art buildings in Hong Kong always keep an attitude of opening door to the public, 7 days a week and 52 weeks a year. In addition to the determination of

---

[16]The Guangdong-Hong Kong-Macau Greater Bay Area includes nine Cantonese cities Guangzhou, Shenzhen, Zhuhai, Foshan, Dongguan, Zhongshan, Jiangmen, Huizhou, Zhaoqing and two special administrative regions Hong Kong and Macau. Its area is 56,000 sq.km. and population 66 million. Its GDP reached US$1.7 trillion in 2017, more than that of Russia and similar as South Korea. It is the most active area in China in terms of economy. With the initiation of "The Silk Road Economic Belt and the 21st-century Maritime Silk Road" in 2015, China state government proposed to deepen the cooperation with Hong Kong, Macau and Taiwan. The aim is to surpass the other three bay areas in the world: Tokyo Bay, New York Bay and San Francesco Bay. See https://www.iyiou.com/p/79655.html, https://www.master-insight.com/category/theme/%e6%96%87%e5%8c%96/, accessed on Dec 25, 2018.

The Hong Kong-Zhuhai-Macau Bridge is a main infrastructure to link the Bay area. However, the construction in the Hong Kong side was obviously slower than the Chinese mainland side. The relevant stories are from the author's own investigation on site.

opening, the government appropriate fund allocation to every theater makes sure that good will be implemented.[17] Such an allocation of theater operation is scarce in the Chinese mainland counterparts. In this way, public buildings in Hong Kong highly uphold their publicness.

Acknowledgements   This chapter is part of a study supported by the Research Grant Council, Hong Kong government, project No. CityU 11658816.

In 1989, I stayed in Hong Kong for nine months as a visiting research student. I attended my first symphony by the Hong Kong Philharmonic Orchestra at City Hall. The music was magnificent. In recent years, I have also viewed performances and visited exhibitions at City Hall, the Hong Kong Cultural Center and the town halls of Shatin, Tsuen Wan and Tun Men, and attending exhibitions held by friends and art groups is my Sunday pastime.

Hong Kong and other Chinese cities are connected in my mind. Compared to the fabulous grand theatres in China, Hong Kong's theaters of the 1980s are plain in appearance but durable in materials and intimate. Lobbies are always open during the day and evening, allowing for chats, meetings, wandering and eating and drinking. The auxiliary rooms can be rented for art activities. Many people use the buildings free of charge in different (or creative) ways. While the building form was fixed in the 1980s, these theaters are continuously providing warmth to people. They add loveliness to this walkable, open and civic city

References

Abercrombie, P. (1948). *Hong Kong Preliminary Planning Report*. Hong Kong Government.
Akers-Jones, D. (2004). *Feeling the stones: Reminiscences by David Akers-Jones*. Hong Kong: Hong Kong University Press.
Bristow, R. M. (1989). *Hong Kong's new towns: A selective review*. Oxford: Oxford University Press.
Carroll, J. (2007). *A concise history of Hong Kong*. Hong Kong: Hong Kong University Press.
Dattner, R. (1995). *Civil architecture—The new public infrastructure*. New York: McGraw-Hill.
Lu, Y., Sarkar, C., & Xiao, Y. (2018a). The effect of street-level greenery on walking behavior: Evidence from Hong Kong. *Social Science and Medicine, 208,* 41–49. https://doi.org/10.1016/j.socscimed.2018.05.022.
Lu, Y., Sun, G., Sarkar, C., Gou, Z and Xiao, Y. (2018). Commuting mode choice in a high-density city: Do land-use density and diversity matter in Hong Kong? *International Journal of Environmental Research and Public Health, 15* (4): 920. MDPI AG. Retrieved from http://dx.doi.org/10.3390/ijerph15050920.
Shelton, B., Karakiewicz, J., & Kvan, T. (2011). *The making of Hong Kong-from vertical to volumetric*. New York: Routledge.
Sit, V. (2015). *Hong Kong: 150 years, development in maps* (p. 2015). Hong Kong: The Joint Publication Ltd.
Tan, Z., & Xue, C. Q. L. (2014). Walking as a planned activity: Elevated pedestrian network and urban design regulation in Hong Kong. *Journal of Urban Design, 19*(5), 722–744.

---

[17]The government's money is used in constructing grand theaters. Most theaters in China have to run on their commercial income or sponsorship. Theaters in Hong Kong all receive government's fund allocation. See annual report of Leisure and Cultural Services Department, Hong Kong Government.

Uduku, O. (2006). Modernist architecture and 'the tropical'. In: West Africa: The tropical architecture movement in West Africa: 1948–1970. *Habitat International, 30*(6), 396–411.

Xue, C. Q. L. (2016). *Hong Kong Architecture 1945–2015: From colonial to global*. Singapore: Springer.

Xue, C. Q. L., & Manuel, K. (2001). The quest for better public space: A critical review of urban Hong Kong. In P. Miao (Ed.), *Public places of Asia Pacific countries: Current issues and strategies* (pp. 171–190). The Netherlands: Kluwer Academic Publishers.

Xue, C. Q. L., Wang, Z., & Mitchenere, B. (2010). In search of identity: The development process of the national grand theater in Beijing, China. *The Journal of Architecture, 15*(4), 517–535.

Zhang, W. Z. (2005). *I am myself—A story of Sze Wing Ching*. Hong Kong: Cosmos Books. 张文中 (2005). 张文中 (2005). 我就是我 – 施永青的故事. 香港:天地图书公司.

Appendix A

Database of grand theaters in China: 1998–2018

Province/municipality	Main prefecture-level city	Name of the theatre	GFA (m²)	Completed year	Designer	Total investment Hundred million Yuan	Total investment Hundred million USD	Number of halls	Total seating capacity
Beijing	–	National Centre for the Performing Arts 國家大劇院	165,000	2007	Paul Andreu, France	30.67	4.60	4	5850
		Beijing Tianqiao Performing Arts Center 北京天橋藝術中心	75,000	2015	Guangzhou Pearl River Foreign Investment Architectural Designing Institute	Undisclosed	Undisclosed	4	3300
Shanghai	–	Shanghai Grand Theatre 上海大劇院	62,803	1998	Arte Charpentier, France	12.00	1.80	3	2506
		Shanghai Oriental Art Center 上海東方藝術中心	39,964	2003	Paul Andreu, France	11.00	1.65	3	3301
		Shanghai Symphony Hall 上海交響樂團音樂廳	19,950	2013	Arata Isozaki, Japan	Undisclosed	Undisclosed	2	1600
		Shanghai Poly Grand Theatre 上海保利劇院	56,000	2014	Tadao Ando, Japan	7	1.05	2	1866
		Shanghai Culture Square 上汽·上海文化廣場	65,000	2016	Beyer Blinder Belle & Shanghai Xiandai, USA and China	11	1.65	1	2010
		Nine Tree Shanghai Future Art Center 九棵樹上海未來藝術中心	71,000	2019	Frederic Rolland Architects, France	9.5	1.43	3	2000
Tianjin	–	Tianjin Grand Theatre 天津大劇院	101,200	2012	gmp. Germany	15.33	2.30	4	3121
		Tianjin Binhai Culture Center 濱海演藝中心	20,000	2017	Bing Thom Architects, Canada	Undisclosed	Undisclosed	1	1200

(continued)

(continued)

Province/municipality	Main prefecture-level city	Name of the theatre	GFA (m²)	Completed year	Designer	Total investment		Number of halls	Total seating capacity
						Hundred million Yuan	Hundred million USD		
Chongqing	–	Chongqing Grand Theatre 重慶大劇院	103,307	2009	gmp, Germany	16	2.40	2	2770
		Chongqing Guotai Art Center 重慶國泰藝術中心	30,200	2013	Cui Kai, CAG	5	0.75	3	1500
		Sanxia Art Center 三峽藝術中心	35,395	–	Cui Kai, CAG,	Undisclosed	Undisclosed	2	2050
Guangdong	Guangzhou	Guangzhou Opera House 廣州歌劇院	73,000	2011	Zaha Hadid, Britain	13.8	2.07	2	2247
		Xinghai Concert Hall 星海音樂廳	18,000	1998	Architectural Design and Research Institute of SCUT	2.5	0.38	3	2060
	Shenzhen	Shenzhen Concert Hall 深圳音樂廳	41,423	2007	Arata Isozaki, Japan	7.76	1.16	2	2183
		Shenzhen Poly Theatre 深圳保利劇院	15,000	2009	Huazhu Design	Undisclosed	Undisclosed	1	1500
	Zhuhai	Zhuhai Grand Theatre 珠海大劇院	46,000	2017	Chen Keshi, Beijing University, Beijing Institute of Architectural Design	10.8	1.62	2	2100
	Dongguan	Dongguan Yulan Theatre 東莞玉蘭大劇院	40,257	2005	Carlos Ott, Canada	6.18	0.93	2	2000
	Shunde	Shunde Arts Center 順德演藝中心	32,000	2005	P&T Group, Hong Kong	3.5	0.53	2	1986
	Huizhou	Huizhou Culture and Art Center 惠州文化藝術中心	36,000	2008	Tongji Architectural Design	4.2	0.63	3	2168

(continued)

(continued)

Province/municipality	Main prefecture-level city	Name of the theatre	GFA (m²)	Completed year	Designer	Total investment		Number of halls	Total seating capacity
						Hundred million Yuan	Hundred million USD		
	Zhongshan	Zhongshan Culture and Art Center 中山市文化藝術中心	47,368	2005	CCDI	5	0.75	2	1948
	Jiangmen	Jiangmen Performing Art Center 江門演藝中心	63,000	2016	Guangzhou Pearl River Foreign Investment Architectural Designing Institute	4	0.60	2	1450
	Meizhou	Jiaying Opera House 嘉應歌劇院	160,000	–	He Jingtang, Design Institute, SCUT	6.8	1.02	2	2300
Jiangsu	Nanjing	Jiangsu Centre for the Performing Arts 江蘇大劇院	270,000	2017	POWERCHINA East China Institute of Architectural Design	26.88	4.04	5	8272
		Nanjing Poly Theater 南京保利劇院	20,000	2014	Zaha Hadid, Britain	Undisclosed	Undisclosed	2	2358
	Wuxi	Wuxi Grand Theatre 無錫大劇院	78,000	2012	PES-Architects, Finland	10	1.50	2	2400
	Changzhou	Changzhou Grand Theatre 常州大劇院	51,000	2009	Institute of Shanghai Architectural Design and Research Co., Ltd.	4.9	0.74	2	1926
	Suzhou	Suzhou Culture and Arts Center 蘇州文化藝術中心	110,000	2007	Paul Andreu, France	17	2.55	2	1672
		Suzhou Poly Theater 蘇州保利劇院	143,700	2017	Tongji Architectural Design	18.5	2.78	3	1791
		Suzhou Grand Theatre 蘇州大劇院	80,000	–	Christian de Portzamparc, France	–	–	2	2200
	Lianyungang	Lianyungang Culture Center 連雲港文化中心	100,000	–	Ni Yang, Design Institute, SCUT	9.98	1.50	3	2550

(continued)

(continued)

Province/municipality	Main prefecture-level city	Name of the theatre	GFA (m²)	Completed year	Designer	Total investment		Number of halls	Total seating capacity
						Hundred million Yuan	Hundred million USD		
	Huaian	Huaian Grand Theatre 淮安大劇院	29,837	2015	UAD, China	3.4	0.51	1	1226
	Yangzhou	Yangzhou New Grand Theatre 揚州新大劇院	109,800	–	Tongji Architectural Design	–	–	4	3200
	Kunshan	Kunshan Culture and Arts Center 昆山文化藝術中心	71,255	2012	Cui Kai and CAG	10	1.50	2	1700
	Suqian	Suyu Grand Theatre 宿豫大劇院	48,000	2016	ZIAD & STI-Studio, China and Germany	Undisclosed	Undisclosed	2	2180
Zhejiang	Hangzhou	Hangzhou Grand Theatre 杭州大劇院	55,000	2004	Carlos Ott, Canada	9.5	1.43	3	2600
	Ningbo	Ningbo Grand Theatre 寧波大劇院	52,000	2004	Frederic Rolland International, France	6.2	0.93	2	2300
	Wenzhou	Wenzhou Grand Theatre 溫州大劇院	36,000	2009	Carlos Ott, Canada	6.54	0.98	3	2239
	Shaoxing	Shaoxing Grand Theatre 紹興大劇院	26,500	2003	Cai Zhenyu, East China Institute of Architectural Design	3.8	0.57	1	1349
	Huzhou	Huzhou Grand Theatre 湖州大劇院	19,120	2008	UAD, China	2.5	0.38	2	1599
	Jiaxing	Jiaxing Grand Theatre 嘉興大劇院	28,000	2003	ZIAD	1.6	0.24	2	1956
		Wuzhen Grand Theatre 烏鎮大劇院	21,750	2010	Kris Yao/ARTECH, Taiwan	4	0.60	2	1800
	Jinhua	Jinhua Grand Theatre 金華大劇院	31,048	2013	Guangzhou Design Institute	3.3	0.50	2	1695

(continued)

(continued)

Province/municipality	Main prefecture-level city	Name of the theatre	GFA (m^2)	Completed year	Designer	Total investment Hundred million Yuan	Hundred million USD	Number of halls	Total seating capacity
	Lishui	Lishui Grand Theatre 麗水大劇院	34,800	2010	UAD, China	3	0.45	1	1305
	Zhoushan	Zhoushan Grand Theatre 舟山大劇院	26,000	2014	Fudan Planning and Architectural Design Institute	2	0.30	3	1774
Heilongjiang	Harbin	Harbin Grand Theatre 哈爾濱大劇院	79,000	2016	MAD Architects	12.79	1.92	2	1952
		Harbin Concert Hall 哈爾濱音樂廳	36,109	2014	Arata Isozaki, Japan	6.9	1.04	2	1600
		Daqing Educational Cultural Center 大慶文化教育中心大劇院	23,426	2007	China Architecture Design Group	Undisclosed	Undisclosed	1	1498
Jilin	Changchun	Changchun International Conference Center 長春國際會議中心	21,787	2008	JLAD	Undisclosed	Undisclosed	2	1800
	Jilin	Jilin City People's Theatre 吉林市人民大劇院	37,000	2015	Fangzhou Architectural Design, Halbin	1	0.15	2	2600
Liaoning	Shenyang	Liaoning Grand Theatre 遼寧大劇院	30,000	2001	China Northeast Architectural Design & Research Institute	2.5	0.38	3	1815
		Shenyang Culture and Art Center 沈陽文化藝術中心	85,000	2014	Auer Weber & ISA Germany & China	6.3	0.95	3	3500

(continued)

(continued)

Province/municipality	Main prefecture-level city	Name of the theatre	GFA (m²)	Completed year	Designer	Total investment		Number of halls	Total seating capacity
						Hundred million Yuan	Hundred million USD		
	Dalian	Dalian Development Zone Grand Theatre 大連開發區大劇院	28,000	2006	Arthur Erickson Corporation, Canada	3.5	0.53	2	1602
		Dalian International Conference Center 大連國際會議中心	117,650	2012	Coop Himmelblau, Austria	Undisclosed	Undisclosed	2	3592
Shandong	Jinan	Shandong Grand Theatre 山東大劇院	136,000	2012	Paul Andreu, France	24.75	3.72	3	3729
	Qingdao	Qingdao Grand Theatre 青島大劇院	87,000	2011	gmp, Germany	13.5	2.03	3	3258
	Yantai	Yantai Grand Theatre 煙臺大劇院	11,400	2009	He Jingtang, Design Institute, SCUT	3.5	0.53	1	1221
	Weifang	Weifang Culture and Art Center 濰坊文化藝術中心	49,000	2018	RSP Architects Planners &Engineers (PTE) LTD, Singapore	Undisclosed	Undisclosed	2	2552
	Zibo	Zibo Cultural Center 淄博市文化中心	60,392	2013	Frank Krueger, France	Undisclosed	Undisclosed	3	1900
	Dezhou	Dezhou Grand Theatre 德州大劇院	38,100	2013	China Architecture Design Group	Undisclosed	Undisclosed	3	2250
	Dongying	Xuelian Grand Theatre 雪蓮大劇院	45,094	2014	China Architecture Design Group	9.8	1.47	2	1800
	Liaocheng	Shuicheng Mingzhu Grand Theatre 水城明珠大劇場	9000	2003	The Architectural Design & Research Institute of Tsinghua University	0.8	0.12	1	3636
	Linyi	Linyi Grand Theatre 臨沂大劇院	70,000	2013	China Architecture Design Group	8	1.20	2	2050
	Heze	Heze Grand Theatre 菏澤大劇院	31,141	2009	CIEDC	2.9	0.44	2	1839

(continued)

(continued)

Province/municipality	Main prefecture-level city	Name of the theatre	GFA (m²)	Completed year	Designer	Total investment		Number of halls	Total seating capacity
						Hundred million Yuan	Hundred million USD		
Anhui	Hefei	Hefei Grand Theatre 合肥大劇院	60,000	2009	DDB Architects Shanghai (Xiang Bingren) and Tongji Architectural Design Institute	6.5	0.98	3	2990
Fujian	Fuzhou	Fuzhou Strait Culture and Art Center 福州海峽文化藝術中心	150,000	2018	PES-Architects, Finland	Undisclosed	Undisclosed	3	3312
		Fujian Grand Theatre 福建大劇院	28,242	2007	China Architecture Design Group	3.6	0.54	2	1820
	Xiamen	Jiageng Grand Theatre 嘉庚大劇院	63,027	2015	Tongji Architectural Design	7.6	1.14	1	1443
		Banlam Grand Theatre 閩南大戲院	27,361	2012	CCDI	4.3	0.65	1	1501
Jiangxi	Nanchang	Jiangxi Arts Center 江西藝術中心	48,720	2010	China Architecture Design Group	5	0.75	2	2500
	Jiujiang	Jiujiang Culture and Art Center 九江市文化藝術中心	27,852	2014	Architects & Engineers Co., Ltd.of Southeast University	3	0.45	2	1700
Henan	Zhengzhou	Henan Art Center 河南藝術中心	75,000	2007	Carlos Ott, Canada	9.26	1.39	3	3004
		Zhengzhou Grand Theatre 鄭州大劇院	125,965	2020	THAD	–	–	4	3430

(continued)

(continued)

Province/municipality	Main prefecture-level city	Name of the theatre	GFA (m²)	Completed year	Designer	Total investment		Number of halls	Total seating capacity
						Hundred million Yuan	Hundred million USD		
Hunan	Changsha	Meixihu International Culture and Arts Center Grand Theatre 梅溪湖國際文化藝術中心大劇院	48,116	2016	Zaha Hadid, Britain	–	–	2	2300
		Changsha Concert Hall 長沙音樂廳	28,161	2015	Architectural Design & Research Institute of SCUT	Undisclosed	Undisclosed	3	2200
Hubei	Wuhan	Qintai Culture and Art Center 琴臺文化藝術中心	65,650	2007	Guangzhou Pearl River Foreign Investment Architectural Designing Institute	15.7	2.36	4	3400
	Shiyan	Shiyan Grand Theatre 十堰大劇院	52,891	–	Tongji Architectural Design	Undisclosed	Undisclosed	3	2338
Hebei	Shijiazhuang	Hebei Arts Center 河北文化中心	32,059	1999	Hebei Institute of Architectural Design & Research Co., Ltd.	3.2	0.48	2	3780
		Xiaguang Grand Theatre 霞光大劇院	50,000	2017	China Architecture Design Group	5.3	0.80	2	1800
		Hebei Grand Theatre 河北大劇院	80,000	–	HH Design	8.8	1.32	3	3400
	Handan	Handan Culture and Art Center 邯鄲文化藝術中心	42,647	2012	BIAD	Undisclosed	Undisclosed	1	1567
Shanxi	Taiyuan	Shanxi Grand Theatre 山西大劇院	85,697	2012	Arte Charpentier, France	7.9	1.19	3	3256
	Datong	Datong Grand Theatre 大同大劇院	47,376	–	Arata Isozaki, Japan	3.3	0.50	2	2300

(continued)

(continued)

Province/municipality	Main prefecture-level city	Name of the theatre	GFA (m²)	Completed year	Designer	Total investment		Number of halls	Total seating capacity
						Hundred million Yuan	Hundred million USD		
Inner Mongolia	Baotou	Baotou Grand Theatre 包頭大劇院	16,000	2013	Jiang Huancheng Architectural Design Ltd.	Undisclosed	Undisclosed	1	1335
	Ordos	Ordos Grand Theatre 鄂爾多斯大劇院	42,688	2009	SHZF Architects	7	1.05	2	2124
	Hohhot	Wulanqiate Grand Theatre 呼和浩特保利劇院	30,627	2007	Yasui Architects & Engineers, Japan	Undisclosed	Undisclosed	1	1370
Ningxia	Yinchuan	Ningxia Grand Theatre 寧夏大劇院	48,610	2012	Cheng Taining and CCTN Design	4.6	0.69	1	1400
Qinghai	Xining	Qinghai Grand Theatre 青海大劇院	36,000	2012	China Architecture Design Group	5	0.75	3	2298
	Yushu	Kangba Art Center 玉樹康巴藝術中心	20,610	2014	Cui Kai and CAG	Undisclosed	Undisclosed	2	1300
Shanxi	Xian	Shanxi Grand Theater 陝西大劇院	51,800	2017	DDB Architects Shanghai and China Northwest Architectural Design Institute	13	1.95	2	2612
		Xian Concert Hall 西安音樂廳 (Grand theater, concert hall, cinema city and art museum are in one complex.)	18,000	2009	DDB Architects Shanghai and China Northwest Architectural Design Institute	Undisclosed	Undisclosed	3	1205 + 1115 cinema city and art museum
Gansu	Lanzhou	Gansu Grand Theatre 甘肅大劇院	31,600	2011	Institute of Shanghai Architectural Design and Research Co., Ltd.	3.5	0.53	2	1800

(continued)

(continued)

Province/municipality	Main prefecture-level city	Name of the theatre	GFA (m²)	Completed year	Designer	Total investment		Number of halls	Total seating capacity
						Hundred million Yuan	Hundred million USD		
Xinjiang	Changji	Xinjiang Grand Theatre 新疆大劇院	100,000	2014	Meng Jianmin and Shenzhen Institute of Arch Design	17.6	2.64	3	2000
Sichuan	Chengdu	Chengdu Contemporary Arts Center 成都當代藝術中心	–	–	Zaha Hadid, Britain	–	–	3	4000
		Sichuan Grand Theatre 四川大劇院	59,000	–	China Southwest Architecture Design & Research Institute	–	–	2	2051
Guizhou	Guiyang	Guiyang Grand Theatre 貴陽大劇院	36,376	2006	China Southwest Architecture Design & Research Institute	4.4	0.66	2	2213
Yunnan	Kunming	Yunnan Grand Theatre 雲南大劇院	47,010	2016	Tongji Architectural Design	7.7	1.16	3	2705
Guangxi	Nanning	Guangxi Culture and Art Center 廣西文化藝術中心	114,835	–	gmp. Germany	–	–	3	3600
Hainan	Sanya	Mid Pennsula Music Hall 半山岛音乐厅	32,300	–	Tadao Ando, Japan	–	–	2	1300
Taiwan	Taipei	Taipei Performing Arts Center 臺北藝術中心	58,658	2018	OMA, Holland	9.3	1.4	3	3100
	Taichung	National Taichung Theater 臺中國家歌劇院	36,000	2014	Toyo Ito & Associates, Japan	9.4	1.41	3	3009
	Kaohsiung	Wei Wu Ying National Kaohsiung Center for the Arts 衛武營國家藝術文化中心	141,000	2018	Mecanoo, Holland	17.75	2.66	4	5861
Hong Kong	–	Xiqu Center 戲曲中心	29,900	2018	Bing Thom Architects, Ronald Lu & Partners, Canada & Hong Kong	27	4.05	2	1273

Compiled by Cong Sun

Appendix B

B.1 Overview of the Performance of the Main Theaters

Grades	First-tier cities		Second-tier cities		Third-tier cities	
Cities	Beijing	Shenzhen	Zhengzhou	Chongqing	Wuzhen	Hohhot
Theaters	The National Center for the Performing Arts	Shenzhen Concert Hall	Henan Art Center	Chongqing Grand Theater	Wuzhen Grand Theater	Hohhot Poly Theater
Total number of performances in 2017	915	185	424	429	28	57

B.1.1 The National Center for the Performing Arts

See Table B.1.1.1; Figs. B.1.1.1, B.1.1.2, B.1.1.3 and B.1.1.4.

Table B.1.1.1 Number of performances in NCPA from 2016 to 2018 or **915** performances a year on average (2016–2018)

Year	2016	2017	2018
Total number of shows	912	915	919

© Springer Nature Singapore Pte Ltd. 2019
C. Q. Xue (ed.), *Grand Theater Urbanism*,
https://doi.org/10.1007/978-981-13-7868-3

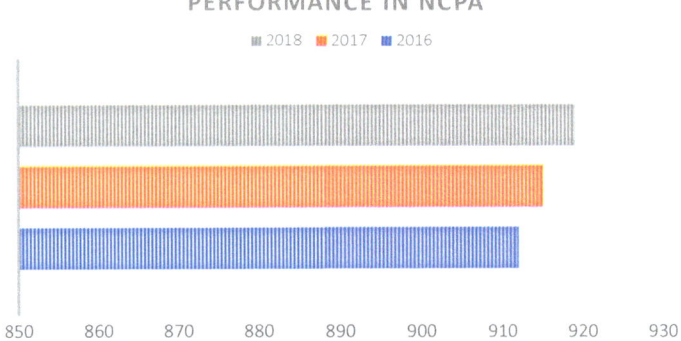

Fig. B.1.1.1 Number of performances in NCPA from 2016 to 2018. Drawn by SUN Cong

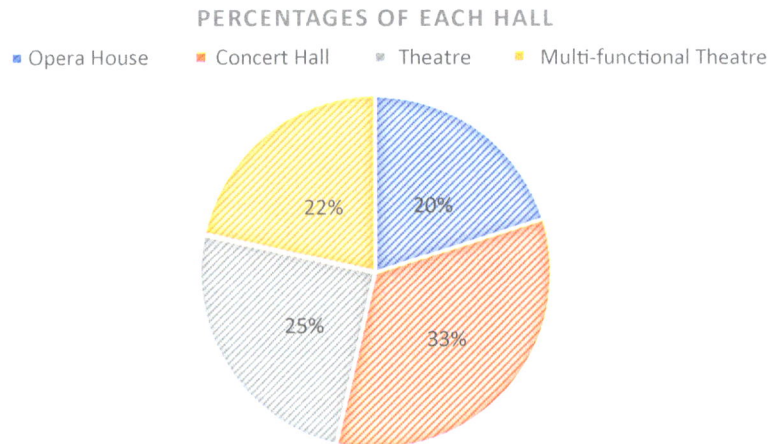

Fig. B.1.1.2 NCPA—percentages of each hall in 2017. Drawn by SUN Cong

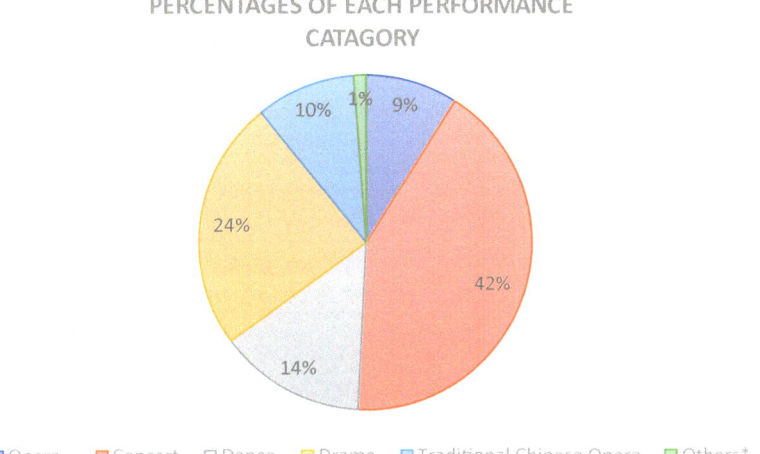

Fig. B.1.1.3 NCPA—percentages of each performance category in 2017 (others include charity performances, art popularization, and educational activities, etc.). Drawn by SUN Cong

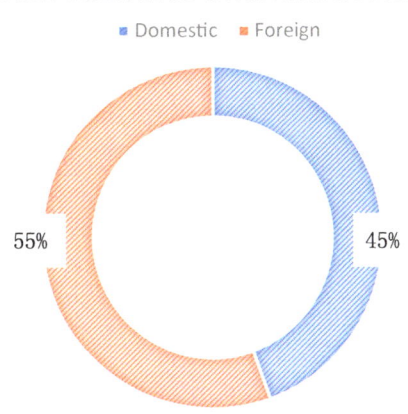

Fig. B.1.1.4 NCPA—percentages of performance organizations in 2017. Drawn by SUN Cong

B.1.2 Shenzhen Concert Hall

See Table B.1.2.1; Figs. B.1.2.1, B.1.2.2, B.1.2.3 and B.1.2.4.

Table B.1.2.1 Number of performances in Shenzhen Concert Hall from 2016 to 2018 or **194** performances a year on average (2016–2018)

Year	2016	2017	2018
Total number of shows	212	185	186

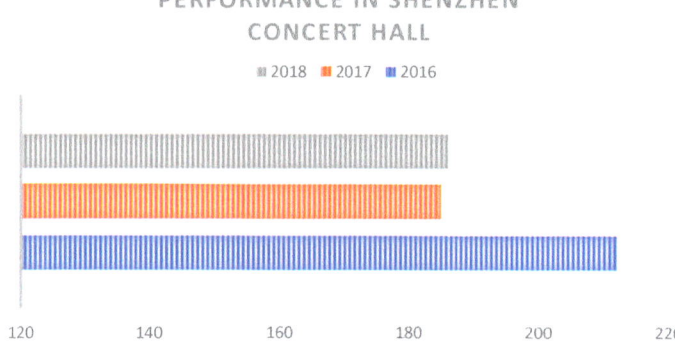

Fig. B.1.2.1 Number of performances in Shenzhen Concert Hall from 2016 to 2018. Drawn by SUN Cong

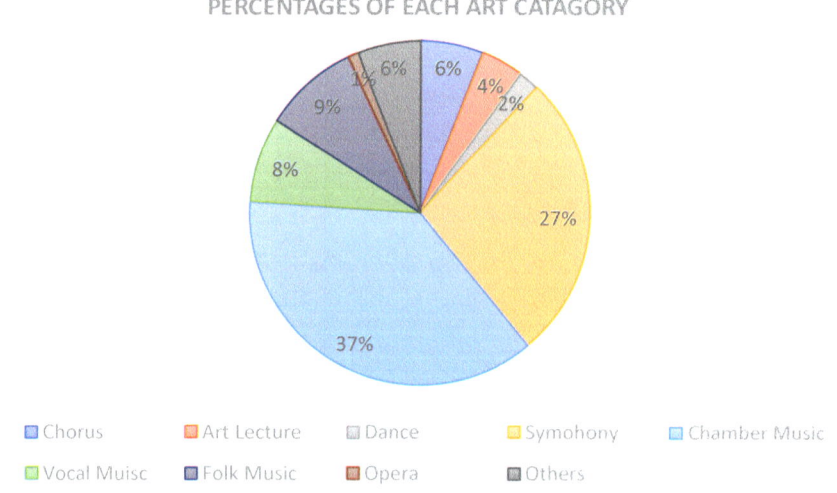

Fig. B.1.2.2 Shenzhen Concert Hall—percentages of each performance category in 2017. Drawn by SUN Cong

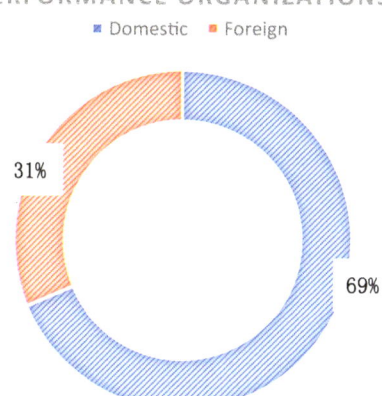

Fig. B.1.2.3 Shenzhen Concert Hall—percentages of performance organizations in 2017. Drawn by SUN Cong

Fig. B.1.2.4 Shenzhen Concert Hall—number of performances in each month of 2017. Drawn by SUN Cong

B.1.3 Henan Art Center

See Table B.1.3.1; Figs. B.1.3.1, B.1.3.2 and B.1.3.3.

Table B.1.3.1 Number of performances in Henan Art Center from 2017 to 2018

Year	2017	2018
Total number of shows	424	454

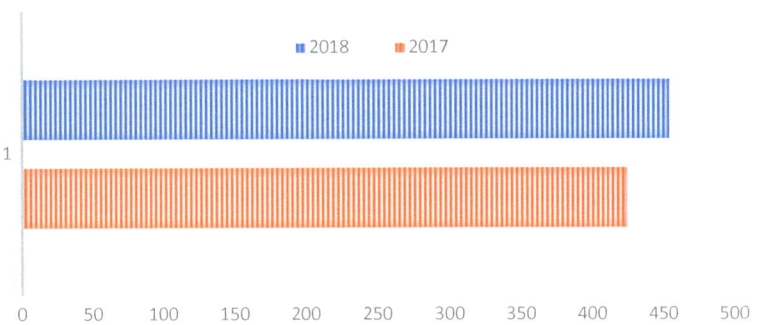

Fig. B.1.3.1 Number of performances in Henan Art Center from 2017 to 2018. Drawn by ZHANG Lujia

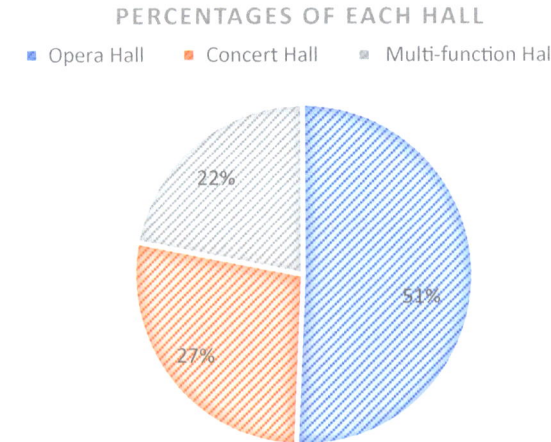

Fig. B.1.3.2 Henan Art Center—percentages of each hall in 2017. Drawn by ZHANG Lujia

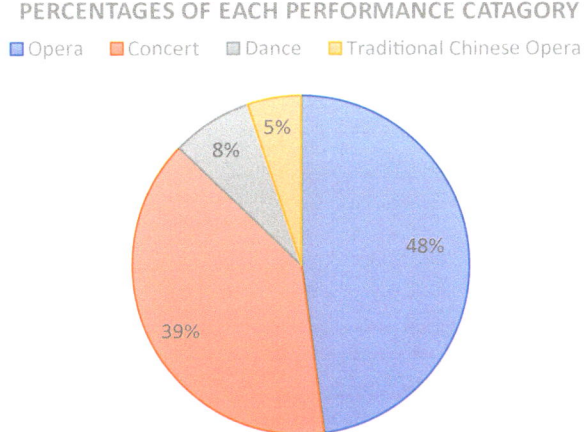

Fig. B.1.3.3 Henan Art Center—percentages of each performance category in 2017. Drawn by ZHANG Lujia

B.1.4 Chongqing Grand Theater

See Figs. B.1.4.1 and B.1.4.2.

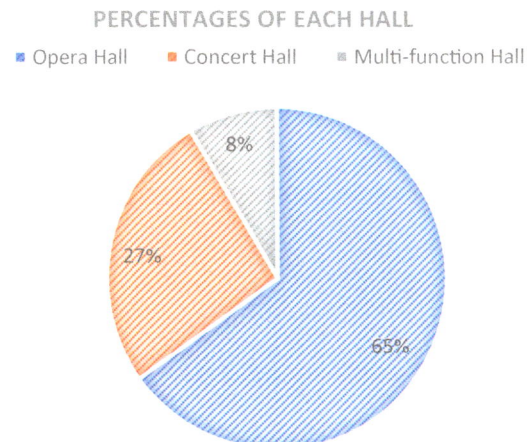

Fig. B.1.4.1 Chongqing Grand Theater—percentages of each hall in 2017. Drawn by ZHANG Lujia

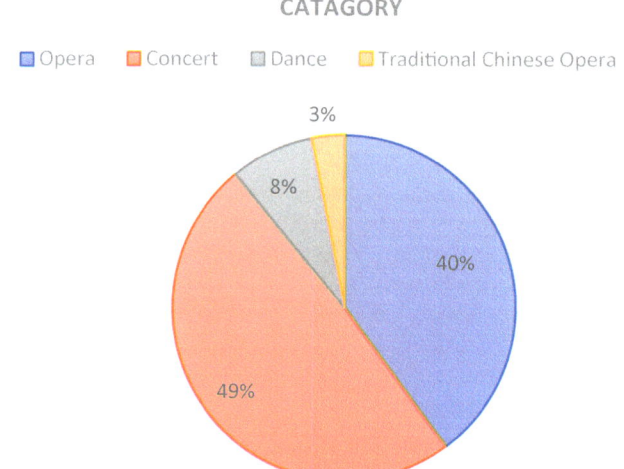

Fig. B.1.4.2 Chongqing Grand Theater—percentages of each performance category in 2017. Drawn by ZHANG Lujia

B.1.5 Wuzhen Grand Theater

See Figs. B.1.5.1 and B.1.5.2.

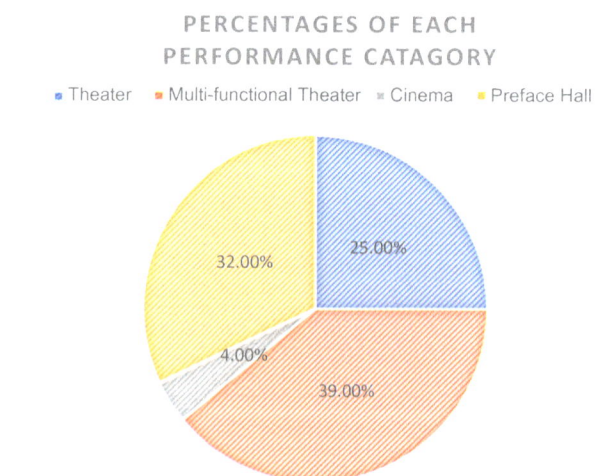

Fig. B.1.5.1 Wuzhen Grand Theater—percentages of each hall in 2017. Drawn by CHANG Wei

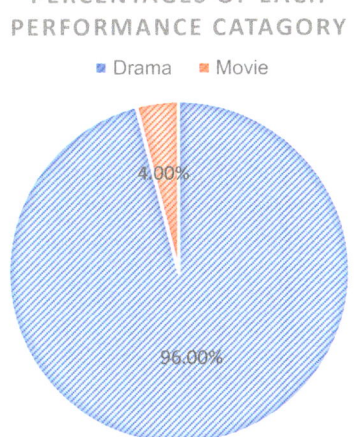

Fig. B.1.5.2 Wuzhen Grand Theater—percentages of each performance category in 2017. Drawn by CHANG Wei

B.1.6 Hohhot Poly Theater

See Figs. B.1.6.1 and B.1.6.2.

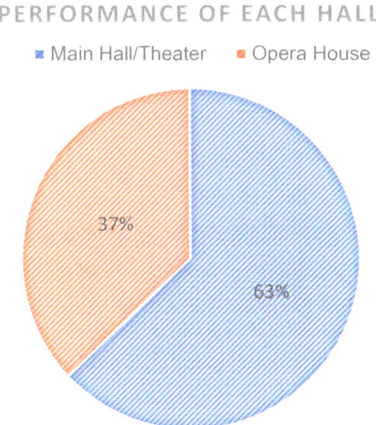

Fig. B.1.6.1 Hohhot Poly Theater—percentages of each hall in 2017. Drawn by CHANG Wei

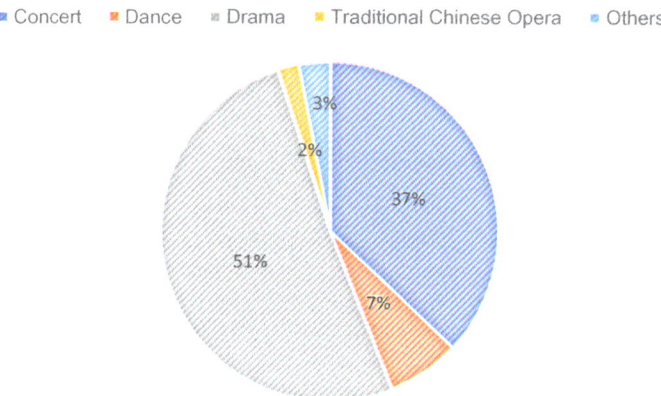

Fig. B.1.6.2 Hohhot Poly Theater—percentages of each performance category in 2017. Drawn by CHANG Wei

Index

© Springer Nature Singapore Pte Ltd. 2019
C. Q. Xue (ed.), *Grand Theater Urbanism*,
https://doi.org/10.1007/978-981-13-7868-3

Printed by Printforce, the Netherlands